Tribal Sovereignty in Alaska

Tribal Sovereignty in Alaska

How It Happened, What It Means

Donald Craig Mitchell

CAROLINA ACADEMIC PRESS
Durham, North Carolina

Library of Congress Cataloging-in-Publication Data

Names: Mitchell, Donald, 1947 January 23- author.
Title: Tribal sovereignty in Alaska : how it happened, what it means / Donald Craig Mitchell.
Description: Durham, North Carolina : Carolina Academic Press, LLC, [2021] | Includes bibliographical references.
Identifiers: LCCN 2021041372 (print) | LCCN 2021041373 (ebook) | ISBN 9781531022242 (paperback) | ISBN 9781531022259 (ebook)
Subjects: LCSH: Alaska Natives—Legal status, laws, etc. | Alaska Natives—Government relations. | Alaska Natives—Politics and government. | Alaska Native corporations—Law and legislation—United States. | Federally recognized Indian tribes—United States. | United States. Alaska Native Claims Settlement Act.
Classification: LCC KIA2395.S68 M58 2021 (print) | LCC KIA2395.S68 (ebook) | DDC 342.79808/72—dc23
LC record available at https://lccn.loc.gov/2021041372
LC ebook record available at https://lccn.loc.gov/2021041373

Carolina Academic Press, LLC
700 Kent Street
Durham, North Carolina 27701
(919) 489-7486
www.cap-press.com

Printed in the United States of America
2025 Printing

For John Baker and Andrea Sitton

Contents

Tribal Sovereignty in Alaska

Introduction

In July 1974 when I moved to Alaska from California to work as an attorney for the Alaska Legal Services Corporation, all I knew about the state was that it was a huge land mass — 365.5 million acres, 571,000 square miles — that in 1867 the United States had purchased from Russia.

When I arrived I learned that 40 percent of Alaska's 567,000 residents lived in one of six towns, Anchorage, Fairbanks, Kodiak, Juneau, Sitka, and Ketchikan, and in the road-connected southcentral region that runs along the Parks Highway from Willow in the Matanuska-Susitna Valley south to Anchorage, along the Glenn Highway from Anchorage east to Glennallen, and along the Seward Highway from Anchorage south to Soldotna and then on to Homer at the tip of the Kenai Peninsula. Most of the other 60 percent lived in one of more than four hundred communities that ranged in size from Lime Village on the Stony River, population 25, to Nome on the coast of the Bering Sea, population 2,488. Many of those communities had names like Aleknagik, Chefornak, Tuntutuliak, and Unalakleet that sounded odd to my cheechako ear.

Each community whose name sounded odd has its own unique history. But to generalize, most began as locations at which the nomadic Indians, Eskimos, and Aleuts who were living in Alaska when the United States purchased the territory from Russia resided during the winter months. Beginning in the 1870s, first missionaries, and then the Bureau of Education, an obscure agency that was part of the Department of the Interior, began building schoolhouses in the winter villages. When the schools opened, the nomadic populations began reducing, and eventually ended, most of their roaming.

In 1971 when it settled aboriginal land claims in Alaska by enacting the Alaska Native Claims Settlement Act (ANCSA),[1] Congress designated every community in Alaska that was "not of a modern and urban character" and that had at least twenty-five Natives* who collectively were a majority of the community's residents as a "Native village." ANCSA then authorized the Native residents of each of the more

* Section 3(b) of ANCSA defines "Native" to mean "a person of one-fourth degree or more Alaska Indian (including Tsimshian Indians not enrolled in the Metlakatla Indian Community), Eskimo, or Aleut blood, or combination thereof." As used in this work, "Natives" are individuals who each are a "Native" as section 3(b) of ANCSA defines the term, and, when a particular context suggests, also individuals who are descendants of those individuals.

than two hundred Native villages to incorporate a business corporation under the laws of the State of Alaska in which each Native resident was issued one hundred shares of stock. The secretary of the interior then conveyed to each corporation fee title to the surface estate of the land within and surrounding the community whose Native residents had incorporated the corporation. Each village corporation also received monetary benefits.

Bethel, the most populous Native village in western Alaska, is located on the Kuskokwim River four hundred miles west of Anchorage, and is where I was sent by the Alaska Legal Services Corporation to work in its office at that location.

Bethel did not begin as a winter village. Rather, the community grew up around a church and a school that Moravian missionaries opened in 1885 near a trading post that had opened in the 1870s.[2]

In 1974 a majority of Bethel's residents were, and they today remain, Natives of Yup'ik Eskimo descent. Because the airport runway can handle commercial jets, by the time I arrived Bethel had become the administrative center for the fifty-six Native villages, almost all populated by Natives of Yup'ik Eskimo descent, that are scattered around the Yukon-Kuskokwim River Delta.

During the years I traveled by bush plane and boat to and from those villages, in every village implementing ANCSA was a controlling preoccupation. And two months after I moved to Bethel, at the regional high school I attended the first shareholders meeting of Calista, the regional corporation that ANCSA required

Bethel, Alaska (1896). Joseph Herman Romig.

Bethel, Alaska (1970s). Ruth A.M. Schmidt. Archives and Special Collections, Consortium Library, University of Alaska Anchorage.

the Yup'ik Eskimo residents of Native villages on the Yukon-Kuskokwim River Delta to incorporate.[3, *]

Section 17(d)(2) of ANCSA directed the secretary of the interior to withdraw up to eighty million acres of public land in Alaska that might be suitable for Congress to add "as units of the National Park, Forest, Wildlife Refuge, and Wild and Scenic Rivers Systems." The secretary then had two years to recommend the specific land he thought Congress should add. Congress then had five years to add to the four systems whatever land it deemed appropriate.

In December 1973 Secretary of the Interior Rogers Morton submitted his recommendations. In January 1977 Representative Morris Udall, the chairman of the House Committee on Interior and Insular Affairs, introduced H.R. 39, a bill whose enactment by Congress would add to the four systems the land Secretary Morton had recommended, plus several million additional acres that the major national environmental organizations had recommended to Udall.[4]

---

* Section 7 of ANCSA divided Alaska into twelve geographic regions, and required Natives residing in each region to incorporate a for-profit corporation under the laws of the State of Alaska in which every Native was issued one hundred shares of stock. The secretary of the interior then conveyed to each regional corporation fee title to the subsurface estate of the land within and surrounding each Native village in its region, as well as fee title to other land surrounding those villages. Each regional corporation also received monetary benefits.

By that date the refusal of the members of the Alaska Board of Fisheries and Alaska Board of Game to regulate fishing and hunting in Alaska in a manner that safeguarded the subsistence harvest by residents of Native villages who were dependent on salmon and other fish stocks and on moose and caribou and other wildlife populations for their sustenance had become a matter of increasing concern throughout the Alaska Native community.

To try to attract Native support for H.R. 39 by responding to that concern, Representative Udall included a provision in the bill, section 701, that authorized the secretary of the interior to establish "subsistence management zones" and a "regulatory subsistence board" for each zone whose members would assist the secretary in regulating the taking of fish stocks and wildlife populations to ensure that subsistence uses of such stocks and populations were given "preference over any competing consumptive use in a subsistence management zone."

By the time Representative Udall introduced H.R. 39, I had relocated from Bethel to the Alaska Legal Services Corporation's headquarters office in Anchorage. When a copy of H.R. 39 came across my desk, because the political and legal history of the regulation of hunting and fishing in Alaska by then had become a subject of professional interest, I sent the Subcommittee on General Oversight and Alaska Lands of the House Committee on Interior and Insular Affairs, which Representative Udall had created to spearhead the committee's consideration of H.R. 39, a brief in which I described that history and offered recommendations regarding how the regulatory system that Congress's enactment of section 701 would create could be improved.[5]

That August the subcommittee held a hearing in Anchorage at which I testified on that subject.[6] When I finished doing so Harry Crandell, the staff director of the subcommittee, sought me out to discuss what he had learned by reading my brief. That began a serendipitous series of events that resulted in me moving to Washington, D.C., where I soon found myself representing the Alaska Federation of Natives (AFN), the organization Alaska Natives had created in 1967 to lobby Congress to settle Alaska Native land claims on fair terms, on Capitol Hill during the Ninety-fifth and Ninety-sixth Congresses' consideration of H.R. 39.

That assignment ended in December 1980 when President Jimmy Carter signed H.R. 39 into law as the Alaska National Interest Lands Conservation Act. I then returned to Anchorage where for the next three years I served as general counsel of the AFN. At the end of 1983 I resigned in order to write a book on the history of the Alaska Native land claims movement that eventually became two books.[7] But during my book-writing, I continued to represent the AFN as its outside general counsel, until 1993 when I ended that representation.

I mention that chronology because it was not until 1982, which was eight years after I had become involved with Alaska Native-related legal issues, that anyone suggested to me that the Native residents of each of the more than two hundred communities that had been designated as Native villages for the purposes of ANCSA were members of a federally recognized tribe whose governing body possessed governmental authority and sovereign immunity.*

In December of that year, I attended a hearing at the U.S. District Court in Anchorage during which District Judge James Fitzgerald heard oral argument on a motion for a preliminary injunction that the defendants had filed in *Native Village of Tyonek v. Puckett*,[8] a lawsuit in which the village council in Tyonek asked Judge Fitzgerald to order four non-Native residents to move out of the village. During his portion of the argument, Bert Hirsch, an attorney from New York who was general counsel for the Association on American Indian Affairs and who represented the Native Village of Tyonek, told Judge Fitzgerald that the village council had "sovereign" governmental authority inside "Indian country" within and surrounding Tyonek. After the hearing when I walked back to my office with several attorneys of my acquaintance who also had attended the hearing, we all agreed that we had no idea what Bert Hirsch had been talking about.

Because I had no idea, and because two months earlier during that year's annual AFN convention a small but vociferous group of delegates had persuaded the convention to pass a resolution that directed the AFN "to make protection of the standing of Alaska Native communities as Indian tribes its top priority for the coming year," I recommended to Janie Leask, the president of the AFN, that the organization sponsor a conference on tribal sovereignty at which Bert Hirsch and other attorneys who were conversant with the subject would be invited to speak.

In March 1983 at the Hilton Hotel in Anchorage, the AFN hosted the conference I organized, after which in December I resigned as the AFN's general counsel to set about writing my book.

That spring I received a telephone call from John Shively, Alaska Governor Bill Sheffield's chief of staff, and Emil Notti, the commissioner of the Alaska Department of Community and Regional Affairs who between 1967 and 1970 had served as the first president of the AFN. They told me that Governor Sheffield had decided to appoint a Task Force on Federal-State-Tribal Relations that Emil would chair and whose members would study, and then make recommendations regarding, the tribal sovereignty issue. They then asked whether I would be willing to serve as the task force's legal counsel, and I said I would as long as Janie Leask, the president of the AFN, had no objection.

My involvement was fine with Janie, the members of the task force were appointed and began holding hearings around the state, and I went to the law library.

I began by reading the Treaty of Cession into which the United States had entered with Russia in 1867 for the purchase of Alaska. Over the next year I read every federal

* In 1940 the U.S. Supreme Court decided that a "federally recognized tribe" has sovereign immunity that prohibits the tribe from being sued without its consent in both state and federal court.

statute, and the legislative history of every federal statute, from 1869 to the present, as well as every judicial decision and government report I could find that was relevant to the tribal sovereignty issue. When I finished I summarized what I had learned in a report that the task force adopted as its report, and which the Alaska Supreme Court subsequently described as a document of "impressive scholarship."[9]

What the report documented was that whether it was a good result or a bad one for there to be more than two hundred federally recognized tribes in Alaska whose governing bodies possess governmental authority and sovereign immunity was a policy question. But the Indian Commerce Clause of the U.S. Constitution gives Congress the exclusive plenary power to decide the nation's Native American-related policies. And beginning in 1884 Congress had repeatedly made it clear that there were to be no federally recognized tribes in Alaska.

In 1986 when the task force released its report, the legal conclusion the report documented was greeted with consternation by members of the nascent tribal sovereignty movement and the attorneys who represented them. Two years later, in its decision in a lawsuit captioned *Native Village of Stevens v. Alaska Management & Planning*, the Alaska Supreme Court provoked even more consternation when, citing the task force report as the controlling authority, the Court concluded that "[i]n a series of enactments following the Treaty of Cession and extending into the first third of this century, Congress has demonstrated its intent that Alaska Native communities not be accorded sovereign tribal status ... No enactment subsequent to the Alaska Indian Reorganization Act [of 1936] granted or recognized tribal sovereign authority in Alaska."[10]

At the time I thought the Court's decision in the *Native Village of Stevens* lawsuit marked the end of the tribal sovereignty movement. But over the past thirty-plus years, events have proven me wrong. And during those years I periodically found myself entangled in many of those events.

Among others, in 1997 I was retained by Alaska Senator Ted Stevens to represent the senator before the U.S. Supreme Court at the petition stage in *State of Alaska v. Native Village of Venetie Tribal Government*, a lawsuit in which the Court held that Congress did not intend land that the secretary of the interior has conveyed in fee title to ANCSA village and regional corporations to be "Indian country." In 1999 I was retained by the Office of Public Advocacy to write a petition for a writ of certiorari that requested the U.S. Supreme Court to review the decision the Alaska Supreme Court had issued in *John v. Baker*, a lawsuit in which the Alaska Supreme Court held that its decision in *Native Village of Stevens* had been superseded and there now were more than two hundred federally recognized tribes in Alaska because in 1993 the assistant secretary of the interior for Indian affairs had said there were. Between 2001 and 2008 I was retained, first by the Legislative Council of the Alaska Legislature, and then by the president of the Alaska Senate, to advise, and occasionally represent, the legislature regarding tribal sovereignty-related legal issues.

Between 2009 and 2012 I represented Edward Parks, and then also Bessie Stearman, in *Simmonds v. Parks*, a lawsuit in which in 2014 the Alaska Supreme Court issued a decision announcing that a tribal court has jurisdiction to terminate the parental rights of a Native parent who is not a member of the federally recognized tribe that created the court. However, because during the course of my representation a conflict developed between Mr. Parks and Ms. Stearman, the Alaska Rules of Professional Conduct required me to withdraw from the lawsuit before it reached the Alaska Supreme Court.

In 2016 I was consulted by the attorney who represented the City of Craig, a small community on Prince of Wales Island in southeast Alaska, regarding the city's situation vis-à-vis the secretary of the interior taking the title to a parcel of land in Craig into trust pursuant to section 5 of the Indian Reorganization Act for the benefit of the Craig Tribal Association. In 2017 I was consulted by the attorney who represented Ronald Oertwich, a non-Native resident of Togiak, a Native village in western Alaska on the northern shore of Bristol Bay. When the tribal court in Togiak banished him from the community and he refused to leave, Oertwich was jailed by tribal police for ignoring the banishment order. And in 2021 I was consulted by the attorney who represented Yvonne Ito regarding Ms. Ito's appeal to the Alaska Supreme Court of the dismissal of an employment discrimination lawsuit she had filed against her former employer, the Copper River Native Association. The lawsuit had been dismissed because the Association's attorneys had persuaded the Alaska Superior Court that, since the Association's members were federally recognized tribes that possessed sovereign immunity, the Association possessed sovereign immunity even though it was a nonprofit corporation that had been incorporated under the laws of the State of Alaska.

So over the years I have had a ringside seat from which I have watched the tribal sovereignty movement evolve from a fringe movement that was begun by a small group of mostly young Natives whose passion for their cause and antipathy to the ANCSA settlement exceeded their understanding of Alaska legal history into what it is today: a broad-based political consensus inside the Alaska Native community whose organizing tenets, not only every Native leader who wants to continue to be one, but the governor of Alaska and the members of Alaska's congressional delegation, no longer question.

How that happened is quite a story.

One

In 1941 Felix Cohen, an attorney in the Office of the Solicitor at the Department of the Interior in Washington, D.C., who today remains an influential commentator on federal Indian law, advised that "the term 'tribe' is commonly used in two senses, an ethnological sense and a political sense." He then cautioned that "it is important to distinguish between these two meanings of the term."[1]

In 1867 when the United States purchased from Russia the right to assert its jurisdiction over the land now known as Alaska, the Indian, Eskimo, and Aleut ancestors of residents of communities that a century later would be designated as Native villages for the purposes of ANCSA were members of ethnological tribes.* But that did not mean that in 1867 or at any subsequent date the United States "recognized" those individuals as members of tribes in a political sense.

With respect to recognition, the Committee on Natural Resources, which in the U.S. House of Representatives exercises jurisdiction over Native American-related legislation, has instructed that:

> "Recognized" is more than a simple adjective; it is a legal term of art. It means that the government acknowledges as a matter of law that a particular Native American group is a tribe by conferring a specific legal status on that group, thus bringing it within Congress' legislative powers. This federal recognition is no minor step. A formal political act, it permanently establishes a government-to-government relationship between the United States and the recognized tribe as a "domestic dependent nation," and imposes on the government a fiduciary trust relationship to the tribe and its members. Concomitantly, it institutionalizes the tribe's quasi-sovereign status, along with all powers accompanying that status....[3]

There are three formal political acts that can confer recognition: a treaty ratified by the Senate, a statute enacted by Congress, and final agency action taken by the secretary of the interior pursuant to authority Congress has delegated to the secretary in a statute.

What formal political act recognized the Native residents in each of more than two hundred Native villages as tribes in a political sense? With a single exception that will be described, to the present day there has been no such act.

* In 1901 the U.S. Supreme Court defined an ethnological tribe as "a body of Indians of the same or a similar race, united in a community under one leadership or government, and inhabiting a particular though sometimes ill-defined territory."[2]

While the United States purchased Alaska in 1867, Congress did not turn its serious attention to the nation's new possession until 1880 when the members began considering whether to create a civil government in Alaska.

On Capitol Hill the principal lobbyist who urged Congress to create a civil government was the Presbyterian missionary Sheldon Jackson. Jackson also was a prominent member of the group of Protestant clergymen who advised Congress and the secretary of the interior on Indian policy.[4] By 1880 the objective of Congress's Indian policy in the coterminous states and territories had shifted from clearing the public domain of the Native Americans who had been occupying it to preparing Native Americans who had survived the clearing for citizenship.[5] Consistent with that new objective, when he testified before the Senate Committee on Territories, Jackson described the Indian policy that he recommended that Congress implement in Alaska as follows:

> JACKSON: The people of Southeastern Alaska, the Indians, live in comfortable plank houses, from 40 feet by 60 feet ordinary size. They have comfortable clothing; many of them dress in European clothing ... They have plenty of comfortable food. It is not necessary that the United States should feed or clothe them, or make treaties with them. This enables us in our Indian policy to take a new departure; and treat them as American citizens. All that is necessary to be done is to afford them government and teachers, which they cannot procure for themselves.
>
> SENATOR: In other words, you mean to say that if we should afford the protection of a well-organized government, they would subordinate themselves to the law of the United States? That is your idea?
>
> JACKSON: That is my idea.[6]

In 1884 when it enacted the Alaska Organic Act,[7] the statute that created a civil government, the Forty-eighth Congress accepted Jackson's recommendation. Rather than recognizing the several hundred ethnological tribes in Alaska as tribes in a political sense, the Act required Alaska Natives living at all locations, including in communities that more than eighty years later would be designated as Native villages for the purposes of ANCSA, to comply with the civil and criminal laws with which the non-Native residents of Alaska were required to comply. In 1886 Alaska District Judge Lafayette Dawson acknowledged the policy choice the Forty-eighth Congress made when he noted, "The United States has at no time recognized any tribal independence or relations among these Indians, [and] has never treated with them in any capacity."[8]

Section 13 of the Alaska Organic Act directed the secretary of the interior to make "proper provision for the education of children of school age in the Territory of Alaska, without reference to race." To implement that directive, with the approval of Secretary of the Interior Henry Teller, in 1885 Commissioner of Education John

Sheldon Jackson (1880). Robert Laird Stewart, *Sheldon Jackson*, New York: Fleming H. Revell Company (1908).

Eaton appointed Sheldon Jackson as general agent for education in Alaska. In that position Jackson supervised the administration of the fifty-nine schools the Bureau of Education opened in Native villages prior to Jackson's retirement in 1908.

Insofar as citizenship being the objective of Congress's Native policy was concerned, in 1895 in a speech at a conference on Indian policy that was held annually at a resort at Lake Mohonk, New York, Jackson explained that

> We have no Indians in Alaska; we have natives. When Alaska began to be developed, some wise man said: "What are you going to do with the natives? Do you want reservations?" The answer was, "No." "Do you want agents?" "No." "Do you want those people to be sheltered behind the Indian policy of the Government." "No: We do not want any Indian government at all." "What do you want, then?" "We want citizenship right from the start, and that the people should simply be called natives." It was at first a constant fight to keep them from being called Indians. We wanted to commence where the friends of the Indian left off. We wanted to avail ourselves of the experience of the past on the Indian question: and so we have no Indians, we have only natives. The natives have all the rights that any white man has. There has never been a time since the establishment of the courts in that land when a native could not go into court, could not sue and be sued, like any white man.[9]

But while they may have had "all the rights that any white man has," in 1908 Alaska District Judge Royal Gunnison described the reality of how Alaska Natives fared in his courtroom as follows:

> The control governmentally of the native has been left to the district court and the commissioners, but that control is punitive only. When the Indian breaks the laws, established, by the way, for white men whose code of morals and habits of life are different, the Indian is hailed before the commissioner or the grand jury or the district court, indicted, tried, usually convicted, and sentenced to jail, oftentimes for matters which under his native customs was not a crime. He serves his term of imprisonment and returns to his people bewildered and embittered, but not bettered. Weeks of time and thousands of dollars in money are annually spent in these futile endeavors to make the Indian understand the white man's way and obey the white man's law.[10]

To cite one example, six years earlier, in 1902 three Tlingit Indians who lived in Hoonah, a Native village on Chichagof Island in southeast Alaska, kidnaped an Indian whose English name was George Smalley because they thought Smalley was a warlock who was practicing witchcraft. When Hiram Folsom, the U.S. commissioner in Juneau, learned that during his confinement Smalley had died from starvation, Folsom asked Smalley's abductors to admit what they had done. Although the three Indians were illiterate, spoke only Tlingit, and were not represented by an attorney, speaking through an interpreter they admitted their involvement in Smalley's death. Based on their statements, they were convicted of manslaughter by an all-white jury and sentenced to four years in federal prison.[11]

In 1932 Secretary of the Interior Ray Lyman Wilbur would reaffirm Judge Dawson's and Judge Gunnison's view of the law when he informed Representative Edgar Howard, the chairman of the House Committee on Indian Affairs, that "the United States has had no treaty relations with any of the aborigines of Alaska nor have they been recognized as the independent tribes with a government of their own. The individual native has always and everywhere in Alaska been subject to the white man's law, both Federal and territorial, civil and criminal."[12]

In 1912 the Sixty-second Congress designated Alaska as a territory and authorized male citizens twenty-one years of age and older to elect a legislature.[13] In 1915 the Alaska Territorial Legislature extended the white man's law into Native villages by enacting a statute that authorized Natives who lived in communities that had forty or more adult inhabitants to "form a self-governing village organization" by petitioning the commissioner of the recording district in which the community was located.

When a petition was granted a community council would be elected that would have authority "to pass such ordinances for the government of the village as shall not be in conflict with federal or territorial laws," including "ordinances to prevent the practice of witchcraft," "levy and collect a tax on dogs," impose "a general tax

Bureau of Indian Affairs School, Noatak, Alaska. Phillip and Retta Reed, Archives and Special Collections, Consortium Library, University of Alaska Anchorage.

not to exceed one percent per annum on assessed valuation of houses, boats, and canoes," "appoint constables," and "provide for the punishment of any violation of its ordinances by fine or imprisonment in the village jail."[14]

In 1929 the legislature repealed the 1915 statute.[15] But that did not mean there was no semblance of local government in Native villages. Rather, the situation at Noatak, a Native village in the northwest arctic, was typical. In 1933 J.B. Henderson, the teacher at the school the Bureau of Indian Affairs (BIA) operated at Noatak,* reported:

> There is a village council of seven men members which are elected by the people. This council discusses and passes on matters of the village which may be brought to its attention and makes regulations as to village life such as pertain to sanitation, police, and public safety, etc., and is very worthwhile. It has no strictly legal powers, of course, but as the community is in support of it, it is an excellent nucleus for dealing with such local matters as are not of sufficient seriousness to bring before a U.S. Commissioner. It derives its very limited powers and local jurisdiction from custom and consent of the community and that is power enough to get along with. It works out very well in practice.[16]

---

* In 1931 Secretary Wilbur transferred responsibility for the administration of schools and other programs for Alaska Natives from the Bureau of Education to the BIA.[20]

In February 1934 Commissioner of Indian Affairs John Collier sent the Seventy-third Congress a bill whose enactment would change Congress's Indian policies in ways that Collier long had advocated. The bill was written principally by Felix Cohen,[17] but the bill's content had been developed by Collier, Assistant Commissioner of Indian Affairs William Zimmerman, and other senior members of Collier's staff.[18]

Introduced in the Senate as S. 2755 by Senator Burton Wheeler, the chairman of the Senate Committee on Indian Affairs, the bill was forty-eight pages long and contained sixty sections.[19] Because the purpose of the bill was to reorder day-to-day life on Indian reservations in the coterminous states, S. 2755 said nothing about Alaska Natives or the Territory of Alaska.

The Senate Committee on Indian Affairs held six hearings on S. 2755, after which, after listening to Commissioner Collier explain the bill, Senator Wheeler rejected it. He then appointed a subcommittee whose members would write a new bill. But before the subcommittee began work, the senator met with Assistant Commissioner Zimmerman (because by then Wheeler had tired of Collier's imperious my-way-or-the-highway arrogance).

At that meeting the senator told Zimmerman what provisions of S. 2755 he would be willing to support.[21] As Wheeler explained when the committee next convened, "I got together with the commissioner of Indian affairs (sic) and went over the important points that I thought were in controversy, and yesterday they sent up this bill, which eliminates, it seems to me, practically all of the matters that are in controversy."[22]

The new bill, which Senator Wheeler introduced as S. 3645 and whose text presumably had been written by Felix Cohen, was only ten pages long and contained only nineteen sections.[23]

Section 19 of S. 3645 contained a three-pronged definition of the term "Indian" that was nearly, although not completely, identical to the definition of the term "Indian" that the Seventy-third Congress would enact as section 19 of the Indian Reorganization Act (IRA).

Section 19 defined "Indian" to mean:

1) "persons of Indian descent who are members of any recognized Indian tribe now under Federal jurisdiction,"
2) "persons who are descendants of such members who were, on June 1, 1934, residing within the present boundaries of any Indian reservation," and
3) "all other persons of one-half or more Indian blood."

Section 19 also contained the sentence: "For the purposes of this Act, Eskimos and other aboriginal peoples of Alaska shall be considered Indians."

When the members of the Senate Committee on Indian Affairs convened to review the new bill and Senator Wheeler asked Commissioner Collier to explain why that sentence had been included in the "Indian" definition, Collier answered: "The law is that [Alaska Natives] are entitled to educational aid, health aid, but otherwise are not under the guardianship of the Government. The effect of [including in section

19 the sentence that designated 'Eskimos and other aboriginal peoples of Alaska' as 'Indians'] will be to extend the land acquisition and credit benefits to these Alaska Indians who are pure-blood Indians and very much in need, and they are neglected, and they are Indians pure and simple."[24]

Section 10 of S. 3645 authorized a "recognized tribal authority" to petition the secretary of the interior to charter a corporation that would be empowered to "take, hold, manage, operate, and dispose of all collective and other corporate assets and property of every description, both real and personal, and to do such other things as are needed for the conduct of its business, except that no authority is granted to sell any of the land included within the limits of the reservation." A corporation also was authorized to borrow money from a revolving loan fund for the purpose of "promoting the economic development of such tribes and of their members." And section 13 of S. 3645 authorized the commissioner of Indian affairs "to provide for the technical education of qualified Indians in the various services and functions now or hereafter performed by the Office of Indian Affairs."

Section 15 of S. 3645 then announced that the provisions of the bill would not apply to any of the territories "except that the provisions dealing with corporations and the educational features of this Act shall apply to Alaska."[25]

Since a "recognized tribal authority" was the only entity that could petition the secretary of the interior for a corporate charter, and section 10 implied that the members of the tribe the authority represented resided on a "reservation," if he did write S. 3645, how Felix Cohen believed that a group of Alaska Natives whose members were not "under the guardianship of the Government" and who did not reside on a reservation would be eligible to petition the secretary for a corporate charter is a mystery whose solution subsequent events would moot.

In the U.S. House of Representatives, Representative Edgar Howard, the chairman of the Committee on Indian Affairs, and the other members of the committee were as opposed to the bill Commissioner Collier had sent to Congress as Senator Wheeler had been. So they wrote their own bill whose text was based on, but was not identical to, the text of S. 3645.[26]

While section 21 of that bill contained a definition of the term "Indian" that stated, "For the purposes of this Act, Eskimos and other aboriginal peoples of the Territory of Alaska shall be considered Indian," section 14 stated that only four sections of the bill would apply to the Territory of Alaska. Inexplicably, those four sections did not include the section 21 "Indian" definition. Rather, they included sections 9, 10, and 11, which authorized the "members of any recognized tribe" to incorporate an "Indian chartered corporation" empowered to borrow money from a revolving loan fund, as well as section 12, which authorized "Indians" to borrow money "for the payment of tuition and other expenses in recognized vocational and trade schools."

The situation vis-à-vis Alaska Natives became even more confused when the members of a conference committee that Senator Wheeler and Representative Howard co-chaired melded the texts of the Senate and House bills into the text the Seventy-third Congress enacted as the IRA.

In that text, section 13 inexplicably continued to not apply to the Territory of Alaska the section 19 definition of the term "Indian" that contained the sentence "For the purposes of this Act, Eskimos and other aboriginal peoples of Alaska shall be considered Indians." Equally inexplicably, section 13 applied to the Territory of Alaska section 9, which authorized funds to be expended for the purpose of organizing "Indian chartered corporations," and section 10, which created the revolving loan fund from which Indian chartered corporations could obtain loans. But section 13 did not apply section 17, which authorized "at least one-third of the adult Indians" of "such tribe" to petition the secretary of the interior to issue a charter for a corporation that would be able to borrow money from the revolving loan fund.

The reference to "such tribe" in section 17 appears to refer back to section 16, which authorized "any Indian tribe, or tribes, residing on the same reservation" to "organize for its common welfare" by adopting "an appropriate constitution and bylaws." Section 13 did apply section 16 to the Territory of Alaska, even though two years earlier Secretary of the Interior Wilbur had advised Representative Howard that Alaska Natives had never been "recognized as the independent tribes with a government of their own," and even though a month earlier Commissioner Collier had told Senator Wheeler that Alaska Natives were "not under the guardianship of the Government."

In 1978 District Judge Robert Kelleher observed that "Congress is constitutionally empowered to launch programs, the scope, impact, consequences, and workability of which are largely unknown, at least to the Congress, at the time of enactment."[27] The disjointed, analytically incoherent manner in which the Seventy-third Congress included Alaska Natives in the IRA confirms the validity of that insight.

Two

In 1934 Anthony Dimond, the Territory of Alaska's delegate in the U.S. House of Representatives,* was a member of the House Committee on Indian Affairs. But he was not a member of the conference committee whose members melded the texts of the bills the Senate and House Committees on Indian Affairs had written into the text of the bill that the Seventy-third Congress enacted as the Indian Reorganization Act. Because he was not, the conference committee's bill inadvertently omitted from section 13, the section that listed the sections of the IRA that would apply to the Territory of Alaska, a reference to section 17. Dimond described the mistake and its consequence as follows:

> The Wheeler-Howard Act [IRA] is the result of bills introduced in both the House and Senate. The Senate bill passed first and got to the House where it was very largely amended. On the last day of the session, the bill went to conference and when the conference committee submitted its report several things originally included in both bills had been inadvertently omitted. The Act itself provides that sections 9, 10, 11, 12, and 16 thereof shall apply to the Territory of Alaska. Through mistake made by the conference committee, however, section 17 was not made applicable to Alaska. Section 17 authorizes the secretary of the interior to issue charters of incorporations to tribes of Indians, and the inference is that they must live on reservations. Section 16 provides that any tribe or tribes residing on the same reservation shall have the right to organize for its or their common welfare. Under section 10, an appropriation of $10,000,000 is authorized as a revolving fund from which the secretary of the interior may make loans to Indian chartered corporations. This section applies to Alaska but, as above stated, section 17 does not, and section 17 provides for the issuance of the charter.
>
> Hence, it appears that through the mistake made in conference in omitting section 17, it is now impossible for any Indian community in Alaska to borrow any of the funds authorized to be appropriated under section 10.[2]

To straighten out the snafu, Dimond asked Commissioner of Indian Affairs John Collier to have one of the attorneys at the Department of the Interior write a bill whose

* In 1906 the Fifty-ninth Congress authorized male citizens of the United States who had resided in Alaska for at least one year to elect a delegate to the U.S. House of Representatives.[1]

Alaska Delegate Anthony Dimond.
John WeirTroy Collection, Alaska State Library.

enactment by the Seventy-fourth Congress would apply section 17 to the Territory of Alaska.[3] The attorney to whom the commissioner gave the assignment was Felix Cohen.[4]

In January 1936 Representative Dimond introduced the bill Cohen wrote as H.R. 9866.

Section 1 of the bill extended section 17 of the IRA to the Territory of Alaska and provided "[t]hat Indian-chartered corporations in Alaska may be organized and carry on business without regard to residence on any reservation." Section 2 of the bill delegated to the secretary of the interior authority to designate land located within the boundaries of certain land withdrawals as well as "other public lands which are actually occupied by Indians or Eskimos within said Territory" as "Indian reservations."

Dimond did not ask to have section 2 included in the bill. Rather, Cohen included it because, as Secretary of the Interior Harold Ickes explained to Representative Will Rogers, who had succeeded Representative Edgar Howard as chairman of the House Committee on Indian Affairs,

> Indian tribes do not exist in Alaska in the same sense as in continental United States. Section 19 of the Indian Reorganization Act defines the word "tribe" as referring to "Any Indian tribe, organized band, pueblo, or Indians residing on one reservation." With a few exceptions the lands occupied by natives of Alaska have not been designated as reservations. In order, therefore, to define

> an Alaskan tribe it is necessary to identify it with the land it occupies and in terms of the language of the act, "reservation." In addition, *if native communities of Alaska are to set up systems of local government, it will be necessary to stipulate the geographical limits of their jurisdictions. Reservations set up by the Secretary of the Interior will accomplish this* (emphasis added).[5]

Shortly after Delegate Dimond introduced H.R. 9866, William Paul, the grand secretary of the Alaska Native Brotherhood (ANB),* arrived in Washington, D.C., to work with Cohen and Dimond on the bill.[6]

After likely having been educated by Paul, Cohen realized that section 13 of the IRA having extended section 16 of the IRA to the Territory of Alaska had created a problem separate from the problem that section 13 not having extended section 17 to the territory had created. As Cohen and Paul explained to Commissioner Collier: "Because of the fact that there are apparently no recognized Indian reservations, tribes, or bands in Alaska (except for the Annette Islands Reservation),** it would be unde-

* In 1912 twelve "civilized" Tlingit, Haida, and Tsimshian Indians, whom the Bureau of Education had gathered in Juneau to discuss how "uncivilized" Indians could be encouraged to assimilate, organized the ANB. The ANB is composed of chapters, called camps, in towns and villages throughout southeast Alaska. The members of the local camps annually hold a convention called a grand camp. William Paul, a Tlingit Indian who was the first Alaska Native admitted to the Alaska bar and the first Alaska Native elected to the territorial legislature, was elected grand secretary at the 1920 grand camp.[7] In 1934 Anthony Dimond sent Paul a copy of the bill Commissioner Collier had sent to the Seventy-third Congress. After reading it, Paul informed Dimond: "There is very little that can apply to Alaska, and that little appears to be entirely beneficial — the matter of education principally. Some people without an understanding of the legal position of the Alaska native would think that these natives would come under the bill. Such questions could be solved when we got to them."[8]

** In 1887 eight hundred Tsimshian Indians, led by the Anglican missionary William Duncan, emigrated from British Columbia to Annette Island on the southern tip of the Alexander Archipelago in southeast Alaska, where they built Metlakatla, a town whose architecture was modeled on that of a nineteenth century English country town. At Duncan's urging, the Tsimshians previously had abandoned their tribal relations.[9] At Duncan's request and with the support of Senator Henry Dawes, the chairman of the Senate Committee on Indian Affairs,[10] in 1891 the Fifty-first Congress designated Annette Island "as a reservation for the use of the Metlakahtla Indians, and those people known as Metlakahtlans who have recently emigrated from British Columbia to Alaska, and such other Alaskan natives as may join them."[11] After the BIA apparently concluded that the Tsimshian residents of Metlakatla were "Indians" as section 19 of the IRA defines that term, in 1944 Assistant Secretary of the Interior Oscar Chapman approved a constitution for the Metlakatla Indian Community pursuant to section 1 of Public Law No. 74-538 and section 16 of the IRA.[12] However, in Article II of the Constitution "the people of the Metlakatla Indian Community" agreed "to obey all applicable laws of the Territory of Alaska." After holding a hearing at which the mayor of Metlakatla testified regarding the history of the Annette Island reserve, in 1958 District Judge Raymond Kelly concluded that "there is no tribal organization in Metlakatla and, in fact, the original settlers expressly renounced their tribal affiliations prior to coming to the Annette Islands." Judge Kelly also concluded that the Annette Island reserve was not an Indian reservation and the land within the boundaries of the reserve was not Indian country.[13] Nevertheless, today the BIA describes the reserve as an Indian reservation, describes the land within the boundaries of the reserve as Indian country, and asserts that residents of Metlakatla of Tsimshian descent are members of a federally recognized tribe.[14] But the Fifty-first Congress established the Annette Island reserve during the assimilation era during which Congress's

William Paul, Grand Secretary, Alaska Native Brotherhood.
Photograph Courtesy of Frances Paul Degermain.

sirable to carry over to this bill the requirement of the Indian Reorganization Act that organization be restricted to the Indians of a single tribe, band, or reservation."[15]

To remedy the problem, Cohen and Paul wrote an amendment to section 1 of H.R. 9866 that removed the sentence "Provided, That Indian-chartered corporations in Alaska may be organized and carry on business without regard to residence on

---

policy objective was to encourage Native Americans on reservations in the coterminous states and territories to abandon their tribal relations. Throughout that era Senator Dawes was Congress's most fervent assimilationist. According to Professor Frederick Hoxie, in 1881 when Dawes became chairman of the Senate Committee on Indian Affairs, "for the next twelve years he used his position to advocate Indian assimilation." Dawes's policy objective "was not a blending of Indian and white societies but Anglo conformity: the alteration of native culture to fit a 'civilized' model ... the senator believed in a single standard of civilization and expected that Indians—like other minority groups—could be made to conform to it."[16] As a consequence, it defies credulity to conclude, as the BIA has, that Senator Dawes and the other members of the Fifty-first Congress intended a create an Indian reservation on Annette Island within whose boundaries members of a federally recognized tribe today reside.[17]

any reservation" and substituted: "Provided, That groups of Indians in Alaska not heretofore recognized as bands or tribes, but having a common bond of occupation, or association, or residence within a well-defined neighborhood, community, or rural district, may organize to adopt constitutions and bylaws and to receive charters of incorporation and Federal loans under sections 16, 17, and 10 of the [IRA]."

Representative Rogers, Delegate Dimond, and the other members of the House Committee on Indian Affairs accepted that amendment, and in the report they filed when they reported H.R. 9866 to the U.S. House of Representatives, they explained that they had done so because "the proposed amendment no. 1 above set out is necessary because of the peculiar nontribal organizations under which the Alaska Indians operate. They have no tribal organizations as the term is understood generally."[18]

On May 1, 1936, President Franklin Roosevelt signed H.R. 9866 into law as Public Law No. 74-538.

In 1937 Assistant Commissioner of Indian Affairs William Zimmerman mailed to the teachers who taught in the schools the BIA was operating in Native villages instructions that they were to follow when assisting the residents of the villages in which the schools were located in writing constitutions that section 1 of Public Law No. 74-538 authorized the secretary of the interior to approve pursuant to section 16 of the IRA.[19] Because, as Secretary of the Interior Harold Ickes had explained a year earlier, "if native communities of Alaska are to set up systems of local government, it will be necessary to stipulate the geographical limits of their jurisdictions," the instructions directed that

> if an Indian reservation has been designated and approved [pursuant to section 2 of Public Law No. 74-538], and if the group of Indians for whom the reservation has been designated are organizing as an entire community..., they may include in their constitutions appropriate powers for the civil government of the area reserved, including police power over their own members and, under the supervision of the Department [of the Interior], the power to tax, license or exclude non-members. If the constitution has been adopted before the reservation became effective, such powers may be added by amendment. If at the time the constitution is being drafted, the designation and approval of an Indian reservation for the community organizing is anticipated, such powers may be included in the constitution, *but limited to take effect only upon the designation and approval of a reservation for such community* (emphasis added).[20]

In July 1940, by which time thirty-eight constitutions had been approved, Assistant Secretary of the Interior Oscar Chapman, who supervised Commissioner Collier and Assistant Commissioner Zimmerman, reaffirmed that "[t]he Department has at no time recognized the existence in Alaska of Indian tribes, with powers of limited sovereignty, similar to the tribes in (sic) continental United States."[21]

Between 1938 and 1950 BIA teachers assisted the Native residents of sixty-nine communities that later would be designated as Native villages for the purposes of ANCSA to write constitutions.[22] As Assistant Secretary Zimmerman's instructions directed, the "Powers of the Village" article in the boilerplate text of the constitutions granted a village council governmental authority only "[t]o control the use by members or nonmembers of any reserve set aside by the Federal Government for the Village and to keep order in the reserve."[23]

Between 1941 and 1946 Assistant Secretary of the Interior Oscar Chapman and Secretaries of the Interior Harold Ickes and Julius Krug designated six Indian reservations in Alaska.[24]

The third reservation was a 1.8 million-acre reserve whose boundaries encircled Venetie and Arctic Village, two communities on the south side of the Brooks Mountain Range in the Alaska interior whose residents were Gwich'in Athabascan Indians.[25] After the reserve was created, Governor Ernest Gruening and other politically influential residents of the territory objected to the secretary of the interior designating any more large tracts of public land in Alaska as Indian reservations.[26] One of those individuals was Anthony Dimond, who in 1947 told Alaska Delegate E.L. "Bob" Bartlett, who in 1944 had been elected delegate when Dimond retired, that

> at the time the legislation [H.R. 9866] was before Congress I had no thought—or even suspicion—that it would be used to reserve anything more than the native settlements and villages with ample space around the same to prevent interference by others, with the necessary facilities including water supply and sea front and harborage areas. There was no suggestion at the time that vast areas would be reserved. Looking back upon the occasion after these intervening years, it seems probable that I would not have sponsored the legislation in its present form had I fully realized that the authority given might be abused. Of course, I should have written reasonable limitations into the bill before its introduction.[27]

That same year, 1947, the public affairs office at the Department of the Interior inadvertently revealed that Secretary Krug was planning to designate public land within and surrounding Hydaburg, a Native village in southeast Alaska, as an Indian reservation.[28] In response, Senator Hugh Butler, the chairman of the Senate Committee on Interior and Insular Affairs who believed that "the solution of the Indian problem in Alaska is not to set [Alaska Natives] apart from other people or from modern life but to give them tools with which to compete with white people,"[29] introduced Senate Joint Resolution No. 162. The resolution's passage by the Eightieth Congress would have abolished the Venetie reserve and the five other Indian reservations and repealed section 2 of Public Law No. 74-538. While the Senate passed Joint Resolution No. 162 by a unanimous voice vote,[30] the resolution died in the House when a procedural objection prevented it from being brought to the floor before the Eightieth Congress adjourned.

A year later Secretary Krug tried to designate as Indian reservations public land within and surrounding not only Hydaburg, but also two other Native villages. That effort failed, and over the succeeding twenty-seven years no secretary of the interior used the authority that section 2 of Public Law No. 74-538 delegated to designate Indian reservations in Alaska, and in 1976 the Ninety-fourth Congress repealed section 2.[31]

The failure of the secretary of the interior to designate an Indian reservation for each community in Alaska whose Native residents had a constitution that the secretary had approved pursuant to section 1 of Public Law No. 74-538 and section 16 of the IRA resulted in the anomaly that in more than fifty communities that later would be designated as Native villages for the purposes of ANCSA, the Native residents had a constitution that authorized them to elect a village council but no reservation within whose boundaries the council had authority to serve as the local government. In 1961 a senior official in the BIA Alaska regional office described the legal situation that anomaly created as follows: "Villages not on reserves or reservations established for or reserved for the use of the resident Natives, even though organized under IRA, do not have legal authority to establish sales tax rates and collect the tax within the village, to enforce curfews, control the use and possession of intoxicants in the village, etc."[32]

Between 1947 and 1957 the Eightieth, Eighty-first, Eighty-third, Eighty-fourth, and Eighty-fifth Congresses held hearings in Alaska and Washington, D.C., on bills whose enactment would admit the Territory of Alaska into the union, as well as oversight hearings in which conditions in Alaska relevant to the question of whether it was advisable for the territory to become a state were investigated.[33] At those hearings numerous Department of the Interior officials, including four secretaries of the interior, testified, as did Alaska Native witnesses.

Those witnesses informed the members of the committees who conducted the hearings that Alaska Natives represented a significant percentage of the territory's population, that the BIA operated schools in eighty-five Native villages,[34] and that Alaska Native land claims based on aboriginal title were an important matter that Congress needed to address.[35]

No witness suggested that the Native residents of communities that later would be designated as Native villages for the purposes of ANCSA were members of federally recognized tribes whose governing bodies, as a consequence of that legal status, possessed governmental authority. Instead, what the witnesses told Congress was that in the 1950s the situation in those communities was the same as it had been in 1933 when J.B. Henderson described the situation at Noatak: Native residents of a community were subject to the civil and criminal laws of the Territory of Alaska, but minor matters, both civil and criminal, were handled informally by village councils that had no legal imprimatur.

In 1955 the Subcommittee on Territorial and Insular Affairs of the House Committee on Interior and Insular Affairs held field hearings in Alaska, including in Barrow, the most populous community on Alaska's North Slope, where most residents were Inupiat Eskimos.

Prior to making the trip, Representative Leo O'Brien, the chairman of the subcommittee, asked the Library of Congress for information about Barrow. The Library informed O'Brien that "Barrow was organized under the Indian Reorganization Act during March of 1940 with a charter, constitution, and bylaws. Under the terms of the Reorganization Act the village has a council, although the tribe owns no land, nor does it operate any enterprises as a tribe. The natives are under the jurisdiction of a United States commissioner located at Barrow ... Minor crimes are handled by the village council, all others are prosecuted under the Territorial laws. The tribe does not have a law and order code."[36]

Two years later the subcommittee held a hearing on Alaska statehood in Washington, D.C.

By that date President Dwight Eisenhower had conditioned his unenthusiastic support for statehood on the inclusion of a provision in the bill that in 1958 the Eighty-fifth Congress would enact as the Alaska Statehood Act that would authorize the president to create "national defense withdrawals" north of a line that began at the location where the Porcupine River crossed the Alaska-Canadian boundary and then ran west along the Yukon and Kukskowim Rivers to the coast of the Bering Sea. During the hearing, when the subject of what laws would be applicable within the national defense withdrawals was discussed, Alaska Delegate E.L. "Bob" Bartlett had the following colloquy with acting Secretary of the Interior Olin Hatfield Chilson in which Bartlett explained to the secretary that in communities located north of the Porcupine, Yukon, Kuskokwim line (that later would be designated as Native villages for the purposes of ANCSA), the Native residents were subject to the civil and criminal laws of the Territory of Alaska:

> BARTLETT: Let us take the little village of Point Hope [an Inupiat Eskimo community on the northwestern coast of Alaska], which, to the best of my information, is not incorporated. Let us say that it is to be involved in a defense withdrawal. They operate, I think, now through a council. They are not incorporated.
>
> CHILSON: I am just trying to think this out. Those natives at the present time are under the Federal trusteeship that pertains to Indians, I assume, and under that trusteeship they have their own tribal government. Now the State laws still pertain in that area. I do not know whether the State laws would have anything to do with those natives or not. If they did, the State law would continue to operate.
>
> BARTLETT: I do not believe that any Federal police laws or similar or associated laws apply to them now. I mean they are not directly under the control of the Bureau of Indians Affairs.
>
> CHILSON: Now, as to whether or not they technically and legally, under the amendments which we have proposed, would continue to have the

right to operate their tribal laws and setup, I do not know. I should think that they would be.

BARTLETT: They are under Territorial now, just as people of any community are. They are certainly not under any municipal law, because they do not have any incorporated municipality.

CHILSON: Then would they not continue to act under the Federal laws relating to Indians, which I assume is what they operate under now?

BARTLETT: No; I do not think so.[37]

Eleven months later, and four months before President Eisenhower would sign the Alaska Statehood Act into law, in February 1958 Assistant Secretary of the Interior Roger Ernst, who supervised the BIA and therefore was better informed than Secretary Chilson had been, reaffirmed that, as had been the situation since 1867, there were no federally recognized tribes in Alaska. Assistant Secretary Ernst told the House Committee on the Judiciary that "it had been the general practice for Territorial officers to apply Territorial law in native villages" and "none of the native villages has ever had any machinery for enforcing law and order. They have no tribal court, no police, and no criminal code."[38]

Three

In 1951 Alaska Delegate E.L. "Bob" Bartlett introduced H.R. 4388, a bill whose enactment by the Eighty-second Congress would have settled Alaska Native land claims.[1] When the Subcommittee on Indian Affairs of the House Committee on Interior and Insular Affairs held a hearing on the bill, Bartlett, in the following colloquy with Representative Wesley D'Ewart, the chairman of the subcommittee, reaffirmed what the House Committee on Indian Affairs had reported in 1936:

> D'Ewart: There is one more point, Mr. Bartlett. On page 2 I notice that the term "community of natives" means any clan, tribe, village, or other community group of natives of Alaska. If this law were passed, would this not be the first time that *tribes* have been recognized by an act of Congress? (emphasis added).
>
> Bartlett: In Alaska?
>
> D'Ewart: Yes.
>
> Bartlett: I cannot say definitively, but that would be my opinion. We do not have, as you know, any tribal concept in the same manner as we find it in the States.[2]

After the hearing the subcommittee took no further action on H.R. 4388.

Twenty years later, in 1971, the Ninety-second Congress settled Alaska Native land claims by enacting ANCSA.

In order to assist Congress in its consideration of the bills that beginning in 1967 were introduced to settle the claims, in 1968 Senator Henry Jackson, the chairman of the Senate Committee on Interior and Insular Affairs, asked a federally funded think tank, the Field Committee for Development Planning in Alaska, to study the land claims issue. In its report submitted that same year, *Alaska Natives and the Land*, the Field Committee explained that

> Most villages in Alaska are organized for government only on a traditional basis. Others are chartered under the Indian Reorganization Act, some are organized as cities under the laws of the State of Alaska, and a few have dual organization. The 84 villages organized only on a traditional basis choose village councils and leaders in varying patterns, sometimes following customs of the past, but most of the time following newer practices of open elections. These villages have no formal legal status.

Members of the House Committee on Interior and Insular Affairs, Subcommittee on Indian Affairs hold field hearing in Alaska on H.R. 4388, November 1951. Representative Wesley D'Ewart (far left). Delegate E.L. "Bob" Bartlett (third from right). E.L. "Bob" Bartlett Collection, Alaska and Polar Regions Department, University of Alaska Fairbanks.

The Field Committee also explained that "State laws, of course, apply in all villages."[3] Between 1968 and 1971 the Senate and House Committees on Interior and Insular Affairs held nineteen hearings on bills whose enactment would settle Native land claims.[4] At those hearings Alaska Natives, attorneys representing Native organizations, and Department of the Interior officials testified. Consistent with what Delegate Bartlett told Representative D'Ewart in 1951 and what the Field Committee explained in 1968, no witness suggested that Native residents of communities that would be designated as Native villages for the purposes of ANCSA were members of federally recognized tribes or were members of a "recognized Indian tribe" within the meaning of that term in the "Indian" definition in section 19 of the Indian Reorganization Act. To the contrary. As Willie Hensley, an Inupiat Eskimo who was a leader of the land claims movement and who later would serve as president of the AFN,[5] explained in 1968 to the Senate Committee on Interior and Insular Affairs, "We have no administratively recognized tribal groups in the State, such as you have in Arizona and some of the other States."[6, *]

By 1971 when the Ninety-second Congress enacted ANCSA, Alaska Natives had created eleven regional organizations, and in 1965 the Eighty-ninth Congress had authorized Tlingit and Haida Indians in southeast Alaska to create the Central Council of Tlingit and Haida Indians of Alaska, a regional organization about which more

* In 1979 Hensley recalled that in the mid-1960s when he attended George Washington University, "I met a lot of Indians, mostly traditional, and I began to wonder why we were different in Alaska, with no tribal organization."[7]

will be said. Section 7(a) of ANCSA described the twelve regional organizations as "Native associations," listed each association by name, and identified the geographic region in which each association was headquartered. Section 7(d) of ANCSA directed five incorporators, "named by the Native association in the region," to "incorporate under the laws of Alaska a Regional Corporation to conduct business for profit."

A year earlier, in 1970, President Richard Nixon sent the Ninety-first Congress a message on Indian policy in which he announced that he soon would send a bill to Capitol Hill whose enactment "would empower a tribe or group of tribes or any other Indian community to take over the control or operation of Federally-funded and administered programs in the Department of the Interior and the Department of Health, Education and Welfare."[8]

In 1971 President Nixon sent the Ninety-second Congress his bill, which was introduced in the Senate as S. 1573. Section 2 of the bill authorized "Indian tribes" to contract with the BIA and Indian Health Service (IHS) to administer programs that the BIA and IHS were administering. Section 1 defined "Indian tribe" to mean "an Indian tribe, band, nation, or Alaska Native Community for which the Federal Government provides special programs and services because of their Indian identity."

After the Ninety-second Congress adjourned without passing S. 1573, in 1973 when the Ninety-third Congress convened Senator Jackson introduced his own bill as S. 1017. Since fourteen months earlier the Ninety-second Congress had enacted ANCSA, section 4 of S. 1017 defined "Indian tribe" to mean "any Indian tribe, band, nation, or other organized group or community, including any Alaska Native community as defined in the Alaska Native Claims Settlement Act, for which the Federal Government provides special programs and services because of its Indian identity."

After the Senate passed S. 1017, in 1974 the Subcommittee on Indian Affairs of the House Committee on Interior and Insular Affairs held a hearing on the bill. One of the witnesses was Ray Paddock, the president of the Central Council of Tlingit and Haida Indians of Alaska. In 1971 the BIA had signed a contract with the Central Council that authorized the Council to administer adult vocational training, old age assistance, foster care placement, and several other programs the BIA had been administering.[9, *]

---

* In 1968 President Lyndon Johnson sent the Ninetieth Congress his own message on Indian policy in which he noted that, "Many tribes have begun to administer activities which Federal agencies had long performed in their behalf."[10] That described an experiment Commissioner of Indian Affairs Robert Bennett had begun a year earlier to allow Indian tribes to contract with the BIA to administer BIA programs.[11] The BIA asserted that the Buy Indian Act, which the Sixty-first Congress had enacted in 1910,[12] delegated the BIA authority to enter into such contracts. But the Buy Indian Act delegates the secretary of the interior authority to employ "Indian labor" and purchase "the products of Indian industry." It does not delegate the BIA authority to contract for the administration of programs. Nevertheless, in 1971 Morris Thompson, the BIA Alaska Regional Director, signed a contract with the Central Council that allowed the Council to begin administering programs that the BIA Southeast Alaska Agency had been administering.

When Representative Lloyd Meeds, the chairman of the subcommittee, asked Paddock whether the "Indian tribe" definition in S. 1017 adequately reflected the situation in Alaska, Paddock recommended that the subcommittee amend the definition to include the Central Council and the other Native associations. Representative Meeds and Paddock then had the following colloquy regarding how the definition should be amended:

> MEEDS: If we were to put right after "Native villages" if we were to put "or Native regional corporations" that would take care of that problem. Was your organization authorized by the Settlement Act? Wasn't it in existence prior to the Settlement Act?
>
> PADDOCK: Yes, it was.
>
> MEEDS: Was it not specifically excluded?
>
> PADDOCK: All of the regional corporations named in the Settlement Act were nonprofit corporations, Mr. Chairman. There have since been named twelve other profitmaking corporations so there are now twenty-four Native corporations in Alaska.
>
> MEEDS: Counsel reminded me of that.
>
> PADDOCK: The profitmaking corporations do not deal in human services.
>
> MEEDS: What we are going to have to do is include those regional corporations and other organizations as chartered by regional corporations, or how do you think we should take care of that?[13]

By describing the Native associations as "regional corporations," Paddock reinforced Representative Meeds's confusion regarding the difference between the associations and the regional business corporations that section 7(d) of ANCSA directed Alaska Natives to incorporate. And after the hearing, the member of the staff of the Committee on Interior and Insular Affairs whom Representative Meeds assigned to write an amendment in the nature of a substitute for the version of S. 1017 that had passed the Senate[14] was similarly confused because the definition he wrote read:

> "Indian tribe" means any Indian tribe, band, nation, or other organized group or community, including any Alaska Native village or regional or village corporation as defined in or established pursuant to the Alaska Native Claims Settlement Act, which is recognized as eligible for the special programs and services provided by the United States to Indians because of their status as Indians.[15]

That is the "Indian tribe" definition that was included in the version of S. 1017 that in 1975 President Gerald Ford signed into law as the Indian Self-Determination and Education Assistance Act (Indian Self-Determination Act).[16]

The definition authorized Native villages and ANCSA regional and village corporations to contract with the BIA and IHS, but not the Native associations with which the BIA and IHS had been contracting.[17] As a consequence, each association now was required to obtain a resolution from each Native village within its region that authorized the association to contract with the BIA and IHS in the village's stead.

During the Ninety-third Congress during which the Indian Self-Determination Act was enacted, Senator Jackson introduced S. 2938, a bill whose enactment would increase the amount of money that could be appropriated to the IHS to provide health services for Native Americans. The bill also authorized the IHS to make grants to "Indian tribes," which the bill defined as "any Indian tribe, band, nation, or other organized group or community, including any Alaska Native village as defined in the Alaska Native Claims Settlement Act, which is recognized as eligible for the special programs and services provided by the United States to Indians because of their status as Indians."

That definition did not include the Native associations.

In 1974 the Senate passed S. 2938, but the House did not consider the bill prior to the adjournment of the Ninety-third Congress.

When the Ninety-fourth Congress convened, in February 1975 Senator Jackson reintroduced S. 2938 as S. 522. In April when the Senate Committee on Interior and Insular Affairs reported an amendment in the nature of a substitute for the original text of S. 522 the amendment retained the "Indian tribe" definition that had been in S. 2938.

Five months later, in September 1975, the members of the AFN Human Resource Board, whose membership was composed of a representative from each of the Native associations, met to discuss the implementation of the Indian Self-Determination Act in Alaska. A month later at a hearing the Subcommittee on Indian Affairs of the House Committee on Interior and Insular Affairs held on the implementation of the Indian Self-Determination Act, Robert Clark, the chairman of the Human Resource Board, explained that

> Our first and foremost problem identified [at the conference] is the definition of "Indian tribe" and "Tribal Organization" of (sic) the act which does not account for the unique Alaska situation. We have recommended to BIA and IHS inclusion of nonprofit regional native associations. It is the position of the Alaska Federation of Natives, Inc. that Congress, in its declaration of policy under Public Law 93-638 [Indian Self-Determination Act], did not intend to exclude those organizations that have been contracting with IHS and BIA in the past and currently. We feel it is the oversight of Congress not to account for the unique Alaska situation.[18]

In March 1976 the members of the Human Resource Board held another meeting at which the problem was discussed, at the conclusion of which they passed a resolution that urged Congress to amend the "Indian tribe" definition in the Indian Self-

Determination Act to limit the definition "to the twelve Native regional associations listed in section 7(a) of the Alaska Native Claims Settlement Act and all Alaska Native villages."[19]

Five months later Alaska Senators Ted Stevens and Mike Gravel arranged with Senator James Abourezk, the chairman of the Subcommittee on Indian Affairs of the Senate Committee on Interior and Insular Affairs, for the subcommittee to hold hearings in Juneau, Anchorage, Bethel, and Fairbanks to allow the leaders of the Native associations to voice their complaints.[20]

At the Juneau hearing Ray Paddock, who two years earlier had unintentionally created the problem about which he now complained, told the subcommittee that the "Indian tribe" definition in the Indian Self-Determination Act prohibited the Central Council of Tlingit and Haida Indians of Alaska from contracting directly with the BIA and IHS, but allowed Native villages in southeast Alaska to do so, even though, "with the exception of the community of Klukwan, which has a very active IRA council," none of the village councils that had been created by the constitutions the secretary of the interior had approved between 1938 and 1948 pursuant to section 1 of Public Law No. 74-538 and section 16 of the IRA had been active for a quarter century. At the Anchorage hearing Sam Kito, the president of the AFN, explained that "[t]he nonprofit Native associations are the current delivery system for [the Indian Self-Determination Act]. However, they do seem to be left out."

Five days after the hearings concluded, on September 9, 1976, the Senate renewed debate on S. 522 when Senator Jackson, whose bill it was, offered an amendment that was a substitute for the text of the bill the House had passed in lieu of the text of the bill the Senate Committee on Interior and Insular Affairs had reported and that had previously passed the Senate.

When he offered it, Jackson explained that most of the changes his amendment made to the House bill were "clarifying or technical." But one that was not was the decision he had made to replace the "Indian tribe" definition in the House bill with the "Indian tribe" definition in the Indian Self-Determination Act, which included ANCSA regional and village corporations but not the Native associations. Jackson explained that the change was necessary because "most of the programs in S. 522 in which Indian tribes would participate would require activities which would be difficult for the usually small native villages and groups to perform. In most cases, the regional corporations with their wider jurisdiction and more skilled manpower, would be the entities most capable of participating effectively in S. 522's programs."[21]

Having been educated by the witnesses who had testified at the hearings the Subcommittee on Indian Affairs had held in Alaska that Jackson had not attended, Alaska Senator Ted Stevens, prior to the vote on the Jackson amendment, offered an amendment to Jackson's amendment whose acceptance would have amended the "Indian tribe" definition to mean "any Indian tribe, band, nation, or other organized group or community, and in the case of Alaska such entity or entities designated by each region defined by the Alaska Native Claims Settlement Act."[22] Stevens explained that his amendment was needed because

> it is a very difficult problem in our State because we have not had recognition of tribes as it has been done in the traditional sense in the South 48.
>
> What this amendment that I propose would do would be to permit each region, as created by the Alaskan Native Land Claims Act, to designate which entity or entities in that region are recognized tribes. It would be a measure of self-determination in letting the people of each area of our State determine which entity is in fact the legal governing body of a tribe and should be the designated entity to participate in the administration of an act such as this pursuant to the Indian Self-Determination Act.[23]

Stevens knew Senator Jackson opposed his amendment. But he offered it in order to obtain from Jackson a promise that "in the next Congress we will endeavor to clarify the situation, either through the process of hearings or through whatever legislation may be needed."[24]

When Jackson made that commitment, Stevens withdrew his amendment. The Senate then passed, and the House subsequently accepted, the Jackson amendment, and S. 522 was enacted as the Indian Health Care Improvement Act.[25]

Taking Senator Jackson at his word, in June 1977 the members of the AFN Human Resource Board began writing a bill whose enactment by the Ninety-fifth Congress would amend the "Indian tribe" definition in the Indian Self-Determination and Indian Health Care Improvement Acts.[26] In July the text of a bill was approved,[27] which in August Alaska Senators Ted Stevens and Mike Gravel introduced as S. 2046.[28]

In September the Senate Select Committee on Indian Affairs[29,*] held a hearing on S. 2046,[30] after which three members of the committee's staff flew to Alaska and held hearings (that because no members participated were called "workshops") on the bill in Ketchikan, Juneau, Fairbanks, Barrow, Nome, Bethel, Aniak, and Anchorage.[31] But the committee then took no further action regarding S. 2046 because the members of the Human Resource Board had overreached by in section 2 of the bill defining the term "Indian tribe" to mean "the body of Alaska Natives represented by a Native Association, or its successor, named in section 7(a) of the Alaska Native Claims Settlement Act, hereinafter referred to as Alaska Regional Tribes," and then announcing that "the definition of Indian tribe as stated herein shall supercede, repeal, or modify the definition of Indian tribe in all other Federal legislation relating to or applicable to Alaska Natives."

* In January 1977 at the beginning of the Ninety-fifth Congress the Senate reorganized its committee structure. As part of the reorganization, the jurisdiction over Native American-related bills that the Subcommittee on Indian Affairs of the Committee on Interior and Insular Affairs had been exercising was transferred to a new Select Committee on Indian Affairs.

Since that definition did not include Native villages and ANCSA regional and village corporations, representatives of those entities objected that if the Ninety-fifth Congress enacted S. 2046 the villages and the corporations would lose the right that the Indian Self-Determination Act conferred to obtain contracts. However, Alaska Attorney General Avrum Gross and Eben Hopson, the mayor of the North Slope Borough (NSB),* objected to S. 2046 because of a different provision: section 6(a), which stated that "all rights, prerogatives, and duties held by federally recognized tribes in the contiguous States of the United States, shall accrue to the Alaska Native Regional Tribes established pursuant to this Act."

Attorney General Gross objected to section 6(a) because its enactment would "vest substantial and partially undefined sovereign or quasi-sovereign powers in racially exclusive groups not within one or more reservations, as it is customary, but rather over the entire territorial extent of the State of Alaska" and "establishing tribal organizations to exercise sovereign or quasi-sovereign powers not with respect to reservations but rather throughout the territory of an entire State is unprecedented and that it has not been shown to be necessary, proper, or desirable from any standpoint."[33] Mayor Hopson objected because section 6(a) went "beyond the establishment of an agency to administer Indian money to constitute a conflict of jurisdiction between the Arctic Slope Regional Tribe and the North Slope Borough established under the laws of the State of Alaska" and the new tribe's "assumption of the functions of the North Slope Borough as a legally constituted government could result in a chaotic situation."[34]

As has been described, section 17(d)(2) of ANCSA directed the secretary of the interior to withdraw up to eighty million acres of unreserved public land in Alaska and then recommend what land within those withdrawals Congress should include "as units of the National Park, Forest, Wildlife Refuge, and Wild and Scenic Rivers Systems." In 1980 the Ninety-sixth Congress implemented the secretary's recommendations by enacting the Alaska National Interest Lands Conservation Act (ANILCA).[35]

In addition to adding public land to the four conservation system units, ANILCA contains a title that establishes a regulatory system to protect the taking of fish stocks and wildlife populations for subsistence uses by Native and other residents of rural Alaska, amendments to ANCSA, and land exchanges between ANCSA regional and village corporations and the federal government.

* In 1972 the State of Alaska approved the incorporation of the NSB, a municipal government whose boundaries encompass 95,000 square miles of land from the crest of the Brooks Mountain Range north to the coast of the Arctic Ocean. Barrow (in 2016 renamed Utqiagvik) and seven communities that have been designated as Native villages for the purposes of ANCSA are located within the NSB.[32]

Between 1977 (the year Alaska Senators Ted Stevens and Mike Gravel introduced S. 2046) and 1980, the House Committee on Interior and Insular Affairs, the House Committee on Merchant Marine and Fisheries, and the Senate Committee on Energy and Natural Resources held seventy-seven hearings, town meetings, and workshops on bills whose enactment would implement the secretary's recommendations.[36] Alaska Natives, attorneys representing Native organizations and ANCSA regional and village corporations, and Department of the Interior officials testified. During those hearings, meetings, and workshops, no witness suggested that the Native residents of communities that had been designated as Native villages for the purposes of ANCSA were members of a federally recognized tribe or of a "recognized Indian tribe" within the meaning of that term in section 19 of the IRA.

Four

In 1978 the BIA decided to publish in the *Federal Register* a list of "Indian tribes which are recognized and receiving services from the Bureau of Indian Affairs."[1] In 1979 when Assistant Secretary of the Interior for Indian Affairs Forrest Gerard published the first list he announced that a "list of eligible Alaskan entities [rather than "tribes"] will be published at a later date."[2]

In 1982 when he republished the 1979 list, Assistant Secretary of the Interior for Indian Affairs Ken Smith published a separate list of "Alaska Native Entities Recognized and Eligible to Receive Services From the United States Bureau of Indian Affairs."[3] Assistant Secretary Smith also published a preamble in which he explained that "while eligibility for services administered by the Bureau of Indian Affairs is generally limited to historical tribes and communities of Indians residing on reservations, and their members, unique circumstances have made eligible additional entities in Alaska which are not historical tribes."[4]

Pursuant to authority that section 1 of Public Law No. 74-538 and section 17 of the Indian Reorganization Act delegated to the secretary of the interior, in 1939 Assistant Secretary of the Interior Oscar Chapman had approved a corporate charter for the Ketchikan Indian Corporation (KIC) that "a group of Indians [who had] a common bond of residence on Revillagigedo Island" on which Ketchikan, the second most populous town in southeast Alaska, is located had submitted.[5]

In 1977 when it became involved in a dispute with the Ketchikan Gateway Borough regarding the borough's assessment of a property tax against a leasehold the KIC owned, the KIC argued that it was not subject to the tax because it was "sovereign." In 1983 in its decision in *Board of Equalization v. Alaska Native Brotherhood*,[6] the lawsuit the KIC filed after the Board of Equalization ruled in the borough's favor, the Alaska Supreme Court held that the borough could subject the leasehold to its property tax. But the court reasoned to that result without deciding "whether KIC is an Indian tribe."[7]

When the KIC petitioned the court to reconsider its decision, the KIC argued that it was a "tribal entity" because Assistant Secretary Smith had included the KIC on the list of Native entities he had published in the *Federal Register*. In response to the petition, the court issued an amended decision. Justice Jay Rabinowitz issued an amended concurring opinion in which he added a footnote noting that it was "doubtful that the KIC has been 'recognized' as a tribe," among other reasons, because in the preamble that he published with his list, Assistant Secretary Smith "expressly avoided characterizing Alaskan Native groups as tribes or Indian communities. Instead, the notice stated that 'unique circumstances have made eligible additional entities in Alaska which are not historical tribes.'"[8]

Three weeks after the Alaska Supreme Court issued its amended decision, David Case, an Anchorage attorney who was the founding legal theoretician of the tribal sovereignty movement,* sent a letter to Scott Keep, the assistant solicitor who handled Alaska Native-related legal matters at the Department of the Interior in Washington, D.C., and with whom Case was acquainted because between 1979 and 1982 he had worked with Keep when Case had been an assistant solicitor in the Anchorage office of the Alaska regional solicitor.[9]

In his letter Case complained that Justice Rabinowitz had reasoned to his "erroneous conclusion" that the members of the KIC were not a federally recognized tribe because he had accepted as true the statement in the preamble that preceded the 1982 list of Native entities that Alaska Natives were not members of "historical tribes."[10] The complaint accomplished its objective because, five months after Case lodged it, when Assistant Secretary Smith published a new list of Native entities, the preamble had disappeared.[12]

By 1983 when David Case sent his letter to Scott Keep, the idea that the Native residents of each community that had been designated as a Native village for the purposes of ANCSA were members of a federally recognized tribe that, as a consequence of that legal status, possessed "inherent" governmental authority had become the core tenet of a nascent political movement that had begun in the Alaska interior. Two years earlier William "Spud" Williams, the president of the Tanana Chiefs Conference (TCC), the Native association headquartered in Fairbanks that had been listed in section 7(a) of ANCSA, described that tenet as follows: "[Alaska Natives have] the right to form IRA governments, even with ANCSA in place," and those governments have "the right to regulate their own fish and game, establish their own police and court systems, levy taxes, and to carry out all other functions of sovereign governments."[13]

In section 19(a) of ANCSA, the Ninety-second Congress revoked all reserves in Alaska other than the Annette Island reserve. And in 1976 the Ninety-fourth Congress repealed section 2 of Public Law No. 74-538, which had authorized the secretary of

* In 1978 David Case authored *The Special Relationship of Alaska Natives to the Federal Government: An Historical and Legal Analysis*, a study of federal Indian policy in Alaska in which he asserted that "The Federal Government has recognized two types of Native government in Alaska—traditional and IRA," and those governments "have inherent governmental authority unless the Federal Government has specifically deprived them of it." Case subsequently would acknowledge that "so far as I can tell [*Special Relationship*] was the first assessment to conclude that the villages were Alaska Native Tribes." While the BIA funded the study, according to Case, "the Department [of the Interior] first tried to embargo its release, but settled for a disclaimer that it did not represent government policy."[11]

William "Spud" Williams, President, Tanana Chiefs Conference.
Chief Peter John Collection, Alaska & Polar Regions Collections,
University of Alaska Fairbanks.

the interior to designate public land in Alaska as Indian reservations. But section 1 of Public Law No. 74-538, which authorized the secretary to approve—pursuant to section 16 of the IRA—constitutions for Alaska Natives "not heretofore recognized as bands or tribes," was not repealed.

Since it had not been, in 1979 Spud Williams directed Michael Walleri, an attorney he had hired to work as a "village government specialist," to assist Athabascan Indian residents of Native villages in the Alaska interior that did not have IRA constitutions to write one.

The first constitution Walleri helped to write was for the Circle Native Community (CNC).*

* Circle was founded in 1893 on the Yukon River by prospectors who stampeded into the area when gold was discovered. By 1896 the town had 700 residents, ten saloons, one church, an opera house, and a newspaper. In 1897 when gold was discovered on the Klondike River in the Yukon Territory, the town emptied out as prospectors stampeded upriver to the new strike. By 1900 Circle had 242 residents, by 1910 144, by 1920 96, by 1930 50. Because in 1970 when the census was enumerated a majority of the 54 residents of Circle were of Athabascan Indian descent, in 1971 the Ninety-second Congress designated Circle as a Native village for the purposes of ANCSA.

When, on the recommendation of the BIA, in October 1981 Secretary of the Interior James Watt approved the CNC's constitution, Walleri was celebratory. "While many state officials question the status of Alaskan Native villages as tribal governments," he told the press, "this decision by the secretary of the interior greatly strengthens the legal position of Native village councils throughout Alaska."[14]

Alaska Governor Jay Hammond responded to Secretary Watt's unexpected action by sending the secretary a letter in which he pointed out that "[t]he creation or recognition of federally-chartered tribal governments subsequent to passage of the Alaska Native Claims Settlement Act in 1971 raises many unanswered questions regarding State-Federal and State-Native legal and political relationships." The letter then posed six questions. The first was: "Do tribes or villages chartered under the IRA have authority to adopt ordinances and regulations, and upon what subjects may they act?" A second question was: "What are the territorial boundaries of jurisdiction of these IRA entities?"[15]

When he read the governor's letter, Spud Williams was disparaging. "What's happening," Williams railed, "is the state is challenging the sovereignty of Alaska Native governments."

> What they're really challenging is the validity of Alaska Natives! They would like to have it so there were no more Alaska Natives, only native Alaskans.
>
> The State of Alaska has only been in existence for how many years? Yet the Indians, Eskimos, and Aleuts have been here for thousands of years. It is ridiculous for the state to say the Natives no longer have the right to govern.[16]

A year later the validity of Williams's assertion that because for thousands of years Native residents of communities that had been designated as Native villages for the purposes of ANCSA had been "sovereign" they had the "right to govern" themselves became an issue that everyone in Alaska would become aware of.

Tyonek is a community on the western shore of Cook Inlet, forty-three miles southwest of Anchorage, that in 1971 the Ninety-second Congress designated as a Native village for the purposes of ANCSA. In 1915 President Woodrow Wilson signed an executive order that created the Moquawkie reserve, a 26,918-acre tract of public land whose boundaries encircled Tyonek.[17] In 1939 Maurice Carmody, the teacher at the school the BIA operated at Tyonek, assisted Tyonek residents to write a constitution pursuant to section 1 of Public Law No. 74-538 and section 16 of the IRA that in May of that year Assistant Secretary of the Interior Oscar Chapman approved.[18]

Article IV of the constitution contained the boilerplate language that granted the village council, which the constitution authorized Tyonek residents to elect, authority "to control the use by members or nonmembers of any reserve set aside by the Federal Government for the Village and to keep order in the reserve." And at the meeting at which that election was held, those in attendance directed the new council to "make any laws, rules, or regulations which it considers to be for the common good of the members of the village."[19]

Rule No. 4, which the village council passed in 1942, prohibited non-Natives from remaining in Tyonek for more than twenty-four hours without the council's permission. Twenty-nine years later, in 1971 in section 19(a) of ANCSA, the Ninety-second Congress revoked the Moquawkie reserve, after which the ANCSA village corporation the Indian residents of Tyonek had incorporated decided to select and be conveyed fee title to the surface estate of public land within and surrounding Tyonek pursuant to the ANCSA land selection and conveyance process.

In 1978 the Alaska regional solicitor of the Department of the Interior issued a legal opinion in which he concluded that "when the Tyonek reserve was terminated on December 18, 1971 by section 19(a) of the Alaska Native Claims Settlement Act, Rule No. 4 became void and unenforceable."[20] Nevertheless, in July 1982 the village council ordered six non-Natives who were living in Tyonek to leave the village. Donald Standifer, the president of the council, asserted that the council had "inherent authority" to do so.[21]

When four of the non-Natives refused to leave, in September 1982 in the U.S. District Court in Anchorage, the village council filed *Native Village of Tyonek v. Puckett*, a civil action in which the council asked the court to enforce Rule No. 4 by issuing an eviction order. In 1997 the lawsuit ended inconclusively.* But in 1982 the news that the lawsuit had been filed was widely reported throughout Alaska.

Every October the AFN holds a convention that delegates from Native villages throughout Alaska attend. Because of Michael Walleri's efforts to assist residents of Native villages in the Alaska interior in writing IRA constitutions and because of the *Native Village of Tyonek v. Puckett* lawsuit, by the October 1982 convention, tribal

* In 1986 District Judge James Fitzgerald issued an oral decision in which he dismissed the claim for relief the Tyonek village council had alleged in its complaint because the claim did not "arise under" federal law, and he dismissed a counterclaim that two of the non-Native defendants had filed because "based upon Tyonek's history and the manner in which the federal government has dealt with Tyonek, … the Village possesses sovereign immunity from suit like that of any other Indian tribes in the contiguous states."[22] In 1989 the U.S. Court of Appeals for the Ninth Circuit reinstated the council's claim for relief, and, without explaining its reasoning, affirmed the dismissal of the counterclaim.[23] The non-Native defendants filed a petition for a writ of certiorari that requested the U.S. Supreme Court to review the circuit court's decision, and in 1991 the Court granted the petition, and then vacated and remanded the circuit court decision "in light of *Oklahoma Tax Commission v. Citizen Band Potawatomi Indian Tribe of Oklahoma*," a decision in which the Court had held that the Citizen Band had not waived its sovereign immunity by filing a lawsuit. In 1992 the circuit court remanded the case to the district court because "the present record fails to set forth sufficient facts to demonstrate that the Village is an Indian tribe in a political sense, and that the real property it owns is Indian country."[24] In 1996 District Judge H. Russel Holland issued an order in which he held that the Indian residents of Tyonek were a federally recognized tribe because, as will be described, in 1993 Assistant Secretary of the Interior for Indian Affairs Ada Deer had said they were.[25] Shortly thereafter, Judge Holland dismissed the lawsuit as moot, and in 1997 the circuit court affirmed the dismissal because the non-Natives whose refusal to leave Tyonek had motivated the village council to file its lawsuit had "moved out of the village in 1983. They have not returned in the 14 years since they left. There is nothing in the record to suggest that they ever will."[26]

sovereignty had become a subject in which enough convention delegates were interested that the AFN board of directors directed the AFN staff to organize a workshop on that subject.

A year earlier when he received Governor Hammond's letter regarding his approval of the Circle Native Community's constitution, Secretary of the Interior James Watt told the BIA that he would not approve any other constitutions while the legal and policy issues the governor had identified in the questions he posed in his letter were being reviewed.

During the workshop, Michael Stancampiano, an attorney who worked for the BIA, told the standing-room-only crowd that the moratorium on approving new constitutions that Secretary Watt had imposed would be lifted for constitutions whose texts were purposely vague regarding the governmental powers the constitutions granted. Then once the constitutions were approved, "individual villages could attempt to exercise whatever powers they wanted, and face state challenges as they arose."[27] According to the *Tundra Times* newspaper, in response to that announcement

> there was widespread agreement among the villagers that the federal government had no business allowing the state to become involved in what has always been a special trust relationship between the federal and tribal governments. Village leaders argued that the IRA governments did not give them sovereignty, it merely recognized those powers which they have always held. Therefore, they said, it was irrelevant what the state thought of the wording of their constitutions.[28]

On the last day of every AFN convention, the delegates pass resolutions that identify the subjects on which the AFN staff is directed to work. Prior to the October 1982 convention, Frank Ferguson, the president of the AFN, told the press that the board of directors had put tribal sovereignty issues "on the back burner" because other issues merited more immediate attention.[29] But the delegates who had attended the workshop brought a resolution to the convention floor whose passage directed the AFN "to make protection of the standing of Alaska Native communities as Indian tribes its top priority for the coming year."[30]

To begin implementing that directive, in March 1983 the AFN hosted a conference at the Hilton Hotel in Anchorage that three hundred Natives from Native villages throughout Alaska attended. For two days they listened to speakers who included Bert Hirsch, the general counsel for the Association on American Indian Affairs who was representing the Tyonek village council in the *Native Village of Tyonek v. Puckett* lawsuit, Larry Jensen, the associate solicitor for Indian affairs at the Department of the Interior in Washington, D.C., David Case, Michael Walleri, Donald Standifer, and Michael Stancampiano discuss the IRA and its application in Alaska post-ANCSA.[31] When it was his turn to speak, Hirsch told the crowd:

> Are there tribes in Alaska? What did ANCSA do to Native sovereign powers? I think you can debate this forever. You do not have to ask permission to

> function as tribes. You do not have to ask the Department of the Interior whether you have sovereign powers. Nonsense. Do it. That's my message to you. If somebody doesn't like what you are doing, they will find the mechanism to challenge you. They will take you to court. There's ample time to fight out the issues then.[32]

During the workshop that had been held during the AFN convention, Theodore Katcheak, the president of the village council in Stebbins, a Native village at the mouth of the Yukon River whose Yup'ik Eskimo residents had obtained an IRA constitution in 1939, had suggested that the leaders of Native villages that had either an IRA constitution or a "traditional" village council that had no legal imprimatur should form their own organization.[33] During the conference that idea gained traction, and in May 1983 Natives who said they represented thirty-seven villages met in Anchorage and organized the United Tribes of Alaska (UTA).[34]

Several days before the October 1983 AFN convention, the UTA held a two-day meeting in Anchorage, which it advertised as a General Assembly, at which various speakers discussed various aspects of the tribal sovereignty issue.[35]

A year later, on the first day of the October 1984 convention, the AFN held another workshop on tribal sovereignty at which Sheldon Katchatag, a thirty-seven-year-old Inupiat Eskimo from Unalakleet, a Native village on the coast of the Bering Sea north of the Yukon River, who was the chairman of the UTA, assured the several hundred Natives in attendance that Native villages "have the power to control their own lands—and they can even expel non-members if they so desire."[36] The next day he delivered a speech at the convention during which he railed that ANCSA was "unfair" because it gave the money and the title to the land Alaska Natives had received as compensation for the extinguishment of their aboriginal titles to regional and village corporations, rather than to tribal governments. Katchatag received a standing ovation.[37]

While the core tenet of the tribal sovereignty movement that Spud Williams had described three years earlier was grounded in an ideology that by 1984 was capturing the hearts and minds of an increasing number of AFN convention delegates, the UTA was a letterhead organization and Sheldon Katchatag was an unpaid volunteer. That became apparent in September 1985 when the UTA rented the Anchorage convention center for a meeting that it now called a Congress. According to the *Tundra Times*:

> Thousands of Alaska Natives were expected at Anchorage's Egan Convention Center to attend the United Tribes of Alaska Second Annual Congress. Many of those expected to attend stayed home. Based on a *Tundra Times* count of registered delegates, approximately 250 Natives were in Anchorage ... While UTA Chairman Sheldon Katchatag claimed, "We'll be representing half the villages in Alaska after this convention," the numbers of people milling in and out of the convention center did not reflect half of Alaska's villages.[38]

The people milling in and out actually reflected considerably less than half because on the second-to-last day of the Congress when Charlie Kairaiuak, the chairman of the village council in Chefornak, a Native village in western Alaska near the coast of the Bering Sea, defeated Sheldon Katchatag in the election for chairman of the UTA, the vote was 38 to 18.[39]

After the Congress adjourned it was discovered that Katchatag had rented the convention center and run up other bills that totaled more than $300,000 by writing bad checks. When the fact that he had became publicly known, Katchatag said that "What we were doing was issuing these checks as a promise to pay and we had that understanding with all of our vendors and clients that everything was conditional on revenues coming in."[40] But when the *Tundra Times* asked three of the vendors whether they had been told that the checks they had been given actually were just promissory notes, none had.[41] Katchatag was not arrested, but the UTA soon thereafter disbanded.

Five

Sections 7 and 8 of ANCSA required each Alaska Native who was alive on December 18, 1971 (the date President Richard Nixon signed ANCSA into law), to be issued one hundred shares of stock in a regional corporation and, if the Native wanted them, one hundred shares of stock in a village corporation, and prohibited Native shareholders from selling their stock until December 18, 1991.

For many Alaska Natives, the possibility that beginning on December 18, 1991 a majority of the shareholders of a corporation might sell their stock to non-Natives and, as a consequence, the shareholders who did not sell would lose control of the corporation that owned the land whose title the secretary of the interior had conveyed to the corporation was a matter of significant concern.

To influence the debate that was beginning inside the Native community regarding how Congress should be asked to amend ANCSA to prevent that possibility, at the urging of representatives from the North Slope Borough, in July 1983 the Inuit Circumpolar Conference (ICC)* created the Alaska Native Review Commission.

The commission was one person: Thomas Berger, a former justice of the British Columbia Supreme Court who had established a reputation in Canada as a stalwart defender of aboriginal treaty and land rights.[2] The ICC tasked Berger with investigating "the history and intent of the Alaska Native Claims Settlement Act" and "the functions of the various Native Corporations in fulfilling the 'spirit' of ANCSA for Alaska Natives." He then was to submit a report containing whatever recommendations he deemed appropriate.[3]

Advised by David Case, whom he hired as the commission's general counsel, Berger held hearings in fifty Native villages and hosted meetings at which various experts expressed their views about ANCSA. He then wrote a report, which in March 1985 he published as a book entitled *Village Journey*.[4]

Chapter six of *Village Journey*, entitled "Native Sovereignty in Alaska," begins with a discourse on the history of federal Indian policy and is sprinkled with quotes from testimony Alaska Natives presented during the hearings he held that Berger selected to bolster a polemical argument, which was that Native residents of Native villages were, and had always been, "sovereign." Here are statements of history and law Berger offered *Village Journey* readers:

* At the instigation of Eben Hopson, the mayor of the NSB, in 1977 Inupiat Eskimos from Alaska, Greenland, and Canada organized the ICC to address issues of common concern.[1]

> Neither Russia nor the United States ever conquered Alaska, nor have Alaska Natives ever voluntarily given up or treated to give up their inherent political powers. They have not been absorbed into the mainstream of American society, and their occupation of their ancestral homelands remains unbroken. Sovereignty inheres in the Native people.[5]
>
> Some seventy Alaska villages have organized IRA councils under its terms. Many villages that do not have IRA councils are governed by traditional councils. Their recognition by Congress is indisputable: all of these villages, whether governed by IRA councils or by traditional councils, have as much right to be called tribes as any Indian community in the Lower 48.[6]
>
> It is apparent that many Alaska Natives hold high hopes for what can be achieved under tribal government. It is apparent that they believe tribal government will protect their interests better than ANCSA corporations or state-chartered local governments can. I believe they are right to think so. No one believes that tribal government can solve all the problems in the villages. Tribal government is, however, essential to the recommendations I intend to make regarding the future of Native lands and Native subsistence [hunting and fishing].[7]

When he later was asked who had advised him regarding the factual accuracy and legal validity of those statements, Berger said he had "relied principally on the advice and counsel of David Case, especially chapter six."[8]

At the end of *Village Journey*, Berger offered these recommendations regarding "Self-Government":

> Tribal governments established in all of Alaska's Native villages should assert their Native sovereignty.
>
> Pending and future applications by villages in Alaska for tribal constitutions and charters under the Indian Reorganization Act should be granted. The State should recognize tribal governments as appropriate local governments for all purposes under state law. These measures, important for Native self-rule, may entail the dissolution of some, but not all, of the state-chartered local governments in Native villages.
>
> I do not recommend the general establishment of Native reservations in Alaska. Instead tribal governments would hold the land in fee simple. But if there are villages that want their land taken into federal trust, this should be done.
>
> I urge that all land subject to the jurisdiction of Native governments should be described as Indian Country or, as the case may be, Eskimo Country or Aleut Country.[9]

On April 17, 1986, Berger testified at a hearing the House Committee on Interior and Insular Affairs held on a bill the AFN had written whose enactment would amend

Thomas Berger. Credit: Erik Hill/Anchorage Daily News.

ANCSA in various ways, but most importantly by continuing the prohibition on the sale of regional and village corporation stock unless and until a majority of the shareholders of a corporation voted to make the stock in their corporation available for sale.[10]

Berger began his testimony by informing the members of the committee that in the Native villages he visited "there is a tribal government. They didn't vanish in 1971. They're still there exercising certain powers under the law. You can call them sovereign powers, if you will, but nobody disputes that those tribal governments are there and that they do have certain powers under U.S. jurisprudence."[11] He then recommended that Congress amend ANCSA to facilitate the ability of regional and village corporations to convey the title to the surface and subsurface estates of the land the corporations owned to "tribal governments."[12]

Thomas Berger had no influence with Alaska Senators Ted Stevens and Frank Murkowski* and Alaska Representative Don Young who would decide the fate of the AFN's bill. But he had a consequential influence with members of the tribal sovereignty movement. Thousands of copies of *Village Journey* were distributed in Native villages and sold in bookstores throughout Alaska. In October 1983 Berger was a featured speaker at the UTA's General Assembly.[13] And in a speech delivered in Sep-

* In the November 1980 Alaska election for the U.S. Senate, Republican Frank Murkowski defeated Democrat Clark Gruening who had defeated Mike Gravel, the Democratic incumbent, in the Democratic primary election.

tember 1985 at the UTA's Congress, Berger told those in attendance that Alaska Native tribal sovereignty was "as American as apple pie."[14]

While Thomas Berger was traveling to Native villages holding hearings, the AFN board of directors had been engaged in a process whose objective was to develop a consensus within the Native community regarding the content of the bill above-described whose enactment would amend ANCSA to continue the prohibition on the sale of regional and village corporation stock.

That objective seemingly was achieved at the October 1985 AFN convention when the delegates approved a proposal to include eight concepts in an AFN bill.[15] As the *Anchorage Daily Times* reported, during the debate that preceded the vote, "[s]overeignty backers ... proposed the drafting of recommendations by Canadian jurist Thomas Berger into legislation. Berger interviewed some 1,450 natives during a two-year study of ANCSA and recommended the transfer of corporate lands to Native governments. However, the proposal adopted only 'acknowledged the testimony' of these Native interviewees."[16]

While the AFN board of directors had avoided including Berger's recommendations in the AFN bill, they did try to placate the members of the UTA and other tribal sovereignty advocates.

On February 6, 1986, Senator Murkowski and Representative Young introduced the AFN bill in the Ninety-ninth Congress as S. 2065 and H.R. 4162.

Section 5 of the bill added a new section 7a to ANCSA that authorized a regional or village corporation to "convey some or all of its assets, including title to the surface and/or subsurface estate of land, or any interest therein, to a qualified transferee entity for no consideration or for such consideration as its stockholders may approve." "Qualified transferee entity" was defined to mean "an entity organized pursuant to or recognized by State or Federal law," an intentionally abstruse way to describe a village council that had been created in a constitution the secretary of the interior had approved pursuant to section 1 of Public Law No. 74-538 and section 16 of the Indian Reorganization Act, as well as a "traditional" village council that had no legal imprimatur.

Caught between the growing number of members of the tribal sovereignty movement who, incited by Thomas Berger, were increasingly committed to "tribalizing" ANCSA and, as will be described, the opposition of Alaska Senators Ted Stevens and Frank Murkowski to that outcome, the AFN board of directors tried to maintain a calibrated neutrality by balancing the qualified transferee entity provision with a provision in the AFN bill that added a disclaimer section, section 7c, to ANCSA that stated: "Nothing in this Act shall be construed as enlarging or diminishing or in any way affecting the scope of any governmental authority of a federally recognized tribe, traditional council or Native council organized pursuant to the Indian Reorganization Act, as amended, or any right, privilege or immunity of Alaska Natives as Native Americans in their relationship with the Government of the United States."

Janie Leask, President, Alaska Federation of Natives, and Native Leader Willie Hensley Discuss ANCSA "1991" Legislation with Alaska Senators Ted Stevens and Frank Murkowski. Ted Stevens Foundation.

On April 17, 1986, the House Committee on Interior and Insular Affairs held a hearing on H.R. 4162. In addition to Thomas Berger and Janie Leask, the president of the AFN, the witnesses included three representatives of the Alaska Native Coalition (ANC), a new organization that members of the defunct UTA had created.[17]

John Borbridge, a Tlingit Indian who was a spokesman for the ANC, told the committee that the ANC had six objections to the AFN bill. The two most consequential were, first, that H.R. 4162 attempted "to side step the critical issue of tribal village status. We find the use of a qualified transferee entity to be ambiguous at best and clearly inadequate to meet our legitimate tribal government needs ... if it is intended that tribal village governments be one of the entities qualified to receive those lands in order to afford them protection, so that Native ownership may continue, let us say that."[18] And second, that the text of section 7c was inadequate "because certain parties who oppose tribal government argue that ANCSA itself removed village governmental powers ... It is our position that ANCSA did not alter in any way the legal nature or status of any of the Alaska Native tribes, nor did it alter the preexisting relationship between the United States and the Alaska Natives as members of such tribes. Particularly, the Settlement Act neither terminated the tribes nor the status as Natives of the members thereof."[19]

When he testified, Thomas Berger told the committee that Congress should amend ANCSA to facilitate the conveyance by regional and village corporations of the title to the surface and subsurface estates of the land they owned to village councils because the corporations doing so would ensure that the land would remain in Native ownership.

But the ANC had a more expansive agenda.

Section 1151 of title 18 of the U.S. Code defines the term "Indian country" to mean (1) "land within the limits of any Indian reservation", (2) "dependent Indian communities within the borders of the United States," and (3) "Indian allotments, the Indian titles to which have not been extinguished." In 1976 in its decision in a lawsuit captioned *Bryan v. Itasca* County,[20] the U.S. Supreme Court had held that a state within whose boundaries a tract of Indian country is located has no authority to assert its criminal and civil jurisdiction within the boundaries of that Indian country, except to the extent Congress has delegated the state that authority.

Similarly, in 1957 in its decision in a lawsuit captioned *In re* McCord,[21] the U.S. District Court in Alaska had held that the public land inside the boundaries of the Moquawkie reserve within which Tyonek was located was an Indian reservation, and hence was Indian country within which the Territory of Alaska had no jurisdiction to enforce its criminal statute that prohibited statutory rape. While the *In re McCord* decision was wrongly decided,[22] rather than the Territory of Alaska appealing the decision to the U.S. Court of Appeals for the Ninth Circuit, Alaska Delegate E.L. "Bob" Bartlett arranged for the Eighty-fifth Congress to amend a statute the Eighty-third Congress had enacted in 1953 that granted several listed states authority to assert their criminal and civil jurisdiction within Indian country.[23] The amendment added the Territory (later State) of Alaska to that list.

At the April 17, 1986, hearing on H.R. 4162, when John Borbridge finished testifying, the next ANC witness was Willie Kasayulie, a Yup'ik Eskimo from Akiachak, a Native village on the Kuskokwim River in western Alaska, who was chairman of the ANC. Kasayulie attached to his written testimony a package of amendments to ANCSA and other statutes that the ANC wanted the committee to include in the bill.[24]

One amendment defined the term "dependent Indian community" in the "Indian country" definition to state that in Alaska a "dependent Indian community" included

> all lands and waters consisting of townsite lands, allotments, village and regional corporation lands, restricted townsite lots, core townships, municipal lands (and all other areas) regardless of ownership, which lie within the exterior boundaries of such lands, and provided such lands lie within the traditional boundaries of those Alaska Native villages made eligible for certain

benefits pursuant to sections 11, 14(h)((2), 14(h)(3), 16 or 19 of the Alaska Native Claims Settlement Act, or any other Alaska Native community.[25]

Another amendment amended section 22 of ANCSA to grant "Alaska Native Tribes" exclusive jurisdiction "to regulate hunting, fishing, and trapping in Indian country."[26]

When they wrote the amendment in the nature of a substitute for the original text of H.R. 4162 that on July 24, 1986, the Committee on Interior and Insular Affairs reported to the U.S. House of Representatives,[27] with one inconsequential exception, Representative Morris Udall, the chairman of the committee, and Alaska Representative Don Young rejected the ANC's amendments; after which on July 28, 1986 the House passed H.R. 4162 without controversy and by an unrecorded voice vote.[28]

Six days later the Subcommittee on Public Lands, Reserved Water and Resource Conservation of the Senate Committee on Energy and Natural Resources held a hearing on S. 2065, as the AFN bill had been denoted in the Senate.[29] The hearing was chaired by Alaska Senator Frank Murkowski.

A banker by profession and training, rather than an attorney familiar with the Talmudic intricacies of federal Indian law, in his opening remarks the senator voiced his confusion regarding how those intricacies might affect the situation in Alaska. But he was clear that, having been educated by the ANC, he opposed its agenda. Senator Murkowski stated:

> The most controversial aspect of this legislation concerns its secondary impacts, how it affects the question of Indian country in Alaska and sovereignty. There are many different opinions on whether Indian country exists in Alaska and to what extent Alaska Natives possess sovereign powers of self-government.
>
> Whatever the 1971 Native Claims Settlement Act allowed or disallowed with respect to these questions will remain unchanged by this bill. Senator Stevens, Congressman Young, and I have consistently stated that the 1991 amendments will not foster sovereignty nor will they detract from any self-government powers which Alaska Natives may now possess under existing law. In short, the bill will not tip the scales on these issues in either direction.
>
> I have stated in my opening remarks in each of the hearings I have held in nine communities in Alaska that I will not support any legislation which leads to the creation of a series of independent sovereign entities in Alaska. One can only imagine the confusion that would exist if the State and Federal Government were required to enter into treaties with various sovereign Indian Nations.
>
> I believe that such a situation is contrary to the best interests of all Alaskans, Native and non-Native alike. From the standpoint of where we go collectively as Alaska citizens, it is our intent to retain the current form of government that we have, and that is the government of the State of Alaska.[30]

After the hearing, members of the AFN's staff began meeting with the Alaska senators and with representatives of Secretary of the Interior Donald Hodel to negotiate a new bill text that all those parties could support.

Secretary Hodel had six objections to the version of H.R. 4162 that had passed the House. During the hearing at which Senator Murkowski presided, Assistant Secretary of the Interior William Horn explained that, for Secretary Hodel, the section that amended ANCSA to facilitate the conveyance of land to qualified transferee entities was particularly problematical because such conveyances

> could lead to attempts to establish independent Indian communities similar to the Indian country or reservation system in the lower 48 states. Efforts to exploit this provision through litigation would likely result. This clearly contravenes the intent of ANCSA as expressed in section 2(b).* We recommend, instead, that an express provision against the establishment of such "Indian country," as defined in 18 U.S.C. section 1151, be substituted, along with an explicit statement that the United States does not bear the same trust responsibility for ANCSA settlement lands as it does for Indian lands. Without these recommended statements, the Administration would be compelled to oppose the bill.[31]

On September 25, 1986, the AFN board of directors announced that the members of the AFN's staff who had been participating in the negotiations would no longer be doing so.[32] The board made that decision because members of the ANC and other tribal sovereignty advocates, who since 1982 had become increasingly influential with rank-and-file delegates who attended AFN conventions, objected to a rewritten text of the disclaimer section of the bill that Senator Murkowski and Secretary Hodel said was nonnegotiable. As Dalee Sambo, a member of the ANC executive committee, explained to the *Anchorage Daily News*: "For tribes, it would have been too high a price to pay. Just yesterday we were coming up with strategies for how we could kill [the bill]. We're pleased it's not going forward."[33]

On October 6, 1986, Senators Murkowski and Stevens published in the *Congressional Record* the text of an amendment in the nature of a substitute for the text of the version of H.R. 4162 that had passed the House that they said they were willing to support.[34]

The substitute text contained the amendment to ANCSA that authorized regional and village corporations to convey title to the subsurface and surface estates of the land they owned to qualified transferee entities. But the disclaimer section of the version of H.R. 4162 that had passed the House was rewritten to provide that no provision in H.R. 4162 was intended to "enlarge or diminish or in any way affect the scope of the governmental authority, if any, of any Native organization, including any federally

---

* Section 2(b) of ANCSA directed that the ANCSA settlement be implemented "without establishing any permanent racially defined institutions, rights, privileges, or obligations, without creating a reservation system or lengthy wardship or trusteeship, and without adding to the categories of property and institutions enjoying special tax privileges."

recognized tribe, traditional Native council, Native council organized pursuant to [section 1 of Public Law No. 74-538 and section 16 of the IRA], or qualified transferee entity over lands (including management of, or regulation of the taking of, fish and wildlife) or over persons in Alaska."

The rewritten disclaimer section also prohibited a land conveyance to a qualified transferee entity or any other change in the ownership of land from being "construed to validate or invalidate or in any way affect any assertion that Indian country, as defined in 18 U.S.C. 1151, exists or does not exist in Alaska," and it prohibited the federal courts from taking such conveyances and changes in ownership into account when determining the governmental authority of a Native organization or "the existence of Indian country within the boundaries of the State of Alaska."[35]

With the Ninety-ninth Congress rushing toward adjournment, on October 17 the 1986 AFN convention convened in Anchorage. During the convention, by a 2-to-1 margin the 1,200 delegates rejected the amendment in the nature of a substitute that Senators Murkowski and Stevens had published in the *Congressional Record*.[36] The next morning the delegates passed a resolution that directed the AFN board of directors to coordinate with "the Alaska Native Coalition and other affected Native organizations" to write a new bill that would maintain "the existing inherent tribal rights of Alaska Native tribes."[37]

When the convention adjourned, the *Anchorage Daily News* summarized the outcome as follows: "Stevens and Murkowski said any 1991 bill should open no new doors to sovereignty claims. But their version of the bill was seen by many within AFN as diminishing existing legal arguments for tribal authority. The result was an upswelling of support in defense of sovereignty this year, compared to past years when tribal activists were a small but vocal minority at annual AFN gatherings."[38]

The disagreement between Senators Murkowski and Stevens and the ANC would not be resolved until the next AFN convention.

On the second day of the One Hundredth Congress, January 7, 1987, Alaska Representative Don Young introduced H.R. 278,[39] a bill whose text was identical to the text of the version of H.R. 4162 the House had passed during the Ninety-ninth Congress. On March 27, 1987, the Committee on Interior and Insular Affairs reported H.R. 287 with four inconsequential amendments,[40] and four days later the House passed the bill by a voice vote after only cursory discussion.[41]

The speed with which H.R. 278 moved from introduction to passage was no accident. On December 18, 1986, Richard Agnew, the chief counsel for the Republican members of the Committee on Interior and Insular Affairs, had reported to the AFN's counsel that Representative Young "wants to be able to argue in committee and on the floor that the 1987 bill is identical to the 1986 bill and that it should be passed without amendment. This, in order to head off the threat of amendments by the environmental community and other interests. Young is convinced that if the bill is opened by the Natives, no matter how inconsequential or technical the amendments may be, everyone will get on the band wagon" and that might "derail the bill."[42]

A month after the House passed H.R. 278, on May 6, 1987, Senators Murkowski and Stevens introduced S. 1145.[43] The bill incorporated changes to H.R. 278 that the leaders of the AFN had negotiated with the senators. The bill included the qualified transferee entity section and a disclaimer section whose text was identical to the text of the disclaimer section in the amendment in the nature of a substitute the senators had published in the *Congressional Record* and which the delegates who attended the 1986 AFN convention had rejected. When S. 1145 was introduced, Senator Murkowski told the Senate:

> Unfortunately, [the qualified transferee entity section] has been tangled up in the sovereignty issue. The status of tribal governmental authority is currently unresolved in Alaska and is not one that should be addressed in this legislation. Thus, I have consistently stated that this legislation will remain neutral on the question of sovereignty—it will neither enhance nor detract from the status quo on that question. This bill attempts to achieve this goal through the use of a sovereignty disclaimer. However, the issue of what neutrality is remains one which will need to be resolved.[44]

On May 19, 1987, when the Committee on Energy and Natural Resources held a hearing on S. 1145 and H.R. 278,[45] Senator Murkowski, who chaired the hearing, made it clear that his view of the situation had not changed. "There are those in the Alaska Native community who seek a greater opportunity for sovereignty in this legislation particularly through this provision [the qualified transferee entity section]," the senator announced to the audience sitting in the hearing room that included two representatives of the ANC. "I personally will not support that position."[46] And Senator Stevens was equally adamant. "So long as the qualified transferee entity provision currently in S. 1145 is retained," he explained, "a comprehensive disclaimer that addresses the issue of a shift in land ownership from a Native corporation to a tribal entity really is necessary. That is the only way we can meet our commitment to keep the 1991 bill out of the Native sovereignty controversy at home in Alaska."[47]

When she testified, AFN president Janie Leask attached to her written testimony the text of a new bill that, because it had been written in conjunction with leaders of the ANC, contained a qualified transferee entity section and a disclaimer section whose text was acceptable to the ANC. Leask explained that AFN's "preference" was that the committee include those sections in the version of H.R. 278 the committee reported.[48] But prior to the hearing, the members of the steering committee the AFN board of directors had created to advise the board had recommended that the board "consider the option of dropping all QTE language provided all disclaimer language is excluded with it and after proper consultation with appropriate members of the Alaska Native Coalition."[49]

The board accepted the recommendation, and during the hearing on S. 1145 and H.R. 278, Leask told Senator Murkowski that, if it was the only way he and Senator Stevens would allow the committee to report H.R. 278, AFN would support removing the qualified transferee entity section from the bill in exchange for "some kind of modified disclaimer."[50]

That is how the impasse was resolved.

On September 23, 1987, the members of the Committee on Energy and Natural Resources reported an amendment in the nature of a substitute for the version of H.R. 278 that had passed the House and whose text reflected the quid pro quo Janie Leask had told the committee was acceptable to the AFN.[51] In its report on the amendment the committee explained that

> the amendment eliminates section 7 of the House-passed bill. Section 7 would amend the Alaska Native Claims Settlement Act to allow the shareholder of a Native Corporation to vote to convey any, or all, of the corporation's assets, including, but not limited to land and interests therein, to a qualified transferee entity. This provision was eliminated in the Committee reported bill. Having eliminated section 7, the Committee also modified the disclaimer in section 8 of the House version of H.R. 278 and contained in section 17 of the Committee amendment to ensure that the language of the disclaimer is viewed by all interested parties as truly neutral on the question of Native sovereignty in Alaska.[52]

Most significantly, the modified disclaimer section omitted the subsection in the disclaimer section in S. 1145 that prohibited the federal courts from considering whether land whose title had been conveyed to a regional or village corporation pursuant to ANCSA had been transformed into Indian country because the corporation had conveyed its title to a village council that had been organized pursuant to section 1 of Public Law No. 74-538 and section 16 of the IRA or to a "traditional" village council that had no legal imprimatur.

The committee reported its amendment over the protestation of the ANC. As the *Tundra Times* explained the week before the committee did so: "Among those who are seeking to stall the 1991 bill are members of the Alaska Native Coalition, who are objecting to the Murkowski version of the bill. They are concerned that the bill does not include a provision authorizing transfer of ANCSA corporation lands to a 'qualified transferee entity,' such as a tribal government."[53]

Three days after the Committee on Energy and Natural Resources reported its amendment to the Senate, on October 23, 1987, the delegates who attended the 1987 AFN convention voted, by a 3-to-1 margin, to reject a resolution the Tanana Chiefs Conference sponsored whose passage would have required the AFN to demand that Senators Murkowski and Stevens amend the committee's amendment by including the qualified transferee entity section.[54]

The dispute between the ANC and Senators Murkowski and Stevens regarding the qualified transferee entity section having been settled in favor of removing the section from the committee's amendment, six days later the Senate accepted the amendment and passed H.R. 278 on a voice vote.[55]

Over the next several months, members of the AFN's staff, Senators Murkowski and Stevens and Representative Young, and representatives of Secretary of the Interior Hodel, Representative Morris Udall, the chairman of the Committee on Interior and Insular Affairs, and Senator Bennett Johnston, the chairman of the Committee on Energy and Natural Resources, negotiated changes to the text of the version of H.R. 278 that had passed the Senate.

On December 21, 1987, the Senate and U.S. House of Representatives passed a new version of H.R. 278 whose text reflected the outcome of those negotiations,[56] and on February 3, 1988, President Ronald Reagan signed that version of the bill into law.[57]

During those negotiations, to placate the ANC, the text of the disclaimer section was modified to state that no provision of the bill was intended to "validate or invalidate or in any way affect"

> any assertion that a Native organization (including a federally recognized tribe, traditional Native council, or Native council organized pursuant to the [IRA], as amended) has or does not have governmental authority over lands (including management of, or regulation of the taking of, fish and wildlife) or persons within the boundaries of the State of Alaska.

That text seemingly put the One Hundredth Congress on record as believing that there were federally recognized tribes in Alaska. However, that was not the understanding of Senator Murkowski, who undoubtedly did not read the disclaimer section to which his staff had agreed. Because prior to the voice vote in the Senate, Senator Murkowski explained to his colleagues that

> There is a great deal of controversy in Alaska over the issue of whether Alaska Native organizations may exercise some degree of governmental authority over lands or individuals. The controversy involves several complex questions — which Native groups might qualify as tribal organizations, what powers such organizations might possess, and whether there is Indian country in Alaska over which such organization (sic) might exercise governmental jurisdiction. The "1991" amendments are scrupulously neutral on this controversy. It is an issue which should be left to the courts in interpreting applicable law. This legislation should play no substantive or procedural role in such court decisions. It was and is my intent that this legislation leave all parties to the sovereignty controversy in exactly the same statue (sic) as if the amendments were not enacted.[58]

Contrary to Senator Murkowski's intention, the inclusion of the reference to federally recognized tribes in the disclaimer section did not leave the sovereignty controversy "in exactly the same state as if the amendments were not enacted." However, six months after President Reagan signed H.R. 278 into law, the Alaska Supreme Court settled the controversy in the senator's favor.

Six

In November 1982 Democrat Bill Sheffield was elected to succeed Republican Jay Hammond as governor of Alaska. In December, when he was sworn into office, the new governor inherited the problem of how the State of Alaska should respond to the nascent tribal sovereignty movement. For Sheffield, the subject was politically problematic because he had been elected in a four-candidate election that he won only because the Republican, Libertarian, and Alaska Independent Party candidates split the conservative vote.

A determinative percentage of the votes that elected Sheffield had been cast by Native voters in communities that the Ninety-second Congress or the secretary of the interior had designated as Native villages for the purposes of ANCSA and in which support for the tribal sovereignty movement was growing. Sheffield defeated Tom Fink, the Republican candidate who had been his principal rival, in Tyonek 85 votes to 11 votes, in Unalakleet, the community in which Sheldon Kachetag, the future chairman of UTA, resided, 210 votes to 47 votes, and in Akiachak, the community in which Willie Kasayulie, the future chairman of the ANC, resided, 164 votes to 10 votes. In total, in 129 coastal Eskimo and interior Indian villages, Bill Sheffield defeated Tom Fink 15,497 votes to 4,115 votes.[1] And he knew he would need those same votes again when he ran for reelection in 1986.

Sheffield's reluctance to alienate that politically important constituency became apparent four months after he was sworn into office when he spoke at the Village Participation Conference, an annual event that was held during the legislative session in Juneau, the state capitol, that representatives from forty-eight Native villages attended and Sheldon Kachatag chaired. After listening to the governor speak, the participants passed a resolution in which they commended Sheffield for recognizing IRA governments.[2] However, his press secretary later clarified that there had been a "misunderstanding" because the governor had said only that he was "interested in exploring the relationship" between the State and village councils in Native villages that had IRA constitutions.[3]

But if he was being pressured by Sheldon Kachatag and other members of the tribal sovereignty movement to agree that village councils that had been issued constitutions pursuant to section 1 of Public Law No. 74-538 and section 16 of the IRA had "sovereign" governmental authority, the governor also was being pressured by Alaska's congressional delegation.

The month after the Village Participation Conference, he received a letter from Alaska Senators Ted Stevens and Frank Murkowski and Alaska Representative Don Young. After noting that the question of whether "certain Alaska Native communities have sovereign authority beyond those powers held by cities and towns organized under State law," was a matter of "continuing concern," the three solons asked the governor to tell them what his position regarding the subject was so that they could be certain that in Washington, D.C., they were "accurately reflecting the position taken by the State concerning the degree of governing authority held by various types of Alaska Native Village government organizations."[4]

Since he had no position, in June Sheffield sent a conciliatory letter to Native leaders of villages that had constitutions the secretary of the interior had approved pursuant to section 1 of Public Law No. 74-538 and section 16 of the IRA, as well as to leaders of other Native organizations. The letter posed four questions that the recipients were asked to answer.[5]

A month later the governor announced his intention to meet with Native leaders.[6] And another two months later when Secretary of the Interior James Watt met with Sheffield, according the governor's press secretary, "Watt agreed to stand back while the State met with Native leaders this fall to develop a consensus on how to respond to claims of sovereignty by individual villages."[7]

However, that meeting was not held because the governor subsequently decided on an alternative plan.[8]

In March 1984 at the annual meeting of Doyon, the ANCSA regional corporation that Athabascan Indians in the Alaska interior had incorporated, Sheffield announced that he was appointing a Task Force on Federal-State-Tribal Relations whose members would study and then make recommendations regarding the tribal sovereignty issue.[9]

The chairman of the task force was Emil Notti, the commissioner of the Alaska Department of Community and Regional Affairs who between 1967 and 1970 had been president of the AFN. Four members were members of the Alaska Legislature. Two others were career BIA employees. Counting Notti, seven of the twelve members were Alaska Natives, including Willie Goodwin, a prominent member of the UTA.[10]

The governor said he was hopeful that the members of the task force would "arrive at some consensus on new laws and policies which will best serve Alaska Natives while protecting the rights of all the public."[11] However, that is not what happened.

After holding hearings around the state,[12] in March 1986 the task force issued a report that contained twenty-one recommendations. Since whether Native residents of Native villages were members of federally recognized tribes, and since whether an IRA village council or a "traditional" village council that had no legal imprimatur possessed "the right of self government over its village area and surrounding lands" were questions of federal, rather than state, law, the principal recommendation was that the governor ask the secretary of the interior what his answers to those questions were.

Alaska Governor Bill Sheffield. Alaska Office of the Governor Photograph Collection, Alaska State Library.

The report also contained an analysis of the history of Congress's Alaska Native-related enactments from 1867 when the United States purchased Alaska to the present that a majority of the members of the task force approved, but only by the margin of a single vote. Two years later that analysis would have a consequential influence.

In the late nineteenth century, four Athabascan Indian brothers settled at a location in the Alaska interior on the north shore of the Yukon River. When steamboats began transporting prospectors and freight from Fort St. Michael, the army post at the mouth of the river, to Dawson, the town near the site of the Klondike River gold strike in the Yukon Territory, the Alaska Commercial Company opened a store in the community the brothers had established. The store was managed by Steven, the youngest brother, and in 1902 the community became known as Stevens Village.[13]

In 1939 Stevens Village had fifty-four residents, most if not all of whom were Athabascan Indians.[14] That same year Assistant Secretary of the Interior Oscar Chapman approved a constitution for the Native Village of Stevens (NVS) pursuant to section 1 of Public Law No. 74-538 and section 16 of the IRA.[15] In 1971 the Ninety-second Congress designated Stevens Village as a Native village for the purposes of ANCSA.

In 1982 the Department of Housing and Urban Development gave the NVS a $369,000 grant to finance construction of an electrical system in the community. In 1983 the NVS contracted with a company based in Fairbanks named Alaska Management & Planning (AM&P) to oversee the construction. When the NVS subsequently abruptly terminated the contract, AM&P filed a breach of contract lawsuit against the NVS in the Alaska Superior Court.

Represented by Michael Walleri, the attorney at the Tanana Chiefs Conference who had assisted the Athabascan Indian residents of Circle and other Native villages in the Alaska interior in filing constitutions with the secretary of the interior pursuant to section 1 of Public Law No. 74-538 and section 16 of the IRA, the NVS filed a motion to dismiss the lawsuit on "the ground that the suit was barred by the doctrine of sovereign immunity."

Superior Court Judge Mary Greene denied the motion. When a jury then awarded AM&P $38,891 as damages for the NVS's breach of its contract, the NVS appealed Judge Greene's denial of its motion to dismiss to the Alaska Supreme Court.

In May 1988 in the decision the court issued in *Native Village of Stevens v. Alaska Management & Planning*,[16] Justice Warren Matthews, writing for a divided court, affirmed Judge Greene's denial of the motion. Relying on the analysis of the history of Congress's Alaska Native-related enactments in the report of the Task Force on Federal-State-Tribal Relations, Justice Matthews concluded that

> in a series of enactments following the Treaty of Cession and extending into the first third of this century, Congress has demonstrated its intent that Alaska native communities not be accorded sovereign tribal status. The historical accuracy of this conclusion was expressly recognized in the proviso to the Alaska Indian Reorganization Act [section 1 of Public Law No. 74-538] and, although that Act afforded a mechanism by which self-governing status might be achieved by Native communities, the mechanism was not utilized in the case of Stevens Village. No enactment subsequent to the Alaska Indian Reorganization Act granted or recognized tribal sovereign authority in Alaska.[17]

Whether the NVS had sovereign immunity because the Athabascan Indian residents of Stevens Village had been designated by Congress (or by the secretary of the interior acting lawfully pursuant to authority that Congress had delegated to the secretary) as a federally recognized tribe was a question of federal law that only the U.S. Supreme Court — rather than the Alaska Supreme Court — could answer definitively. But as Lloyd Miller, an attorney who four years earlier had opened an office in Anchorage for Sonosky, Chambers & Sachse, a Washington, D.C., law firm that specialized in representing Indian tribes, explained to the *Tundra Times*, "Unless reversed, the majority opinion in the Stevens Village case strikes a severe blow to village self-government in Alaska."[18]

To try to reverse the opinion, represented by Miller and nine other attorneys, including David Case and Bert Hirsch, the ANC, eight of the twelve Native associations listed in section 7(a) of ANCSA, three of the twelve ANCSA regional corporations, and Tyonek, Akiachak, and three other Native villages petitioned the Alaska Supreme Court to rehear the NVS's appeal. And the AFN signed on as a petitioner because as AFN president Janie Leask explained, "We needed to get on the band-wagon."[19]

In August 1988 the Alaska Supreme Court denied the petition.[20] And four years later, in the decision it issued in an appeal captioned *Hydaburg Cooperative Association v. Hydaburg Fisheries*,[21] after reaffirming its holding in *Native Village of Stevens*, the court reiterated that "Alaska Native associations generally do not have sovereign immunity" because "[v]illage reorganization under section 16 [of the IRA] by itself is not sufficient to establish tribal status for purposes concerning the doctrine of tribal sovereign immunity."

Seven

Headquartered in Boulder, Colorado, the Native American Rights Fund, known by its acronym as NARF, is a nonprofit law firm that was established in 1971 to assist Indian tribes to "maintain their government-to-government relationship with the United States" and assist unrecognized and terminated tribes to "establish or re-establish such a relationship."[1] In 1984 NARF opened an office in Anchorage because, as John Ecohawk, the organization's executive director, explained, "Requests for assistance from Alaska Native villages increased to the point that a separate office in Alaska was the most feasible way to address the important Native issues of sovereignty and subsistence hunting and fishing that emerge as Native protections in the Alaska Native Claims Settlement Act move toward expiration in 1991."[2]

The attorneys NARF sent to Anchorage were Lawrence "Lare" Aschenbrenner and Robert Anderson.

When they arrived, Aschenbrenner and Anderson joined a self-appointed attorney "working group" that included David Case and Lloyd Miller that during the spring of 1985 developed eleven amendments to ANCSA, the Indian Reorganization Act, and several other statutes whose enactment by Congress would establish the "sovereign" status of Native residents of Native villages.

One amendment amended the "Indian country" definition in 18 U.S.C. 1151 to include all land within the "traditional boundaries" of Native villages, including "townsite lands, allotments, village and regional corporation lands, restricted townsite lots, core townships, municipal lands and private lands." Another amendment overturned a legal opinion, about which more will be said, that Associate Solicitor for Indian Affairs Thomas Fredericks had issued in 1978 by amending section 5 of the IRA to authorize the secretary of the interior to take the title to land in Alaska into trust. A third amendment "clarified" that Congress did not intend ANCSA to "abridg[e] in any way the governmental powers of Alaska Native Tribes either over their members or over any areas of Indian country within their respective jurisdictions."[3]

That September at the Congress the UTA held at the Anchorage convention center, Robert Anderson and Lloyd Miller presented the working group's amendments.[4] When the UTA disbanded and members of that organization created the ANC, Aschenbrenner and Anderson began representing the ANC in its failed effort to persuade Alaska Senators Ted Stevens and Frank Murkowski and Alaska Representative Don Young, first to include the working group's amendments in the ANCSA "1991" bill that the One Hundredth Congress would enact in 1987, and then to keep the qualified transferee entity section in the bill.[5]

As has been described, in 1982 Assistant Secretary of the Interior for Indian Affairs Ken Smith published in the *Federal Register* a list of 197 Native entities that were eligible to receive services from the BIA even though, as Assistant Secretary Smith explained in the preamble that preceded the list, Alaska Natives who were members of the entities were not members of "historical tribes."[6]

With the preamble removed after David Case complained about its inclusion, in 1983, 1985, and 1986, Smith and his successors as assistant secretary republished the 1982 list.[7]

The month before he and other Reagan administration political appointees departed the Department of the Interior, in December 1988 Assistant Secretary of the Interior for Indian Affairs Ross Swimmer again republished the list. But rather than 197, the list contained 500 Native entities.[8]

Swimmer explained the reason for the increase in a new preamble.[9] After asserting that the preamble that preceded the 1982 list had been omitted from the subsequent lists "inadvertently," he explained that the 1988 list was not a list of federally recognized tribes that, as a consequence of that legal status, possessed powers of self-government. Instead, it was a list of Native entities that were eligible to receive services from the BIA. And insofar as those entities were concerned, Congress had provided "guidance as to whom we should provide services." The preamble explained that

> The 1936 amendments to the Indian Reorganization Act [Public Law No. 74-538], applicable only to Alaska, authorized groups to organize as tribes which are not historical tribes and are not residing on reservations. They include groups having a "common bond of occupation or association, or residence within a well-defined neighborhood, community, or rural district." More recently, Indian statutes, such as the Indian Self-Determination Act, specifically include Alaska Native villages, village corporations and regional corporations defined or established under the Alaska Native Claims Settlement Act.[10]

Because, as the preamble noted, in 1974 the Ninety-third Congress had included ANCSA regional and village corporations in the "Indian tribe" definition in the Indian Self-Determination Act, Assistant Secretary Swimmer included the corporations on the 1988 list.

After reading the new list and preamble, NARF attorney Lare Aschenbrenner complained: "One of our stronger arguments in support of tribal status has been our position that inclusion on the prior list of Alaska Native entities constituted federal recognition. The new list, by including ANCSA corporations, which admittedly are not tribes, negates the argument that all entities on the new list have tribal government status."[11]

In June 1989 the Senate confirmed Eddie Brown, a member of the Pascua Yaqui Indian tribe in Arizona, whom President George H.W. Bush had nominated to succeed Ross Swimmer as assistant secretary of the interior for Indian affairs. Eight months later, Lare Aschenbrenner, writing on NARF letterhead stationery as one of the attorneys who represented the ANC, sent Assistant Secretary Brown and Associate Solicitor for Indian Affairs William Lavell a letter that David Case, Lloyd Miller, Michael Walleri, Bert Hirsch, and ten other attorneys who were active in the tribal sovereignty movement signed. The letter requested Assistant Secretary Brown to rescind the list Assistant Secretary Swimmer had published and publish a new list "which corrects the errors and ambiguities of the 1988 list and explicitly recognizes the tribal status of Alaska Native villages and other tribes" because "[i]t is clear that Alaska Native villages are tribes and that the 1988 BIA list substantively and procedurally violated federal law."[12]

When Assistant Secretary Brown did not do so, four months later Aschenbrenner tried again.

In 1980 the Alaska Legislature added chapter 89 to title 29 of the Alaska Statutes to create a program that allowed municipalities to receive revenue-sharing monies.[13]

Because the residents of many communities that had been designated as Native villages for the purposes of ANCSA had not organized a municipal government, A.S. 29.89.050 directed the State to pay $25,000 to every "Native village government for a village which is not incorporated as a city under this title." And the statute defined "Native village government" to mean "a local governing body organized by authority of [section 1 of Public Law No. 74-538 and section 16 of the IRA]," or "a traditional village council or, if there is no traditional village council, the paramount chief or other governing body of a Native village which meets the requirements of [ANCSA]."

In 1981 Assistant Attorney General Laura Davis advised Lee McAnerney, the commissioner of the Alaska Department of Community and Regional Affairs, that A.S. 29.89.050 was "unconstitutional if read literally" because limiting eligibility for the $25,000 payment to "unincorporated communities which are identified as Native villages ... exclude[s] from participation a number of similarly situated communities which are not Native villages."[14]

Rather than then, as she should have, advising Commissioner McAnerney that she should inform the legislature that the Department of Community and Regional Affairs could not implement A.S. 29.89.050 until and unless the legislature amended the statute to create community eligibility criteria that were constitutional, Davis advised McAnerney that she could cure the statute's unconstitutionality on her own by disregarding the words "Native" and "government" in the term "Native village government" and disregarding the definition of the term "Native village government" in its entirety.

When Commissioner McAnerney accepted that advice and interpreted the text of A.S. 29.89.050 as Davis recommended, the consequence was that the number of communities eligible to participate in the revenue-sharing program increased.

When the legislature then appropriated money to fund the program, each community that had a "Native village government" received less than $25,000, both because Commissioner McAnerney had increased the number of eligible communities and because the legislature did not appropriate enough money to pay each "Native village government" $25,000 even if the commissioner had not done so.

In response, representing the Native villages of Akiachak, Noatak, and Circle, in 1985 in the U.S. District Court in Anchorage, NARF attorneys Lare Aschenbrenner and Robert Anderson filed *Native Village of Akiachak v. Notti*,[15] a lawsuit that requested the court to order the State of Alaska to pay Native village governments $853,587 to which they would have been entitled if Commissioner McAnerney had implemented A.S. 29.89.050 in the manner the text of the statute required and if the legislature had appropriated enough money to pay each Native village government $25,000.

In their complaint Aschenbrenner and Anderson alleged 28 U.S.C. 1362 as the basis for the district court's jurisdiction. That statute states: "The district courts shall have original jurisdiction of all civil actions, brought by any Indian tribe or band with a governing body duly recognized by the secretary of the interior, wherein the matter in controversy arises under the Constitution, laws, or treaties of the United States."

The Eighty-ninth Congress had enacted 28 U.S.C. 1362 in 1966 in response to *Yoder v. Assiniboine and Sioux Tribes*,[16] a decision in which the U.S. Court of Appeals for the Ninth Circuit held that the district court had no jurisdiction pursuant to 28 U.S.C. 1331 to adjudicate a claim for relief the Assiniboine and Sioux Tribes had alleged in a complaint the two tribes had filed because the tribes had not demonstrated that the matter in controversy exceeded $10,000 (the showing that at that time section 1331 required every plaintiff to make).[17]

Because S. 1356, the bill the Eighty-ninth Congress enacted as 28 U.S.C. 1362, passed the Senate and House by voice votes after only a cursory explanation in the Senate and no explanation in the House,[18] it is not possible to determine whether the Eighty-ninth Congress intended the term "Indian tribe" in section 1362 to mean "tribe" in its ethnological sense or "tribe" in its political sense.

In 1987 District Judge Andrew Kleinfeld dismissed the *Native Village of Akiachak v. Notti* lawsuit for two reasons. First, because the Eleventh Amendment to the U.S. Constitution prevented the State of Alaska from being sued without its consent. And in the alternative because the claims Aschenbrenner and Anderson had alleged in their complaint did not "arise under the Constitution, laws, or treaties of the United States."[19] Because he did not need to do so, Judge Kleinfeld did not decide whether the Inupiat Eskimo residents of Noatak and the Athabascan Indian residents of Circle were members of "Indian tribes" within the meaning of that undefined term in section 1362.*

In 1989 in its decision in *Native Village of Noatak v. Hoffman*,[20] a divided panel of the U.S. Court of Appeals for the Ninth Circuit reversed Judge Kleinfeld. The two deciding judges held that the Eleventh Amendment did not bar the lawsuit and that the claims alleged in the complaint arose under the Constitution and laws of the United

* Because the Yup'ik Eskimo residents of Akiachak had incorporated a municipal government, Akiachak was not eligible to receive a grant made pursuant to A.S. 29.89.050. For that reason, Judge Kleinfeld determined that the Native Village of Akiachak did not have standing to be a plaintiff in the lawsuit.

States. They also held that the Inupiat Eskimo residents of Noatak and the Athabascan Indian residents of Circle were, for the purposes of 28 U.S.C. 1362, "Indian tribes with governing bodies duly recognized by the secretary of the interior."

The deciding judges reasoned to their result by assuming that the Eighty-ninth Congress intended the term "Indian tribe" in 28 U.S.C. 1362 to mean "tribe" in its ethnological sense and that the Inupiat Eskimo residents of Noatak and the Athabascan Indian residents of Circle were members of ethnological tribes because they were of the "same race" and were "united in a community under a single government in a particular territory." They then concluded that the governing body in each village had been "duly recognized by the secretary of the interior."

In the latter regard, with respect to Noatak, the deciding judges said, "We see no reason to suppose that the secretary of the interior needs to issue a special document conferring a right to sue under the statute. Noatak Village has a governing body approved by the secretary [pursuant to section 1 of Public Law No. 74-538 and section 16 of the IRA]. It is therefore a tribe with a duly recognized governing body and qualifies for the benefits of section 1362."[21] And with respect to Circle, they announced that the governing body of the community had been "duly recognized by the secretary of the interior" because the Ninety-second Congress had designated Circle as a Native village for the purposes of ANCSA and because in three other statutes — the Indian Self-Determination Act, the Indian Financing Act, and the Indian Child Welfare Act — "Congress treated the Native Villages as Indian Tribes," albeit "only for the particular purposes of each piece of legislation."[22]

In May 1990 the State of Alaska filed a petition for a writ of certiorari that requested the U.S. Supreme Court to review the panel's decision.[23] The petition presented three questions. The second question was: "Is an Indian group automatically a tribe for purposes of 28 U.S.C. section 1362 (federal jurisdiction over suits by Indian tribes) because it has received the same treatment as an Indian tribe in or received benefits under certain federal statutes?"

A month later, and writing again on NARF letterhead stationery, Lare Aschenbrenner sent to his home (rather than to his office at the Department of the Interior) a letter to Associate Solicitor for Indian Affairs William Lavell that David Case, Lloyd Miller, Reid Chambers (Miller's law partner), and two other attorneys who were active in the tribal sovereignty movement signed. Aschenbrenner told Associate Solicitor Lavell:

> As you are aware it is critical that the Bureau issue a new list of federally recognized tribes in Alaska before the Supreme Court rules on the State's cert. petition in *Noatak v. Hoffman*. We thought it would be helpful; so we are enclosing a draft 1990 BIA list of federally recognized tribes in Alaska. In the preamble we attempt to set forth the circumstances giving rise to publication of the 1988 list, the problems it presented and the changes required to resolve them in the proposed 1990 list. Most importantly the 1990 draft unequivocally and expressly acknowledges the tribal status of the listed villages and regional tribes."[24]

If Associate Solicitor Lavell passed Aschenbrenner's letter on to Assistant Secretary Brown, he ignored the back-channel lobbying and did not publish a new list.*

A year and a half later Aschenbrenner (and David Case, Lloyd Miller, Michael Walleri, Bert Hirsch, and nine other attorneys who were active in the tribal sovereignty movement) tried again.

In a letter dated January 14, 1992, that Aschenbrenner sent (and that the other attorneys signed) to Lynn Forcia, the chief of the BIA Branch of Acknowledgment and Research, he urged the BIA "to rescind its 1988 list and publish a new list which explicitly recognizes [Alaska Native] tribal status" because "the 1988 list casts into doubt the political status of the listed Villages not only because it includes Native corporations, which obviously are not 'tribes' in the political sense, but also because its preamble can be read as an attempt to rescind the government's prior recognition of their tribal status as expressed in the secretary's earlier lists and numerous Acts of Congress."[26]

While the 1988 list was not rescinded, by the time Aschenbrenner sent his letter, the solicitor of the Department of the Interior was conducting a review of the tribal sovereignty situation in Alaska.

In June 1991 Manual Lujan, whom President Bush had appointed to succeed Donald Hodel as secretary of the interior, directed Thomas Sansonetti, the solicitor of the Department of the Interior, "to develop the legal position of the United States on the nature and scope of so-called governmental powers over lands and non-members that a Native village can exercise after ANCSA." Secretary Lujan explained that: "This opinion will be useful in resolving questions which arise in the context of approving the constitutions put forward by villages seeking recognition under the Indian Reorganization Act. My request to the solicitor will aid me in deciding whether jurisdictional claims made by the villages under this procedure are consistent with law."[31]

In response to that directive, in January 1993 Solicitor Sansonetti sent Secretary Lujan, and released to the public, Solicitor Opinion M-36975, entitled "Governmental Jurisdiction of Alaska Native Villages Over Land and Nonmembers."[32]

---

* On October 1, 1990, the U.S. Supreme Court granted the State of Alaska's petition for a writ of certiorari.[25] Several days later Lloyd Miller informed the Native villages and organizations he represented that because the Court would "review *all* aspects of the *Noatak* decision, including whether Alaska villages are tribes" the Court's decision to grant the State's petition posed "a direct threat to tribal status and tribal self-governance in Alaska" (emphasis in the original).[27] However, in its decision in *Blatchford v. Native Village of* Noatak,[28] a divided Court reversed the panel of the U.S. Court of Appeals for the Ninth Circuit and dismissed the lawsuit on the ground that the lawsuit was barred by the Eleventh Amendment. The Court did not reach the question of whether the two deciding judges had been correct that, for the purposes of 28 U.S.C. 1362, the Inupiat Eskimo residents of Noatak and the Athabascan Indian residents of Circle were members of "Indian tribes." For that reason, Lare Aschenbrenner told the *Anchorage Daily Times* that "all the court has done is postpone the day in which we get a definite answer to the question of whether the 200 villages have the same tribal status as Indians,"[29] and that "the decision just marks the end of Round 1. The issues of whether a village has tribal status and whether or not states can deal with tribes on a government-to-government basis has (sic) been returned to the lower courts."[30]

Stuffed to bursting with historical analysis, the 133-page opinion concluded that "while the Department [of the Interior]'s position with regard to the existence of tribes in Alaska may have vacillated between 1867 and the opening decades of this century, it is clear that for the last half century, Congress and the Department have dealt with Alaska Natives as though there were tribes in Alaska."[33] However, which groups of Alaska Natives were federally recognized tribes and which groups were not was a fact-driven question that would have to be decided group-by-group.

The story of the politics inside the Department of the Interior bureaucracy that led to Solicitor Sansonetti announcing in his opinion that there were groups in Alaska, which he pointedly declined to identify, whose Native members were members of federally recognized tribes is a subject beyond the scope of this narrative other than to say that the evidence on which the opinion relied was cherry-picked and apparently intentionally miscited.

Four examples.

First, the opinion cites a solicitor's opinion entitled "Status of Alaska Natives" that Solicitor Edward Finney wrote and Secretary of the Interior Ray Lyman Wilbur approved on February 24, 1932.[34]

A year earlier Secretary Wilbur had transferred the administration of Alaska Native programs from the Bureau of Education to the BIA.[35] After he did so, a question arose regarding whether Congress had intended to include Alaska Natives within the purview of the undefined word "Indians" in statutes the BIA administered, particularly the Snyder Act,[36] which authorizes the BIA to spend money that Congress appropriates "for the benefit, care, and assistance of the Indians throughout the United States."

In his opinion Solicitor Finney concluded that because "no distinction has been or can be made between the Indians and other natives of Alaska so far as the laws and relations of the United States are concerned," Alaska Natives "are entitled to the benefits of and are subject to the general laws and regulations governing the Indians of the United States."[37]

That legal conclusion had nothing to do with the question of whether Congress, or the secretary of the interior acting lawfully pursuant to authority Congress had delegated to the secretary, had previously "recognized" Native residents of communities that decades later would be designated as Native villages for the purposes of ANCSA as "tribes" in a political sense that, as a consequence of that designation, possessed "sovereign" powers of self-government.

With respect to that question, on the page of the Sansonetti opinion on which Solicitor Finney's opinion is discussed, a footnote references a letter that Secretary Wilbur sent to Representative Edgar Howard, the chairman of the House Committee on Indian Affairs, three weeks after Secretary Wilbur approved Solicitor Finney's opinion.[38] But the footnote did not describe the content of the letter. The reason it did not is that, as has been described, in that letter Secretary Wilbur informed Representative Howard that "[t]he United States has had no treaty relations with any of the aborigines of Alaska nor have they been recognized as the independent tribes with a government of their own. The individual native has always and everywhere in Alaska been subject to the white man's law, both Federal and territorial, civil and criminal."[39]

Second, as also has been described, in 1937 when the BIA began implementing Public Law No. 74-538, Assistant Commissioner of Indian Affairs William Zimmerman issued written instructions to the teachers who taught in the schools the BIA operated in Native villages that the teachers were to follow when they assisted residents of the villages in which the schools were located write constitutions that section 1 of Public Law No. 74-538 authorized the secretary of the interior to approve pursuant to section 16 of the IRA.

While it acknowledged that Assistant Commissioner Zimmerman had issued them,[40] the Sansonetti opinion made no mention of the fact that the instructions told the teachers that a constitution could contain language that granted a village council "powers for the civil government" within the boundaries of the reservation that Assistant Commissioner Zimmerman assumed that the secretary of the interior would establish for each community pursuant to authority section 2 of Public Law No. 74-538 delegated to the secretary. But with the understanding that the civil government powers would "take effect only upon the designation and approval of a reservation for such community."[41]

Third, the administrative record on which the Sansonetti opinion was based includes a letter dated June 26, 1940, that Assistant Commissioner Zimmerman sent to Claude Hirst, the general superintendent of the BIA in Alaska, in which he advised that Tlingit Indians living in the southeast Alaska communities of Klukwan and Haines were not eligible to obtain a constitution pursuant to section 1 of Public Law No. 74-538.[42] While in that letter Assistant Commissioner Zimmerman advised Superintendent Hirst that "the Department has at no time recognized the existence in Alaska of Indian tribes, with powers of limited sovereignty, similar to the tribes in the continental United States," the Sansonetti opinion made no mention of the letter.

Fourth, as has been described, section 1151 of title 18 of the U.S. Code defines the term "Indian country" to mean (1) "land within the limits of any Indian reservation," (2) "dependent Indian communities," and (3) "Indian allotments, the Indian titles to which have not been extinguished."

After "reject[ing] the notion that there are no tribes in Alaska,"[43] the Sansonetti opinion concluded by announcing that Congress did not intend the subsurface and surface estates of public land the secretary of the interior had conveyed in fee title to ANCSA regional and village corporations to be "dependent Indian communities," and hence "Indian country," within whose boundaries "tribes" could exercise governmental authority.[44] But the opinion made no mention of the fact that that had not always been the solicitor's legal position.

Sections 1154 and 1156 of title 18 of the U.S. Code prohibit the possession and sale of intoxicating liquors in Indian country. However, section 1161 of title 18 waives that prohibition if possession or sale is lawful in the state in which a parcel of Indian country is located, has been authorized by "an ordinance duly adopted by the tribe having jurisdiction over such ... Indian country," and the secretary of the interior certifies the ordinance and publishes a notice in the *Federal Register* that announces the certification.

In 1980 the village council in Allakaket, a Native village in the Alaska interior, submitted a liquor ordinance to the secretary. In response, Hans Walker, the associate solicitor for Indian affairs, issued a memorandum opinion in which he advised the commissioner of Indian affairs that Alaska Native allotments located in the vicinity of Allakaket and "the village townsite and lands owned by the village or village corporation" were Indian country because those lands collectively constituted a "dependent Indian community."[45]

For unrelated reasons the secretary did not certify the ordinance. But seven months later, in May 1981, Associate Solicitor Walker and James Canan, the acting deputy assistant secretary of the interior for Indian affairs, told the Senate Select Committee on Indian Affairs that, while not all of the surface estate of the land surrounding a Native village whose title the secretary had conveyed to the local village corporation pursuant to ANCSA was Indian country, "the village itself, the land—could be considered Indian country for the purposes of enforcement of the Indian liquor law" and "we did have a ruling on that."[46]

Chalkyitsik, Northway, and Minto are three other Native villages in the Alaska interior. In May 1983 John Fritz, the acting assistant secretary of the interior for Indian affairs, published a notice in the *Federal Register* in which he certified that an ordinance "relating to the application of the Federal Indian Liquor Laws within an area of Indian country was duly adopted by the Chalkyitsik Village Council on March 18, 1982."[47] A month later Assistant Secretary of the Interior for Indian Affairs Ken Smith published a notice in which he certified "that Ordinance No. 83-4 relating to the application of the Federal Indian Liquor Laws within an area of Indian country was duly adopted on January 20, 1983 by the Northway Native Village Council." And in August 1986, Assistant Secretary of the Interior for Indian Affairs Ross Swimmer published a notice in which he certified "that the Minto Liquor Ordinance was duly adopted by the Village Council of Minto on February 14, 1985."[48]

In response to Assistant Secretary Swimmer's certification of the Minto Liquor Ordinance, Alaska Governor Bill Sheffield sent Secretary of the Interior Donald Hodel a letter in which he noted that the certification "appears to be a significant change of position" because "to our knowledge the secretary [of the interior] has never stated that Indian country exists in Alaska, except for reservations and allotments."[49] The letter then posed several questions, including whether the Department of the Interior now believed that land ANCSA regional and village corporations owned in fee title was Indian country, and whether the village council in Minto and other village councils had authority to regulate alcohol consumption by non-Natives and preempt the authority of the Alaska Legislature to regulate alcohol consumption.

Although the administrative record on which the Sansonetti opinion was based contains documents that reference the Chalkyitsik, Northway, and Minto liquor ordinances, the opinion made no mention of Associate Solicitor Walker's memorandum, his subsequent testimony, the three ordinances, or of Governor Sheffield's letter.

With respect to the land within the boundaries of the revoked Venetie reserve whose fee title, as will be described, the Venetie Indian Corporation and the Neets'ai Corporation had conveyed to the Native Village of Venetie, the Sansonetti opinion further opined that that land was not Indian country because "the ANCSA statutory scheme simply does not permit tribes to create Indian country in Alaska by unilateral action."[50]

The Alaska Native Allotment Act,[51] which the Fifty-ninth Congress enacted in 1906, authorized Alaska Natives to each obtain a restricted title to up to 160 acres of public land as "the homestead of the allottee and his heirs in perpetuity." In section 18 of ANCSA, the Ninety-second Congress repealed the Alaska Native Allotment Act. But in 1993 there were more than 16,000 allotment parcels whose validity the secretary of the interior had approved or whose approval was pending.

The Sansonetti opinion announced that land within the boundaries of approved allotment parcels was Indian country. However, that conclusion was wrong. Because even if the Eightieth Congress that in 1948 enacted the "Indian country" definition intended the term "Indian allotments" in the definition to include Alaska Native allotments (and the legislative history indicates that the Eightieth Congress intended no such result), the definition was limited to "Indian allotments" whose "Indian titles have not been extinguished." Because "Indian title" and "aboriginal title" are synonymous legal terms of art, and because in section 4(b) of ANCSA the Ninety-second Congress extinguished "[a]ll aboriginal titles ... in Alaska," contrary to the legal conclusion the Sansonetti opinion announced, there were no Alaska Native allotments whose Indian titles had not been extinguished.

But even if Alaska Native allotments were Indian country, at the conclusion of his analysis Solicitor Sansonetti announced that "after examining the statute and circumstances related to Alaska allotments, we are not convinced that any specific villages or groups can claim jurisdictional authority over allotment parcels," and "particularly in the absence of a tribal territorial base (e.g., a reservation), there is little or no basis for an Alaska village claiming *territorial* jurisdiction over an Alaska Native allotment" (emphasis in original).[52]

By the fall of 1992, the Sansonetti opinion was circulating in draft form inside the Department of the Interior, and in Alaska the content of the opinion became known.

Because the conclusion that there was no Indian country in Alaska within whose boundaries federally recognized tribes could exercise governmental authority was anathema for members of the tribal sovereignty movement, at the request of NARF and the AFN, on November 9, 1992, Senator Daniel Inouye, the chairman of the Senate Committee on Indian Affairs, met with Secretary Lujan to try to persuade him to order Solicitor Sansonetti not to issue his opinion because, as the senator argued in a letter he gave to the secretary at that meeting, "the issuance of a solicitor's opinion at this time, such as that contemplated to address the status of tribal governments in Alaska, would serve to seriously undermine the ability of the incoming administration [Bill Clinton having been elected president a week earlier] to determine the federal government's policies as they relate to the legal status of Alaska Native governments."[53]

When Secretary Lujan ignored the senator's request and Solicitor Sansonetti issued his opinion, the *Anchorage Daily News* reported:

> "The solicitor's opinion essentially leaves the villages in the same position they were in as a result of recent federal court rulings," said Lare Aschenbrenner of the Native American Rights Fund in Anchorage. "It is positive in that it rejects the Alaska Supreme Court's position [announced in the decision the Court had issued in *Native Village of Stevens v. Alaska Management & Planning*] that there are not tribes in Alaska, but it means that each of the 230 Native villages will have to bring separate federal lawsuits to prove their tribal status," he said.
>
> Julie Kitka, the executive director (sic) of the Alaska Federation of Natives, complained that the opinion flatly rejects any Native powers over their lands beyond what ordinary land-owning citizens would have over their property. "This impinges on the desire of Natives to exercise their aboriginal and inherent self-government powers," Kitka said. She said the conclusion that Natives gave up their self-government powers with the enactment of the 1971 settlement act is a policy conclusion of the Bush administration that no federal court has yet endorsed and which she hopes the Clinton administration will reject.[54]

Nine days after Solicitor Sansonetti issued his opinion, on January 20, 1993, Bill Clinton was sworn into office. A day later the Senate confirmed President Clinton's nomination of former Arizona Governor Bruce Babbitt to succeed Manual Lujan as secretary of the interior. Three weeks later NARF attorneys Lare Aschenbrenner and Robert Anderson sent Secretary Babbitt a letter, written on NARF letterhead stationery, that David Case, Bert Hirsch, and nine other attorneys active in the tribal sovereignty movement signed. The letter urged Babbitt to "publish a new list of Federally Acknowledged Tribes that expressly recognizes the tribal status of Alaska Native villages; and withdraw the former Solicitor's Opinion of January 11, 1993 insofar as it denied the existence of Indian country and tribal territorial powers in Alaska."[55]

On March 20 Aschenbrenner and Anderson sent the other attorneys who had signed the letter a memorandum in which they reported:

> Please find for your review a draft letter to the assistant secretary [of the interior for Indian affairs], a draft 1993 *Federal Register* list of federally recognized tribes in Alaska and a draft explanation and rationale for the new list.
>
> We have been in contact with [Assistant Solicitor] Scott Keep [in Washington, D.C.] and he believes the time is right to follow up on our letter to Secretary Babbitt. The plan is to get [Assistant Secretary of the Interior for Indian Affairs] Eddie Brown (who is still in office) to direct the Bureau [of Indian Affairs] to review the proposed new *Federal Register* list and come up with its own draft list, and to give this matter priority starting *now*!
>
> If we wait for the appointment and confirmation of the new assistant secretary before we start this process, we will be just that much further behind.
>
> We plan to have John Ecohawk [the executive director of NARF] ask Bruce Babbitt to *direct* Eddie Brown to take this action, if necessary ... So *now* is the time to strike! (emphases in original).[56]

Two days later Aschenbrenner sent Scott Keep a copy of the March 20 memorandum, as well as a copy of the letter, the new *Federal Register* list, and the explanation and rationale for the new list to which he had alluded in the memorandum. He also sent a note written on NARF letterhead stationery in which Aschenbrenner told Keep: "Here is the package we hope to send back to D.C. later in the week after all the attorneys & the [BIA] Juneau Area Office have had their final input. Please review & if we have made some gross error please give me a call as we want it as error free as possible."[57]

If John Ecohawk did ask Secretary Babbitt to direct Assistant Secretary Brown to publish NARF's new list, nothing came of it because no new list was published.

Three months later, on June 30, President Clinton nominated Ada Deer to replace Eddie Brown as assistant secretary of the interior for Indian affairs.[58] Who was Ada Deer? As she explained to the Senate Committee on Indian Affairs during the hearing the committee held on her nomination, Deer was a former "client, a staff member, a board member, a board chair, and finally, chair of the National Support Committee of the Native American Rights Fund."[59]

On July 16 the Senate confirmed Deer's nomination.[60] Soon thereafter Lare Aschenbrenner and Robert Anderson renewed their effort to have the assistant secretary publish in the *Federal Register* a new list of Native entities and a new preamble that would announce that the act of publication had the legal consequence of transforming each entity into a federally recognized tribe. As Aschenbrenner and Anderson explained in a letter dated August 4 that they sent to Scott Keep and John Trezise, the acting associate solicitor for Indian affairs:

> It will not, in our view, be enough to merely state in a single paragraph that Alaska Native villages have the same tribal status as tribes in the lower 48. To the contrary, in order to eliminate altogether, or at least reduce to the absolute minimum, any possible misconception as to the Department's po-

Assistant Secretary of the Interior for Indian Affairs Ada Deer.
U.S. Department of the Interior.

> sition we believe it is essential for the preamble to expressly state *how* the earlier *Federal Register* lists have been *misconstrued*. According, we have no objection to reducing the narrative description of the misconstruction of the earlier lists *provided* the essential particulars are retained. In particular, we believe it is essential that the changes and defects in the 1988 list be specifically detailed.
>
> Finally, the operative language which we believe is indispensable ... is as follows:
>
> > The purpose of the present publication is to eliminate any doubt as to the Department [of the Interior]'s intention by expressly and unequivocally acknowledging that the Department has determined that the villages and regional tribes listed below are distinctly Native communities and have the same tribal status as tribes in the contiguous states. Such acknowledgment of tribal existence by the Department is a prerequisite to the protection, services, and benefits from the federal government available to Indian tribes. This list is published to clarify that the villages and regional tribes listed below are not simply eligible for services, or recognized as tribes for certain narrow purposes. Rather, they have the same inherent protection, immunities and privileges available to other federally acknowledged Indian tribes by virtue of their status as Indian tribes with a government-to-government relationship with the United States (emphases in original).[61]

On August 11 Secretary Babbitt arrived in Alaska to spend three weeks touring the state.[62] He soon was joined by Assistant Secretary Deer.[63] On August 13 Deer met privately in Fairbanks with Dalee Sambo, the executive director of the Alaska

Inter-Tribal Council (AITC), the organization that in December 1992 tribal sovereignty advocates had created to replace the by then defunct ANC,[64] as well as with other members of the AITC. After the meeting the *Tundra Times* reported: "According to AITC spokesperson Dalee Sambo, lengthy memos written by Deer — who's only been in office since last month — for Babbitt's consideration, as well as remarks she made in Fairbanks, have been heartening to sovereignty advocates. 'Ada Deer supports the position of AITC,' said Sambo."[65]

What was the position of the AITC?

On August 19 Secretary Babbitt and Assistant Secretary Deer met with members of the AFN board of directors and other Native leaders in Dillingham, the largest Native village in the Bristol Bay region of southwestern Alaska.[66] Prior to the meeting, Dalee Sambo held a press conference during which she announced that "[t]he [AITC] wants the Clinton administration's support on two key points in the debate over tribal sovereignty. First, says the council, the feds should formally recognize that Alaska Native villages are, in the legal sense, tribes. Second, the feds should recognize that Alaska tribes can exercise the same legal powers as tribes in the Lower 48."[67]

When she returned to Washington, D.C., Assistant Secretary Deer set about implementing the AITC agenda.

In September John Trezise, the acting associate solicitor for Indian affairs, sent Lloyd Miller for his private review and comment a copy of the preamble Assistant Secretary Deer would publish in the *Federal Register* when she published a new list of Native entities. On September 30 Miller faxed Trezise his changes, along with a note that read: "John, I think the redraft is excellent, and I am glad the NARF submission we all worked on was helpful. I have proposed a sentence for page 3, and made a comment on page 5, a correction on page 6, and joined in Bob [Anderson]'s correction on page 7. I look forward to seeing your final (if possible) and to seeing the list itself at your earliest convenience."[68]

Three weeks later Assistant Secretary Deer flew to Anchorage where, in a speech she delivered at that year's AFN convention, she announced that, "Today, I'm releasing the 1993 revised list of Alaska Native entities with which the federal government has a government-to-government relationship. The preamble to the list expressly states that the listed villages are distinctly Native communities and have the same powers and attributes as tribes in the Lower 48, except to the extent that those powers or attributes have been limited by Congress."[69]

On October 21 Assistant Secretary Deer published her list and preamble in the *Federal Register*.[70]

What statute delegated Assistant Secretary Deer authority to turn more than a century of Congress's Alaska Native policy inside out by, in Congress's stead, creating 212 federally recognized tribes in Alaska simply by publishing a new list of Native entities and a preamble in the *Federal Register*? The preamble stated: "This notice is published in exercise of authority delegated to the assistant secretary — Indian affairs under 25 U.S.C. 2 and 9."[71]

But neither statute delegated the authority that Assistant Secretary Deer purported to exercise.

The Twenty-second Congress enacted 25 U.S.C. 2 in 1832.[72] As now codified, the statute reads: "The commissioner of Indian affairs shall, under the direction of the secretary of the interior, and agreeably to such regulations as the president may prescribe, have the management of all Indian affairs and of all matters arising out of Indian relations." The circumstances that motivated the Twenty-second Congress to enact 25 U.S.C. 2 are as follows:

In 1806 the Ninth Congress created the office of superintendent of Indian trade inside the War Department to manage the trading posts, called factories, that the president was operating on the frontier.[73] In 1816 President James Madison appointed Thomas McKenney superintendent.[74] In 1822 the Seventeenth Congress ordered the president to close the factories. As a consequence, Superintendent McKenney no longer had any statutorily mandated duties. To fill the vacuum, in 1824 "Secretary of War [John C.] Calhoun, by his own order, and without special authorization from Congress, created in the War Department what he called the Bureau of Indian Affairs. To head the bureau Calhoun appointed McKenney and assigned him two clerks as assistants."[75]

Because Secretary Calhoun had no authority to create the BIA or hire Thomas McKenney to run it, in 1826 McKenney wrote a bill whose enactment would create the position inside the War Department that he already occupied.[76] In 1832 the Twenty-third Congress enacted McKenney's bill, which today is 25 U.S.C. 2.

When the bill passed, the secretary of war was annually distributing more than $1 million in gratuities to Indians, operating fifty-four schools for Indian children, and as recently as 1830 had issued ninety-eight licenses to traders doing business in Indian country. As Senator Hugh White, the chairman of the Senate Committee on Indian Affairs, informed his colleagues when the bill McKenney had written reached the floor of the Senate, "To all these different branches the personal attention of the secretary of war is now required. The creation, therefore, of such an officer [the commissioner of Indian affairs] as is provided by the bill, be deemed to be indispensably necessary."[77]

If Assistant Secretary Deer was to be believed, in 1832 the Twenty-second Congress intended its enactment of the bill that would be codified as 25 U.S.C. 2 to delegate an obscure subordinate employee of the War Department* unfettered authority to decide on his (and later her) own which groups of Native Americans would be designated as federally recognized tribes whose members, as a consequence of having obtained that legal status, would have a "government-to-government" relationship with the United States. That interpretation of the intent of the Twenty-second Congress stretches credulity past breaking.

---

* In 1849 the Thirtieth Congress moved the BIA from the War Department to the Department of the Interior.

The Twenty-third Congress enacted 25 U.S.C. 9 in 1834. As now codified, the statute reads: "The President may prescribe such regulations as he may think fit for carrying into effect the various provisions of any act relating to Indian affairs, and for the settlement of the accounts of Indian affairs." On its face, 25 U.S.C. 9 delegated Assistant Secretary Deer no authority whatsoever.

Even if the Twenty-second and Twenty-third Congresses had intended 25 U.S.C. 2 and 9 to delegate Assistant Secretary Deer authority to create federally recognized tribes in Alaska in Congress's stead simply by publishing a list of Native entities and a preamble in the *Federal Register*, the U.S. Supreme Court has instructed that, while Congress may enact a statute in which it delegates a portion of its legislative authority to the executive branch, the constitutional doctrine of separation of powers requires that the text of the statute contain an "intelligible principle to which the person or body authorized to [exercise the delegated authority] is directed to conform," and that a statute that delegates legislative authority is invalid if its text contains "an absence of standards for the guidance of [executive branch action], so that it would be impossible in a proper proceeding to ascertain whether the will of Congress has been obeyed."[78]

The texts of 25 U.S.C. 2 and 9 do not contain any intelligible principles or identifiable standards that could have guided Assistant Secretary Deer's decision-making. Because they do not, for that reason alone, Assistant Secretary Deer's attempt to create 212 federally recognized tribes in Alaska by unilateral agency fait was, and today remains, *ultra vires*.

Eight

Because as Secretary of the Interior Ray Lyman Wilbur noted in 1932, "The individual native has always and everywhere in Alaska been subject to the white man's law, both Federal and territorial, civil and criminal," the territorial, and later state, laws to which Alaska Natives living in communities that would be designated as Native villages for the purposes of ANCSA were subject included laws that regulate domestic relations, including adoptions. For example, it is a common practice in Native villages for Native children to be adopted without the Native adoptive parents complying with the State of Alaska's adoption statute. In 1977 in its decision in *Calista Corporation v.* Mann,[1] the Alaska Supreme Court held that in Native villages Native adoptive parents were as subject to the State's adoption statute as all other adoptive parents. But as an exercise of its power in equity, the court directed the State to treat *de facto* adoptions by Native adoptive parents as if they were *de jure* adoptions for the limited purpose of implementing state laws relating to inheritance.

That same year the American Indian Policy Review Commission, which the Ninety-third Congress created in 1974 to study federal Indian policy, recommended that tribal courts be granted exclusive jurisdiction to adjudicate child custody disputes involving Indian children who are domiciled on Indian reservations, and that, with respect to a state child custody proceeding involving an Indian child who was not domiciled on a reservation, the child's "tribe of origin" should be granted the right to intervene in the proceeding.[2]

In 1978 the Ninety-fifth Congress implemented that recommendation by enacting the Indian Child Welfare Act (ICWA).[3]

Because there were no federally recognized tribes and no reservations in Alaska, to afford Native parents and children the procedural protections in state child custody proceedings that the ICWA mandated, and to afford Native villages an opportunity to intervene in those proceedings, the Ninety-fifth Congress defined "Indian tribe" in section 4(8) of ICWA to include "Alaska Native village[s] as defined in section [3(c) of ANCSA]."

Significantly, section 108 of the ICWA authorized an ICWA "Indian tribe" that had no jurisdiction to conduct child custody proceedings to petition the secretary of the interior to grant that jurisdiction within the boundaries of the tribe's reservation or former reservation. If a tribe had no reservation or former reservation, section 108(b) authorized the tribe to petition the secretary to grant the tribe jurisdiction to conduct child custody proceedings within "limited community or geographic areas without regard for the reservation status of the area affected."

Section 108 was included in H.R. 12533, the bill the Ninety-fifth Congress enacted as the ICWA, by the House Committee on Interior and Insular Affairs. When it reported H.R. 12533, the committee explained that it included section 108 in the bill "in order to take into consideration special circumstances, such as those occurring in Alaska."[4] But petitioning the secretary of the interior to grant an ICWA "Indian tribe" jurisdiction was inconsistent with the tenet of the tribal sovereignty movement that the governing bodies of federally recognized tribes in Alaska possess "inherent" governmental authority, including authority to issue adoption decrees.

Allakaket is a community on the Koyukuk River in the Alaska interior at which several Athabascan Indian families settled after the Episcopal Church established a mission at the site in 1906. In 1971 the Ninety-second Congress designated Allakaket as a Native village for the purposes of ANCSA. In 1975 the adult residents of Allakaket, whose total population was 174, incorporated a municipal government. But they did not disband the village council that, while it had no legal imprimatur, had been functioning as the local government. In 1986 the village council issued an adoption decree and then requested the Bureau of Vital Statistics in the Alaska Department of Health and Social Services to issue a new birth certificate for the child who was the subject of the decree.

When the attorneys who represented the village council asserted that the Bureau had a legal duty to issue the certificate because section 101(d) of the ICWA requires a state to give "full faith and credit" to the judicial proceedings of an ICWA "Indian tribe," John Pugh, the commissioner of the Department of Health and Social Services, asked Alaska Attorney General Harold Brown for advice.

In April 1986 Douglas Mertz, the assistant attorney general who advised Attorney General Brown regarding tribal sovereignty-related legal issues, told Commissioner Pugh that the Bureau of Vital Statistics should not issue a new birth certificate unless the village council that had issued the adoption decree for which the certificate was needed had petitioned the secretary of the interior pursuant to section 108 of the ICWA for jurisdiction to involve itself in child custody proceedings and the secretary had granted the petition. He then advised that since the Native village of Allakatek had not filed a petition, "[t]he Bureau of Vital Statistics is not obligated to issue a substitute birth certificate pursuant to a decree from the Allakaket village council, at least as long as the council's jurisdiction is in as much legal doubt as it is today."[5]

Mertz later would recall that around that same time he discussed the situation with the attorneys in the Anchorage office of NARF and at the Alaska Legal Services Corporation who were representing many village councils. According to Mertz: "My thought was that one of the worst things that could happen to a Native family was to have an adoption declared invalid years after the placement of the child with the family. So if a tribe wanted to do a tribal adoption, as NARF and ALSC were advocating, they should do a dual adoption, both tribal and state, so that if the tribal one was declared invalid there would still be a fallback legal adoption, i.e., the state adoption. The NARFees and ALSC went crazy, as if this would be some kind of betrayal of their clients instead of a practical move to avoid a possible terrible consequence."[6]

Consistent with Mertz's recollection of their attitude, in November 1986 in the U.S. District Court in Fairbanks, Andrew Harrington and Judith Bush, attorneys who worked in the ALSC office in Fairbanks and who in 1990 would sign the letter that NARF attorneys Lare Aschenbrenner and Robert Anderson sent to Assistant Secretary of the Interior for Indian Affairs Eddie Brown, filed *Native Village of Venetie I.R.A. Council v. State of Alaska*, a lawsuit that District Judge Andrew Kleinfeld described as "a test case brought by the plaintiffs to determine unsettled questions of the scope of the Indian Child Welfare Act."[7]

Courts that the village councils in Venetie and Fort Yukon, a Native village located southeast of Venetie at the confluence of the Yukon and Porcupine Rivers in the Alaska interior, had created had issued adoption decrees that, based on the advice Assistant Attorney General Mertz had given to Commissioner Pugh, the Bureau of Vital Statistics and the Division of Public Assistance and other state agencies refused to recognize. In their complaint the Venetie and Fort Yukon village councils asserted that, even though they had not petitioned the secretary of the interior for jurisdiction pursuant to section 108 of the ICWA, the courts they had created had "inherent" jurisdiction to issue adoption decrees.

After observing that "the fundamental question in this case is whether the tribal courts have jurisdiction to issue adoption decrees, even though they have not complied with statutory provisions for reassuming such jurisdiction," Judge Kleinfeld held that the two courts had no jurisdiction. In so holding, he observed that "the law of aboriginal peoples in Alaska has remained distinct from Indian law for the continental United States, because of the different historical path taken in Alaska."[8]

But rather than basing his decision exclusively on that ground, Judge Kleinfeld suggested that the courts in Venetie and Fort Yukon might have had inherent jurisdiction if in 1958 the Eighty-fifth Congress had not reversed the decision of the U.S. District Court in Anchorage in the *In re McCord* lawsuit[9] by enacting Public Law No. 85-615, the statute that added the Territory (later State) of Alaska to the list of states in Public Law No. 83-280 whose civil laws were given "the same force and effect within ... Indian country as they have elsewhere within the State."

In 1990 a three-judge panel of the U.S. Court of Appeals for the Ninth Circuit reversed Judge Kleinfeld.[10]

The judges first accepted the legal validity of the doctrine of "inherent" tribal sovereignty* and the application of the doctrine in Alaska by announcing that

---

* "Inherent" tribal sovereignty is a legal fiction that Felix Cohen, the assistant solicitor in the Department of the Interior who was the principal author of the text of the IRA, invented in a solicitor's opinion Cohen wrote in 1934 entitled "Powers of Indian Tribes."[12] As Vine Deloria Jr., a scholar of

> if native groups in Alaska were sovereign prior to the incorporation of the land mass [of Alaska] into the United States, they could lose their sovereignty only by express act of Congress or assimilation by the natives into the non-native culture.
>
> Indian sovereignty flows from the historical roots of the Indian tribe. Tribal sovereignty exists unless and until affirmatively divested by Congress. Thus, to the extent that Alaska's natives formed bodies politic to govern domestic relations, to punish wrongdoers, and otherwise provide for the general welfare, we perceive no reason why they too, should not be recognized as having been sovereign entities. If the native villages of Venetie and Fort Yukon are the modern-day successors to sovereign historical bands of natives, the villages are to be afforded the same rights and responsibilities as are sovereign bands of native Americans in the continental United States.[11]

They then concluded that, because the texts of Public Law No. 83-280 and of the ICWA both were ambiguous,

> resolving the jurisdictional ambiguities in favor of the villages, we hold that neither the Indian Child Welfare Act nor Public Law 280 prevents them from exercising concurrent jurisdiction. If the native villages of Venetie and Fort Yukon are sovereign entities which may exercise dominion over their members' domestic relations, Alaska must give full faith and credit to any child-custody determinations made by the villages' governing bodies in accordance with the full faith and credit clause of the Indian Child Welfare Act.[14]

The judges then sent the lawsuit back to Judge Kleinfeld to "determine whether the Native villages of Venetie and Fort Yukon are the modern-day successors to an historical sovereign band of Native Americans."[15]

In February 1986 the Yukon Flats School District awarded Unalakleet/Neeser Construction Joint Venture (UNCJV) a contract to construct an addition to the high school the district operated in Venetie.

In 1971 in section 19(a) of ANCSA the Ninety-second Congress had revoked the 1.8 million-acre Venetie reserve that Assistant Secretary of the Interior Oscar Chapman had created in 1943 pursuant to section 2 of Public Law No. 74-538. In 1979 the secretary of the interior conveyed fee title to the public land within the boundaries of the revoked reserve to the Venetie Indian Corporation and the Neets'ai Corporation, the ANCSA village corporations the Gwitch'in Athabascan Indian residents of Venetie and Arctic Village had incorporated.

---

the history of federal Indian policy who today remains revered throughout Indian country, has noted, "Modern tribal sovereignty ... begins with this opinion."[13]

In 1939 Assistant Secretary of the Interior Oscar Chapman had approved a constitution for an organization called the Native Village of Venetie (NVV) that "a group of Indians having the common bond of living together in the village of Venetie" had submitted pursuant to section 1 of Public Law No. 74-538 and section 16 of the IRA.[16]

When they were conveyed the fee titles to the public land within the boundaries of the revoked reserve, the Venetie Indian Corporation and the Neets'ai Corporation conveyed their titles to the NVV.*

In May 1986 the village council in Venetie adopted an ordinance that imposed a business activity tax on construction projects within the boundaries of the revoked reserve and established a "tax commission" whose members were the members of the council. In November the tax commission notified the UNCJV that it owed $100,751 in back taxes, which the commission later increased to $161,203.

When UNCJV ignored the notice, represented by NARF attorney Robert Anderson, in July the NVV filed a lawsuit against UNCJV in a "tax court" the village council had created, one of whose "judges" was Anchorage attorney David Case.

When the owners of UNCJV complained to the State of Alaska, in October 1987 the State filed a lawsuit in the U.S. District Court in Fairbanks, captioned *State of Alaska ex rel. Yukon Flats School District v. Native Village of Venetie Tribal Government*,[18] to obtain an order enjoining the NVV from enforcing its business activity tax. Three weeks later Judge Andrew Kleinfeld issued the order. And in September 1988, a three-judge panel of the U.S. Court of Appeals for the Ninth Circuit affirmed Judge Kleinfeld.[19]

When it did so, the panel noted that the questions of whether the members of the NVV were a federally recognized tribe that, as a consequence of that legal status, possessed the power to impose a business activity tax, and whether the land within the boundaries of the revoked Venetie reserve was Indian country within which a federally recognized tribe could impose a tax, were "quite factually dependent."[20]

Because the *Native Village of Venetie I.R.A. Council v. State of Alaska* and *State of Alaska v. Native Village of Venetie Tribal Government* lawsuits both required Judge Kleinfeld to determine whether the members of the NVV were members of a federally recognized tribe, the lawsuits were consolidated. When President George H.W. Bush then appointed Judge Kleinfeld to the U.S. Court of Appeals for the Ninth Circuit, the consolidated lawsuits were transferred to District Judge H. Russel Holland.

Because the assistant attorneys general who represented the State did not ask them to, the six judges who were members of the panels that had decided the two appeals did not consider the question of whether, as the House Committee on Natural Resources would note in 1994, for a group of individuals of Native American descent to be designated as a federally recognized tribe requires a "formal political act" in

* The constitution Assistant Secretary Chapman approved in 1939 authorized the residents of Venetie to elect a village council. In 1976 Venetie residents voted to expand the membership of the council to include council members from Arctic Village.[17]

the guise of a treaty, a statute, or final agency action of the secretary of the interior acting lawfully pursuant to authority Congress has delegated to the secretary in a statute. As a consequence, in the appeal in the *Native Village of Venetie I.R.A. Council* lawsuit, the panel had announced that if the NVV was the "modern-day successor" to a "sovereign historical band of natives," then the members of NVV were a federally recognized tribe.[21] And in the appeal in the *State of Alaska v. Native Village of Venetie Tribal Government* lawsuit, a different panel reasoned to the same result, holding that "tribal status may ... be based on conclusions drawn from careful scrutiny of various historical factors."[22]

Bound by that direction, in November 1993 Judge Holland conducted a trial at which NARF attorney Robert Anderson presented evidence regarding the question of whether the Gwich'in Athabascan Indian residents of Venetie and Arctic Village were "modern-day successors" to a "sovereign historical band of natives."

On December 23, 1994, Judge Holland issued a decision[23] in which he answered that question in the affirmative because, even though "the Venetie Council and Tribal Government has failed to convince the court that their tribal status has been acknowledged by the federal government," he had been persuaded by the evidence Anderson had presented that the Gwich'in Athabascan Indian residents of Venetie and Arctic Village "are a sovereign tribe as a matter of common law" and, as a consequence, the adoption degree the court in Venetie had issued was "entitled to full faith and credit from the State of Alaska."

In the *State of Alaska v. Native Village of Venetie Tribal Government* lawsuit, the three judges who were members of the panel that decided that appeal had noted that, even if the Gwich'in Athabascan Indian residents of Venetie were a federally recognized tribe, insofar as the tribe's authority to require the UNCJV to pay the NVV's business activity tax was concerned, "a tribal tax is only valid within the confines of Indian country."

As has been described, 18 U.S.C. 1151 defines the term "Indian country" to include the undefined term "dependent Indian communities."

On August 2, 1995, Judge Holland issued a second decision in which he announced that the land within the boundaries of the revoked Venetie reserve that since 1979 the NVV had owned in fee title was not Indian country because Venetie was not a dependent Indian community.[24]

In reasoning to that result, Judge Holland began by noting that "Indian country cannot exist ... without proof of three elements." First, "a claim of Indian country must be brought by an Indian tribe." Second, "the tribe must be under the active superintendence of the federal government." And third, "the tribe must have had land set aside by the federal government for its people as Natives."[25] He then noted that in section 19(a) of ANCSA the Ninety-second Congress had not only revoked the Venetie reserve, but in section 2(b) of ANCSA it had directed that the ANCSA land settlement be accomplished "without establishing any permanent racially defined institutions, rights, privileges, or obligations," and "without creating a reservation system or lengthy wardship or trusteeship."[26] He further noted that

> This court finds that the conveyance of lands by the federal government to village business corporations was not intended to be and in fact was not a set-aside of lands "for the use of Indians *as such*...." The court is not aware of any court having ever held that a government patent conveying fee title to a corporate entity (even one controlled by Indians) constituted a set-aside for Indians as such. The Native Village of Venetie Tribal Government had the right to acquire the land in question from the village corporations; but that unilateral decision of those corporations and the tribe (both of which are controlled by the Neets'aii Gwich'in) did not constitute "action ... by the federal government indicating that it set aside the land for the use by the ... [tribe as such]." The lands of the Neets'aii Gwich'in do not meet the set aside factor necessary to support a finding that the Neets'aii Gwich'in are a dependent Indian community (emphasis in original).[27]

As a consequence, Judge Holland concluded that "the lands of the Neets'aii Gwich'in are not Indian Country; and, therefore, the Tribal Government does not have the power to impose a tax upon non-members of the tribe."[28]

Represented by NARF attorney Heather Kendall,* the NVV appealed to the U.S. Court of Appeals for the Ninth Circuit Judge Holland's decision that the land located within the boundaries of the revoked Venetie reserve was not Indian country. But Alaska Attorney General Bruce Botelho did not appeal Judge Holland's decision that the Gwich'in Athabascan Indian residents of Venetie and Arctic Village were "a sovereign tribe as a matter of common law."

Attorney General Botelho would tell the Senate and House Judiciary Committees of the Alaska Legislature that the reason he did not file an appeal was that Alaska Governor Tony Knowles, at whose pleasure he served,** had decided "not to have a battle over [the tribal status] issue" in order to "try to develop a better, happier relationship with the villages throughout Alaska." And he told the speaker of the Alaska House of Representatives that

> the decision by the Knowles Administration to withdraw the challenge to federal recognition of tribes in Alaska was not driven by litigation considerations. Instead, it was motivated by a commitment to working with Alaska villages to achieve a healthier, safer environment in which the community

---

* Five months earlier Heather Kendall had replaced Robert Anderson as the attorney who represented the NVV when Anderson left NARF to become associate solicitor for Indian affairs at the Department of the Interior.[29] A committed tribal sovereignty ideologue, in 2010 Kendall told *First Alaskans* magazine, "If it were not for my passion for Native rights work, I would not be an attorney, because I don't particularly like the law."[30]

** Alaska is one of only five states in which, rather than being an elected public official, the attorney general is appointed by, and serves at the pleasure of, the governor.

is an active participant in solutions. Litigation over the issue of tribal status was viewed as a major impediment to this state-local partnership.[31]

While that explanation may have been true as far as it went, a year earlier Knowles, a Democrat, had been elected governor by defeating Jim Campbell, the Republican candidate, by 539 votes in an election in which 213,435 votes were cast and that Campbell would have won if Jack Coghill, the Alaska Independence Party candidate who was even more politically conservative than Campbell was, had not won 27,838 votes.[32]

But even with Coghill on the ballot, Knowles would have lost if he had not courted Native voters by supporting the tribal sovereignty movement.

In 1986 Steve Cowper, a former member of the Alaska House of Representatives from Fairbanks, defeated Bill Sheffield in the Democratic primary election and then won the general election to succeed Sheffield as governor.

Prior to the primary election when candidate Cowper was asked what his position on tribal sovereignty was, he answered:

> I don't have any problem with a tribal government or a tribal organization rendering services to the public through contractual means. I think that when federal money which is designated for Native people is concerned, of course those services would be rendered to the Native people. When state money is being administered, then the money has to be administered without regard to race or culture.
>
> Now in terms of the types of tribal governments which are envisioned by some groups, which would be roughly equivalent to reservations in other areas of the country, I don't think that that's in the best interest of the people of the state of Alaska. I think that we are basically all one people, and I don't think that it would be in anybody's best interest to set up independent jurisdictional units which are not answerable to anybody except the federal government. I realize that view is not held by many people in rural Alaska, but that's the view that I take.[33]

Consistent with that view, after candidate Cowper became Governor Cowper, in October 1987 his attorney general filed *State of Alaska v. Native Village of Venetie Tribal Government*, the lawsuit that requested District Judge Andrew Kleinfeld to prohibit the NVV from enforcing its business activity tax.

As will be described, a year later Governor Cowper attempted to appease the delegates who attended the 1988 AFN convention by announcing that he supported tribal "sovereignty" as long as village councils exercised governmental authority in a manner that did not contravene the Alaska Constitution.

Several months later Governor Cowper unexpectedly announced that he would not run for a second term.

Alaska Governor Steve Cowper. Alaska Office of the Governor Photograph Collection, Alaska State Library.

Although he now was a lame duck who no longer needed to try to curry favor with Native voters, two months before he left office, in September 1990 Governor Cowper signed Administrative Order No. 123 in which he announced that the State henceforth would "treat as a tribe any Alaskan Native group that meets the common sense of the word."[34]

Cowper did so even though four years earlier he had said that he did not think "it would be in anybody's best interest to set up independent jurisdictional units which are not answerable to anybody except the federal government," and two years earlier in its decision in *Native Village of Stevens v. Alaska Management & Planning*, the Alaska Supreme Court had held that more than a century earlier Congress had made a policy decision not to afford Native residents of Native villages "sovereign tribal status."

Years later when he was asked why at the end of his term in office he had decided to concede — if only symbolically — the validity of the tribal sovereignty movement's principal contention, Cowper recalled that he had had no qualms about signing Administrative Order No. 123 because in 1968 when he had been an assistant district attorney he had traveled regularly to Native villages on the Yukon-Kuskokwim River Delta. So he understood that the day-to-day reality of village life had not changed appreciably from the situation J.B. Henderson, the BIA teacher at Noatak, had described in 1933. According to Cowper,

> When I was a prosecutor the protocol was, the village councils would call John Malone [the Alaska State Trooper stationed at Bethel] whenever there was something they couldn't handle. John had a Cessna 195. We would go get Nora Guinn [the district court judge in Bethel] and off John and Nora and I would go to Crooked Creek or Hooper Bay or some other village and sort it out. Sticklers for procedural due process would not have approved. But the village council members did and that was good enough for us.[35]

Based on that experience, Cowper believed that "a tribal organization would likely serve about as well as a city bureaucracy of whatever class" because, "after all, the village people were the ones making the decisions."

But while he was willing to end his term in office by telling members of the tribal sovereignty movement what they wanted to hear, as had been his position when he had run for governor, Cowper continued not to be willing to agree that village councils had the governmental authority that NARF attorneys Lare Aschenbrenner and Robert Anderson and David Case, Lloyd Miller, and the other attorneys who were active in the tribal sovereignty movement said they had. For that reason, Administrative Order No. 123 announced: "When the State treats a Native group outside of a reservation as a tribe, it does not recognize that the tribe has the governmental powers of a tribe on a reservation. Whether governmental powers exist in a tribe in any particular instance is a completely separate question from tribal status."

Governor Cowper also understood that his limited concession regarding tribal status had no force of law. Rather, according to Cowper, "As far as I was concerned the administrative order was just a statement of how I intended to treat village governments. Whether it had any legal effect beyond that was in the eye of the various beholders. I certainly don't recall thinking the order would survive my term in office."[36]

And it did not.

In November 1990 Walter Hickel, a bombastic Anchorage businessman who, although he had been a stalwart lifelong Republican, had arranged to be the candidate of the fringe Alaska Independence Party, was elected to succeed Steve Cowper as governor.

For Hickel, his predecessor's symbolic acquiescence to the tribal sovereignty movement was anathema. In January 1991 in his first State of the State address the new governor vowed that "we will not bow to those who would bring Native sovereignty in a legal sense into the sovereign state of Alaska."[37] Seven months later, Hickel signed

Administrative Order No. 125, which revoked Administrative Order No. 123 because, as he explained when he did so, "This administration is not going to stand by and wait for the balkanization of Alaska."[38]

Administrative Order No. 125 announced that, because Alaska was "one country, one people," "the State of Alaska opposes expansion of tribal governmental powers and the creation of 'Indian country' in Alaska."[39]

Fairbanks attorney Charles Cole, whom Hickel had appointed attorney general, was of a similar mind. As Cole explained when he spoke at the Alaska Mayors' Conference:

> Fifteen years ago we all thought we knew the legal status of Alaskan Natives. The Alaska Native Claims Settlement Act became law in 1971, and we thought it settled the matter ... Many Native villages had become municipalities and were receiving state funding for local projects. The combination of municipal corporations and ANCSA corporations was bringing new benefits to Native villages.
>
> But by the late 1970s, some individual Alaska Natives began making claims that they had special privileges under federal law—that their communities were the equivalent of Indian reservations in the Lower 48. Some even claimed that Native villagers were exempt from state laws, and that Native councils could impose their own laws on non-members and even on the state.
>
> The result was widespread confusion and litigation. Over the last decade, there has been constant litigation in the courts over the rights and privileges of Alaska Natives. The result, frankly, has not only been unhelpful, the litigation has added confusion.
>
> ...
>
> As attorney general, I have the legal duty to oppose the most extreme sovereignty claims, those that would result in dozens of small states within our state of Alaska.[40]

Implementing the policy that Administrative Order No. 125 had announced, Attorney General Cole and the attorneys at the Department of Law he supervised continued to aggressively litigate the consolidated *Native Village of Venetie* lawsuits.

In January 1994 Attorney General Cole and Governor Hickel had a falling out, Cole resigned,[41] and Hickel appointed Bruce Botelho, a career attorney in the Department of Law who had been Cole's deputy, to succeed Cole as attorney general.[42] When his appointment was announced, Attorney General Botelho said that at the Department of Law there would be no "change in the general direction" Governor Hickel had "charted." As a consequence, the attorneys whom Attorney General Botelho supervised continued to contest NARF attorney Robert Anderson's assertion in the consolidated lawsuits that the Gwich'in Athabascan Indian residents of Venetie were a federally recognized tribe.

Then in August 1994, Governor Hickel announced that he would not run for a second term. His withdrawal significantly advanced the chances of Tony Knowles, the former mayor of Anchorage whom Hickel had defeated in the 1990 gubernatorial election and who would be the Democratic Party's candidate in the 1994 gubernatorial election.

Knowing that Native voters in Native villages were a core Democratic constituency, less than two weeks prior to the 1990 gubernatorial election when he, Hickel, and Arliss Sturgulewski, the Republican candidate, had appeared at that year's AFN convention, Knowles told the delegates that he supported the tribal sovereignty movement. As the *Anchorage Daily News* reported: "Knowles picked up more points with many Natives when he said he'd support Gov. Steve Cowper's declaration recognizing the tribal status of Alaska Native groups. Sturgulewski and Hickel both said no to the question and both wavered when asked if they'd support giving tribal councils the same powers as state-sanctioned local governments. Knowles said he would."[43]

Four years later Knowles promised those same Native voters that if they elected him governor, "I will withdraw Gov. Hickel's divisive and unrealistic executive (sic) order [that had repealed Administrative Order No. 123 and] that denied the existence of tribes."[44] And in an advertisement printed in the *Tundra Drums*, the newspaper in Bethel that was distributed in Native villages throughout the Yukon-Kuskokwim River Delta, Knowles vouched that it was "time for tribal or village courts to handle many misdemeanors and civil matters."

Courting members of the tribal sovereignty movement paid its dividend when, for the first time in the history of the AFN, the delegates who attended the October 1994 convention endorsed a gubernatorial candidate. As the *Tundra Times* reported three weeks before the election: "The Alaska Federation of Natives delegates at its (sic) convention last week endorsed Democratic candidate Tony Knowles for governor, primarily due to his stand on subsistence, tribal self-governance, village sanitation, and the capital move issue."[45]

On election day, in Venetie and Arctic Village, Knowles defeated Jim Campbell, the Republican candidate, 77 votes to 5 votes. In Akiachak, the village in which Willie Kasayulie, the former head of the ANC who now was chairman of the AITC resided, he defeated Campbell 109 votes to 13 votes. And he did the same in other Native villages in which the tribal sovereignty movement had taken root.[46]

So in 1995 when Governor Knowles directed Bruce Botelho, whom he had retained as attorney general,[47] not to appeal Judge Holland's decision that the members of the NVV were a federally recognized tribe, Knowles knew he would need those same votes again when he ran for reelection in 1998. And three weeks before the 1998 election, the *Anchorage Daily News* would report that prior to the 1994 election candidate Knowles had promised that Governor Knowles would "drop[] the portion of the [consolidated] lawsuit that opposed recognition of tribal status for Venetie and other Alaska villages, a move criticized by Republican legislators."[48]

Alaska Governor Tony Knowles with Athabascan Indian Patriarch Peter John, Elsie John, and Mike Irwin, Commissioner of the Alaska Department of Community and Regional Affairs. Chief Peter John Collection, Alaska & Polar Regions Collections, University of Alaska Fairbanks.

On November 20, 1996, a three-judge panel of the U.S. Court of Appeals for the Ninth Circuit issued its decision in the appeal NARF attorney Heather Kendall had filed in the *State of Alaska v. Native Village of Venetie Tribal Government* lawsuit. In that decision the judges reversed Judge Holland's determination that the land within the boundaries of the revoked Venetie reserve was not a dependent Indian community and hence was not Indian country.[49]

Since only a federally recognized tribe can occupy Indian country, if the members of the NVV were not one, whether the land within the boundaries of the revoked reserve was Indian county was a question the panel had no reason to decide. But when Attorney General Botelho did not appeal Judge Holland's decision regarding tribal status, the State of Alaska conceded that the members of the NVV were a federally recognized tribe.

After assuming tribal status, the two judges who issued the panel's controlling decision began their analysis by assuming that "a dependent Indian community requires a showing of federal set aside and federal superintendence."[50]

With respect to the set-aside requirement, they concluded that in ANCSA the Ninety-second Congress intended to set aside public land for Alaska Natives "as such" when it directed the secretary of the interior to convey fee title to the land to village and regional corporations. The purported reason was that the Ninety-second Congress had intended the corporations to be "the instruments of, and owe obligations to, the Native villages."[51]

With respect to the superintendence requirement, they announced that that element of the dependent Indian community test was "designed to determine the extent to which the traditional trust relationship between the federal government and Native Americans remains intact in a particular case."[52] They then concluded that the Ninety-second Congress did not intend ANCSA to "extinguish federal superintendence of Alaska Natives," and that "the federal government continues to execute its trust responsibilities toward Alaska Natives."[53]

At the conclusion of their analysis, the two judges announced: "In sum, we hold that ANCSA neither eliminated a federal set aside for Alaska Natives, as such, nor terminated federal superintendence over Alaska Natives. As a result, Indian country may still exist in Alaska."[54]

They then applied the federal set aside and superintendence standards they had invented and concluded that Venetie was a dependent Indian community, and, because it was, the land within the boundaries of the revoked reserve was Indian country. After so holding, they directed Judge Holland to determine whether the NVV had "the power to impose a tax upon a private party where the State of Alaska will ultimately pay the obligation."[55]

As has been described, in 1953 the Eighty-third Congress had assumed that states have no jurisdiction to enforce their criminal and civil laws within Indian country and had enacted Public Law No. 83-280, a statute that granted that jurisdiction to five listed states. And at the instigation of Alaska Delegate E.L. "Bob" Bartlett, in 1958 the Eighty-fifth Congress added the Territory (later State) of Alaska to that list.[56]

In 1976 in its decision in *Bryan v. Itasca County*[57] and then in 1987 in its decision in *California v. Cabazon and Morongo Bands of Mission Indians*,[58] the U.S. Supreme Court held that the Eighty-third Congress did not intend Public Law No. 83-280 to grant the listed states jurisdiction to enforce their civil regulatory laws in Indian country.

If, as Assistant Secretary of the Interior for Indian Affairs Ada Deer had announced in 1993, there were more than two hundred federally recognized tribes in Alaska whose members resided in communities that had been designated as Native villages for the purposes of ANCSA, and if, as the panel of the U.S. Court of Appeals for the Ninth Circuit had announced in its decision in *State of Alaska v. Native Village of Venetie Tribal Government*, the forty-four million acres of land whose fee title the secretary of the interior was conveying to ANCSA regional and village corporations was transformed into Indian country whenever a corporation conveyed its title to a village council, the jurisdictional consequences for the State of Alaska would be adverse in the extreme.

When Governor Knowles finally belatedly realized the seriousness of the situation, he directed Attorney General Botelho to petition the U.S. Court of Appeals for the

Ninth Circuit to reconsider the panel's decision.[59] When the court refused to do so, Governor Knowles directed Attorney General Botelho to petition the U.S. Supreme Court to issue a writ of certiorari and review the decision.[60]

During its 1996 term, the U.S. Supreme Court received 6,633 petitions and would grant fewer than one hundred.[61] So why would the Court grant a petition that would require it to review a decision that affected only one state and that involved a question of statutory construction—the intent of the Eightieth Congress embodied in the undefined term "dependent Indian communities" in 18 U.S.C. 1151—that if the panel had misconstrued that intent a future Congress could remedy the error by amending the statute?

To improve the odds that the Court would grant the State's petition, Attorney General Botelho hired John Roberts, the head of the appellate section of Hogan & Hartson, a prominent Washington, D.C., law firm, to write it. A former assistant solicitor general who had argued twenty-five cases in the U.S. Supreme Court, Roberts had been a law clerk for, and was a protege of, Chief Justice William Rehnquist.[62]

To further improve the odds, Attorney General Botelho also arranged for attorneys general representing twenty-five states to file a brief in which they told the Court that they feared tribes in their jurisdictions would take "unilateral actions to acquire land and, based on minimal federal presence in the area, successfully assert the lands are Indian country as a 'dependent Indian community'" by invoking the federal set-aside and federal superintendence tests the Ninth Circuit panel had invented.[63]

Alaska Senator Ted Stevens also filed a brief.

A graduate of the Harvard Law School, between 1956 and 1961 Stevens had been a senior official at the Department of the Interior.[64] And at the end of the Eisenhower administration he had served for four months as the acting solicitor.[65]

Since he was knowledgeable about principles of federal Indian law and the history of Congress's decision not to apply many of those principles in Alaska, from its inception the senator had been an opponent of the tribal sovereignty movement.

In 1971 the U.S. Supreme Court issued a decision, *Kennerly v. District Court of Montana*,[66] in which it held that a federally recognized tribe had no authority to grant the state in which the tribe's reservation was located authority to assert the states' criminal and civil jurisdiction within the boundaries of the reservation.

In February 1978 South Dakota Senator James Abourezk, the chairman of the Senate Select Committee on Indian Affairs, introduced S. 2502, a bill whose enactment would give tribes that authority. The bill defined "Indian tribe" to mean "any Indian tribe, band, nation, or other organized group or community exercising powers of self-government which is recognized as eligible for services provided by the United

Alaska Senator Ted Stevens. Vasilly Ushanoff Photography Collection, Alaska State Library.

States to Indians because of their status as Indians, including any Alaska Native villages included in the Alaska Native Claims Settlement Act."[67]

In March the select committee held a hearing on S. 2502 during which no mention was made of the situation in Alaska.[68]

Six months later when the members of the select committee voted to send S. 2502 to the Senate, their report on the bill explained the inclusion of "Alaska Native villages" in the "Indian tribe" definition as follows:

> Questions have been raised about the status of Alaska Native villages. The inclusion of these villages in this bill is intended to cover those villages which are recognized by the Department of the Interior as having powers of self-government springing from their own inherent sovereignty. It is noted that some villages in Alaska are organized under state law as second class cities. As such they are creatures of the State and are not authorized under this legislation to negotiate as Indian tribes. Other villages, and in fact some that are also organized as second class cities, are also organized under the Indian

> Reorganization Act and some have traditional governments which are recognized by Interior as having powers of self-government independent of State or Federal law. These entities are included within the meaning of the definition.[69]

The Senate passed S. 2502 on a voice vote and with no explanation of the bill's content or legal consequence.[70] But the House did not consider S. 2502 prior to the adjournment of the Ninety-fifth Congress.

In May 1979, Senator Abourezk having retired, Arizona Senator Dennis DeConcini, who had joined the select committee at the beginning of the Ninety-sixth Congress, reintroduced S. 2502 as S. 1181. The bill contained the same "Indian tribe" definition as the definition in S. 2502.[71]

In March 1980 the select committee held a hearing on S. 1181 at which again no mention was made of the situation in Alaska.[72] However, in May when the members of the select committee voted to send S. 1181 to the Senate they amended the "Indian tribe" definition to state that, for the purposes of the bill, an "Indian tribe" was "any Indian tribe, band, nation, or other organized group or community, including any Alaska Native Village as defined in section 3(c) of the Alaska Native Claims Settlement Act, which is exercising powers of self-government and which is recognized by the secretary of the interior as eligible for services provided by the United States to Indians because of their status as Indians."[73]

In its report on S. 1181 the select committee explained that the "Indian tribe" definition had been amended "to avoid any inference that the Congress is determining that all Alaska Native Villages included in the Alaska Native Claims Settlement Act are exercising powers of self-government."[74] That explanation implied that Senator DeConcini and the other members of the select committee believed that the Native residents of some villages were exercising such powers.

Alaska Senator Ted Stevens was not a member of the select committee. However, before S. 1181 reached the Senate floor the bill came to his attention. As a consequence, before the Senate passed S. 1181 on a voice vote,[75] Senator DeConcini offered an amendment whose acceptance by the Senate removed "Alaska Native Villages" from the "Indian tribe" definition. Senator DeConcini subsequently included a statement in the *Congressional Record* in which he explained that "the amendment which deletes the reference to Alaska Native villages, was suggested by Senator Stevens. It attempts to clarify the applicability of [S. 1181] regarding those Villages. Lands selected by native villages or regional corporations under the Alaska Native Claims Settlement Act are not considered Indian country within the meaning of section 1151, title 18, USC. Thus, the purposes of S. 1181 would not be applicable to lands acquired under the Alaska Native Claims Settlement Act."[76]

A year later, Wyoming Senator Malcolm Wallop, the chairman of the subcommittee of the Senate Finance Committee that had jurisdiction over the subject matter, introduced S. 1298, the Indian Tribal Government Tax Status Act,[77] a bill whose enactment would allow "Indian tribal governments" to be treated as if they were municipal governments for certain tax purposes.

S. 1298, whose text likely was written by attorneys at the Department of the Interior rather than the Department of the Treasury,[78] defined "Indian tribal government" to mean "the governing body of any tribe, band, community, village, or group of Indians or Alaska Natives which is determined by the secretary [of the treasury], after consultation with the secretary of the interior, to exercise governmental functions."[79]

However, when the Senate considered H.R. 5470, an omnibus tax bill into which the text of S. 1298 had been included, before the Senate passed the bill Senator Stevens arranged for the "Indian tribal government" definition to be amended by removing the reference to "Alaska Natives" and at the end of the definition adding "and in Alaska shall include only the Metlakatlia (sic) Indian Community."[80]

When leaders of the nascent tribal sovereignty movement discovered what Stevens had done and complained, the senator relented. Before H.R. 5470 was sent to the president to be signed into law, Stevens arranged for the Ninety-seventh Congress to pass a concurrent resolution that reinserted the reference to "Alaska Natives" in the "Indian tribal government" definition. But he included a paragraph in the definition that stated: "Nothing in the Indian Tribal Government Tax Status Act of 1982, or in the amendments made thereby, shall validate or invalidate any claim by Alaska Natives of sovereign authority over lands or people."[81]

Six weeks later during his annual address to the Alaska Legislature, Stevens explained his position as follows:

> I have worked to ensure that Alaska's villages are treated equally with lower 48 tribes for purposes of receiving social and health benefits. It has not been my assumption that such treatment implied that Alaska Native villages had the same police powers, taxation ability, and fish and game management authority as those reservations in the lower 48.
>
> Some have sought a federally-derived Native sovereignty—sovereignty not dependent upon our state's constitution or our laws. It has, and will continue to be, my position that village sovereignty is a matter for our state through this legislature and the governor to determine.
>
> However, there have been bills dealing primarily with reservation tribal powers that have led to some misunderstanding of my position on the issue. It is my hope Congress will pass a tribal state compact law that authorizes states to negotiate with Native tribes or villages, such as IRA Councils, to resolve the sovereignty issue. Meanwhile, I intend to ask Congress to follow the pattern of the Indian Tribal Government Tax Status Act, which we passed last year, which specifically stated that that Act cannot be interpreted "to validate or invalidate any claim by Alaska Natives of sovereign authority over lands or people."[82]

The senator having settled on neutrality as his response to the tribal sovereignty movement, to placate Stevens, in 1985 the AFN included a disclaimer section in its

ANCSA "1991" bill that announced that nothing in the bill could be construed to enlarge or diminish "the scope of any governmental authority of a federally recognized tribe, traditional council or Native council organized pursuant to the Indian Reorganization Act."

Ten years later, in 1997, in the brief he filed in support of the State of Alaska's petition for a writ of certiorari in *State of Alaska v. Native Village of Venetie Tribal Government*, Stevens urged the Court to grant the petition because "unless corrected, the [Ninth Circuit panel's] decision will irreparably harm the people of Alaska, both Native and non-Native, who until now have largely escaped the damage that Congress's early nineteenth century Indian policies inflicted in the coterminous states, and will severely damage the institutions Congress created to implement the ANCSA settlement."[83]

Independent of the legal merit of that argument, Stevens had the ability to influence the Court's decision regarding whether it would grant the State's petition in two extrajudicial respects. First, Stevens was chairman of the Senate Committee on Appropriations in which the bills were written whose enactment appropriated the money on which Chief Justice William Rehnquist depended to fund the federal judiciary. Second, Stevens and Rehnquist had been personal friends for more than forty years.* So Stevens's name on the brief sent the chief justice the message that his old friend who never before had asked for it needed his help.

On June 23, 1997, the Court granted the State's petition.[85]

When she heard the news, NARF attorney Heather Kendall-Miller,** who would represent the NVV before the Court, said she was "optimistic that the Venetie tribe will prevail in the end."[86] But it did not. In the decision the Court issued on February 25, 1998,[87] Justice Clarence Thomas, writing for a unanimous Court, announced that "[a]fter the enactment of ANCSA, the [1.8 million acres of land within the revoked Venetie reserve] are neither 'validly set apart for the use of the Indians as such,' nor are they under the superintendence of the Federal government."[88]

In reasoning to that result, Justice Thomas explained that ANCSA transferred reservation lands to private, state-chartered Native corporations, without any restraints on alienation or significant use restrictions, and with

> the goal of avoiding "any permanent racially defined institutions, rights, privileges, or obligations." By ANCSA's very design, Native corporations can immediately convey former reservation lands to non-Natives, and such corporations are not restricted to using those lands for Indian purposes. Because Congress contemplated that non-Natives could own the former Venetie Reservation, and because the Tribe is free to use it for non-Indian purposes, we must conclude that the federal set-aside requirement is not met.[89]

---

* In 2005 when Chief Justice Rehnquist died, Stevens reminisced that, "I first met Bill Rehnquist in 1952. We were both young lawyers here in Washington, D.C. We each had taken jobs here in Washington after finishing law school and in the course of many months became very good friends. In fact, my first date with my first wife was double-dating with Bill Rehnquist."[84]

** In 1996 Heather Kendall married Lloyd Miller and changed her name to Kendall-Miller.[90]

Heather Kendall-Miller. Fran Durner/Anchorage Daily News.

And that

> After ANCSA, federal protection of the Tribe's land is essentially limited to a statutory declaration that the land is exempt from adverse possession claims, real property taxes, and certain judgments as long as it has not been sold, leased, or developed. These protections, if they can be called that, simply do not approach the level of superintendence over the Indians' land that existed in our prior cases.... Finally, it is worth noting that Congress conveyed ANCSA lands to state-chartered and state-regulated private business corporations, hardly a choice that comports with a desire to retain *federal* superintendence over the land (emphasis in original).[91]

Although it dealt only with the status of the land within the boundaries of the revoked Venetie reserve, the practical legal consequence of the Court's decision was that none of the forty-four million acres of land the secretary of the interior would convey in fee title to ANCSA regional and village corporations qualified as a dependent Indian community and hence as Indian country. However, because Governor Knowles had directed Attorney General Botelho not to appeal Judge Holland's decision that the members of the NVV were a federally recognized tribe to the U.S. Court of Appeals for the Ninth Circuit, in their decision Justice Thomas and the other justices simply assumed that the members of the NVV had that legal status.

Nine

In 1988 in its decision in *Native Village of Stevens v. Alaska Management & Planning*, the Alaska Supreme Court announced that Congress had "demonstrated its intent that Alaska Native communities not be accorded sovereign status." However, as NARF attorneys Lare Ashenbrenner and Robert Anderson and David Case, Lloyd Miller, and the other attorneys who in 1993 had orchestrated Assistant Secretary of the Interior for Indian Affairs Ada Deer's publication in the *Federal Register* of her list of Native entities that she said was a list of federally recognized tribes hoped it might, in 1999 the Alaska Supreme Court reversed course.

In 1941 when the U.S. Army built an airfield in the Alaska interior forty-two miles west of the Canadian border, several Athabascan Indian families settled near the field. They named the community they established Northway after Walter Northway, a locally prominent Athabascan patriarch.[1] Because in 1970 a majority of Northway's forty residents were Athabascan Indians, in 1971 the Ninety-second Congress designated Northway as a Native village for the purposes of ANCSA. And in 1993 Assistant Secretary Deer included "Northway Village" on the list of Native entities she published in the *Federal Register*.[2]

In 1994 John Baker, an Athabascan Indian who lived near Northway, asked the court in Northway, which the Tanana Chiefs Conference had assisted the village council to create, to decide a dispute regarding the custody of his two sons that he was having with their mother, Anita John, an Athabascan Indian who lived in Mentasta, a Native village ninety-four miles west of Northway. In 1995 when the court in Northway held a hearing regarding his custody dispute and John Baker discovered that Lorraine Titus, the "judge" of the court, had invited Katie John, Anita John's grandmother, who was a "judge" of the court the village council in Mentasta had created, to participate in deciding how the dispute would be resolved, he realized that the court in Northway was not an impartial tribunal. When, after consulting with Katie John and Nora David, Anita John's adoptive sister who was "first chief" of the Native Village of Mentasta, Titus issued an "order" in which she directed John Baker and Anita John to share custody of their sons, Baker drove to Fairbanks and hired an attorney named Rita Allee who on his behalf filed a custody action against Anita John in the Alaska Superior Court.[3]

Because she was income eligible, Anita John was represented in that action by Andrew Harrington, one of the attorneys in the Fairbanks office of the Alaska Legal

Services Corporation who in 1986 had filed the *Native Village of Venetie I.R.A. Council v. State of Alaska* lawsuit. And between 1990 and 1993, Harrington had been a member of the group of attorneys led by NARF attorneys Lare Aschenbrenner and Robert Anderson that lobbied, first Assistant Secretary of the Interior for Indian Affairs Eddie Brown and then Assistant Secretary of the Interior for Indian Affairs Ada Deer, to transform the Native residents of more than two hundred communities that had been designated as Native villages for the purposes of ANCSA into federally recognized tribes by publishing a new list of Native entities and a new preamble in the *Federal Register*.

On Anita John's behalf, Harrington filed a motion in which he requested Superior Court Judge Ralph Beistline to dismiss the custody action Rita Allee had filed on the ground that the court in Northway had already asserted its jurisdiction over the custody dispute that was the subject of the action.

Judge Beistline denied the motion.

At that point, John Baker ran out of money to pay Rita Allee. However, because Anita John was being represented by an ALSC attorney, John Franich, the supervising attorney at the Fairbanks office of the Office of Public Advocacy (OPA), a state agency that represents indigent individuals in certain types of cases, took over John Baker's representation.

After a trial, in April 1997 Judge Beistline awarded John Baker custody of his sons after finding that "Ms. John drinks when the children are around," "always drinks until she blacks out," and has "experienced serious bouts of depression with suicidal components."[4]

Andrew Harrington then appealed to the Alaska Supreme Court Judge Beistline's denial of the motion to dismiss that Harrington had filed.

Insofar as the legal status of the Athabascan Indian residents of Northway as a federally recognized tribe whose village council possessed authority to create a court that had jurisdiction to involve itself in child custody matters was concerned, in his opening brief Harrington asserted that "on October 21, 1993, the Department of the Interior published a new list of recognized Alaska tribes. Northway appears on that list. The list is preceded by an introduction which makes it clear that Alaska tribes have the same sovereign status as tribes in the lower 48 states ... Any continued distinction between tribes in Alaska and tribes in the contiguous United States is thus no longer tenable."[5]

Because he was not knowledgeable about federal Indian law and its application (and nonapplication) in Alaska, John Franich recommended to OPA that the agency contract with a Fairbanks attorney named Deborah Niedermeyer to write the briefs Franich would file on behalf of John Baker and to then argue the appeal.[6]

While Deborah Niedermeyer knew more about federal Indian law than John Franich did, unfortunately for John Baker, as Niedermeyer later would acknowledge, she had "supported Alaska Native sovereignty from the get-go."[7] As a consequence, the brief she wrote on behalf of John Baker did not challenge the validity of Andrew

Harrington's assertion in his brief that the Athabascan Indian residents of Northway were a federally recognized tribe because in 1993 in the preamble she published in the *Federal Register* with her list of Native entities Assistant Secretary Deer had said they were.

Instead, Niedermeyer argued that the Eighty-third Congress that enacted 28 U.S.C. 1360, the statute the Eighty-fifth Congress amended in 1958 to grant the State of Alaska "jurisdiction over civil causes of action between Indians or to which Indians are parties which arise in the areas of Indian country," intended to grant the State exclusive jurisdiction to adjudicate custody disputes that involve Native parents and children who are members of the federally recognized tribes that she implicitly conceded existed.[8]

In October 1997 when Andrew Harrington filed his reply brief, the *John v. Baker* appeal was ready for the Alaska Supreme Court to hear oral argument. However, no date for the argument was set because four months earlier the U.S. Supreme Court had granted the petition for a writ of certiorari the State of Alaska had filed and agreed to review the validity of the decision the panel of the U.S. Court of Appeals for the Ninth Circuit had issued in *State of Alaska v. Native Village of Venetie Tribal Government.* So the Alaska Supreme Court justices decided not to schedule oral argument in the *John v. Baker* appeal until after the U.S. Supreme Court issued its decision in that case.

On February 25, 1998, the U.S. Supreme Court issued its decision and in *State of Alaska v. Native Village of Venetie Tribal Government* held that the land within the boundaries of the revoked Venetie reserve (and, by inference, the more than forty million acres of other land whose fee title ANCSA required the secretary of the interior to convey to village and regional corporations) did not qualify as a "dependent Indian community" and, as a consequence, was not "Indian country."

A week after the U.S. Supreme Court issued its decision, the Alaska Supreme Court directed Andrew Harrington and Deborah Niedermeyer to file supplemental briefs that would answer six questions, one of which was, "Can a tribe have sovereignty over its members even if the tribe does not occupy Indian country?"

In her brief Niedermeyer conceded that "the Native Village of Northway [NVN] is a federally recognized tribe."[9] And during the oral argument she would tell the Alaska Supreme Court that John Baker, whom she had never met, believed "the wisest decision this Court could make is to recognize tribal jurisdiction in Alaska as long as tribal court decisions meet the law of comity."[10]

In addition to directing Andrew Harrington and Deborah Niedermeyer to file supplemental briefs, the Alaska Supreme Court requested the State of Alaska "to express its views on the issues presented in this case."

For Alaska Governor Tony Knowles, who in nine months would be the Democratic Party's candidate in the 1998 gubernatorial election, the Court's request presented a fortuitous opportunity to try to repair his relationship with members of the tribal sovereignty movement whose votes had elected him to his first term and whose votes he believed he would need again to win a second one.

In November 1996 when Attorney General Botelho announced two days after the panel of the U.S. Court of Appeals for the Ninth Circuit issued its decision in the *State of Alaska v. Native Village of Venetie Tribal Government* appeal that the State would ask all of the Ninth Circuit judges, sitting *en banc*, to reconsider the decision, and, if they declined to do so, would petition the U.S. Supreme Court to issue a writ of certiorari and review the decision, leaders of the tribal sovereignty movement were outraged.

In March 1997 when Governor Knowles spoke at the annual Tanana Chiefs Conference convention in Fairbanks, he reminded the two hundred participants from Native villages throughout the Alaska interior that he had made good on the pledge he had made prior to the 1994 gubernatorial election to end the State's opposition to tribal status. But Mitch Dementieff, a prominent leader of the tribal sovereignty movement in the Alaska interior, was not impressed. "He [Knowles] knows we were a big help in terms of his election," Dementieff answered when asked what he thought of the governor's remarks. "We're disappointed in what we've received to date."[11]

Five months later when Knowles hosted the governor's picnic, an annual summer event held on the park strip in Anchorage, he was surrounded by Native protesters waving signs that read "Native Sovereignty Now" and "Free Venetie."[12] And in October when he spoke at the AFN convention the *Anchorage Daily News* reported:

> The governor's cool reception was a far cry from past ovations for Knowles, who was the first-ever candidate for governor endorsed by the AFN in 1994. It was also a far cry from the loud standing ovation given not long after Knowles left to Native rights attorney Heather Kendall-Miller, who is taking Venetie's case to the U.S. Supreme Court. In her speech, Kendall-Miller blasted the state for promoting distrust, "hiring an army" of Outside lawyers, and for predicting "mass chaos" if Venetie wins its case.
>
> ...
>
> Knowles, who relied on heavy Native support at the polls to win in 1994, had sought to blunt such criticism in his speech. He told the convention he has pursued Venetie's Indian country case to protect the state's basic governmental functions like taxation and fish and game management. But that does not mean he does not support tribes, he said. He pointed out that he dropped an appeal of an earlier court decision recognizing Venetie's tribal status "despite considerable criticism."[13]

Four months later when on February 25, 1998 the U.S. Supreme Court issued its decision in *State of Alaska v. Native Village of Venetie Tribal Government*, Myron Naneng, the president of the Association of Village Council Presidents, spoke for all members of the tribal sovereignty movement when he lamented that February 25 was "a day of mourning."[14]

To try and repair the damage to his political support in the Native community that the State's victory in the U.S. Supreme Court would inflict, five days before the Court issued the decision that would give the State that victory, Governor Knowles signed Administrative Order No. 174, which established what became a twenty-two-member Commission on Rural Governance and Empowerment that would examine "the responsibilities and relationships in the delivery of services in rural Alaska by all governance institutions, including municipalities, federally recognized tribes and other state, federal and local institutions that affect rural Alaska."[15] The members included fifteen regionally prominent Native leaders, including Byron Mallott, a Tlingit Indian from Juneau who was a former president of the AFN and who in 1990 had been chairman of Knowles's gubernatorial campaign,[16] Willie Kasayulie, the former chairman of the Alaska Native Coalition, and Steve Ginnis, an Athabascan Indian from Fort Yukon who was chairman of the Alaska Inter-Tribal Council.[17]

When the commission met in April, Attorney General Botelho used the occasion to announce that, in response to the Alaska Supreme Court's request that he do so, he would file a brief in the *John v. Baker* appeal that would inform the Court that the State of Alaska (in the guise of the Knowles administration) not only agreed with Andrew Harrington and Deborah Niedermeyer that the Native residents of Northway and more than two hundred other communities that had been designated as Native villages for the purposes of ANCSA were federally recognized tribes, but also that courts such as the court the village council in Northway had established had concurrent jurisdiction with the Alaska District and Superior Courts — which Botelho described as "a fundamental change of point of view of the state."[18]

In the brief he filed, Botelho argued that, as a consequence of Assistant Secretary Deer's publication in 1993 in the *Federal Register* of the preamble that accompanied her list of Native entities, the One Hundred-third Congress's enactment in 1994 of the Federally Recognized Indian Tribe List Act (FRITLA),[19] and the decision District Judge H. Russel Holland had issued in 1994 in which he announced that the members of the Native Village of Venetie were a federally recognized tribe, the State had concluded that "Alaska villages were recognized as tribes" that "could exercise the retained powers possessed by all tribes in the United States."[20] The brief then urged the Court to "hold that under Pub. L. 280, Alaska tribes retained concurrent jurisdiction with the state over civil matters involving the domestic relations of their members."[21, *]

---

* In May when Attorney General Botelho filed his brief, the outcome could not have been predicted, but in November Tony Knowles was reelected to a second term as governor with 51 percent of the vote in an election in which his loss of support from Native voters proved inconsequential. Because two weeks before the election the Alaska Republican Party Central Committee repudiated the Republican candidate, John Lindauer, a former member of the Alaska House of Representatives. The committee did so after Lindauer admitted that he had lied about the source of $1.7 million the Lindauer for Governor campaign had been spending to try and win the election. Lindauer initially said the $1.7 million was money he had earned from investments and consulting work. But he eventually admitted that the $1.7 million was an illegal campaign contribution that his wealthy second wife, who lived in Chicago, had made.[23]

Although the Alaska Supreme Court had not requested it to do so, the Department of the Interior filed a brief that informed the court that "it has consistently been the Interior Department's view that Congress did not intend ANCSA to 'terminate' the sovereign status of tribes in Alaska or to divest those tribes of authority to regulate their internal relations."[22] The brief concluded by asserting that "the Native Village of Northway is a sovereign Tribe," and "the absence of Indian country is not a barrier to Northway tribal court jurisdiction over domestic relations cases involving the village's members and their children."[24,] *

The Native Village of Venetie and the Alaska Inter-Tribal Council, represented by NARF attorney Heather Kendall-Miller and her husband, Lloyd Miller, and the Native Village of Northway also filed briefs that made the same argument.**

More than thirty years earlier, the U.S. Supreme Court had instructed that it is important for disputed questions of law to be "presented in an adversary context"[25] in order, as the Court explained in a subsequent decision,[26] "to assure that concrete adverseness which sharpens the presentation of issues upon which the court so largely depends for illumination of difficult ... questions."

Because Andrew Harrington and Deborah Niedermeyer and all the *amici curiae*[27] urged the Alaska Supreme Court to conclude that the Athabascan Indian members of the NVN were a federally recognized tribe and that, as a consequence of that legal status, the village council in Northway was a "sovereign" that possessed "inherent" governmental authority to create a court that had jurisdiction to involve itself in the custody dispute between John Baker and Anita John, the requisite "concrete adverseness" regarding whether either of those propositions was legally correct was not present. So it is no surprise that in the decision it issued in the *John v. Baker* appeal,[30] the Alaska Supreme Court concluded what it had been urged to conclude.

Writing for a unanimous court,[31] Justice Dana Fabe began by observing that "prior to 1993, no ... recognition of Alaska villages had occurred. In *Native Village of Stevens v. Alaska Management & Planning*, we conducted an historical analysis and concluded that the federal government had never recognized Alaska villages as sovereign tribes."[32] Then, rotely accepting the arguments that had been presented in all the briefs, Justice Fabe perorated:

* Five months earlier Secretary of the Interior Bruce Babbitt had promoted former NARF attorney Robert Anderson from associate solicitor for Indian affairs to counselor to the secretary, a position whose duties included advising Babbitt on "policy matters, including Native American ... issues."[28] Whether Anderson arranged for the Department of the Interior to file a brief in the *John v. Baker* appeal is not known.

** Deborah Niedermeyer later would recall that after the oral argument in the *John v. Baker* appeal "Heather [Kendall-Miller] assured everybody on her team that I was indeed on the sovereignty side, and invited me out to eat with all the attorneys and *amici* to celebrate what we thought might end up as an important achievement. It was a great conversation, largely celebrating how the attorneys had sort of ganged up on the judges—quite an unusual situation."[29]

> In 1993, however, the Department of the Interior issued a list of federally recognized tribes that included Northway Village and most of the other Native villages in Alaska. In the list's preamble, the Department of the Interior explained that it was issuing the list in order to clarify confusion over the tribal status of various Alaska Native entities.
>
> . . .
>
> The language in the preamble to the 1993 list unquestionably establishes that the Department of the Interior views the recognized Alaska villages as sovereign entities.
>
> . . .
>
> And for those who may have doubted the power of the Department of the Interior to recognize sovereign political bodies, a 1994 act of Congress appears to lay such doubts to rest. In the Federally Recognized Indian Tribe List Act of 1994, Congress specifically directed the Department to publish annually "a list of all Indian tribes which the Secretary recognizes to be eligible for the special programs and services provided by the United States to Indians because of their status as Indians." The Department published tribal lists for 1995 through 1998, all of which include Alaska Native villages such as Northway, based on this specifically delegated authority.
>
> The text and legislative history of the Tribe List Act demonstrate that Congress also views the recognized tribes as sovereign bodies. In the Act's findings section, Congress discusses the "sovereignty" of federally recognized tribes. Similarly, the House report to the Act provides that federal recognition "institutionalizes the tribe's quasi-sovereign status. Acknowledging that federal recognition "is no minor step," the report states that such recognition "permanently establishes a government-to-government relationship between the United States and the recognized tribe as a "domestic dependent nation."
>
> Through the 1993 tribal list and the 1994 Tribe List Act, the federal government has recognized the historical tribal status of Alaska Native villages like Northway. In deference to that determination, we also recognize such villages as sovereign entities.[33]

After deciding that, because neither John Baker nor any of its other members resided within the boundaries of Indian country, "Northway's jurisdiction to adjudicate child custody disputes between village members" was not exclusive, but instead was concurrent with the jurisdiction of the Alaska courts,[34] Justice Fabe sent the case back to Judge Beistline and instructed him to "determine whether the tribal court's resolution of the custody dispute between Ms. John and Mr. Baker should be recognized under the doctrine of comity."[35, *]

---

* When the case returned to his court, Judge Beistline declined to recognize the custody order the court in Northway had issued under the doctrine of comity because the hearing the court held

Alaska Supreme Court Justice Dana Fabe. Chris Arend Photography.

The Association of Village Council Presidents (AVCP) is one of the Native associations listed in section 7(a) of ANCSA. First organized in 1965, in 1977 the AVCP was incorporated under the Alaska Nonprofit Corporation Act "to promote the common good and the general social welfare of the residents in the Bethel-AVCP region."[36] The AVCP's membership is composed of a representative from each of the fifty-six communities on the Yukon-Kuskokwim River Delta that the Ninety-second Congress or the secretary of the interior has designated as Native villages for the purposes of ANCSA. In 1993 Assistant Secretary of the Interior for Indian Affairs Ada Deer

prior to issuing the order had not afforded John Baker due process. Anita John, again represented by Andrew Harrington, appealed that decision to the Alaska Supreme Court. And Deborah Niedermeyer again represented John Baker. In 2001 in *John v. Baker II*,[38] a decision again written by Justice Dana Fabe, the court concluded that the court in Northway had not denied John Baker due process, even though it lost the audio recording of the hearing it conducted, as well as "other crucial documents and/or transcripts," and even though Lorraine Titus, the judge who had issued the order, had privately discussed John Baker's custody dispute with Nora David, Anita John's adoptive sister. Justice Fabe then remanded the custody dispute between John Baker and Anita John "to the Northway Tribal Court to conduct further child custody proceedings."

included those Native villages on the list of Native entities she published in the *Federal Register*.[37]

In 2001 a child was sexually molested and another child was physically injured while participating in a Headstart program AVCP administered. When their parents filed civil actions in the Alaska Superior Court in which they alleged that the AVCP had been negligent in its administration of the program, the court dismissed both actions on the ground that federally recognized tribes possess sovereign immunity,[39] the Yup'ik Eskimo residents of each of the AVCP's member Native villages were members of a federally recognized tribe, and the AVCP could invoke its member tribes' sovereign immunity. The parents then appealed the dismissals.

The Alaska Supreme Court described the question the appeal presented as "whether AVCP may be sued by private parties, or whether the sovereign immunity of its member tribes extends to bar such suits." However, when it appeared as an *amicus curiae*, the Legislative Council of the Alaska Legislature* urged the court to "reconsider, and then correct, the conclusions of law it announced in *John v. Baker* regarding the lawfulness of Assistant Secretary Deer's administrative action in 1993 and regarding the intent of One Hundred and Third Congress embodied in [the FRITLA]" because "those were not conclusions of law on which the Court settled after adversarial briefing and argument."[40]

With respect to Assistant Secretary Deer's publication of her list of Native entities, after pointing out that an executive branch agency "has no power to act ... unless and until Congress confers power upon it,"[41] the Legislative Council argued that 25 U.S.C. 2 and 9, the statutes on which Assistant Secretary Deer relied as authority from Congress for her administrative action, had delegated no such authority. With respect to the Court's conclusion in its decision in *John v. Baker* that the One Hundred-third Congress intended its enactment of the FRITLA to ratify Assistant Secretary Deer's *ultra vires* administrative action, the Legislative Council pointed out that the FRITLA simply directed the secretary of the interior to publish annually in the *Federal Register* "a list of all Indian tribes which the Secretary recognizes to be eligible for the special programs and services provided by the United States to Indians because of their status as Indians," and, on its face, that statutory text did not delegate the secretary authority to create new federally recognized tribes in Congress's stead, nor did it mention, much less did it ratify, Assistant Secretary Deer's attempt to create federally recognized tribes in Alaska by publishing a list of Native entities in the *Federal Register*.

The Legislative Council also pointed out that the congressional findings in the FRITLA, which in her decision in *John v. Baker* Justice Fabe had found determinative, had no force of law,[42] and that in its report on the bill that the One Hundred-third Congress enacted as the FRITLA the House Committee on Natural Resources had

* Article II of the Alaska Constitution establishes the Legislative Council as a permanent interim committee of the Alaska Legislature.

explained that the bill made "no changes in existing law,"[43] and that insofar as the situation in Alaska was concerned the report stated:

> The committee is aware that in January 1993 the solicitor of the Department of the Interior issued an opinion which concluded that Congress has restricted the sovereign powers of Alaska Native tribes. As the BIA stated in the October 21, 1993 Federal Register Notice of Alaska Native Entities Recognized and Eligible to Receive Services, "[the solicitor] concluded, construing general principles of Federal Indian law and ANCSA, that 'notwithstanding the potential that Indian country exists in Alaska in certain limited cases, Congress has left little or no room for tribes in Alaska to exercise governmental authority over land or nonmembers.' M-36,975 at 108. That portion of the opinion is subject to review, but has not been withdrawn or modified."
>
> The committee notes that the solicitor's opinion has generated controversy and that there is extensive litigation on the subject of the precise sovereign powers of Alaska Native tribes. While these issues deserve further review by Congress, nothing in this Act should be construed as enhancing, diminishing or changing in any way the status of Alaska Native tribes.
>
> It is the intent of the Committee that its previous position taken in the 1987 amendments to the Alaska Native Claims Settlement Act be maintained and that nothing in this Act shall "confer on, or deny to, any Native organization any degree of sovereign governmental authority over lands (including management or regulation of the taking of fish and wildlife) or persons in Alaska." P.L. 100-241, Section 2(8)(B). The Act merely requires that the secretary continue the current policy of including Alaska Native entities on the list of Federally recognized tribes which are eligible to receive services.[44]

In its decision in *Runyon v. Association of Village Council Presidents*,[45] written by Justice Fabe, the Alaska Supreme Court did not acknowledge, much less did it address, those arguments. Instead, in a footnote the court announced, "We decline the invitations of the Runyons and *amicus* Legislative Council to revisit *John v. Baker*."[46]

In 1965 several families that had been living in Perryville, a community on the Alaska Peninsula five hundred miles southwest of Anchorage, relocated to Ivanof Bay thirteen miles east of Perryville. Because in 1970 a majority of the forty-eight residents of Ivanof Bay were of Aleut descent, in 1971 the Ninety-second Congress designated the community as a Native village for the purposes of ANCSA. And in 1993 Assistant Secretary of the Interior for Indian Affairs Ada Deer included "Ivanof Bay Village" (IBV) on the list of Native entities she published in the *Federal Register*.[47]

By 2009 Ivanof Bay was deserted because the individuals who once lived there had moved to Anchorage. That year Michael McCrary filed a breach of contract action against the IBV in the Alaska Superior Court.[48]

Represented by David Case, the IBV moved Superior Court Judge Peter Michalski to dismiss the action on the ground that "the Alaska Supreme Court held in *John v. Baker* that Alaska Native Villages on the Department of the Interior's list of federally (sic) tribes are sovereign entities" and "Ivanof Bay is a sovereign tribe based on its inclusion on the Department of the Interior's list."[49] In 2010 Judge Michalski granted the motion and Michael McCrary appealed the dismissal of his breach of contract action to the Alaska Supreme Court.

As the Legislative Council had six years earlier in the *Runyon v. Association of Village Council Presidents* appeal, in his appeal McCrary urged the court to revisit its decision in *John v. Baker* because the court had reasoned to its result in that decision without the benefit of adversarial briefing and oral argument.[50] But, as it had in *Runyon*, in *McCrary v. Ivanof Bay* Village,[51] the court declined to do so because, as the decision written by Justice Daniel Winfree explained, "Our conclusion regarding the Executive Branch's tribal recognition and Congress's approval through the Tribe List Act was carefully considered and adopted by the entire court."[52]

Ten

J.M. was born in Anchorage in 1984. While the identity of his father was unknown, his mother was an Athabascan Indian who was a resident of Kaltag, a community on the Yukon River in the Alaska interior. Because the Ninety-second Congress had designated Kaltag as a Native village for the purposes of ANCSA, pursuant to section 4(8) of the Indian Child Welfare Act (ICWA)[1] the Athabascan Indian residents of Kaltag were an "Indian tribe," and pursuant to section 4(4) of the ICWA[2] J.M. was an "Indian child." When J.M. was two months old his

> mother brought the child from Kaltag to the Indian Health Service facility in Fairbanks, and hospitalized the child. After a brief stay in the hospital, the child recovered and was available for discharge. Unfortunately, the mother was not available to assume custody of the child. IHS contacted the Kaltag Village Council about this situation, through Tanana Chiefs Conference, Inc., and the Council issued an order assuming custody of the child ... The Council, working in cooperation with TCC, placed the child in a foster home in Galena, Alaska.[3]

A month later the Alaska Department of Health and Social Services petitioned the Alaska Superior Court to declare J.M. a child in need of aid and terminate his mother's parental rights.

Section 101(c) of the ICWA[4] authorizes an "Indian child's tribe" to intervene in a state court proceeding that involves the child's foster care placement. Represented by TCC attorney Michael Walleri, the Native Village of Kaltag (NVK) intervened in the child in need of aid proceeding involving J.M. and then moved the Superior Court to dismiss the department's petition.

Section 101(a) of the ICWA[5] provides: "An Indian tribe shall have jurisdiction exclusive as to any State over any child custody proceeding involving an Indian child who resides or is domiciled within the reservation of such tribe, except where such jurisdiction is otherwise vested in the State by existing federal law. Where an Indian child is a ward of a tribal court, the Indian tribe shall retain exclusive jurisdiction, notwithstanding the residence or domicile of the child."

In its motion, the NVK argued that the petition should be dismissed because J.M. was "a ward of the tribal court" and "under the Indian Child Welfare Act—specifically [section 101(a)]—the tribe had exclusive jurisdiction over the child."[6] When the Superior Court denied the motion, the NVK appealed the denial to the Alaska Supreme Court.

In that appeal Assistant Attorney General Rebecca Snow, who represented the Department of Health and Social Services, conceded that before the department filed the petition whose validity was the subject of the appeal the NVK had assumed exclusive jurisdiction of J.M. pursuant to section 101(a) of the ICWA. She did so even though the House Committee on Interior and Insular Affairs, which had written section 101(a), had explained that it intended section 101(a) to confirm "the developing Federal and State case law holding that the tribe has exclusive jurisdiction when the child is residing or domiciled on the reservation"[7] and at Kaltag and Galena there were no reservations for J.M. to have resided on. Instead, Snow argued that the chairman of the village council in Kaltag had waived the NVK's exclusive jurisdiction.

Years later when she was asked why she had conceded that the NVK had exclusive jurisdiction to initiate a child in need of aid proceeding pursuant to a statute that, on its face, did not apply to the situation, Snow said that

> The Fairbanks region of the Division of Family & Youth Services, for whom we were the lawyers, stretched from the border at Tok to Barrow and Bethel; it thus covered a large number of Native villages ... The practice during that time was for each of the Attorney General Office's Human Services Sections [in Anchorage, Fairbanks, and Juneau] to operate pretty autonomously. That changed some in the 1990s when the three sections occasionally met together in an effort to increase everyone's understanding of ICWA and to develop consistent responses to the arguments being presented by village attorneys around the state. However, in the 1980s, everyone — social workers, assistant attorneys general, villages, tribal attorneys — was trying to understand how ICWA applied to Alaska.
>
> ...
>
> Many of the cases in those early days were testing grounds for interpretation of ICWA and the fleshing out generally of how the well-developed principles of Indian law might apply in Alaska's anomalous situation. As it happened, I had a particular interest in Indian law and had studied it in law school before it was a generally available course. It is probably safe to say that I knew more about Indian law then than any other assistant attorney general in the Human Services Sections at that time, which I say only to indicate why I felt fine about reacting to the different arguments that were put forward as they arose without seeking guidance from Juneau.
>
> As to *J.M.*, the practice during my whole time at the attorney general's office, at least in Fairbanks, was for the assistant attorney general who handled the child protection case at the trial level to do the appeal. So I am pretty sure that *J.M.* was mine from the beginning. You ask who made the decision to concede Kaltag's jurisdiction. It was probably I (sic); I am certain that I had no orders to do so from any supervisor, up to the attorney general at that time ... We certainly never heard from the governor's office.[8]

If, as she recalled, Rebecca Snow decided on her own that the Department of Health and Social Services would concede the validity of the NVK's assertion of jurisdiction, for the Alaska Supreme Court, that concession was determinative. In its decision in *In the Matter of J.M.*,[9] after noting that "the State did not dispute that J.M. was a ward of a tribal court or that Kaltag had exclusive jurisdiction under [section 101(a) of ICWA]," the Court concluded "that the trial court erred in finding that Kaltag had waived its jurisdiction over J.M." The Court reasoned to that result without analyzing the text and investigating the legislative history of section 101(a).

A month after it issued its decision in *In the Matter of J.M.*, the Alaska Supreme Court issued its decision in *Native Village of Nenana v. State.*[10]

In 1983 A.N. had been born in Anchorage to unwed parents. His mother was a non-Native resident of Anchorage. His father was an Athabascan Indian from Nenana, a community located at the confluence of the Nenana and Tanana Rivers in the Alaska interior that the Ninety-second Congress had designated as a Native village for the purposes of ANCSA.

When he was eleven months old, the Department of Health and Social Services placed A.N. in foster care after it received a report that when he was living in his mother's home he had been abused. The department then petitioned the Alaska Superior Court to declare A.N. a child in need of aid.

Pursuant to section 101(c) of the ICWA and represented by TCC attorney Michael Walleri, the Native Village of Nenana (NVNe) intervened in the child in need of aid proceeding. While the NVNe had no legal imprimatur, because the Ninety-second Congress had designated Nenana as a Native village for the purposes of ANCSA, the Athabascan Indian residents of Nenana were an "Indian tribe" for the purposes of the ICWA.

Section 101(b) of the ICWA[11] authorizes an "Indian child's tribe" to petition a state court to transfer a child in need of aid proceeding involving an "Indian child" who is "not domiciled or residing within the reservation of the Indian child's tribe" to the "jurisdiction of the tribe," and requires the state court to make the transfer, unless one of the child's parents objects or the court determines that there is "good cause" not to do so.

Pursuant to section 101(b), the NVNe petitioned the Superior Court to transfer to the NVNe the Superior Court's jurisdiction to decide whether A.N. was a child in need of aid. While A.N.'s parents did not object to the transfer, the Department of Health and Social Services did.

Section 108 of the ICWA[12] authorizes an Indian tribe that "became subject to state jurisdiction pursuant to the provisions of [28 U.S.C. 1360 (the statute that allows the listed states to apply their civil laws of general applicability within Indian country)] or pursuant to any other Federal law" to petition the secretary of the interior to "reassume jurisdiction over child custody proceedings."

Because the NVNe had not petitioned the secretary to reassume jurisdiction, the Superior Court denied the NVNe's petition.

In its decision in *Native Village of Nenana*, the Alaska Supreme Court affirmed the Superior Court. As it had in its decision in *In the Matter of J.M.*, the Court reasoned to its result without investigating the legislative history of the ICWA. Had it done so, the Court would have discovered that the House Committee on Interior and Insular Affairs, which had written section 108, had explained that petitioning the secretary of the interior to "reassume" jurisdiction was a concept the committee had adopted "in order to take into consideration special circumstances, such as those occurring in Alaska."[13] Instead, the Court based its decision on the policy ground that

> there are more than 200 ... [Native] villages "listed" in sections [11 and 16 of ANCSA] alone. Some of these entities already may have systems for dispute resolution in place capable of adjudicating custody matters in a reasonable and competent fashion; others, no doubt, do not. It seems highly unlikely that Congress was unaware of this when it enacted the Indian Child Welfare Act, or that it intended the Indian tribes in Alaska to exercise jurisdiction in child custody matters until such time as there is satisfactory proof that a particular tribe has the ability to properly adjudicate such cases.[14]

In 1987 in its decision in *In the Matter of K.E.*,[15] the Alaska Supreme Court reaffirmed the holding it had announced in *Native Village of Nenana*. A year later in the Court's decision in *Native Village of Stevens v. Alaska Management & Planning*, three members of the Court that had decided *Native Village of Nenana* concluded that between 1867 and 1988 Congress had not afforded the Athabascan Indian residents of Nenana or the Native residents of any other Native village "sovereign tribal status." And in 1992 in its decision in *In the Matter of F.P.*,[16] the Court again reaffirmed the holding it had announced in *Native Village of Nenana*.

Then in 1999 the Alaska Supreme Court, a majority of whose members had not been members of the Court when the Court decided *Native Village of Nenana* and *Native Village of Stevens*, decided in *John v. Baker* that in 1993 Assistant Secretary of the Interior for Indian Affairs Ada Deer had negated the conclusion regarding the intent of Congress to which the Court had reasoned in its decision in *Native Village of Stevens* by creating more than two hundred federally recognized tribes in Alaska in Congress's stead by publishing a list of Native entities in the *Federal Register*, and that in 1994 the One Hundred-third Congress had intended its enactment of the Federally Recognized Indian Tribe List Act to ratify Assistant Secretary Deer's action.

Relying on that reasoning, in 2001 the Alaska Supreme Court reversed *Native Village of Nenana*.

C.R.H. was born in Anchorage in 1999. Her mother was an Athabascan Indian from Nikolai, a community on the Kuskokwim River in the Alaska interior that the

Ninety-second Congress had designated as a Native village for the purposes of ANCSA. Her father was an Indian from Chickaloon, a community northeast of Anchorage that the secretary of the interior had designated as a Native village for the purposes of ANCSA. In 1993 Assistant Secretary Deer included "Nikolai Village" and "Chickaloon Native Village" on the list of Native entities she published in the *Federal Register*.[17]

As a consequence of her mother's alcohol abuse and both parents' disinterest in parenting, four days after C.R.H. was born, the Alaska Department of Health and Social Services petitioned the Alaska Superior Court to declare C.R.H. a child in need of aid.

Represented by attorneys employed by TCC, the Native Village of Nikolai (NVNk) intervened in the child in need of aid proceeding and then, pursuant to section 101(b) of the ICWA, filed a motion that requested the Superior Court to transfer the petition to a court that the village council in Nikolai had established. Since the NVNk had not petitioned the secretary of the interior for jurisdiction pursuant to section 108 of the ICWA, as the Alaska Supreme Court had directed in its decision in *Native Village of Nenana*, the Superior Court denied the motion. The NVNk then appealed the denial to the Alaska Supreme Court.

In the appeal the Department of Health and Social Services was represented by Assistant Attorney General Donna Goldsmith.

After graduating from law school in Washington, D.C., in 1986 and then working as a law clerk for a Superior Court judge in Juneau, in 1987 Goldsmith was admitted to the Alaska bar. After also being admitted to the California bar, Goldsmith moved to Portland where in 1992 she was admitted to the Oregon Bar. She also joined the Federal Bar Association and by 1996 was the deputy chairperson of the association's Indian Law Section. That same year when Goldsmith submitted testimony to the Senate Committee on Indian Affairs regarding a bill whose enactment would have amended the ICWA in various ways, she touted her credentials as an expert on the ICWA by explaining that "from January of 1993 through October of 1995 I represented Indian children and parents in hundreds of ICWA proceedings involving members of numerous Indian families."[18]

In 1999 Theresa Tanoury, the director of the Division of Family & Youth Services (DFYS) of the Department of Health and Social Services, met Goldsmith at a conference, was impressed with her experience, and arranged for the department to hire Goldsmith as the DFYS's in-house ICWA expert. However, Tanoury and Goldsmith soon had a falling out, after which Goldsmith arranged with Attorney General Bruce Botelho to transfer to the Department of Law.

Like Deborah Niedermeyer, Donna Goldsmith was a proponent of the tribal sovereignty movement who, subsequent to her employment as an assistant attorney general, would become executive director of the Alaska Inter-Tribal Council.[19]

In the brief she filed in the *In re the Matter of C.R.H.* appeal, Goldsmith told the Alaska Supreme Court that the State of Alaska joined the NVNk in requesting the court "to revisit *Nenana*, *K.E.*, and *F.P.* in light of intervening events, to clarify the law concerning inherent tribal authority over child protection matters affecting member children, and to overturn *Nenana* and its progeny."[20] And during the oral argument she urged the Court to do even more.

When she was asked whether a court that a village council had established had jurisdiction to initiate—rather than just accept the transfer of—a child in need of aid proceeding, Goldsmith answered: "Yes. It is clear under federal law that the tribes retain jurisdiction over their members and the Indian Child Welfare Act underscores that. Membership is really the key ... If the tribe is the first to the plate, the tribe acts before the state acts, the tribe has jurisdiction if the child is a member or is eligible for membership and is the biological child of a member of the tribe."[21]

When Justice Warren Matthews then asked what the legal authority was on which she relied for that assertion of purported law, Goldsmith could cite none because there was none. Nevertheless, she remained unrepentant, since later during her oral argument she told the Court that "the legislative history makes a statement to the effect that Congress intended when it enacted the Indian Child Welfare Act to be recognizing that the tribes had concurrent authority off reservation." But when Justice Matthews asked her to identify that legislative history, Goldsmith could not do so because there was no such history.

At the beginning of the oral argument, Justice Matthews, who had been a member of the court that had decided the *John v. Baker* appeal without the benefit of adversarial briefing and oral argument, suggested that "as a matter of jurisprudence shouldn't the Court proceed with quite a measure of caution in a case like the present one where there is no adversity whatsoever?" But rather than reflecting caution, while it did not go as far as Donna Goldsmith urged, in an opinion written by Justice Dana Fabe in its decision in *In the Matter of C.R.H.*, the Court announced:

> Subsection [101](b) [of ICWA] tribal transfer jurisdiction over ICWA custody cases was expressly approved by Congress in enacting ICWA. The language and structure of section [101] reflect congressional intent that all tribes, regardless of their P.L. 280 status, be able to accept transfer jurisdiction of ICWA cases from state courts. We therefore hold that Nikolai may assume jurisdiction over this case under ICWA's subsection [101](b) transfer provision. To the extent that *Nenana*, *F.P.*, and *K.E.* are inconsistent with this decision, those cases are overruled.[22]

The U.S. Supreme Court has instructed that statutes are to be "construed by the courts with reference to the circumstances existing at the time of passage."[23] But, as had been the situation in the *John v. Baker* appeal, because Justice Fabe and the other justices reasoned to the result they announced in their decision in the *In the Matter of C.R.H.* appeal without the benefit of adversarial briefing and oral argument, they did not consider the fact that in 1978 when the members of the House Committee on Interior and Insular Affairs wrote section 101(b) of the ICWA there were no, nor since 1867 had there ever been, federally recognized tribes in Alaska.

As Daniel Branch, an attorney in the Bethel office of the Alaska Legal Services Corporation, had explained a year earlier to the Senate Select Committee on Indian Affairs: "Much of title I [of S. 1214, the ICWA bill the committee reported to the Senate in 1977] assumes the existence of an effective tribal structure in the Native villages that simply does not exist in the Yukon-Kuskokwim Delta."[24] And Michael Jeffrey, the supervising attorney at the Alaska Legal Services Corporation office in Barrow, told the committee that, because the bill was "oriented heavily toward the tribal government and tribal reservation system of the Lower 48," "your staff will need to take some time to include language that will make the bill more applicable to the situation in Alaska."[25]

To make the bill more applicable to the situation in Alaska was the reason the members of the House Committee in Interior and Insular Affairs included the section 108 petition procedure in the bill they reported and the U.S. House of Representatives subsequently passed as the version of S. 1214 President Carter signed into law as the ICWA. And that is why the committee had pointed out in its report on the bill that section 108 had been written to "to take into consideration special circumstances, such as those occurring in Alaska."

The result to which the Alaska Supreme Court reasoned in its decision in *John v. Baker* had turned procedurally on the fact that John Baker had voluntarily submitted himself to the jurisdiction of the court the village council in Northway had created before he hired Rita Allee to file his custody action against Anita John in the Alaska Superior Court. In recognition of that fact, in the opinion she wrote in *John v. Baker*, Justice Dana Fabe pointedly promised that "Alaska Natives who for any reason do not wish to have their disputes adjudicated in a tribal court will retain complete and total access to the state judicial system."[26] However, in the dissenting opinion he wrote in *John v. Baker*, Justice Warren Mathews was less sanguine.

While he agreed with Justice Fabe that the Athabascan Indian residents of Northway were a federally recognized tribe because Assistant Secretary of the Interior for Indian Affairs Ada Deer had said they were, he argued that neither the court in Northway nor any other court that a federally recognized tribe in Alaska created had jurisdiction to adjudicate child custody and other domestic relations matters that involved members of the tribe because "under established principles of federal Indian law, state law governs outside of Indian country unless Congress provides otherwise, and Congress has not so provided."[27] He also predicted that

> Today's opinion changes Alaska society. Alaska law no longer applies to every Alaskan. The doors of Alaska's courts will no longer by open to all Alaskans. More than one-sixth of Alaskan children, regardless of where they reside, will be subject to the laws of one of 226 village tribal organizations. More than one-sixth of Alaskan adults, regardless of where they reside, will be subject to the domestic relations laws of one of 226 village tribal organ-

> izations. These laws, written or unwritten, may be different from the laws of the state, indeed they may conflict with the laws of the state. But their reach will be statewide, and even beyond, governing cases that arise in cities, towns, and villages which may be hundreds of miles from the village whose tribal laws are applied. And the family law cases of more than one out of six Alaskan children and adults will be subject to adjudication not in the Alaska Court System, but in the tribal courts of one of 226 villages. Some tribal court cases will be decided fairly. Others will not be. But the only remedy Alaskans aggrieved by the application of conflicting laws or unfair decisions will have is to pursue "comity" litigation in the state courts. Relief through this vague doctrine will be uncertain, hard to obtain, and expensive.[28]

That expression of concern would prove prescient.

In its decision in *In the Matter of C.R.H.*, the Alaska Supreme Court had announced that, in Justice Dana Fabe's and the other justices' view, the Ninety-fifth Congress that enacted the ICWA had intended section 101(b) to delegate a court that had been created by Natives who were members of an ICWA "Indian tribe" jurisdiction to accept the transfer of a child in need of aid proceeding that had been filed in the Alaska Superior Court even though the tribe had not petitioned the secretary of the interior pursuant to section 108 of the ICWA to grant the tribe that jurisdiction. Assuming *arguendo* that that was what the Ninety-fifth Congress intended, section 101(b) provides that the parent of a Native child who is the subject of such a proceeding can prevent the transfer by objecting for any reason. So no parent could be subjected to the jurisdiction of a court a village council created involuntarily.

That arrangement was eviscerated seven months after the Alaska Supreme Court issued its decision in *In the Matter of C.R.H.*, when in March 2002 Assistant Attorney General Donna Goldsmith sent Jay Livey, the commissioner of the Department of Health and Social Services, a memorandum in which she provided legal advice regarding the decision.[29] Goldsmith instructed that henceforth a "tribe may initiate child custody proceedings in tribal court pursuant to tribal law. Where the tribe initiates proceedings and makes the child a ward of its court before the state court issues an order regarding the child, tribal jurisdiction over those proceedings becomes exclusive, in which case the state lacks any authority over the child at issue."

Not only in its decision in *In the Matter of C.R.H.* had the Alaska Supreme Court rejected Goldsmith's request that it say what she now advised Commissioner Livey was the law, as authority for that legal advice, Goldsmith cited section 101(a) of the ICWA. But section 101(a) grants an ICWA "Indian tribe" exclusive jurisdiction only when a child custody proceeding involves an Indian child "who resides or is domiciled within the reservation of such tribe." Subsection (a) also authorizes an ICWA "Indian tribe" that has acquired exclusive jurisdiction over an Indian child because the child was residing or domiciled within the tribe's reservation to retain that jurisdiction if the child acquired a new residence or domicile outside the boundaries of the reservation.

Despite the fact that neither of those provisions were applicable in Alaska, which had no reservations, seven months after Donna Goldsmith sent Commissioner Livey her memorandum, the DFYS amended its Child Protective Services Manual, which sets out the protocols DFYS social workers are required to follow.

It is a blackletter rule of administrative law that, because state agencies "are creatures of statute," they "must find within the statute [that created each agency] the authority for the exercise of any power they claim."[30]

Alaska Statute 47.17.020(b) authorizes any person to report to the DFYS that he or she suspects that a child may be suffering harm as a consequence of abuse or neglect. A.S. 47.17.025 requires the DFYS to — within 72 hours of its receipt of a report of harm — provide a written report of its investigation regarding the report to the Alaska Department of Law. A.S. 47.17.040(b) mandates that reports of harm are confidential.

Nevertheless, in October 2002 the DFYS amended section 2.1 of its Child Protective Services Manual to require DFYS social workers, when they received a report of harm, to ask the reporter whether the child who was the subject of the report was a Native child and, if the child was a Native child, the identity of the child's, and the child's parents', tribe and village.

Section 2.1 was further amended to require the social worker who received a report of harm involving a Native child to "contact the child's tribe" and ask whether the tribe already had "custody/jurisdiction" of the child. If the tribe said that it had already asserted jurisdiction, the amendment directed that "once verification [of the tribe's assertion of jurisdiction] has been received the information [the social worker received from the reporter] will be shared with the tribe and the Report of Harm transferred to the tribe." Finally, another amendment directed the social worker to "forward a copy of the Report of Harm to the child's tribe if the tribe has custody of the child," but to provide the tribe the name of the individual who made the report "only if the reporter has given permission."

For parents of Native children, those changes would prove consequential.

Tok is a community on the Alaska Highway in the Alaska interior fifty-six miles west of Northway. Ninety percent of Tok's 1,200 residents are Caucasian.

In 1989 when she was a senior in high school, Andrea Sitton, a Caucasian resident of Tok, became pregnant by Darrel Felix, whose father was Caucasian and whose mother, Daisy Northway, was an Athabascan Indian from the village of Healy Lake who lived in Tok with her husband who was an Athabascan Indian from Northway.

Andrea Sitton and Darrel Felix did not marry. In 1990 their daughter, H.F., was born. A year later Andrea Sitton ended her relationship with Felix after she repeatedly had been subjected to domestic violence. When she then applied to the Division of Public Assistance of the Department of Health and Social Services for financial support, the division filed a child support enforcement action against Felix. When he found that out Darrel Felix petitioned the court the village council in Northway had created to grant him "sole physical custody" of H.F.

When Lorraine Titus, the judge of the court, signed an order that purported to grant him custody, Felix gave a copy of the order to the Division of Public Assistance, which then dismissed the child support enforcement action. The division did so even though, as Andrea Sitton subsequently would attest: "I did not know that Darrel had petitioned the tribal court for custody of H.F., did not know that Lorraine Titus held a hearing on February 20, 1992, and did not know that the tribal court had issued an order granting Darrel's petition."

As she had from birth, H.F. continued to live with her mother. However, when H.F. was old enough to begin doing so, Andrea Sitton encouraged her daughter to spend time with her father.

One evening in January 2003 when H.F. was spending the night with her father at his grandmother's house in Tok, Darrel Felix telephoned Andrea Sitton and told her that the next day he was taking H.F. and her six-year-old half-sister, R.F., to Fairbanks, where he and the girls would live with Felix's aunt and uncle in an apartment the couple were renting.

The next day Andrea Sitton applied to the District Court in Tok for a protective order. After issuing an emergency order, the magistrate held two hearings at which Andrea Sitton told the magistrate that several years earlier when Darrel Felix's aunt and uncle had foster children living in their home in the village of Tanacross the children had been sexually molested by Joseph Beaver, the aunt's nephew. Andrea Sitton told the magistrate that she feared that when he visited Fairbanks Joseph Beaver would stay with Darrel Felix's aunt and uncle at the apartment into which Felix intended to move with H.F.

Disregarding that expression of concern, the magistrate vacated the emergency order and Darrel Felix, who had continued to have H.F. in his physical custody, took H.F. and R.F. to Fairbanks.

Two months later, R.F. told her mother that she had been sexually molested in the aunt and uncle's apartment by Joseph Beaver. When R.F.'s mother told Andrea Sitton what R.F. had told her, Sitton, who was in Tok, telephoned the DFYS office in Fairbanks and filed a report of harm regarding H.F. with a social worker named Jennifer Reynolds.

Several days later Andrea Sitton received a telephone call from Reynolds's supervisor, a social worker named Judy Wangstad. Wangstand assured Andrea Sitton that the DFYS would initiate an investigation to determine whether H.F. was a child in need of aid. When several more days passed and she had not heard whether the DFYS had done so, Andrea Sitton's mother, Shirley Marshall, who lived in Tok, telephoned the DFYS and spoke with Jennifer Reynolds.

During that conversation Reynolds asked Marshall whether H.F. was an Alaska Native, and if she was, what the name of the tribe was that she was a member of. Marshall answered that H.F. was one-quarter Native (because Darrel Felix was half-Native). She also told Reynolds that, although he lived in Tok, she thought Darrel Felix was a member of the Native Village of Northway (NVN). In response to that information, Reynolds told Marshall that she was required by law to contact the NVN.

When she finished her conversation with Shirley Marshall, Jennifer Reynolds telephoned the NVN. Her call was answered by Crystalena Sam, the NVN employee who implemented the ICWA in the village, Darrel Felix's mother, Daisy Northway, who, while she lived in Tok, worked in Northway as the NVN tribal administrator, or by some other female employee of the NVN. Reynolds told the woman with whom she spoke about the report of harm Andrea Sitton had filed.

Shortly after that call ended, Daisy Northway telephoned Darrel Felix in Fairbanks and told him about the call from Jennifer Reynolds. She also had Cheryl Silas, one of the judges of the court in Northway, sign an order that granted her physical custody of H.F.

Less than an hour after Shirley Marshall finished what by law was a confidential telephone conversation with Jennifer Reynolds, Darrel Felix telephoned Andrea Sitton to rage that her "fucking bitch mother" had reported him to the DFYS. He also told Sitton that his mother was driving to Fairbanks to take physical custody of H.F.

After Daisy Northway did so, Andrea Sitton filed two lawsuits. The first was *Sitton v. Felix*, a custody action filed in the Alaska Superior Court in Fairbanks against Darrel Felix and Daisy Northway in which she sought legal and physical custody of H.F.[31] The second was *Sitton v. Native Village of Northway*, a civil action she filed in the U.S. District Court in Anchorage against the NVN, the court in Northway and the judges thereof, and the Department of the Interior in which she sought a declaratory judgment that neither Congress nor the secretary of the interior, the assistant secretary of the interior for Indian affairs, nor any other executive branch official acting lawfully pursuant to authority delegated to such official by Congress had recognized the Athabascan Indian members of the NVN as a federally recognized tribe whose village council possessed governmental authority to establish a court that had jurisdiction to adjudicate the dispute between Andrea Sitton and Darrel Felix regarding the custody of H.F.[32]

The *Sitton v. Native Village of Northway* lawsuit was assigned to District Judge H. Russel Holland who in 1994 and 1995 had issued the unpublished decisions in the consolidated lawsuits regarding tribal status and Indian country that in 1998 had resulted in the decision the U.S. Supreme Court issued in *State of Alaska v. Native Village of Venetie Tribal Government*.

When the Department of the Interior moved the district court to dismiss, or in the alternative to stay, the *Sitton v. Native Village of Northway* lawsuit, Judge Holland granted the motion and stayed proceedings for twelve months in the hope that during that time a decision by the Superior Court in the *Sitton v. Felix* lawsuit might moot the need for him to have to decide the merits of the claims for relief regarding the NVN's tribal status (or lack thereof) that the *Sitton v. Native Village of Northway* lawsuit presented for decision. As his rationale for refusing to decide a legal dispute that, the district court's jurisdiction having been properly invoked, he had a duty to decide, Judge Holland explained:

> Plaintiffs' complaint, both as regards the question of the Native Village of Northway's governmental authority as well as plaintiffs' due process claims, raises extraordinarily important and politically sensitive issues which, if plaintiffs were to prevail on them, would have very far-reaching impact in the state of Alaska. For example, it is the court's impression that a determination that the Native Village of Northway tribe lacks governmental authority to adjudicate custody disputes, as is contended by the plaintiffs, could impact all or very nearly all of the more than 200 Native villages in the state of Alaska.[33]

Andrea Sitton appealed the order that imposed the stay to the U.S. Court of Appeals for the Ninth Circuit. But while the appeal was pending, through the *Sitton v. Felix* lawsuit, she regained physical custody of H.F. As Judge Holland had hoped it might, that outcome mooted the *Sitton v. Native Village of Northway* lawsuit and, at Andrea Sitton's request, the U.S. Court of Appeals for the Ninth Circuit dismissed her appeal.[34]

Over the years since, the U.S. District Court in Alaska, citing procedural grounds as its rationale for doing so, has repeatedly refused to decide the federal question regarding tribal status in Alaska that the U.S. Supreme Court had not been asked to decide in *State of Alaska v. Native Village of Venetie Tribal Government* and that Judge Holland refused to decide in *Sitton v. Native Village of Northway*.[35]

Eleven

In June 1999 the Commission on Rural Governance and Empowerment, which Governor Tony Knowles had created a year-and-a-half earlier to try and brunt the animosity toward Knowles that the anticipated decision of the U.S. Supreme Court in the *State of Alaska v. Native Village of Venetie Tribal Government* lawsuit would ignite prior to the 1998 gubernatorial election, submitted its report. Given the composition of the commission's membership, it is no surprise that the report announced that

> The existence of tribes in Alaska predates both the federal and state constitutions. While the United States Supreme Court established in *Venetie* that Alaska Native Claims Settlement Act lands are not Indian country, its decision did not affect the federally recognized status of Alaska tribes.
>
> Tribal governments, as with municipalities, provide needed services for their people. In many rural Alaska communities, tribes are the only forms of government. Alaska Native tribes have a government-to-government relationship with the federal government. The United States confirmed this relationship by recognizing Alaska's tribes. A tribe's status as a sovereign depends exclusively on the actions of the federal government, independent of state action.[1]

The report contained thirty-two recommendations. The first was that the governor "issue a proclamation officially acknowledging and accepting the existence of tribes and tribal governments," and then "invite all tribes to the table for a summit to forge a two-way, permanent framework for a working relationship.[2]

To try to further repair his relations with tribal sovereignty advocates, four months later Knowles hired Will Mayo, an outspoken tribal sovereignty advocate in the Alaska interior who had been a member of the commission, to advise him on Native issues. Then several days later at the October 1999 AFN convention, Knowles announced that it was time for the State to "acknowledge and embrace" Alaska tribes.

Earning his new paycheck, Will Mayo spun the press that Knowles's announcement was "unprecedented" because "no governor has talked like this before"[3] — which was hyperbole that ignored the fact that nine years earlier Alaska Governor Steve Cowper had said the same thing.

Six weeks later at a meeting of the Alaska Inter-Tribal Council (AITC), Knowles followed up on the recommendation of the Commission on Rural Governance and Empowerment by inviting the group to enter into a "government-to-government"

Alaska Governor Tony Knowles Dances at Alaska Native Heritage Center Before Signing Administrative Order No. 186. Erik Hill/Anchorage Daily News.

negotiation with the State of Alaska that Will Mayo would coordinate and at which Attorney General Bruce Botelho would serve as the governor's negotiator.[4]

The invitation was enthusiastically accepted. But in February 2000 at a meeting AITC hosted in Anchorage, those in attendance could not agree on who would meet with Botelho. So they appointed a forty-five-member negotiating team.[5] And by May when the first "government to government" meeting was held, the negotiating team had expanded to forty-nine members.[6]

Over the next four months, additional meetings were held. Then in September at an event the AITC hosted at the Alaska Native Heritage Center in Anchorage, after dancing for the crowd with a costumed Eskimo dancer, Knowles signed Administrative Order No. 186, which revoked the administrative order Alaska Governor Walter Hickel had signed in 1991 that had revoked the administrative order Governor Cowper had signed in 1990. Administrative Order No. 186 also announced that the order was "intended to make clear for all state and federal agencies, the courts, the tribes, and the public that the State of Alaska recognizes and respects the governmental status of the federally recognized tribes within the boundaries of Alaska."[7]

The day previous Knowles had faxed a copy of Administrative Order No. 186 to Alaska Senators Ted Stevens and Frank Murkowski and Representative Don Young, who responded by faxing back their own letter in which they told the governor:

> The extraordinary implications of the creation of tribal authority and jurisdiction in the state require a full and open dialogue through an inclusive public process. We request that you suspend any further administrative

> action and allow all Alaskans to participate in a process to review the implications of this proposed order. We also request that you provide us with the Alaska Department of Law's economic and legal analysis of the implications of your administrative order.[8]

Knowles then responded with a letter in which he informed the solons that "the administrative order I will sign later today is the culmination of years of an extensive public process within Alaska, some of which each of you has participated in, and all of which you have been informed about." He then concluded by lecturing: "Permit me to remind you that a state administrative order serves to set a direction for state government. In this case, I am directing state agencies how to better work with federally recognized tribes to improve the delivery of services to Alaskans. As it explicitly stated in the administrative order, this work shall be 'consistent with the constitutions of the United States and the State of Alaska.'"[9]

But insofar as the Alaska Constitution was concerned, when it reported on the event at the Alaska Native Heritage Center, the *Anchorage Daily News* related that:

> Rep. Brian Porter, R-Anchorage and speaker of the State House, said Knowles aides briefed him on the Order earlier in the week. But their explanations left him puzzled and concerned, Porter said. "I asked what he's recognizing them as, and quite frankly the answer was unsatisfactory," Porter said. "I can't remember the precise words, but it begged the question, 'Are you saying they have sovereign rights?' And the answer was, 'Yes, but it has to be within the confines of the state and federal constitutions,'" Porter said, adding that he's not sure the Alaska Constitution permits sovereign tribes.[10]

By December the text of a document that Attorney General Botelho negotiated during the "government to government" meetings, which now was called a Millennium Agreement, had been agreed to except by several outlier members of the AITC negotiating team who objected that the inclusion of language that acknowledged that the State of Alaska was as sovereign as tribal governments were sovereign was an admission that might persuade the United Nations that the AITC negotiating team had "signed away our rights to sovereignty."[11]

The content of the Millennium Agreement was entirely procedural since the text merely established a framework for future "government to government" relations that consisted of the creation of a State-Tribal Forum, which was code for "more meetings." The agreement also created a committee consisting of four state officials and four tribal leaders that would submit recommendations regarding how "a centralized office, council, or commission to oversee tribal-state relations" should be "constituted, structured, and governed."

For Tony Knowles, the Millennium Agreement was a triumph of political theater that in April in the ballroom of an Anchorage hotel culminated with a signing ceremony at which, with the press looking on, the governor and representatives from sixty-two Native villages signed the document.[12] The next morning the *Anchorage*

Daily News editorialized that "for the state and the tribes to have government-to-government relations, they must recognize one another, acknowledge the sovereignty of one another. How exactly these relations will work out remains to be seen."[13]

The way they worked out was that the Millennium Agreement soon was forgotten. When he was asked years later, Botelho could not recall whether the committee the agreement established ever met, and, according to Botelho, "I certainly don't recall any recommendations regarding how a 'centralized office, council, or commission to oversee tribal-state relations' should be 'constituted, structured, and governed.'"[14] However, what Botelho did recall was that, because the Millennium Agreement directed them to do so, officials at the Department of Health and Social Services and the Department of Public Safety "embarked on their own consultations with the tribes."[15]

In November 2002 Alaska Senator Frank Murkowski was elected to succeed Tony Knowles as governor. When he assumed office, Murkowski appointed Gregg Renkes, a longtime member of his Senate staff, to replace Bruce Botelho as attorney general.

By that time, with the assistance of the Tanana Chiefs Conference, the Association of Village Council Presidents, NARF, the Alaska Legal Services Corporation, and other organizations whose members and employees were part of the tribal sovereignty movement, Native residents of a number of communities that the Ninety-second Congress or the secretary of the interior had designated as Native villages for the purposes of ANCSA had created courts that, as Cheryl Silas, the judge of the court in Northway, would do in 2003 when she signed the order that purported to grant Daisy Northway custody of H.F., had begun initiating their own child in need of aid proceedings.

In October 2004 Attorney General Renkes issued an opinion letter in which he advised Joel Gilbertson, whom Governor Murkowski had appointed to succeed Jay Livey as commissioner of the Department of Health and Social Services, regarding "the question of when tribes in Alaska may exercise jurisdiction over tribal children in child custody proceedings under the Indian Child Welfare Act."[16]

The opinion letter began by revoking the legal advice Assistant Attorney General Donna Goldsmith had given in the memorandum she had sent Commissioner Livey two years earlier.[17] The letter then advised Commissioner Gilbertson that "Alaska state courts have exclusive jurisdiction over child custody proceedings involving Alaska Native children unless (1) the child's tribe has successfully petitioned the Department of the Interior to reassume exclusive or concurrent jurisdiction under [section 108 of] the Indian Child Welfare Act or (2) a state superior court has transferred jurisdiction of the child's case to a tribal court in accordance with [section 101(b) of the Indian Child Welfare Act] and the tribal court is exercising its jurisdiction."[18]

After he received the opinion letter, Commissioner Gilbertson directed the Office of Children's Services (OCS), as the DFYS had been renamed, to amend section 2.1 of its Child Protective Services Manual to eliminate the changes that had been made to reflect the legal advice Donna Goldsmith had given to Commissioner Livey.[19]

Three weeks after Attorney General Renkes sent Commissioner Gilbertson the opinion letter, the Native Villages of Tanana, Nulato, Kalskag, Akiak, and Lower Kalskag, represented by NARF attorney Heather Kendall-Miller, filed a civil action in the Alaska Superior Court against the State of Alaska to invalidate the legal advice Attorney General Renkes had given in the letter. In the prayer of their complaint the plaintiff villages requested the Superior Court to issue a judgment declaring that Alaska Native tribes "possess inherent and concurrent jurisdiction to adjudicate children's proceedings and issue tribal court decrees," as well as an injunction that would require the State to afford tribal court child custody decrees full faith and credit.

In August 2008 Superior Court Judge Sen Tan entered the judgment and issued the injunction the plaintiff villages had requested, after which the State appealed Judge Tan's decision to enter the judgment to the Alaska Supreme Court.[20]

Two years earlier Sarah Palin had succeeded Frank Murkowski as governor and had appointed an attorney of her hometown acquaintance named Talis Colberg to serve as attorney general.

Attorney General Colberg began his opening brief in the *State v. Native Village of Tanana* appeal by gratuitously conceding that "there are 229 tribes in Alaska."[21] In its decision in *State v. Native Village of* Tanana[22] the Alaska Supreme Court found that concession determinative when the justices observed, "Notably, the state does not ask that *John v. Baker* be overruled."[23] The Court then proceeded to do what, seven years earlier during her oral argument in the *In the Matter of C.R.H.* appeal, Assistant Attorney General Donna Goldsmith had urged the justices to do. The decision announced that

> in light of our foundational decision *John v. Baker*, ICWA, federal case law regarding Alaska Native tribal sovereignty, and the absence of express contrary Congressional intent, we hold that federally recognized Alaska native tribes that have not reassumed exclusive jurisdiction under [section 108 of ICWA] still have concurrent jurisdiction to initiate ICWA-defined child custody proceedings, both inside and outside of Indian country. Necessarily, federally recognized Alaska Native tribes are entitled to all of the rights and privileges of Indian tribes under ICWA, including procedural safeguards imposed on states and [section 101(d) of ICWA] full faith and credit with respect to ICWA-defined child custody orders to the same extent as other states' and foreign orders."[24]

The decision then concluded by announcing that "among the issues we are not deciding today are: (1) whether, parallel to ICWA [section 101(b)] transfer jurisdiction limitations, parents of Indian children might have the right to object to tribal jurisdiction; (2) the extent of tribal jurisdiction over non-member parents of Indian children; and (3) the extent of tribal jurisdiction over Indian children or member parents who have limited or no contact with the tribe."[25]

However, three years later the justices would do so.

S.P. was born in Fairbanks in 2007. Her father was Edward Parks, whose father was Caucasian and whose mother was an Athabascan Indian from Stevens Village. Parks had been raised in, and was a lifelong resident of, Fairbanks. S.P.'s mother was Bessie Stearman, an Athabascan Indian who had been raised in Minto, a community on the Tolovana River 130 miles west of Fairbanks.

In 1939 Assistant Secretary of the Interior Oscar Chapman approved a constitution for an organization called the Native Village of Minto (NVM) that "a group of Indians having the common bond of living together in the Village of Minto" had submitted pursuant to section 1 of Public Law No. 74-538 and section 16 of the IRA.[26] In 1971 the Ninety-second Congress designated Minto as a Native village for the purposes of ANCSA. And in 1993 Assistant Secretary of the Interior for Indian Affairs Ada Deer included the "Native Village of Minto" on the list of Native entities she published in the *Federal Register*.[27] In 2000 258 individuals, almost all of Athabascan Indian descent, lived in Minto. In 2001 Bessie Stearman left Minto with no intention of ever returning.

In 2008 Edward Parks and Bessie Stearman, who did not marry, were living with S.P. in Fairbanks when Stearman, who had a history of alcohol and substance abuse problems, was told that she was going to be incarcerated for a probation violation. Because Edward Parks was working on the North Slope, Stearman asked her cousin, Jeff Simmonds, and his wife, Rozella Simmonds, who lived in Fairbanks, to take physical custody of S.P. while she was incarcerated.

After Bessie Stearman gave them physical custody of S.P., Jeff and Rozella Simmonds informed Mishal Gaede, a social worker who worked for the Tanana Chiefs Conference, of the situation. Gaede then arranged a teleconference with Lori Baker, a judge of the court the village council in Minto had created. At the conclusion of the teleconference, Baker signed an order in which the court purported to take legal custody of S.P. and give physical custody to Jeff and Rozella Simmonds.

When he learned of those events, Edward Parks quit his job, returned to Fairbanks, and began attempting to regain physical custody of his daughter.

That began a convoluted series of interactions between Edward Parks, Mishal Gaede, Jeff and Rozella Simmonds, and, via teleconferences, Lori Baker, that, after Parks obtained an attorney, included Parks's attorney informing Baker that, because the Athabascan Indian residents of Minto had not been lawfully designated as a federally recognized tribe, the NVM and the court it had created in Minto had no governmental authority to involve themselves in matters involving the custody of S.P.

Those interactions concluded in May 2009 when Lori Baker and the other judges of the court in Minto held a teleconference that Edward Parks and Bessie Stearman attended at the TCC office in Fairbanks and during which Parks's attorney was not allowed to speak. At the conclusion of the teleconference, Baker signed an order that purported to terminate Edward Parks's and Bessie Stearman's parental rights.

In September 2009 in the Alaska Superior Court in Fairbanks, Edward Parks filed *Parks v. Simmonds*,[28] a civil action in which he sought an order directing Jeff and Rozella Simmonds to give him custody of his daughter. The lawsuit was assigned to Superior Court Judge Paul Lyle.

Section 101(d) of the ICWA[29] requires states to give "full faith and credit" to the "judicial proceedings of any Indian tribe applicable to Indian child custody proceedings." While the Alaska Supreme Court had not yet issued its decision in *State v. Native Village of Tanana*, in January 2010 the Fairbanks attorney TCC had hired to represent the Simmondses filed a motion in which he requested Judge Lyle to dismiss the *Parks v. Simmonds* lawsuit on the ground that the May 2009 order in which the court in Minto had terminated Edward Parks's parental rights was entitled to full faith and credit.

In November 2010 Judge Lyle denied the motion.

Two years earlier in its decision in *Starr v.* George,[30] the Alaska Supreme Court had instructed that the Superior Court was not to afford a resolution of a village council approving an adoption full faith and credit pursuant to section 101(d) of the ICWA if the council had not afforded a complaining party due process of law because the party had not been given "notice and an opportunity to be heard." In the decision in which he denied the Simmonds's motion to dismiss, Judge Lyle concluded that

> Parks' jurisdictional objections to the exercise of tribal authority in this case are complex, esoteric, rooted in a complicated history and well beyond the ken of most lay people or lay advocates to understand or explain. Minimal due process requires that a party be afforded "an opportunity to present their objections," to the court including the opportunity to contest jurisdiction. Tribal proceedings must "be addressed to the issues involved in a meaningful fashion." Parks sought to raise a jurisdictional issue before the tribal court. When Parks' attorney was prohibited from speaking at the outset of the termination trial, Parks was denied a meaningful opportunity to present his jurisdictional objections to the exercise of Minto's tribal authority. Therefore, he was denied minimal due process under the U.S. and Alaska Constitutions."[31]

The NVM, whose membership was composed of residents of a community whose population by 2010 had declined to only 210 persons, said that, in addition to the court over which Lori Baker presided, it also had created a court of appeals, although who the judges were and whether the court of appeals existed other than on paper would never be explained. With respect to the contention of the Fairbanks attorney who represented the Simmondses that Edward Parks waived his jurisdictional argument because he did not appeal to the court of appeals the refusal of the court in Minto to allow his attorney to present his jurisdictional argument, Judge Lyle concluded that

> The Minto appeal procedures permit only a "brief statement" of the reasons for the appeal and Minto apparently applies the same rule (that attorneys may not speak) in all of its proceedings. The evidence thus indicates that Parks' attorney would not have been allowed to speak and raise his jurisdictional argument on appeal. Given the limited statement permitted under the appeal procedures, the rule that lawyers may not speak before the Minto tribal courts, and the reasons given at oral argument for the rule—that Minto Tribal Court judges are not law-trained and therefore do not permit lawyers to speak—requiring exhaustion of tribal remedies would not cure the due process denial that occurred here—the refusal to permit a jurisdictional objection to be raised and heard in a meaningful fashion. It does not appear that Parks would have been permitted to raise his jurisdictional arguments at his appellate hearing in the only effective manner available to him—through counsel or through detailed legal briefing prepared by counsel and reviewed and decided by the court... The provision for tribal appellate review that excluded the opportunity to argue jurisdictional challenges would not have cured the due process denial and, therefore, exhaustion of tribal remedies is not required under the circumstances of this case.[32]

At that point, attorneys in NARF's Anchorage office took over the Simmondses' representation and petitioned the Alaska Supreme Court to review Judge Lyle's decision denying the motion to dismiss, and the Court granted the petition.

Fifteen years earlier in the decision she had written in *John v. Baker*, Justice Dana Fabe had promised that "Alaska Natives who for any reason do not wish to have their disputes adjudicated in a tribal court will retain complete and total access to the state judicial system."[33] But touting *John v. Baker* as "our foundational decision on tribal jurisdiction over child custody" in her decision in *Simmonds v.* Parks,[34] Justice Fabe repudiated that assurance by announcing:

> We will not allow a party to challenge a tribal court's judgment in an ICWA-defined child custody proceeding in Alaska state court without first exhausting available tribal court appellate remedies. Because Parks failed to exhaust available tribal court remedies by appealing to the Minto Court of Appeals, and because none of the exceptions to the exhaustion doctrine apply, we conclude that he is not permitted to relitigate his minimal due process and jurisdictional claims in Alaska state court. Therefore, we accord full faith and credit to the Minto Tribal Court's judgment terminating Parks's parental rights, and we reverse, remanding to the superior court to order dismissal of Parks's state court action.[35]

Judge Lyle had determined that it would have been futile for Edward Parks—on his own and without an attorney—to have presented to the Minto court of appeals, whose members would not have understood them, jurisdictional arguments that were "complex, esoteric," and "well beyond the ken of most lay people or lay advocates to understand or explain." But Justice Fabe dismissed that determination as "misplaced" because, even though the paper he had been given that described the rules of the Minto court of appeals stated that he could only submit a "brief statement," Edward Parks should have known that that restriction did not prohibit him from submitting "meaningful written briefing" that his attorney could have written.[36]

After so holding, Justice Fabe reviewed federal court decisions she considered relevant, the most important of which was *Strate v. A-1 Contractors*.[37]

In that decision the U.S. Supreme Court held that a court that had been organized by three federally recognized tribes whose members reside on the Fort Berthold Indian Reservation in North Dakota had no authority to subject to its jurisdiction a non-Indian company whose employee had been involved in an automobile accident on a state highway at a location within the boundaries of the reservation. The case had reached the Court after the company filed a civil action in the U.S. District Court against the tribal court to obtain an injunction that prohibited the tribal court from subjecting the company to its jurisdiction.

After reaffirming that, as a general rule, "a federal court should stay its hand until after the Tribal Court has had a full opportunity to determine its own jurisdiction," the U.S. Supreme Court noted in a footnote that in situations in which it was "plain" that a tribal court had no authority to subject a non-member of the tribe to the court's jurisdiction, "the otherwise applicable exhaustion requirement must give way, for it would serve no purpose other than delay."[38]

In her decision in *Simmonds v. Parks*, Justice Fabe acknowledged the U.S. Supreme Court's recognition in its decision in *Strate v. A-1 Contractors* that a plaintiff could dispense with exhausting his remedies in a tribal court when pursuing those remedies would serve no purpose, and then disregarded it by announcing that, even though Edward Parks was not a member of the NVM, had never lived in Minto, and had had no prior contact with the NVM, "the Minto Tribal Court's claim to jurisdiction, based on S.P.'s membership or eligibility for membership in the Native Village of Minto, is colorable or plausible." And because it was, "Parks does not satisfy the exception to the exhaustion of tribal remedies doctrine identified in *Strate*."[39]

Kaltag is a community on the Yukon River in the Alaska interior 335 miles west of Fairbanks that in 1971 the Ninety-second Congress designated as a Native village for the purposes of ANCSA. In 1993 Assistant Secretary of the Interior for Indian Affairs Ada Deer included the "Village of Kaltag" on the list of Native entities she published in the *Federal Register*.[40]

In 2004 a court the village council in Kaltag had created issued an order in which it terminated the parental rights of an Athabascan Indian resident of Kaltag and an

Athabascan Indian resident of the community of Koyukuk to their daughter, N.S. In 2005 the court in Kaltag issued a degree that authorized an Athabascan Indian couple from the community of Huslia to adopt N.S.

When the court in Kaltag requested the Bureau of Vital Statistics of the Department of Health and Social Services to issue a new birth certificate for N.S., the Bureau denied the request. Relying on the opinion letter Attorney General Renkes had issued a year earlier, the Bureau informed the village council that "as of October 25, 2005, the Bureau will only be accepting Tribal Court granted adoption paperwork from the following 3 entities: Barrow, Chevak, and Metlakatla."*

Apparently because Judge Tan had not yet issued his decision in the *Native Village of Tanana v. State* lawsuit, in September 2006 NARF attorney Heather Kendall-Miller filed *Kaltag Tribal Council v. Jackson*[41,]** in the U.S. District Court in Anchorage to obtain a judgment "declaring that plaintiff Kaltag Tribal Council, as a federally recognized tribe, possesses the inherent right of self-governance which includes the authority to adjudicate tribal adoptions, and that Kaltag Tribal Court orders of adoption are entitled to full faith and credit under the Indian Child Welfare Act."[44]

Because it would be another four years before the Alaska Supreme Court would announce in its decision in *State v. Native Village of Tanana* that "federally recognized Alaska Native tribes that have not reassumed exclusive jurisdiction under [section 108 of the ICWA] still have concurrent jurisdiction to initiate ICWA-defined child custody proceedings, both inside and outside of Indian country," when Assistant Attorney General Jan Rutherdale, who represented Commissioner Jackson, requested District Judge Timothy Burgess to dismiss the *Kaltag Tribal Council v. Jackson* lawsuit, she argued that while the Native Village of Kaltag — whose members she described as a "reservation-less tribe" — could accept transfers of child in need of aid proceedings from the Alaska Superior Court pursuant to section 101(b) of the ICWA, the village council could not initiate a proceeding and terminate a parent's parental rights unless and until it petitioned the secretary of the interior pursuant to section 108 of the ICWA to reassume jurisdiction over child custody proceedings and the secretary granted the petition.[45]

---

* Pursuant to section 108 of the ICWA, in 1997 the Chevak Traditional Council (CTC), and in 1998 the Native Village of Barrow (NVB), filed petitions that requested the secretary of the interior to allow them to "reassume" jurisdiction over Indian child custody proceedings.[42] In 1999 the BIA approved both petitions, granting the CTC "exclusive jurisdiction over Indian child custody proceedings involving Indian children who are enrolled or eligible for enrollment with the Chevak Traditional Council of Chevak, Alaska, and who reside or are domiciled within the Native Village of Chevak, Alaska," and granting the NVB "exclusive jurisdiction over Indian child custody proceedings involving Indian children who are enrolled or eligible for enrollment with the Native Village of Barrow and who reside or are domiciled within the Native Village of Barrow in the State of Alaska."[43] To date, those are the only Native villages that have petitioned to reassume jurisdiction pursuant to section 108 of the ICWA.

** In 2005 Governor Frank Murkowski appointed Karleen Jackson to succeed Joel Gilbertson as commissioner of the Department of Health and Social Services.

In February 2008 Judge Burgess rejected that contention in a memorandum order in which he announced that the decision the three-judge panel of the U.S. Court of Appeals for the Ninth Circuit had issued seventeen years earlier in *Native Village of Venetie I.R.A. Council v. State*[46] was controlling. In reasoning to that conclusion, Judge Burgess announced that U.S. Supreme Court precedent required him to resolve ambiguities in the text of section 101 of the ICWA "in favor of the tribe," and that in its decision in *Native Village of Venetie I.R.A. Council v. State*, the panel had instructed that "when a question of tribal power arises, the relevant inquiry is whether any limitation exists to *prevent* the tribe from acting, not whether any authority exists to *permit* the tribe to act" (emphases in original).[47]

In 2009 another three-judge panel of the U.S. Court of Appeals for the Ninth Circuit affirmed Judge Burgess in a cursory decision in which the judges concluded that "[t]he district court's decision that full faith and credit be given to the Kaltag court's adoption judgment is compelled by this circuit's binding precedent. *See Native Village of Venetie I.R.A. Council v. Alaska*."[48]

In 2010 the State of Alaska petitioned the U.S. Supreme Court to issue a writ of certiorari in *Hogan v. Kaltag Tribal Council** and review the panel's decision because

> the Ninth Circuit grounded its decision in this case on precedent — *Venetie I.R.A. Council* — that not only was decided before this Court issued its landmark decision in *Alaska v. Native Village of Venetie Tribal Gov't* on the scope of Indian country in Alaska, but that predates many significant pronouncements by this Court on the scope of tribal sovereignty as to nonmembers off-reservation, including *Plains Commerce Bank*, *Hicks*, and *Atkinson Trading Co.* Without even recognizing the import of those controlling precedents, the Ninth Circuit simply invoked *Venetie I.R.A. Council* and held that the district court's decision ordering the state to give full faith and credit to the tribal court's adoption decree was "compelled" by that case. There is no reason for this Court to leave the Ninth Circuit case law frozen in time — at *Venetie I.R.A. Council*.[49]

As has been described, in *Native Village of Venetie I.R.A. Council v. State*, the three judges who were members of the panel of the U.S. Court of Appeals for the Ninth Circuit that issued that decision decided that a group of Alaska Natives whose legal status as a federally recognized tribe had not been conferred by a treaty or statute or by the secretary of the interior acting lawfully pursuant to authority that Congress had delegated to the secretary in a statute nevertheless was a federally recognized tribe if the group could demonstrate that its members were "the modern-day successors to an historical sovereign band of native Americans."

The panel's invention of its "common law" theory of tribal recognition was clear error because as the House Committee on Natural Resources has explained,

---

* In 2008 Governor Sarah Palin appointed William Hogan to succeed Karleen Jackson as commissioner of the Department of Health and Social Services.

"'Recognized' is more than a simple adjective; it is a legal term of art" that requires "a formal political act."[50] But in 1995 the State of Alaska waived its opportunity to ask the U.S. Supreme Court to correct that error when, at the direction of Alaska Governor Tony Knowles, Attorney General Bruce Botelho did not appeal to the U.S. Court of Appeals for the Ninth Circuit District Judge H. Russel Holland's unpublished decision in the *Native Village of Venetie I.R.A. Council v. State* lawsuit in which he found that the Gwich'in Athabascan Indian residents of Venetie were a federally recognized tribe because they were "the modern-day successors to a historical sovereign entity."[51]

And in the petition for a writ of certiorari it filed in *Hogen v. Kaltag Tribal Council*, the State of Alaska not only did not contest the respondent's assertion that it was the governing body of a federally recognized tribe, the petition described the lawsuit that had produced the decision that was the subject of the petition as "a dispute between the State of Alaska and the Native Village of Kaltag—a federally recognized tribe."[52] For those reasons, it is no surprise that the Court denied the petition.[53]

Twelve

In 1981 Professor John Angell, the director of the Justice Center at the University of Alaska Anchorage, surveyed available data regarding law enforcement in fifty-five communities that the Ninety-second Congress or the secretary of the interior had designated as Native villages for the purposes of ANCSA. Angell summarized his conclusions as follows:

> In addition to the influence of the customary perspectives concerning right and wrong on behavior, traditional practices for dealing with deviants also influence the way Native communities deal with present day deviancy.
>
> . . .
>
> The broader community became involved only after the behavior of an aggressor was perceived as a substantial threat to the entire community. Repeated acts of community-damaging misbehavior were commonly handled by serious discussions between elders of the community and the wayward person. Several such discussions — or warnings — usually preceded any overt action against the person. People who engaged in unacceptable behavior were tolerated until their cumulative behavior became a basis for direct action. When the day of reckoning was reached — often after several years of tolerating misconduct — action was taken. In such cases the person might be banished from the community.
>
> The federal and state constitutions that have been imposed on the Natives hamper continued use of banishment; however, the influence of this traditional way of handling unacceptable behavior is apparent in the present day procedures for handling deviancy in some communities. Native communities still initially dispose of most cases of minor deviancy themselves. The normal practice involves a village council accepting referrals from the village police and rendering decisions about the disposition of the accused. For first offenses, the offender is almost inevitably issued a warning.
>
> Where the case involves a matter that causes widespread concern, the council may call a meeting of all village people and a consensus is reached on the appropriate course of action ... Repeated misbehavior or misbehavior that is considered extremely offensive is nearly always referred to the Alaska State Troopers.
>
> On occasion, Alaska State Troopers are summoned to villages and presented with someone the villagers wish removed for committing crimes. Upon

> checking the facts, it often becomes apparent that the accusations against a person involve crimes which have occurred over a period of 10 to 15 years, and little evidence of the criminal acts still exists. Even if the evidence is strong statutes of limitation prevent prosecution. Troopers are placed in a difficult position of explaining why it is not possible for them to remove the person from the village.
>
> ...
>
> Native communities have been encouraged to enact their own ordinances for handling situations and behavior the villagers find objectionable. These ordinances usually deal with curfews for people under 18, stray dogs, trash and garbage, the operation of snow machines, consumption of alcohol, and use of citizen band radios ... In many cases these ordinances were adopted in response to suggestions by Alaska State Troopers who visited the various villages and trained village police officers. These troopers persuaded villagers that no enforcement was possible unless written descriptions of the undesirable behavior existed. Many city ordinances have legally questionable provisions. Some are saliently unconstitutional. Since nearly all villages are second class cities, the use of improperly constructed ordinances places the municipalities in a vulnerable position of liability for damages.[1]

In other words, while the Native residents of the surveyed communities were subject to the criminal jurisdiction of the State of Alaska, day-to-day life in those communities was little different from what J.B. Henderson, the BIA teacher in Noatak, described in 1933, except that some communities now had "village police officers."

Who were those officers?

As will be described, by 1981 residents in more than one hundred Native villages had incorporated municipal governments pursuant to Alaska law. In a number of those communities, the city councils used money they received from the Alaska Legislature to hire police officers. In other communities money from the BIA was used for that purpose.

For example, Nunapitchuk is a community on the Kuskokwim River twenty-five miles downriver from Bethel. In 1939 Assistant Secretary of the Interior Oscar Chapman approved a constitution for an organization called the Native Village of Nunapitchuk that "a group of Eskimos having the common bond of living together in the Village of Nunapitchuk" had submitted pursuant to section 1 of Public Law No. 74-538 and section 16 of the IRA. In 1977 Robert Nick, the president of the village council the constitution had authorized the Yup'ik Eskimo residents of Nunapitchuk to elect, informed the Senate Select Committee on Indian Affairs that "[t]he IRA council hires the village policemen who govern and watch the safety of the people of that community. We have done that for many, many years."[2]

Two years later, in 1979, the Alaska Legislature created the Village Public Safety Officer (VPSO) program to hire residents of Native villages to serve as unarmed law enforcement officers. By 1981 fifty-two VPSOs had been hired.[3,*] But more than half of the more than two hundred communities that had been designated as Native villages for the purposes of ANCSA had no law enforcement presence in the community. However, both in communities that had a law enforcement presence and in communities that did not, the fact that for generations the Native residents of those communities had, of necessity, informally governed themselves would take on a political patina when that reality became increasingly entangled with the ideology of the tribal sovereignty movement.

The year before Professor Angell conducted his survey, in 1980 the Alaska Legislature enacted a statute that authorized residents of an "established village" to vote to prohibit the importation of alcohol into the community,[4] and the residents of seventy-four Native villages voted for prohibition.

When an individual violated the prohibition, the remedy was for a village resident, or, if the village had a VPSO or other law enforcement officer, the VPSO or officer, to report the violation to the Alaska State Troopers and to the district attorney in Bethel, Nome, Kotzebue, or one of the other larger communities where the State maintained a court.[6] But too frequently that was no remedy at all. Here is how in 1985 Paul Longpre, the VPSO in Sleetmute, a Native village on the Kuskokwim River upriver from Bethel, described the situation he confronted:

> I've been doing this job for at least three months now, and I admit that because of alcohol abuse throughout the community that this is the most depressing and discouraging job on earth.
>
> . . .
>
> As VPSO, alone, with the nearest help about 90 miles away, and in regards to alcohol abuse, all I can do is pick up the pieces, so to speak, after the alcohol binge is over, and care for the victims, usually the innocent, young children who are neglected and sometimes abused, older persons, and women, or weaker men who get beat upon by the drunks who the next day no longer have any recollection of their actions.
>
> . . .
>
> This is a community that voted for banning the importation and sale of alcoholic beverages. A law that cannot be enforced most of the time. The booze comes in by way of Red Devil and McGrath [communities on the Kuskokwim River that had liquor stores], stowed away beneath groceries, personal baggage, hidden on a person or mailed in mixed with groceries shipped into the community by a friend or relative.[7]

---

* In 2014 more than a hundred Native villages had a VPSO. As a consequence of low pay and the dangerous nature of the work (in 1986 and 2013 VPSOs were shot to death when they responded to calls for assistance), in 2020 only forty-nine villages did.[5]

When faced with a similar situation, in August 1987 members of the village council in Kipnuk, a Native village on the Kugkaktlik River eighty-five miles southwest of Bethel whose Yup'ik Eskimo residents had voted to prohibit the importation of alcohol,[8] directed the VPSO to search every individual, Native and non-Native, resident and non-resident, when the plane in which he or she had flown to Kipnuk landed at the airstrip. When Michael Fagan, a reporter for the *Tundra Drums* newspaper, visited Kipnuk, he was searched. According to Fagan:

> The search, conducted in a small, heated building located at the airport, required nearly one hour's time. All pockets — in pants, shirt and parka — were emptied for inspection. All pockets in two backpacks were emptied, also. Clothes taken from the backpack were searched, as was a sleeping bag and the reporter's boots. Items as small as a box of wooden matches were also inspected. This reporter also was given a pat-down — much like ones conducted by state-employed law enforcement officers — on the upper body and legs.[9]

When what was happening in Kipnuk became known and he was asked to identify the legal authority that gave the village council in Kipnuk the power to direct the VPSO to conduct searches at the airstrip, John Paul Jones, a spokesperson for the Association of Village Council Presidents, whose membership included Kipnuk, answered that Kipnuk was Indian country within which the village council had the "right to do that."[10]

That was not the view of Alaska Governor Steve Cowper.

In February 1988 Rosita Worl, the special assistant who advised the governor regarding Alaska Native-related matters, informed the chairman of the village council in Kipnuk that the State had

> come to the conclusion that the searches you are conducting are, in all likelihood, not legal, and we cannot assist in violations of the civil rights of persons being subjected to the searches. It does not matter whether the searches are conducted under the authority of a council ordinance or by individuals on their own; as presently carried out, the searches have the same legal problems. Anyone who is and has been involved in these searches has exposed themselves to serious legal problems and liability.
>
> . . .
>
> The state cannot permit its facilities to be used for purposes of doubtful legality. Therefore, should you choose to continue the searches in the same manner, you may not do so on the airport property or in the adjacent buildings owned by the state. State funds, including revenue sharing money, may not be used to support the searches in any way, for example, for use as a payment for the personnel involved in the searches.
>
> We sympathize with your goals, but we cannot allow the state itself to be a party to what may be serious violations of peoples' rights.[11]

In response to Worl's demand that the VPSO stop conducting searches in the building the State owned, the searches were moved to a building the State did not own.[12]

Three months later the Alaska Supreme Court issued its decision in *Native Village of Stevens v. Alaska Management & Planning* in which the Court announced that Congress had not accorded Native residents of Native villages "sovereign tribal status." Another two months later the *Anchorage Daily News* reported:

> Gov. Steve Cowper says he supports Native efforts to increase local control in rural Alaska. But that support doesn't extend to creation of tribal governments with authority equal to the state's. Cowper says he wants to encourage creation of new village courts and councils that would meet the need for traditional forms of local government while operating under state law. "The traditional way may well have worked better than the way we work it right now," Cowper said in a recent interview. "But everyone in the village has to be able to vote and be entitled to benefits. The problem with tribal sovereignty is that it's exclusive."
>
> . . .
>
> Cowper says he would like to find ways to 'legitimize' efforts already under way in the Bush to re-establish tribal courts for local civil and criminal cases. "Within the confines of the Alaska Constitution, we think that communities ought to assume responsibility for solving their own problems," Cowper said. "But there have got to be some rules. As the word gets around that the state is just looking the other way, people will be tempted to set up systems that we don't necessarily want." Cowper said he will seek legislation if necessary to find alternatives to the existing system of municipalities and regional state courts in the Bush.
>
> Native rights lawyers say Cowper appears to be trying to have it both ways, to protect the distinctive Native culture of the Bush with color-blind institutions. "Most of my clients have philosophical problems with having to knuckle under to the state," said Bob Anderson of the Native American Rights Fund. "They were here first, and they already have organizations that serve their needs."[13]

That October Governor Cowper spoke at the 1988 AFN convention whose theme—"We Are Sovereign"—demonstrated the extent to which, since the AFN had sponsored a workshop on the subject during the 1982 convention, convention delegates had embraced the ideology of the tribal sovereignty movement.

As has been described, when he had been asked during the 1986 gubernatorial election what his position on tribal sovereignty was, candidate Cowper had said he had no "problem with a tribal government or a tribal organization rendering services to the public through contractual means" but he did not "think that it would be in anybody's best interest to set up independent jurisdictional units which are not answerable to anybody except the federal government."

1988 Alaska Federation of Natives Convention. Mike Mathers/Fairbanks Daily News-Miner, Alaska & Polar Regions Collections, University of Alaska Fairbanks.

In his speech to the AFN convention Governor Cowper expressed that same view by equating "local control," which he told the convention delegates he was committed to giving residents of Kipnuk and other Native villages more of, with "sovereignty." As a policy statement the governor released after the speech explained: "State government will support initiatives to strengthen local government and empower people at the local level. The State believes this can be done under the Alaska State Constitution and by adapting existing state institutions to meet these objectives."

That attempt at appeasement was unavailing, since, as the *Associated Press* reported, "The new policy statement outlines a more limited concept of local authority than that sought by many sovereignty advocates" who "contend the Alaska Constitution has no authority to define the powers they seek and that federal law developed over the years in dealing with Indian tribes in the Lower 48 will be the basis for Native self-government in this state."[14]

Governor Cowper could have ordered Alaska State Troopers to arrest the VPSO in Kipnuk. But he decided to avoid a physical confrontation. However, five months after the AFN convention in another Native village on the Yukon-Kuskokwim River Delta, a situation arose that demonstrated that the misguided belief in the legal validity of the ideology that the leaders of the tribal sovereignty movement and the attorneys who advised them had spent seven years encouraging had the potential to get both people who believed what they had been told and Alaska State Troopers seriously hurt or worse.

Tununak is community located fifty-nine miles northwest of Kipnuk. In 1939 "a group of Eskimos having the common bond of living together in the Village of Tununak" submitted to the secretary of the interior a constitution for an organization called the Native Village of Tununak that Assistant Secretary of the Interior Oscar Chapman approved pursuant to section 1 of Public Law No. 74-538 and section 16 of the IRA.[15] In 1971 the Ninety-second Congress designated Tununak as a Native village for the purposes of ANCSA, and in 1975 the three hundred Yup'ik Eskimo residents of Tununak incorporated a second class city under the laws of the State of Alaska.

In April 1989 an Alaska State Trooper stationed in Bethel flew to Tununak to arrest two residents, Leo Kanrilak and Peter Pitka, for violating commercial fishing regulations. Both men resisted arrest; Pitka because he said that the members of an elders' council that had been organized in Tununak had told him that his fishing violation would be handled by a court in the village that recently had been created. Pitka believed that because when the elders' council had been organized the members announced that henceforth Tununak was "sovereign."

When the trooper asked the VPSO in Tununak to assist him in arresting Kanrilak and Pitka and the VPSO refused, the trooper flew back to Bethel.

Three days later he returned accompanied by five other troopers commanded by Corporal Simon Brown. Peter Pitka was not home. But Leo Kanrilak was, and when two troopers told him he was under arrest, Kanrilak resisted. During the melee that ensued, Kanrilak was handcuffed, and to stop him from kicking the troopers hobbled Kanrilak's feet with a rope.

When the troopers began walking Kanrilak to the airstrip, they were surrounded by a crowd of men angry that Kanrilak had been arrested by troopers who were in Tununak without permission from the elders' council. The confrontation escalated, and according to Corporal Brown, "If it had been just those two troopers, either there would have been troopers hurt or there would have been citizens hurt." But Brown arrived at the scene and talked the crowd down. With Leo Kanrilak in tow, the troopers completed the walk to the airstrip and flew Kanrilak to jail in Bethel.[16]

Thirteen

In 1956 the delegates who attended the Alaska Constitutional Convention included in the Alaska Constitution fifteen sections — collectively denoted Article X — that were devoted to local government.

Section 3 provided that "the entire State shall be divided into boroughs, organized and unorganized." Section 4 provided that in each organized borough an elected assembly would be the governing body. Section 6 provided that the Alaska Legislature would function as the governing body in an unorganized borough. And section 7 provided that "cities shall be incorporated in a manner prescribed by law, and shall be part of the borough in which they are located."

Those sections of Article X were written by a seven-member Local Government Committee.

When Article X was discussed on the floor of the convention, John Rosswog, the chairman of the Local Government Committee, explained that "the committee, being from all over Alaska, knowing its problems in the thinly populated areas and in the smaller cities and also in the larger cities, we tried to fit this proposal to each section."[1]

The members of the committee from the "thinly populated areas" were John Cross, a non-Native bush pilot from Kotzebue, and Maynard Londborg, a non-Native clergyman from Unalakleet. Since most residents of both communities were Inupiat Eskimos, in 1971 the Ninety-second Congress would designate Kotzebue and Unalakleet as Native villages for the purposes of ANCSA.

In 1939 "a group of Eskimos having the common bond of living together in the Village of Kotzebue" and "a group of Eskimos having the common bond of living together in the Village of Unalakleet" submitted to the secretary of the interior constitutions for organizations called the Native Village of Kotzebue and the Native Village of Unalakleet that Assistant Secretary of the Interior Oscar Chapman approved pursuant to section 1 of Public Law No. 74-538 and section 16 of the IRA.[2]

The constitutions authorized the Inupiat Eskimo residents of Kotzebue and Unalakleet to elect village councils that by 1956 had functioned for almost twenty years as the local government in both communities even though neither council had the legal authority to do so.

Nevertheless, throughout the discussion that preceded the vote to include Article X in the Alaska Constitution, Delegates Cross and Londberg made no mention of that fact. Nor did any other delegate mention that in most of the more than two hundred communities that would be within the boundaries of the new boroughs, and that the

Ninety-second Congress or the secretary of the interior later would designate as Native villages for the purposes of ANCSA, a village council that had been authorized by a constitution that had been approved pursuant to section 1 of Public Law No. 74-538 and section 16 of the IRA or a "traditional" village council that had no legal imprimatur were the only forms of local government. Instead, the delegates assumed that the residents of those communities would incorporate municipal governments.*

In anticipation that they would, a year later two members of the Territorial Legislature who had been delegates to the Constitutional Convention, Victor Fischer, who also had been a member of the Local Government Committee, and John Coghill, introduced a bill that the legislature enacted as the Village Incorporation Act.[3]

Section 2 of the act explained that its purpose was "to provide for limited self-government through the establishment of incorporated villages in rural areas where the local residents are unable to bear the financial burden of supporting an incorporated city or other type political subdivision as is now provided by law, but do desire to undertake some of the obligations and burdens generally assumed at the local level." The act authorized the residents of a village to petition for incorporation, and when the petition was approved, to elect a city council empowered to adopt ordinances for impounding dogs, establishing a curfew, regulating the use of intoxicating beverages, and establishing a sales tax.[5]

In 1959 when Alaska entered the union, the Alaska Legislature amended the Village Incorporation Act to designate incorporated villages as "cities of the fourth class" and expand the authority of the city councils to include adopting ordinances that prohibited "drunkenness, gambling, houses or places of ill fame," as well as disorderly conduct. The amendments authorized a city council to maintain a "village jail," and gave a "village magistrate" jurisdiction to enforce the council's ordinances by imposing fines of up to $25 and jail sentences not to exceed five days.[6]

Between January 1959 when Alaska entered the union and December 1971 when the Ninety-second Congress enacted ANCSA, sixty-eight communities that Congress or the secretary of the interior would designate as Native villages for the purposes of ANCSA incorporated municipal governments pursuant to either the Village Incorporation Act or other Alaska laws that authorized the incorporation of municipal governments.[7]

Because Alaska Senators Ted Stevens and Mike Gravel, Alaska Representative Nick Begich, and the other members of the Ninety-second Congress that enacted ANCSA assumed that the residents of all Native villages would incorporate a municipal government, they included section 14(c)(3) in ANCSA, which required each

---

* The delegates included Marvin "Muktuk" Marston who during the Second World War had organized Yup'ik and Inupiat Eskimo men in more than sixty villages located on the coast of the Bering, Chukchi, and Beaufort Seas into units of the Alaska Territorial Guard. In *Men of the Tundra*, the book in which he described doing so, Marston noted, "During 1943, 1944, and 1945, I traveled the Arctic constantly."[4] As a consequence of those travels, Marston would have been familiar with how local government worked in the communities he visited. But he made no mention of it during the discussion that preceded the vote to approve Article X.

village corporation to which the secretary of the interior conveyed title to the surface estate of land pursuant to ANCSA to reconvey "to any Municipal Corporation in the Native village or to the state in trust for any municipal corporation established in the Native village in the future" its title to the surface estate of not less than 1,280 acres consisting of "the improved land on which the Native village is located," as well as "additional land as is necessary for community expansion, and appropriate rights-of-way for public use, and other foreseeable community needs."

No representative of the AFN, the Native associations that would be listed in section 7(a) of ANCSA, or of any other Native organization objected to the Ninety-second Congress including section 14(c)(3) in ANCSA. The land reconveyance process that section 14(c)(3) mandated was noncontroversial, and between 1971 and 1982, thirty-six more communities that the Ninety-second Congress or the secretary of the interior had designated as Native villages for the purposes of ANCSA incorporated municipal governments.[8]

One of those communities was Akiachak, a Native village on the Kuskokwim River eighteen miles upriver from Bethel.

In 1948 "a group of Eskimos having the common bond of living together in Akiachak" submitted to the secretary of the interior a constitution for an organization called the Akiachak Native Community that Assistant Secretary of the Interior William Warne approved pursuant to section 1 of Public Law No. 74-538 and section 16 of the IRA. The constitution authorized the Yup'ik Eskimo residents of Akiachak to elect a village council.[9] The constitution also included the boilerplate text the BIA had instructed the teachers in its schools to include in the constitutions that authorized the village council "to control the use by members or nonmembers of any reserve set aside by the federal Government for the community and to keep order in the reserve." But as was the situation in most of the communities for which constitutions were approved, the secretary of the interior did not withdraw any land within and surrounding Akiachak as a reserve.

In 1974 when the several hundred adult residents of Akiachak voted to incorporate a second class city, the individual who was most influential in persuading them to do so was Willie Kasayulie.

In 1974 twenty-three years old, after graduating from the BIA grade school in Akiachak, Kasayulie had attended BIA boarding schools, first a junior high school in southeast Alaska, and then the Chemawa Indian School in Oregon. Taking advantage of a federal program for disadvantaged Native American students, in 1968 Kasayulie transferred to a high school in Vermont, from which he graduated in 1971.[10] He then returned to Akiachak where, because he could read and write English while many members of the village council could not, he became involved in council activities.

Three years later he was instrumental in incorporating a municipal government in Akiachak whose principal attraction was that it enabled the city council to receive municipal assistance, revenue-sharing, and grant monies from the state.

That created a situation in which Akiachak had a village council that operated under the auspices of the constitution Assistant Secretary Warne had approved in 1948 and a city council. In 1983 Kasayulie decided that the city council should be disbanded so that Akiachak could be governed exclusively by a "tribal government." He was educated to that view by David Case, Michael Walleri, and the other tribal sovereignty advocates who spoke at the workshop on tribal sovereignty that the AFN sponsored during its October 1982 convention, the conference the AFN hosted in March 1983, and at the meeting in Anchorage in May 1983 at which the United Tribes of Alaska was organized. According to Kasayulie, "In going to meetings and workshops we heard a lot of talk of sovereignty ... During the UTA convention, I made a comment: if the villages were to practice sovereignty, it's up to the community to decide."[11]

At Kasayulie's urging, in September 1983 the members of the Akiachak city council resigned. Two months later when he was asked what his objection was to the municipal government he had been instrumental in creating, Kasayulie explained,

> Tribal governments establish their membership under protection of federal law. That membership consists of Natives born in the community. Under state laws, anybody can be a member. All they have to do is live in the community for thirty days and they can vote in the city council and run for office. One example we use to make our people understand is the city of Bethel. When it was first organized as a city government, all of the council members were Native people. Now it has really changed. There are only two Natives out of seven council members. We realized that eventually there would be people living in our community who were non-Native. We had to do something to protect our language, our culture, and our lifestyle.[12]

Because Bethel is the administrative center for the fifty-six Native villages on the Yukon-Kuskokwim River Delta, non-Natives employed by the BIA, the Indian Health Service, and other federal and state agencies reside there, as do non-Natives of diverse ethnicities (Albanian, African American, Korean, etc.) attracted to the jobs and other economic opportunities that an administrative center generates. But as Kasayulie knew as well as anyone, there was no reason for anyone to move to Akiachak other than the schoolteachers who periodically cycled through the community. For that reason, as recently as 2010, of Akiachak's 627 residents, 603 (96.1 percent) were of Yup'ik Eskimo descent. That suggests that Kasayulie's actual motivation for wanting to dissolve the municipal government in Akiachak was his allegiance to the ideology of the tribal sovereignty movement about which in 1983 he had only recently been educated.

When Mark Lewis, the commissioner of the Alaska Department of Community and Regional Affairs, learned that the members of Akiachak city council had resigned, he informed Kasayulie, who by then was chairman of the village council, that the only way a municipal government could be dissolved was by following the procedure for doing so in title 29 of the Alaska Statutes.[13] However, even though, because that procedure had not been followed, the municipal government in Akiachak still existed, because there was no city council there was no one to administer $450,000 the Alaska Legislature had appropriated to the city of Akiachak in the form of municipal assistance and revenue-sharing, and grants to construct a water and sewer system, a fire station, and a fish hatchery. For that reason, Lewis refused to allow those funds to be disbursed.[14]

Having been informed of what title 29 required, in 1984 Kasayulie and more than sixty other Akiachak residents petitioned the Alaska Local Boundary Commission to allow registered voters in Akiachak to vote to dissolve the municipal government.[15] But the commission denied the petition, first because debts the municipal government owed remained outstanding,[16] and then because an attorney in the Department of Law advised that title 29 limited dissolution to municipal governments in communities that had become ghost towns.[17]

Represented by NARF attorney Robert Anderson, in December 1985 Kasayulie and the other petitioners appealed the Boundary Commission's decision to the Alaska Superior Court in Bethel.[18] In 1986 when he lost there, Kasayulie turned to Johne Binkley.

A non-Native from Fairbanks who had moved to Bethel to operate a freight business, in 1984 Binkley had narrowly defeated the Yup'ik Eskimo incumbent to win election to the Alaska House of Representatives from an election district that included Bethel and twenty-one surrounding communities, including Akiachak. In November 1986 Binkley was elected to the Alaska Senate from an election district that also included Akiachak.

In January 1987 when the Alaska Legislature convened, Senator Binkley introduced SB 50, a bill whose enactment would amend title 29 to authorize the Local Boundary Commission to allow an election to dissolve a municipality if the members of the commission determined that the dissolution was in the "best interest of the state." The bill also authorized the assets of a municipal government that had been dissolved to be given to a village council that had been organized pursuant to a constitution the secretary of the interior had approved pursuant to section 1 of Public Law No. 74-538 and section 16 of the IRA.

Two months before Senator Binkley introduced SB 50, Steve Cowper had been elected to succeed Bill Sheffield as governor of Alaska. In October 1988 Governor Cowper would tell the delegates who attended that year's AFN convention that "initiatives to strengthen local government and empower people at the local level" should be undertaken "under the Alaska State Constitution and by adapting existing state institutions to meet these objectives." But if that is what he believed, Cowper inexplicably did not care if "existing state institutions" were dissolved in order to clear the way for village councils operated by Willie Kasayulie and other tribal sovereignty advocates who wanted nothing to do with the State of Alaska and its institutions.

After the Senate Committee on Community and Regional Affairs amended SB 50 to require the assets of a municipality that had been dissolved to be transferred to the State, Jan Faiks, the president of the Alaska Senate, asked Grace Schaible, whom Governor Cowper had appointed attorney general, how the legislature's passage of SB 50 would affect the tribal sovereignty situation. Schaible responded:

> We believed that the original version of SB 50 did have sovereignty implications because of a section that would have permitted the assets of a dissolved municipality to be conveyed to a Native council formed under the Indian Reorganization Act. We conveyed our opinion to the first committee on referral, the [Community & Regional Affairs] committee, which deleted that section ... As to the balance of [the bill] we do not believe it would affect the current sovereignty debate. It is true that several villages are looking at dissolution as a first step toward establishment of a Native council as a substitute local government, but we believe that that view is based on the mistaken assumption that a Native council could succeed to the assets and powers of a state-chartered municipality. Without that possibility, a Native council occupies the same legal position whether or not it coexists with a municipal government: It cannot exercise governmental powers or control public assets. Thus making it easier for a municipality to dissolve ... does not make it easier for a Native council to claim governmental or sovereign status.[19]

That sanguine explanation demonstrated an astounding lack of understanding of the agenda of Willie Kasayulie and other tribal sovereignty activists.

Nine months later David Hoffman, whom Governor Cowper had appointed commissioner of the Department of Community and Regional Affairs, went even further, telling the Alaska House of Representatives that his department "firmly" supported the legislature's enactment of SB 50 because the bill "clearly speaks" to "the needs of communities desiring dissolution in favor of a return to unincorporated status."[20]

Since the governor and his attorney general did not oppose the bill, and since most members of the legislature, most of whom had spent little, if any, time in communities such as Akiachak, did not care enough about the potential adverse consequences for the future of the state as a cohesive multi-racial polity to educate themselves regarding what those consequences might be, SB 50 passed both houses without controversy.

In May 1988 Governor Cowper signed SB 50[21] into law even though two months later, seemingly oblivious that his signing had furthered the opposite result, he would announce that while he wanted "to see if we can't arrive at forms of local government more conducive to villages," those forms had "to be under state guidelines."[22]

After SB 50 was enacted, Senator Binkley, who was neither an attorney nor a historian knowledgeable about the history of Congress's Alaska Native-related enactments, explained why he had made it possible for the residents of Akiachak and any other Native village who wished to do so to dissolve their municipal government:

> Historically, Alaska's Native peoples have always had a system of self government within their tribes and villages that had a strong cultural basis. Over

the years, layer upon layer of new government structures have been added so that now, whether consciously or by accident, we have created a very complicated system. Today, in many of our communities you can see: a state municipality, an IRA council, a traditional council, and a village corporation created under the Alaska Native Claims Settlement Act. But somehow the people can get lost in this maze, and what many Alaska Natives are trying to do is to regain control and maintain their strong ties to their culture and the land. Local control means that people need to decide which governmental entity is going to serve them best. That, I believe, is up to the community to decide. And that's why I introduced and saw into passage legislation which allows communities to dissolve their municipal government and choose some other form of government, if they desire.[23]

In February 1989 Willie Kasayulie filed a new petition that asked the Local Boundary Commission to allow registered voters in Akiachak to vote to dissolve their municipal government.[24] After the members of the commission decided that dissolution would be in the "best interest of the state,"* in January 1990 an election was held and by a vote of 122 to 7 the municipal government in Akiachak was dissolved.[25] The month after the vote was certified. Commissioner Hoffman publicly opined that

> Akiachak's bold move to replace its municipal form of government may or may not work for others, but it holds valuable lessons for those seeking a local government that works best in their community … Akiachak's quest for a single local government — the tribal government — began more than six years ago. Community leaders had become concerned by what they perceived as a deterioration of community values. They also felt that they were virtually unable to control persons who had violated local laws and customs.
>
> The leaders decided that having both a municipal government and a tribal government was contributing to local problems. They felt that having both was confusing, inefficient, and caused tension in the community.

* How was it in the "best interest of the state" to allow a municipal government in which all Akiachak residents could participate and whose city council was required to comply with the bill of rights in the U.S. and Alaska Constitutions to be replaced by a local government in which only the Yup'ik Eskimo residents could participate and whose village council was not required to comply with those constitutional safeguards? When it passed SB 50, the Alaska Senate adopted a Letter of Intent that had been written by the Finance Committee, which Senator Binkley co-chaired.[26] The letter directed the Local Boundary Commission to find that the dissolution of a municipal government was in the "best interest of the state" if (1) the municipal government had been abandoned, (2) "alternative entities" in the community could deliver essential services, and (3) "dissolution would not be adverse to the interests of the region in which the city is located and the state" because the dissolution would not reduce a "viable tax base" or require the State to be responsible for schools the municipality had been operating.[27] Akiachak had no tax base, and the State already was operating the grade and high schools.

> They also believed their municipal government was hamstrung by senseless rules and procedures. Akiachak decided that having a single federally chartered tribal government would help the community return to a more traditional way of doing things and would promote traditional community values.
>
> Akiachak's tribal leaders promise a local government system that is responsive both in terms of timeliness and community values and not dependent on outsiders. Whether all that Akiachak hopes for can be obtained remains to be seen, but clearly they have taken a major step toward their goal of effective self-governance ... Willie Kasayulie and the other leaders of Akiachak should be saluted for developing their own vision of how local governance should work—and then laboring six years to implement that vision.[28]

In 1972 the Alaska Legislature had created the Department of Community and Regional Affairs in order to "render maximum state assistance to government at the community and regional level."[29] The legislature did so at the urging of Governor Bill Egan who had argued that "the time is now ripe with the adoption of the Alaska Native Claims Settlement bill" for the Local Boundary Commission to divide the unorganized borough into "administrative units" and within the boundaries of each unit provide for "local self rule."[30]

To achieve that objective the governor appointed Byron Mallott, the former mayor of the city of Yakutat and former director of the Rural Affairs Agency, to head the new department, and in that guise Mallott and the state employees he supervised set about facilitating "local self rule" by encouraging the incorporation of municipal governments.

The fact that almost twenty years later one of Mallott's successors as commissioner would celebrate the dissolution of a municipal government while two years earlier the governor for whom the commissioner worked had told the delegates who attended the 1988 AFN convention that "existing state institutions" that operated "under the Alaska State Constitution" were the means they should employ to "strengthen local government and empower people at the local level" demonstrates the vacillation and disarray that—under the leadership of governors from both political parties—have characterized the State of Alaska's response to the ever-escalating demands of the tribal sovereignty movement.

The dissolution of the municipal government in Akiachak having established the precedent, by 1997 the residents of five other Native villages on the Yukon-Kuskokwim River Delta—Atmautluak, Kasigluk, Newtok, Tuluksak, and Tununak—had dissolved their municipal governments.

The residents of the twenty-seven other Native villages on the delta that had a municipal government did not dissolve theirs, and their decisions not to do so derailed a related project Willie Kasayulie had begun more than a decade earlier.

In July of 1984, the year that he first petitioned the Local Boundary Commission to allow registered voters in Akiachak to vote to dissolve their municipal government,

Willie Kasayulie. Tundra Times Collection. Courtesy of Ukpeagvik Inupiat Corporation and Tuzzy Consortium Library of Utqiagvik, Alaska.

Kasayulie hosted a meeting in Akiachak during which participants from Akiachak and the nearby villages of Akiak and Tuluksak organized the Yupiik Nation, which Kasayulie envisioned would be a regional tribal government that would operate its own schools and courts and regulate hunting and trapping on land within the nation's jurisdiction.[31] In October the members of the nascent organization adopted a constitution.

In 1986 the *Tundra Times* reported: "An important current goal of the organization, said Chief Kasayulie, is expanding the number of member villages. His dream is to see all the Yup'ik villages, wherever they are in the state, joined together under the banner of the Yupiit Nation."[32]

Setting about to achieve that objective, in January of that year Kasayulie hosted a meeting in Akiachak of the Yupiik Nation that individuals from twenty-one Native villages on the Yukon-Kuskokwim River Delta attended.[33] A month later the members of the village councils in Atmautlauk and Kasigluk (whose residents later would dissolve their municipal governments) voted to join the organization.[34] When the members of the village council in Nunapitchuk did so as well, Kasayulie jubilantly announced, "That's a total of six, only forty-nine more to go."[35]

By September 1987 another thirteen villages had joined.

But that was the apogee.

One of the conundrums of the tribal sovereignty movement of which Willie Kasayulie and other leaders of the movement make no mention is that, while they assert that village councils are "sovereign governments," those governments have no source of revenue other than whatever funds the BIA and other federal agencies deem to make available. The Yupiit Nation being no exception, Kasayulie applied to the Administration for Native Americans, an agency inside the federal Department of Health and Human Services, for a three-year $150,000 per year grant.

The grant application explained that the money would be spent to create a regional "tribal government" that, "rather than the State of Alaska, will be able to rule on matters concerning Yup'ik persons." The application described the need for such a government as follows:

> Among the 19 member villages of the Yupiit Nation ... there is growing concern about losing control over our home lands which include Native village townsites, allotments, traditional and current hunting, fishing, and food gathering lands, historical and cemetery sites, and ANCSA lands. We also see an erosion of our control over renewable resources as federal and state agencies write laws and regulations without taking our needs and wishes into consideration. We are apprehensive about the erosion of our cultural identity and our right to self-determination. We see a continued influx of non-Natives into the region, and we're concerned that in the next 20–25 years their numbers and influence will dominate our own and that they might then take over our governance.[36]

Rather than providing funding for three years, the Administration for Native Americans approved a one-year $119,000 grant. According to the *Tundra Drums*, the money was spent on "salaries for two Yupiit Nation positions, a project director and a secretary/bookkeeper," as well as to pay office and "conference-related" expenses. The *Tundra Drums* also reported that additional funding was "contingent on whether Yupiit Nation can attract further member villages."[37]

But no other villages joined, and while the Yupiit Nation would continue to exist as the paper organization it had been from the outset, in December 1990 Kasayulie resigned as the organization's titular head because, as he explained when he did so, "I had done what I wanted to do; that is, get people excited and talking about regional tribal government."[38]

Even the paper organization soon ceased to exist. But, as Kasayulie noted, orchestrating the dissolution of the municipal government in Akiachak and creating the Yupiik Nation did get people in Native villages throughout the Yukon-Kuskokwim River Delta talking about tribal governments and in several villages asserting the "sovereignty" Kasayulie told them they had always possessed.

In 1980 the Ninety-sixth Congress designated all federally-owned public land on the Yukon-Kuskokwim River Delta as the Yukon Delta National Wildlife Refuge. In September 1987 U.S. Fish and Wildlife Service enforcement agents cited Edward Berlin and Ambrose Aguchak, two Yup'ik Eskimo residents of Atmautluak, a Native village on the Kuskokwim River twenty miles downriver from Bethel, for having illegally harvested two moose. The agents also confiscated the meat. Seven months earlier Atmautluak had joined the Yupiit Nation and had created a Traditional Elders Court. When Berlin and Ambrose complained to the Elders Court that their moose meat had been confiscated, the court ordered the refuge manager to return the meat or pay a $10,980 fine and to "submit to ten hours of instruction by the Elders Council of Atmautluak so that he may recognize the jurisdictional boundaries of Atmautluak."[39] The refuge manager ignored the edict, the citation against Berlin was dismissed, Aguchak pleaded no contest in the district court in Bethel, and in 1996 the residents of Atmautluak voted to dissolve their municipal government.

Quinhagak is a Native village located at the mouth of the Kanektok River on the shore of Kuskokwim Bay seventy-one miles southwest of Bethel. In 1948 "a group of Eskimos having a common bond of living together in the Village of Kwinhagak (sic)" submitted to the secretary of the interior a constitution for an organization called the Native Village of Kwinhagak that Assistant Secretary of the Interior William Warne approved pursuant to section 1 of Public Law No. 74-538 and section 16 of the IRA. The constitution authorized the two hundred Yup'ik Eskimo residents of Quinhagak to elect a village council.[40] In 1975 Quinhagak residents incorporated a municipal government. While the municipal government was not dissolved, in 1987 Quinhagak joined the Yupiik Nation.

Quinhagak residents fished commercially for salmon that spawn in the Kanektok River while upriver from the community several non-Natives operated sport fishing lodges. Because of low escapements, during the 1987 fishing season the Alaska Department of Fish & Game (ADF&G) closed the Kanektok River to commercial fishing but continued to allow sportfishing. Several weeks before U.S. Fish & Wildlife Service enforcement agents cited Atmautluak residents Edward Berlin and Ambrose Aguchak for illegally shooting two moose, several ADF&G biologists came to Quinhagak. According to the *Anchorage Daily News*, residents "angry about the closure" of the Kanetok River to commercial fishing held the biologists "hostage in the community hall for most of a day," although they eventually were released unharmed.[41]

A year and a half later, in March 1989, in the Kilbuck Mountains east of Quinhagak, Alaska State Trooper Scott Gibbons discovered the carcasses of thirty caribou that had been shot in an area of the Yukon Delta National Wildlife Refuge that had been closed to hunting to allow the caribou herd to rebuild. Gibbons followed the tracks of the snow machines the hunters had ridden to Quinhagak where he identified the individuals who were responsible. When Gibbons confiscated their snow machines, sleds and rifles, and the caribou meat they had in their possession, he was confronted by as many as a hundred angry Quinhagak residents. Gibbons called Trooper Captain Glen Godfrey at the trooper office in Bethel for back-up, locked the snow machines, sleds, and caribou meat in a warehouse, and locked the rifles in the evidence locker in the building city of Quinhagak police officers used as their headquarters.

Accompanied by three other troopers and a VPSO named Max Olick, Godfrey flew to Quinhagak and tried to calm the crowd by convening a meeting at the community hall. While the meeting was underway, the snow machines, sleds, and meat disappeared from the warehouse and the rifles were stolen from the evidence locker.[42] However, Olick diffused the situation by negotiating the return of the items that had disappeared and been stolen and persuading the individuals who Gibbons had tried to arrest to allow themselves to be taken into custody.[43]

A month later when Alaska State Troopers arrested Leo Kanrilak in Tununak, they were surrounded by a crowd of men angry that the troopers had entered the village without the permission of the elder's council.

After the near violence in Quinhagak and Tununak, Alaska Commissioner of Public Safety Arthur English flew to Bethel and held a press conference in which Trooper Colonel Jack Jordan, the director of the Division of Fish and Wildlife Protection, participated. Commissioner English told the *Tundra Drums* and KYUK, the public radio station in Bethel, that "there are certain laws, rules and regulations that we have to enforce, regardless of the sovereignty issues ... When those rules and regulations have been violated and the court of Alaska issues a warrant for some individual, we have no choice but to go in and enforce the warrant," to which Colonel Jordan added: "We're not trying to make any comments about whether they should be a sovereign nation or not. We're just saying that until it gets through the courts, we have a job to do."[44]

In Tununak that message initially was received.

After the confrontation that the troopers' arrest of Leo Kanrilak provoked, Mike Albert, the chairman of the elder's council, announced that "we want no interference" and "the state out."[45] But five months after the press conference, the village council in Tununak requested trooper assistance when an intoxicated resident named Bernard Lincoln began firing a rifle through the village. When they arrived in Tununak, in addition to arresting Lincoln, the troopers arrested Peter Pitka and Leo Kanrilak (for having violated the terms of his release after his arrest the previous March), a Tununak resident named Christopher Oscar who had threatened two other residents with a handgun, and Phillip James, who was arrested for sexually abusing a minor.

According to the *Tundra Drums*, when they were making those arrests Mike Albert "advised investigating troopers that although the tribal council wished to handle the majority of misdemeanor problems in the village, the council recognized a need for state trooper assistance in serious matters. Albert added that the council was becoming concerned some persons may be taking advantage of the council's attempts at handling problems in the village and he wanted it understood the council would request Alaska State Trooper assistance in the future for serious problems."[46]

While that may have been Albert's view at the time, in Tununak the tribal sovereignty movement continued to gain supporters and in 1994 Tununak residents dissolved their municipal government (although the dissolution would not become official until 1997).

In September of that year, Alaska State Trooper Dan Donaldson and another trooper flew to Tununak to arrest a Tununak resident named Jack Evan for having committed the type of crime — sexual assault — with which five years earlier Mike Albert had said the village council wanted trooper assistance. When the troopers arrested Evan and also took another man, Gregory Angaiak, into protective custody after he had threatened suicide, Lawrence Kanrilak, the "tribal" police officer, told Donaldson that he had no authority to take Evan and Angaiak out of Tununak without the permission of the elders council. Donaldson then went to the building in which the elders council had its office and told Peter Pitka, the administrator of the elders council who in 1989 had been one of the men the troopers had flown into Tununak to arrest, and a Caucasian tribal sovereignty activist named Hank Ostrosky, not to interfere with Evan's arrest.

In response, Pitka and Ostrosky ordered Kanrilak to arrest Donaldson. An altercation then ensued during which Donaldson pepper-sprayed Kanrilak.

When Donaldson and the other trooper, with Jack Evan and Gregory Angaiak in tow, reached the airstrip, a dozen members of the elders council surrounded their plane, and Pitka and Ostrosky told the two troopers that they were being charged with trespassing and kidnaping because Tununak was sovereign territory within which the State of Alaska had no authority. Donaldson eventually talked the crowd down, after which Donaldson, the other trooper, and Evan and Angaiak flew to Bethel.[47]

A week later Ostrosky was arrested in Bethel, and a week after that fourteen troopers returned to Tununak and arrested Kanrilak and Pitka. When he was arraigned in the Alaska Superior Court in Bethel, Pitka protested that his "indigenous rights" were being violated.[48]

After their arraignments Kanrilak and Pitka returned to Tununak. When they refused to appear in Bethel for court appearances, in June 1995 troopers returned to Tununak and arrested Kanrilak. Pitka eluded arrest and later told a reporter that he had no intention of turning himself in "because the state of Alaska is a third-party court and they're not supposed to mess with us" because "we have our own jurisdiction, our own territory, and our own tribal law."[49]

Despite that bravado, Pitka was apprehended, after which he and Kanrilak pled no contest to resisting arrest and hindering trooper Donaldson's arrest of Jack Evan.[50]

Fourteen

Throughout recorded history banishment has been employed to rid communities of individuals of whose conduct or political or religious views a majority of the members of a community disapproves.[1]

The code of laws the Babylonian king Hammurabi wrote in 1754 B.C. imposed banishment as the punishment to which a man "guilty of incest with his daughter" was subjected. According to one scholar, "During the Middle Ages, banishment was used by the Franks, the Danes, and other Germanic peoples," and, "As Europe emerged from the Middle Ages, banishment was used ever more frequently, especially in England."[2]

In England between the thirteenth and sixteenth centuries, an accused felon could flee to a designated sanctuary. Once there, if he confessed his guilt and promised to leave the country, the king allowed him to do so. In 1718 the British parliament banished to the American colonies individuals who had committed various crimes. Between that date and the beginning of the American Revolution, 50,000 English, Irish, and Scottish convicts were transported across the Atlantic Ocean by ship, most to Maryland and Virginia.

Banishment also was imposed in the colonies. In 1637 the Massachusetts General Court banished the Puritan minister John Wheelwright because he had espoused heretical religious views. And through the end of the eighteenth century, an individual could not settle in a New England town without the permission of the town selectmen. If after receiving permission a new resident behaved in a manner that a majority of residents deemed opprobrious, he or she was "warned out" and banished. According to historian Michael Zuckerman, "town records continued to be studded with such warnings to the time of the Revolution itself, and constables continued to be paid for the bodily removal of undesirables from the towns."[3]

After the Revolutionary War, the Georgia Legislature banished Georgia residents who had sided with the British.[4] More than half a century later, banishment was a routine punishment in mining camps in the American West. During the California gold rush, for example, in 1850 in Rough and Ready, a mining camp in the Sierra Nevada foothills, a miner caught stealing "was given thirty-nine lashes, after which he was banished, and warned never again to appear in that camp."[5]

In September 1945 when Japan's surrender ended the Second World War, men who had come to Anchorage during the war to work found themselves unemployed. So many so quickly became socially disruptive inebriants that a meeting in the high school auditorium was convened that more than five hundred residents attended and at which a hat was passed to create a "vagrancy fund" that was used to buy miscreants a steamship ticket to Seattle because "the crux of the problem hinges upon ridding Anchorage of its undesirable population."[6] Six hundred dollars were raised, which C.E. Crosswhite, the chief of the Anchorage police department, used to buy nine tickets. "All of the men were taken from the city jail," the *Anchorage Daily Times* reported, where they had been incarcerated for public drunkenness.[7]

Two weeks after the vagrancy fund was created the *Associated Press* reported that "Seattle is fast becoming the dumping ground for roughnecks and criminals being shipped out of Alaska via the so-called 'blue ticket' route," and quoted a city official in Anchorage explaining that "between selective service and the war industries all we got up here was the scrapings. We found some men had prison records or dishonorable discharges. Now we're getting rid of them as fast as we can."[8]

Elsewhere in Alaska, according to Richard Burton, who twice served as the Alaska commissioner of public safety and who began his career in law enforcement in 1954 in Ketchikan, prior to statehood police in Ketchikan and other towns in southeast Alaska rid their communities of undesirables by, as Chief Crosswhite had, buying them a ticket to Seattle.[9] And to the present day, state judges and magistrates banish criminal defendants when they deem doing so appropriate.

In 1985, for example, James Edison, a resident of Marshall, a Native village on the Yukon River, was arrested for driving drunk on his snow machine. After serving a jail sentence Edison was released on probation, with a condition that he not return to Marshall for a year because the mayor had asked Magistrate Craig McMahon to banish Edison because he had a string of misdemeanor convictions for disruptive behavior. The Alaska Court of Appeals subsequently vacated the banishment order on the ground that, based on the particular facts in Edison's case, banishment was not warranted. But the court acknowledged that "there may be situations in which a probationer may reasonably be required to temporarily vacate a specific geographical area that is associated with criminal activity."[10]

And in 2014 when a Superior Court judge in Bethel sentenced a Quinhagak resident named Adolph Rivers who had committed a sexual assault in Quinhagak, he imposed a probation condition that was tantamount to banishment from Quinhagak for the five-year period of probation. In 2018 the Alaska Court of Appeals approved the imposition of that condition.[11]

Given the ubiquity of banishment as a means of social control, it is no surprise that Alaska Natives living in small geographically isolated communities would employ banishment as a means to rid a community of individuals of whose conduct a majority of the residents disapprove.

According to former Commissioner Burton who joined the Alaska State Troopers in 1961, in 1962 when he was sent to the post the troopers had opened in Dillingham, the largest Native village in the Bristol Bay region of southwest Alaska, "My biggest responsibility, the first month, was traveling to all the villages, and meeting with the village councils."[12]

The law enforcement system Burton worked out with the councils worked as follows: when he was called into a village to deal with a crime that under state law was a misdemeanor, Burton let the members of the village council be the judges and decide the sentence. According to Burton:

> For the first offense, there was always an elderly widow in the village to cut wood for, or who needed to have her drinking water hauled. The offender also had to kill and dress meat for her. For second or more serious offenses, the individuals were made to unload the river barge when it delivered fuel to the village. They would have to take the barrels to the individual houses in the village, and this always involved a lot of work. For repeat offenders the penalty was banishment from the village, usually for a year. This is sometimes practiced even today. Most would come into Dillingham. No one from their village would talk to them, or have anything to do with them during the banishment period.[13]

But not every individual who was banished moved to Dillingham. Again according to Burton: "They had this guy they banished in Ekok. I don't remember why exactly, but I think he was a continual problem from drinking. They banished him for a year. He had to live across the Nushagak River by himself. I didn't get involved in it. I just observed it. It was their tradition."[14]

As has been described, after surveying the law enforcement situation in fifty-five Native villages, in 1981 Professor John Angell, the director of the Justice Center at the University of Alaska Anchorage, reported that "the federal and state constitutions that have been imposed on the Natives hamper continued use of banishment; however, the influence of this traditional way of handling unacceptable behavior is apparent in the present day procedures for handling deviancy in some communities."

In 1972 the village council in Venetie, the Gwich'in Athabascan Indian community on the south side of the Brooks Mountain Range in the Alaska interior, prohibited the possession of alcohol. The first two times an individual was caught violating the prohibition he was fined. The third time he was banished. In 1988 the *Anchorage Daily News* reported that "no one knows exactly how many people have been banished from Venetie. Residents say it may be as many as a couple dozen. Some came back; some were never heard from again. One man, who asked that his name not be used, was banished in 1980. He recalled being put on a plane for Fairbanks with no money in his pocket after ignoring two fines and then being caught with a bottle of whiskey. The council sent him off with a letter saying he was welcome to return in six months."[15]

In 1997 William Walters, who the Tanana Chiefs Conference had hired to assist Athabascan Indian residents of Native villages in the Alaska interior in creating courts, reported that over the previous five years the courts had banished eleven individuals. "The power is very rarely invoked," Walters explained, "and in my experience there's always been a series of events that have been very disturbing to the community."[16]

A year later, in 1998, the village council in Perryville, a Native village on the south side of the Alaska Peninsula, banished a Native resident of Perryville named John Tague after he had been arrested for assault. When Tague was released from jail, the council relented and rescinded the banishment order. However, when he returned to Perryville, Tague beat a Perryville resident with a wrench, choked another, and knocked a third unconscious. Tague again was arrested, again was jailed, and again was banished.[17]

In 2004 the village council in Quinhagak banished Adolph Rivers for a year a decade before the Superior Court judge in Bethel did. In 2015 the village council in Togiak, a Native village south of Quinhagak, banished a nonresident suspected of selling drugs and alcohol.[18]

In June 2016 the village council in Nunan Iqua, a Native village at the mouth of the Yukon River, banished a Nunan Iqua resident named Derek Adams who had started a house fire in which three people died. When the members of the village council in Alakanuk, a Native village near Nunan Iqua and in which Adams was living, learned that he had been banished from Nunan Iqua, they banished Adams from Alakanuk. When Adams then moved to Emmonak, another Native village near Nunan Iqua, the village council in that community issued its own banishment order.[19]

A month later in Quinhagak where four residents had overdosed on heroin, the village council banished six individuals who were suspected of having brought the drug into the village.[20] And another five months later, in February 2017 in Allakaket, a Native village on the Koyukuk River in the Alaska interior, the members of the village council convened a community meeting after receiving complaints that four individuals, two Allakaket residents and two nonresidents, had been selling methamphetamine.

According to Pollack Simon, the chairman of the village council, "The elders spoke, the young men spoke, the women spoke," after which, when Simon asked, "Who wants the meth out of this village?" every hand in the room went up. Simon and several dozen other residents then proceeded to the house where the four men, one of whom was believed to be armed, were staying. "We didn't know if we would be shot," Simon later recalled. "We were an unarmed SWAT team. We showed up at their house and escorted them out of town."[21]

Those examples demonstrate that banishment can be an effective means to rid Native villages of individuals whose conduct threatens public safety or violates community norms.

But is banishment lawful?

The U.S. Supreme Court has held that the governing body of a group composed of individuals of Native American descent whose legal status as a federally recognized tribe is unquestioned has authority to banish individuals, both tribal members and nonmembers, from land located within the boundaries of the tribe's reservation whose title the United States owns in trust for the tribe, which Congress, in 18 U.S.C. 1151, has designated as Indian country. As the Court explained in 1990 in its decision in *Duro v. Reina*, a federally recognized tribe possesses the "traditional and undisputed power to exclude persons whom they deem to be undesirable from tribal lands."[22]

But in Alaska, what if—notwithstanding the Alaska Supreme Court's pronouncement in its decision in *John v. Baker*—the Native residents of communities that the Ninety-second Congress or the secretary of the interior has designated as Native villages for the purposes of ANCSA are not members of federally recognized tribes? If they do not have that legal status, village councils in those communities have no governmental authority. And if the Alaska Supreme Court was correct in its decision in *John v. Baker*, does a village council that is the governing body of a federally recognized tribe have governmental authority to banish an individual from land the tribe does not own?

In 2003 when former Alaska Senator Frank Murkowski became governor of Alaska, his attorney general posed that question regarding the authority of the village council in Perryville to banish John Tague.

Perryville was founded in 1912 when Captain Kirtland Perry, the commander of the U.S. Revenue Cutter *Manning*, relocated seventy-eight Aleuts and a Bureau of Education school teacher to a new village site on the south side of the Alaska Peninsula after the Katmai volcano erupted and buried the village in which the Aleuts had been living under volcanic ash.[23]

In 1949 "a group of Natives having the common bond of living together in the Village of Perryville" submitted to the secretary of the interior a constitution for an organization called the Native Village of Perryville (NVP) that Assistant Secretary of the Interior Mastin White approved pursuant to section 1 of Public Law No. 74-538 and section 16 of the IRA. The constitution contained the boilerplate text that the teachers in the BIA schools included in most of the constitutions the secretary of the interior approved, which authorized the Native residents of Perryville to elect a village council that would have authority to "control the use by members or non-members of any reserve set aside by the Federal Government for the Village and to keep order in the Reserve," although no reserve was established at Perryville.[24]

In 1971 the Ninety-second Congress designated Perryville as a Native village for the purposes of ANCSA. And in 1993 Assistant Secretary of the Interior for Indian Affairs Ada Deer included the NVP on the list of Native entities she published in the *Federal Register*.

In 1891 the Fifty-first Congress enacted the Alaska Townsite Act, which authorized the secretary of the interior to convey the legal title to up to 640 acres of public land in and immediately surrounding a town or village in Alaska to a townsite trustee. After the land within the boundaries of a townsite was subdivided into blocks, streets, and house lots, the trustee conveyed legal title to the house lots to the individuals who occupied them.[25] In 1908 the solicitor of the Department of the Interior decided that the Alaska Organic Act, which the Forty-eighth Congress had enacted in 1884, prohibited the townsite trustee from conveying house lots to Alaska Natives.[26]

In response to that decision and at the urging of Territorial Governor George Parks, who believed that encouraging Natives to own land would advance their "progress toward municipal government in their own communities," in 1926 the Sixty-ninth Congress enacted the Native Townsite Act, which authorized the townsite trustee to create townsites in villages "claimed or occupied by Indians or Eskimos of full or mixed blood," subdivide the land within the townsites into blocks, streets, and house lots, and convey the legal title to the house lots to the Native occupants, although the deeds they received prohibited the occupants from selling their lots without the approval of the secretary of the interior.[27]

Pursuant to the Native Townsite Act, in 1969 the townsite trustee surveyed a seventy-eight-acre townsite in Perryville that contained ninety-nine house lots.[28] The townsite trustee conveyed the legal title to forty-one of the house lots to individual occupants or their heirs. However, in 1992 he conveyed the legal title to fifty-eight lots that were unoccupied, plus the land within the townsite that had not been subdivided, to the NVP.[29]

Seven years later, in 1999, John Tague was released from jail and returned to Perryville where he soon was arrested for committing a new series of assaults. When Tague again was incarcerated, the members of the village council adopted a resolution in which they banished Tague "from entering into the Native Village of Perryville for any reason whatsoever."[30]

Like every landowner, the NVP, acting through the village council, could prohibit Tague from trespassing on the land the NVP owned. But the NVP did not own the house lots within the Perryville townsite whose legal title had been conveyed to the individual occupants. It did not own the surface estate of the land surrounding the townsite whose title the secretary of the interior had conveyed to the Oceanside Corporation, the ANCSA village corporation the Native residents of Perryville had incorporated in 1973. And it did not own the surface estate of the 1,280 acres of land, including the airstrip, whose title the Oceanside Corporation had conveyed to the State of Alaska, which, pursuant to section 14(c)(3) of ANCSA, the State held in trust for a municipal government that might be incorporated in the future.

In 2000 when John Tague again was released from jail, concerned that he would ignore the banishment resolution they had adopted, the members of the village council directed the council's attorney to file in the Alaska Superior Court in Anchorage *Native Village of Perryville v. Tague*, a lawsuit that requested "an injunction to permanently enjoin defendant John W. Tague from entering into or remaining within the borders of the Native Village of Perryville." In its complaint the council alleged that it had the "inherent sovereign authority of a tribal government, recognized by Congress under the Indian Tribal Justice Act,* to enact and enforce tribal laws, in-

---

* The Indian Tribal Justice Act, which the One Hundred-third Congress enacted in 1993, authorizes the secretary of the interior to give grants to Indian tribes "for the development, enhancement, and

cluding the right to banish assaultive members," and that "the State of Alaska has the duty to give full force and effect to any tribal ordinance or custom adopted by an Indian tribe, band, or community in the exercise of its authority which it may possess, if not inconsistent with any applicable civil law of the State."[31]

Because his whereabouts were unknown, the village council's attorney did not notify John Tague that the lawsuit had been filed. And because the State of Alaska was not a party, the attorney did not notify Attorney General Bruce Botelho.

After having heard only from the village council's attorney, in March 2001 Superior Court Judge Peter Michalski signed an order that the attorney had written, which stated: "Defendant John W. Tague shall remove himself from the Native Village of Perryville, and shall not reenter or remain within the Village, absent a court order or prior approval of the Perryville IRA Council. Any law enforcement official may assist the plaintiff to enforce this permanent injunction."[32]

In 2003 John Tague returned to Perryville. By chance, an Alaska State Trooper named John Holm flew into the village on the same plane. When he was asked to enforce the order Judge Michalski had signed, Holm asked his superiors for instructions and was told not to do so unless Judge Michalski reaffirmed the validity of the order.

The village council's attorney then filed a motion in the *Native Village of Perryville v. Tague* lawsuit that requested Judge Michalski to issue a writ of assistance.[33] The writ, which the village council's attorney wrote, directed "any peace officer" to enforce the order Judge Michalski had issued in 2001 by directing John Tague to "immediately vacate the Native Village of Perryville upon the next aircraft" and then escorting "Tague to said aircraft with directions that he leave and not return to the Native Village of Perryville or its surrounding areas unless authorized to do so by further order of the court."[34]

Without notifying Tague that the motion had been filed and providing him an opportunity to respond to the motion if he wished, on the day it was filed Judge Michalski granted the motion and signed the writ.

When the writ was faxed to Trooper Holm, he contacted the Alaska Department of Law, which was when the department's attorneys first learned that three years earlier the *Native Village of Perryville v. Tague* lawsuit had been filed, that two years earlier Judge Michalski had issued an injunction, and that he now had signed a writ of assistance. The attorneys instructed Holm to try to enforce the writ but not to arrest Tague if he ignored it. However, when Holm told him that Judge Michalski

---

continuing operation of tribal justice systems, and traditional tribal judicial practices by Indian tribal governments." The act defines "Indian tribe" to include "any Alaska Native entity, which administers justice under its inherent authority or the authority of the United States and which is recognized as eligible for the special programs and services provided by the United States to Indian tribes because of their status as Indians." That definition does not state that any Alaska Native entity has such "inherent authority." The One Hundred-third Congress passed the Indian Tribal Justice Act a month after Assistant Secretary of the Interior for Indian Affairs Ada Deer published in the *Federal Register* her list of Native entities and the preamble in which she purported to transform, through her act of publication, the members of those entities into more than two hundred federally recognized tribes.

had issued a writ of assistance that required him to leave Perryville, Tague departed voluntarily.[35]

The month before Judge Michalski signed the writ, former Alaska Senator Frank Murkowski was sworn into office to succeed Tony Knowles as governor of Alaska and appointed Gregg Renkes to succeed Bruce Botelho as attorney general.

In his 1994 and 1998 gubernatorial campaigns, Knowles had not only embraced the tribal sovereignty movement, he had recruited Willie Kasayulie, the former chairman of the Alaska Native Coalition and the founder of the Yupiit Nation, to appear in advertisements that promoted his candidacy. After Knowles was elected, in 1995 Attorney General Botelho made good on a promise candidate Knowles had made to Kasayulie and other tribal sovereignty advocates: In the *State of Alaska v. Native Village of Venetie Tribal Government* lawsuit the attorney general abandoned the State's long held legal position and conceded that the Native residents of Venetie, and by implication the Native residents of the more than two hundred other communities that the Ninety-second Congress or the secretary of the interior had designated as Native villages for the purposes of ANCSA, were members of federally recognized tribes because in 1993 Assistant Secretary of the Interior for Indian Affairs Ada Deer had published in the *Federal Register* a preamble with her list of Native entities in which she had said they were.

In 1999 Attorney General Botelho expressed that view to the Alaska Supreme Court in the *amicus* brief he filed on behalf of the State of Alaska in the *John v. Baker* appeal. And he told the court that the State believed that the court the village council in Northway had created had authority to decide the dispute between John Baker and Anita John regarding the custody of their children even though the land within and surrounding Northway was not Indian country.

Attorney General Renkes had a decidedly different view regarding the legal consequence of the fact that there was no Indian country in Alaska.

Two months after Judge Michalski issued the writ of assistance in the *Native Village of Perryville v. Tague* lawsuit, in March 2003 Attorney General Renkes sent Judge Michalski a letter in which he expressed "serious concerns about the legal underpinnings of the permanent injunction and the writ of assistance." The letter listed six concerns. The first was that "the tribal decree of banishment (and any injunction based on that tribal decree) is invalid because [the Native Village of] Perryville has no Indian country over which it can assert sovereignty."[36]

After reading the letter, Judge Michalski issued an order in which he directed the NVP to show cause why, as a consequence of the concerns Attorney General Renkes had expressed, he should not vacate the injunction and writ of assistance.

The village council's attorney then filed a brief to which Attorney General Renkes responded with a brief, and John Tague continued not to appear. In his brief, the attorney general argued: "There is no question that 228 out of 229 federally-recognized Alaska tribes, including Perryville, do not have a reservation from which to banish tribal members* ... But if Alaska tribes do not need sovereign territory from which to banish, then this inevitably leads to the conclusion that they have the legal authority to banish tribal members from anywhere in Alaska, indeed from anywhere in the country."[37]

After considering that argument, Judge Michalski rejected it, vacated the order to show cause, and explained his rationale for doing so as follows:

> The unfairness of subjecting an unwilling non-native citizen to the authority of a native governing body is simply not allowed by the authority claimed by [the Native Village of] Perryville. But as the record indicates, Mr. Tague is a tribal member of Perryville ... The law allows tribes to "regulate the internal affairs of its members." *John v. Baker.* Mr. Tague is a member of Perryville. The state is concerned that without requiring "Indian Country" for banishment, banishment will be applied by tribes in small villages to try to keep the banished person out of such places as Anchorage or Fairbanks in addition to the specific small village. The court recognizes that with many members of various tribal groups living in Anchorage and Fairbanks, not to mention Seattle and other cities, this concern about the extreme limits of such orders by tribes is not just academic. But this isn't such a case. Here the people of Perryville simply want Mr. Tague to stay away from tribal members in Perryville.[38]

Sympathy for the desire of Perryville residents to rid themselves of a violent miscreant undoubtedly explains why Judge Michalski glossed over Attorney General Renkes's observation that if the village council had the authority to banish John Tague from Perryville, it had the authority to banish him from Anchorage or Seattle.

Because the State of Alaska was not a party in the *Native Village of Perryville v. Tague* lawsuit, Attorney General Renkes could not appeal Judge Michalski's decision to the Alaska Supreme Court. As a consequence, the disagreement between the attorney general and the judge regarding the authority of the village council in Perryville to banish John Tague soon was forgotten, and two years later Renkes resigned as attorney general.

Since then village councils and the courts that many village councils have created have continued to banish individuals in situations in which the community consensus was that an individual deserved to be banished.

Since, like John Tague in Perryville and Adolph Rivers in Quinhagak, most of those individuals have been Alaska Natives, no questions were asked regarding the village councils' and the courts' authority to do so.

But in 1978 and 1981, in its decisions in *Oliphant v. Suquamish Indian Tribe* and *Montana v. United States*, respectively, the U.S. Supreme Court ruled that the gov-

---

* The reservation Attorney General Renkes did not name was the Annette Island reserve. However, as has been described, the Fifty-first Congress that in 1891 created it did not intend the reserve to be an Indian reservation.

erning body of a federally recognized tribe has no criminal jurisdiction over non-Native Americans and no civil jurisdiction over non-Native Americans unless a particular non-Native American consents to the exercise of that jurisdiction. So even if the Native residents of Native villages in Alaska are members of federally recognized tribes, village councils and the courts they have created have no authority to banish non-Natives. However, during Tony Knowles's tenure as governor, village councils did so anyway with the approval of the governor and his attorney general.

The month after Tony Knowles was sworn into office, in January 1995 in Kipnuk, the Native village on the Yukon-Kuskokwim River Delta where in 1987 the VPSO had begun searching individuals at the airstrip, the village council banished a non-Native named James Boan.

According to the council, Boan, who had lived in Kipnuk for two years with his Yup'ik Eskimo girlfriend, was a "troublemaker, gambler, and drug dealer who refused to abide by village laws." According to Boan, he had continually been harassed because he objected to being searched.

Boan eventually departed Kipnuk voluntarily after Alaska State Troopers flew into the village and persuaded him to leave. The troopers did so with the approval of Colonel Glenn Godfrey, who now was the head of the troopers, and Deputy Attorney General Laurie Otto, whom Governor Knowles had appointed to supervise attorneys in the Criminal Division of the Alaska Department of Law. As the *Anchorage Daily News* explained when it reported that the troopers had persuaded Boan to leave, "Both Godfrey and Laurie Otto of the attorney general's office say Gov. Tony Knowles' administration is putting a new emphasis on trying to work out the legal relationships involving villages, the state, and the federal government."

A spokesman for the village council told the *Anchorage Daily News* that "Natives have their own laws here and their own code of regulation within the boundaries of Kipnuk" and "[w]e've been banishing Natives for years." Colonel Godfrey's response was simply to say that "village self-government" was a "sensitive situation." As the head of the Alaska State Troopers, Godfrey saw no need to explain to the members of the village council that Kipnuk was as much a part of the State of Alaska as any other location, that the Native residents of Kipnuk the council had banished were state citizens who had the same legal rights as all other state citizens, or that, even if the village council had the authority to banish Native residents of Kipnuk from Kipnuk, it had no authority to banish James Boan.

As has been described, in 2006 when Sarah Palin was elected to succeed Frank Murkowski as governor of Alaska, she appointed Talis Colberg attorney general.

Palin, who had been a local television news reporter, a housewife, and a small-town mayor, knew nothing about federal Indian law and its application (and non-application) in Alaska. And her attorney general, who in private practice had specialized in workers' compensation law, knew next to nothing.

But the new governor's policy instinct was that the tenets of the tribal sovereignty movement contravened the idea of Alaska as a socially cohesive multi-ethnic society. Consistent with that conclusion, she appointed a non-Native as her rural affairs advisor, a position that traditionally had been filled by a Native. And while the attorneys he supervised at the Department of Law did not contest the assertion by the Alaska Supreme Court in its *John v. Baker* decision that there were more than two hundred federally recognized tribes in Alaska because in 1993 Assistant Secretary of the Interior for Indian Affairs Ada Deer had said there were, Attorney General Colberg did not rescind the opinion letter Attorney General Renkes had issued in 2004, and Department of Law attorneys continued to defend the validity of the legal advice contained in the letter in *Native Village of Tanana v. State*, the lawsuit NARF attorney Heather Kendall-Miller had filed during the Murkowski administration to invalidate it. And when in August 2008 Superior Court Judge Sen Tan issued a final judgment in the *Native Village of Tanana* lawsuit, Attorney General Colberg appealed the judgment to the Alaska Supreme Court.

That provoked Kendall-Miller and her husband, Lloyd Miller, to publicly rail in *Indian Country Today* and other publications that during her almost two years in office Governor Palin had waged "a battle against tribal sovereignty" because

> while Palin pays lip service to the fact that Alaska tribes are federally recognized, it is an empty statement because she insists they have no authority whatsoever to act as sovereigns despite that recognition unless, she argues, the state first permits a tribe to take some particular action. Palin has sought to block Alaska tribes from even exercising authority over the welfare of Native children again, unless the state through its courts first authorizes a tribe to act. It is a position that is so extreme that not only have the federal courts rejected it, but even her own state courts have rejected it. Nonetheless, Palin stubbornly refuses to relent, regardless of the consequence for village children caught in the middle of the resulting jurisdictional nightmare.[39]

One grievance the Millers did not mention was the Department of Law's position regarding the authority of village councils and the courts that a number of village councils by then had created to banish individuals of whom the members of the councils and courts disapproved.

Togiak is a community located at the mouth of a river of the same name on the northern shore of Bristol Bay in southwestern Alaska. In 1880 when Ivan Petroff conducted the first census in Alaska, he recorded that 1,826 Yup'ik Eskimos lived in seven settlements along the river,[40] and that in those settlements "the Togiak Eskimo ... seem to live without any tribal authority or organization, and have no chiefs, each family managing its own affairs, coming and going with perfect freedom, without regard for the wishes of other members of the community."[41]

By 1959 when the State of Alaska became one, those settlements had been abandoned and the descendants of the Yup'ik Eskimos who had lived along the river when

Petroff reconnoitered the area had congregated around a trading post at the mouth of the river whose existence Petroff had noted in his census.[42]

In 1966 the BIA reported that Togiak, as the community was known, population 409, had "a traditional organizational set up, being neither organized under federal nor state statutes. There is a president, vice president, treasurer, secretary, and two councilmen, all elected yearly." The BIA also reported that in 1961 Togiak residents had asked the secretary of the interior to designate the public land within the curtilage of the community as a townsite. The BIA also predicted that "after the survey is made and property lines established, the village will most likely petition to become a fourth class city."[43]

In 1969 a townsite was surveyed and subdivided into blocks, streets, and 139 house lots.[44] That same year Togiak residents incorporated a municipal government to which the townsite trustee subsequently conveyed the legal title to nineteen house lots that were unoccupied, plus the land on which the school and the cemetery were located, plus the land within the townsite that had not been subdivided.

In 1971 the Ninety-second Congress designated Togiak as a Native village for the purposes of ANCSA. In 1973 the Native residents of Togiak incorporated a village corporation, Togiak Natives Limited (TNL), in order to be conveyed the title to the surface estate of the land surrounding the townsite that ANCSA made available. When it was conveyed the title to that land, in 1998 the TNL conveyed the title to 498 acres to the city of Togiak, including 181 acres surrounding the airstrip that the city then conveyed to the State of Alaska.[45, *]

Using the procedure the State's local option law had created, in 1986 the city of Togiak held an election in which a majority of the Togiak residents who participated voted to prohibit the possession of alcoholic beverages.[46] But for the next twenty years, the prohibition was routinely ignored by bootleggers, as well as by Togiak residents who manufactured home brew.

In 2006 Gary Carlos, the member of the city council whom the other members of the council had selected to serve as mayor, hired a non-Native named Aaron Parker to be chief of the city's police department.

Parker had been employed as chief of police in Tanana, an Athabascan Indian village in the Alaska interior. And before that he had been a police officer in Kotzebue, the largest Inupiat Eskimo village in the northwest arctic. At both locations Parker had departed after less than six months on the job, and in Kotzebue he had been fired for "honesty and ethical reasons."[48]

---

* In 1980 the Ninety-sixth Congress amended section 14(c)(3) of ANCSA to authorize village corporations, municipal corporations, and the State of Alaska acting as the trustee for municipal corporations that would be incorporated in the future to negotiate agreements that would authorize a village corporation to reconvey to the municipal corporation or to the state in trust less than 1,280 acres.[47]

When Parker arrived in Togiak he began enforcing the law in a manner that was, by all accounts, brusque and authoritarian. Looking back, while she thought Parker's time as chief of police had been a "plus" for a community that had had too little law enforcement, Fanny Parker, a teacher at the school, would recall that Parker was condescending and "you really feel stupid when he talks to you."[49]

In June 2007 a group of Togiak residents who wanted Parker fired tried to recall Mayor Carlos because he refused to do so.[50] While the recall effort went nowhere, that October Kevin Ramey, one of the leaders of the group, was elected to the city council.[51]

The month after Ramey was sworn into office, a joint meeting of the city council, the village council, which had not disbanded after the city of Togiak was incorporated, and the leaders of the TNL was held, the purpose of which was to allow Ramey and other Togiak residents to complain that Mayor Carlos had hired Parker "without any public process," that Parker did not have the certifications from the Alaska Police Standards Council that he was required to have, and that Parker had repeatedly violated the civil rights of individuals he had arrested."[52]

Parker rejected those accusations as "fabrications," and that winter he announced that the Togiak police department had identified thirteen bootleggers whom he intended to soon arrest.[53] He also arrested a Togiak resident named Nancy Coopchiak for manufacturing home brew.

When Coopchiak failed to appear in the Superior Court in Dillingham to answer that charge, an arrest warrant was issued that an Alaska State Trooper flew to Togiak to execute. When he arrived at Coopchiak's house, the trooper was confronted by Coopchiak's brother and several other Togiak residents who told him that the judge who had issued the warrant "doesn't have any jurisdiction here."

To prevent the confrontation from escalating into violence, the trooper flew back to Dillingham without Coopchiak. However, two weeks later he returned with six other troopers who, when she refused to open it, kicked in Coopchiak's front door. During the altercation that ensued, Coopchiak attacked one of the troopers.[54] She later would be convicted of assault and resisting arrest.[55]

After his sister was arrested, Coopchiak's brother and eight other Togiak residents sent Chief Parker, Governor Palin, and Attorney General Colberg a notice in which they announced that they were members of the Nutmlak Iupiak Provinces of Nasarlurmiut, Ingritchuarmiut, and Manokotarmiut, an organization they said was the successor to the governments that had operated in Togiak and two other nearby villages before the United States purchased Alaska in 1867, and that, because the purchase had been illegal, the United States—and by inference the State of Alaska—had no authority to enforce their laws in the three communities. The notice also complained that Chief Parker had harassed the residents of Togiak by enforcing laws whose validity they did not recognize.[56]

Several days later, on March 6, the city council, the village council, and the leaders of the TNL held another joint meeting that several troopers and any resident of

Togiak who wanted to do so attended. During the meeting complaints about Parker were voiced that ranged from being "insensitive to the Yup'ik culture of the tribal community of Togiak" to arresting intoxicated individuals on "trumped up charges."

In 1998 the village council had created a "tribal" court. Initially, the judges limited their activities to dealing with misbehaving teenagers. But by 2008 they had expanded their ersatz jurisdiction.

The month after the March 6 meeting, the judges signed an order that banished Parker from Togiak.[57]

Parker faxed a copy of the order to Attorney General Colberg. The next day Assistant Attorney General Monica Jenicek informed Parker that after reviewing the order "in light of relevant federal and state law," the attorneys at the Department of Law who had done so had concluded that the order had "no legal basis."[58]

Because it did not, Parker ignored the order. However, six months later Mayor Carlos and his son, Sean Carlos, who also was a member of the city council, lost their seats in a municipal election that had become a referendum on the mayor's refusal to fire Parker. As Togiak resident Olia Sutton explained after the vote, "There was a banishment, and they went ahead and kept him on." And according to Andrew Franklin, the candidate who defeated Sean Carlos, he decided to run for Carlos's seat because he had seen "some wrong things going on" because "people weren't feeling right about the cop here."[59]

Soon after the new members of the city council were sworn into office, Aaron Parker was suspended as chief of police and in December terminated.[60]

Nine years later attorneys at the Department of Law who worked for a different attorney general who served at the pleasure of a different governor had a different view of the authority of the court in Togiak to banish a non-Native.

On January 24, 2017, a plane operated by an air cargo service on a flight that had originated in Anchorage delivered a plastic tote to the airport in Togiak addressed to Ronald Oertwich, a seventy-two-year-old non-Native who in a house he leased near the airport operated the Airport Inn, a bed & breakfast that catered to sport fishermen. Oertwich had been a resident of Togiak and the surrounding area for more than thirty years.

When the tote was off-loaded Roger Wassillie, the Village Public Safety Officer whose position the State of Alaska funded in Togiak, told Leroy Nanalook, the "tribal" police officer,* that the tote looked suspicious. So Nanalook confiscated the tote and

* In 1994 the One Hundred-third Congress created the Community Oriented Policing Services (COPS) program, which authorized the U.S. Department of Justice to award grants to state, local, and tribal law enforcement agencies.[61] When the department began awarding grants, it began awarding grants to village councils in Alaska because the statute that created the COPS program defined "Indian tribe" to mean "a tribe, band, pueblo, nation, or other organized group or community of Indians, including an Alaska Native village (as defined in or established under the Alaska Native Claims Settlement Act), that is recognized as eligible for the special programs and services provided by the United States

asked the tribal court to issue a search warrant. Based on no evidence other than Roger Wassillie's suspicion, three of the tribal court judges issued the warrant. When Nanalook then opened the tote, mixed in with dog food he found twenty-two bottles of whiskey that Oertwich later said a friend had sent to him without his knowledge.[63, *]

If the whiskey belonged to Oertwich he was guilty of a Class A misdemeanor. But instead of contacting the Alaska State Troopers in Dillingham, more than a month later Nanalook filed a complaint against Oertwich in the tribal court.

On March 27 all five tribal court judges called a meeting to discuss the complaint that all Togiak residents who were interested in doing so attended. Oertwich was notified but refused to attend. At the conclusion of the meeting a vote was taken and, according to Anecia Kritz, one of the judges, "[Ronald Oertwich] was found guilty from the community, and their wishes were to banish."[64]

After informing him that he had been banished, Leroy Nanalook and another man took Oertwich to the Airport Inn to gather whatever personal belongings he wanted to take with him and then drove him to the airport.[65]

When his plane landed in Dillingham, Oertwich phoned an attorney of his acquaintance named David Henderson who, according to Henderson, told Oertwich that "they didn't have a right to banish him from his home and his business."[67] Acting on that legal advice, the next day Oertwich flew to Twin Hills, a Native village four miles east of Togiak, where a friend gave him a ride on an all-terrain vehicle back to the Airport Inn.

When they discovered that he had returned to Togiak, Leroy Nanalook and Roger Wassillie arrested Oertwich for having violated the tribal court's banishment order and transported him to the city of Togiak's public safety building, where he was locked in one the building's two jail cells.

On March 29 the tribal court judges held another community meeting that Oertwich was allowed to attend. Another vote was taken and Oertwich again was banished.

Oertwich was returned to his cell and told he would stay there until he agreed to leave Togiak. When Oertwich refused to agree to do so he remained incarcerated for another four days.

On day six Leroy Nanalook, Jimmy Coopchiak, the chairman of the village council, and three other men entered Oertwich's cell, handcuffed his hands behind his back, and wrapped his legs with duct tape because, according to Coopchiak, "he was resisting" and "didn't want to leave." They then carried Oertwich to a vehicle in which he was driven to the airport and forcibly put on a plane that was flown to Dillingham.[68]

---

to Indians because of their status as Indians." In 2015 the department awarded a COPS grant to the village council in Togiak that the council used to hire a "tribal police officer" to "enforce tribal laws and ordinances."[62]

* In 2010 Ronald Oertwich's then-wife was arrested in Dillingham for being in possession of a shipment of alcoholic beverages that she intended to transport to Togiak for the purpose of making the libations available for guests at the Airport Inn. In 2011 she pled guilty to that misdemeanor offense and was sentenced to thirty days in jail with twenty-seven days suspended.[66]

When he first was jailed Oertwich was able to reach David Henderson by cell phone to tell Henderson that he had been. Henderson then called the Alaska State Trooper post in Dillingham and told the trooper who took the call that Oertwich had been incarcerated in Togiak because he had refused to agree to be banished.

Under Alaska's criminal statutes, at a minimum, Leroy Nanalook and Roger Wassillie were guilty of misdemeanor assault and coercion, a felony that is committed when a person tries to compel an individual to engage in conduct—in Oertwich's case leaving Togiak—that the individual had a legal right not to have to engage in. Nevertheless, after speaking with his superiors, the trooper told Henderson that he had been told not to intervene.

According to Richard Burton, the former commissioner of the Alaska Department of Public Safety who at the beginning of his career as an Alaska State Trooper had been stationed in Dillingham:

> I was shocked when I read the news about the Togiak incident and the lack of response of the Department of Public Safety to the illegal detention of someone over whom the village council and tribal court had no jurisdiction or authority of any kind. As a trooper stationed in Dillingham in the early 1960s I responded to a similar instance in Togiak and rescued a pilot who was held by the village council for a "violation." I don't know who considers banishment legal. It is an old custom. But I ask anyone to show me where it is legal. The conduct of the state is an embarrassment to me personally and professionally.[69]

While former Commissioner Burton may have been embarrassed, Jahna Lindemuth, an Anchorage attorney whom Alaska Governor Bill Walker had appointed attorney general the previous June, not only was not embarrassed, but the order the trooper was given reflected her policy and that of the governor at whose pleasure she served since, as a reporter at the public radio station in Dillingham later confirmed, when the trooper in Dillingham asked his superiors how he should respond, "the situation went immediately up the chains of command of both the Department of Law and Department of Public Safety, and Governor Walker was made aware."[70]

Five months later when *Alaska Dispatch News* reporter Lisa Demer asked Lindemuth what her and Governor Walker's policy was regarding when the troopers would intervene when an individual whom a village council or court had banished refused to leave the community, she answered: "We recognize that [banishment] presents constitutional challenges. But I don't think it's the state's place to approve or disapprove of anything. We are not looking for a test case. It is not the state's challenge to bring. Tribes are sovereigns. [Banishment] arises between a private person and that particular sovereign."[71]

Another two months later, on October 19, 2017, Governor Walker, wearing a blue Eskimo kuspuk jacket and standing next to his lieutenant governor, Byron Mallott, who was wearing the beaded Tlingit vest in which he frequently appeared, addressed several thousand delegates at the annual AFN convention. Several hours earlier At-

Alaska Attorney General Jahna Lindemuth explains her position on banishment at the Annual Conference of the Alaska Native Law Section of the Alaska Bar Association, October 17, 2017. Alaska Bar Association.

torney General Lindemuth released an attorney general's opinion entitled "Legal Status of Tribal Governments in Alaska" in which she told the governor (and the convention delegates who were the opinion's intended audience) that "the law is clear. There are 229 Alaska Tribes and they are separate sovereigns with inherent sovereignty and subject matter jurisdiction over certain matters."[72]

In the section that described the governmental powers that an Alaska tribe possesses, the opinion made no mention of the power to banish either members of the tribe or nonmembers. However, two days before she released the attorney general's opinion, Attorney General Lindemuth was the keynote speaker at the annual conference of the Alaska Native law section of the Alaska Bar Association. During that presentation she told the attorneys in attendance that, in her (and Governor Walker's) view, banishment was "a civil matter, rather than a criminal matter," and that "the state's not in the business of running around protecting an individual's civil rights." After describing tribes as "law enforcement partners," she explained that:

> In most instances what happens is a tribe will ask the Department of Public Safety, the troopers, to help enforce the [banishment] order. We look very closely about what the legalities of that are. And it may be that that's not something that the troopers will help with. On the flip side of that, if somebody who has been banished or excluded from a community makes a complaint to the state the state will investigate and evaluate that. But we may not be taking action in every situation or being involved in any particular claim.
>
> But in most instances we are working behind the scenes with our law enforcement partners. So if we have a tribal police officer who is working on these kinds of issues, the state, behind the scenes, is communicating and

working with the tribe so that we have good communication and collaboration between the law enforcement partners who are dealing with these particular matters.[73]

In November 2018 Mike Dunleavy, a right of conservative former Republican member of the Alaska Senate, was elected to succeed Bill Walker as governor. And in December the new governor appointed Kevin Clarkson, an equally right of conservative Anchorage attorney, to succeed Jahna Lindemuth as attorney general.

Ten months after Clarkson began his tenure as attorney general, in September 2019 the members of the village council in Kiana banished an Inupiat Eskimo named Thomas Nay, who had been living in Kiana, after Nay was accused of selling methamphetamine.[74]

Early in the twentieth century Inupiat Eskimos living along the Kobuk River in the northwest arctic began congregating around a trading post that had opened to supply prospectors who were working mining claims on the nearby Squirrel River. By 1915 when a post office was opened, the trading post had expanded into a community that had been named Kiana.

Prior to 1964 the local government in the community was a "traditional" village council that had no legal imprimatur. However, in that year the residents of Kiana incorporated a municipality. As a consequence, in 1971 when the Ninety-second Congress designated Kiana as a Native village for the purposes of ANCSA, the community's 278 residents had two governments: the village council and the city council. In 1993 when Assistant Secretary of the Interior for Indian Affairs Ada Deer published her list of Native entities in the *Federal Register*, she included the Native Village of Kiana (NVK) on her list.

When after he was told he had been banished Thomas Nay agreed to leave, the NVK and the city of Kiana split the $600 it cost to charter the airplane that flew Nay to Kotzebue.

When the *Anchorage Daily News* reported that the village council in Kiana had banished Nay, the paper's reporter asked Cori Mills, the Department of Law's spokesperson, whether what the village council had done was lawful. As she had when she had been the department's spokesperson during Attorney General Lindemuth's tenure, Mills obfuscated.

First, by saying that the question had no "easy, straightforward answer," and then by noting that "even if we [Attorney General Clarkson and the attorneys at the Department of Law he supervised] do know the facts, we would have to thoroughly evaluate the situation before commenting."[75] And seven months later when she was asked whether the Department of Law had conducted the thorough evaluation to which she had earlier alluded, Mills, through her own spokesperson, answered, "There is no further information that the department will be providing."[76]

Fifteen

It has been thirty-nine years since the *Native Village of Tyonek v. Puckett* lawsuit was filed, which began the effort by the small group of attorneys who staffed the tribal sovereignty movement to tribalize Alaska by judicial decision and executive branch agency fait. To date they have enjoyed considerable success, principally because, with the exception of Walter Hickel and Charles Cole, the nine men and one woman who have served as governor of Alaska during those years, and their attorneys general, responded to the tribal sovereignty movement ad hoc and with little to no understanding of the history of Congress's Alaska Native-related enactments or appreciation for the policy consequences their decisions.

During those same years, the response of Alaska's congressional delegation was the same.

The neutrality policy on which Alaska Senator Ted Stevens settled in 1982 has been described, as has his and Alaska Senator Frank Murkowski's and Alaska Representative Don Young's embrace of the neutrality policy as their response to the efforts of the Alaska Native Coalition and NARF to tribalize ANCSA during the Ninety-ninth and One Hundredth Congresses' consideration of the "1991 amendments" to ANCSA.

Because they illustrate the extent to which the members of Alaska's congressional delegation have responded to the tribal sovereignty movement by vacillating between opposition, inattention, acquiescence, and back again, only to find themselves confronted with new demands, three other delegation actions merit description.

Tlingit and Haida Status Clarification Act

The Tlingit-Haida Central Council was one of the Native associations listed in section 7(a) of ANCSA.

In 1935 the Seventy-fourth Congress enacted a statute that authorized the "Tlingit and Haida Indians of Alaska" to file a civil action in the Court of Claims to obtain a judgment awarding monetary compensation for the extinguishment of the Tlingit and Haida Indians' aboriginal title to land in southeast Alaska that had been included within the Tongass National Forest and Glacier Bay National Monument. The statute designated the judgment as an "asset" of the villages in which Tlingit and Haida Indians resided and required the money to be used to purchase "productive economic instruments and resources of public benefit to such Indian communities." The statute also referenced a "Tlingit and Haida central council" that, although no such organization existed, was directed to prepare a roll of Tlingit and Haida Indians.[1]

In 1941 the BIA decided on its own to hold village elections to create a central council for the purpose of having the members of the council select an attorney to file the lawsuit,[2] which the attorney they selected finally filed in 1947.[3]

In 1965 the Eighty-ninth Congress enacted a second statute that authorized a central council to be officially organized by selecting members in an election conducted pursuant to rules that the secretary of the interior approved. The statute provided that the council's sole purpose was to develop a plan for the use of the money judgment the Court of Claims would award.[4]

In 1968 the Court of Claims awarded $7.5 million.[5]

In 1970 the Ninety-first Congress enacted a third statute that authorized the "Central Council of the Tlingit and Haida Indians of Alaska," with the approval of the secretary of the interior, to spend the $7.5 million however it wished.[6]

In 1971 Commissioner of Indian Affairs Louis Bruce appointed Morris Thompson, a prominent leader of the Athabascan Indian community in Fairbanks, as director of the BIA Alaska Regional Office.[7] A month later Thompson and John Borbridge, the president of the Central Council who fifteen years later would become a spokesperson for the Alaska Native Coalition, signed a contract that allowed the Central Council to begin administering programs that the BIA Southeast Alaska Agency had been administering.[8]

In 1973 the Central Council adopted a constitution in which the organization granted itself authority not only to spend the $7.5 million but "to serve as the general governing body of the Tlingit and Haida Indians of Alaska."[9] Eight months later President Richard Nixon appointed Thompson to succeed Louis Bruce as commissioner of Indian affairs.[10] In January 1975 President Gerald Ford, who the previous August had become president when President Nixon resigned, signed into law the Indian Self-Determination and Education Assistance Act, which authorized "Indian tribes" to contract with the BIA to administer programs such as the programs that since 1971 the Central Council had been contracting to administer.

After the Indian Self-Determination Act was enacted, the director of the BIA Alaska Regional Office questioned whether, because the Central Council was not an "Indian tribe" as that term had been defined in the Indian Self-Determination Act, the BIA could continue to contract with the Central Council.

In July 1975 Commissioner Thompson informed the director that "it was reported that some questions had been raised as to whether the Bureau recognized the Tlingit and Haida Tribes and the Central Council as empowered to speak on behalf of those Tlingit and Haida people that adhere to the organization," and "we were surprised that doubts continued to exist among our Juneau staff as to whether the Tlingit and Haida Central Council was a recognized tribal organization." Commissioner Thompson then advised that "the general explanations offered in this letter will clarify for all concerned that it is the view of the Bureau that the Tlingit and Haida Central Council is a tribal entity representing the Tlingit and Haida Indians of Alaska."[11]

That was a view regarding the Central Council's legal status on which Commissioner Thompson apparently settled without consulting the attorneys in the Office of the Solicitor who advised the BIA. Because in 1977 Ray Paddock, the president of the Central Council (who in 1974 had unintentionally been responsible for the House Committee on Interior and Insular Affairs not including the Central Council and the other Native associations listed in section 7(a) of ANCSA in the "Indian tribe" definition in the bill it reported to the U.S. House of Representatives that the Ninety-third Congress would enact as the Indian Self-Determination Act) would complain: "For the past two years, the Bureau of Indian Affairs in Alaska has been enforcing their interpretation of Indian tribe which provides first priority recognition to those groups of Indians organized pursuant to the provisions of the Wheeler-Howard Act [IRA] and the Alaska Indian Reorganization Act of May 1, 1936 [Public Law No. 74-538]."[12]

As has been described, five years later, in 1982, Assistant Secretary of the Interior for Indian Affairs Ken Smith published in the *Federal Register* the first list of Native entities that were "not historical tribes" but to which BIA gave "priority for purposes of funding and services." Without explaining why, he included the "Tlingit & Haida Indians of Alaska" on the list.[13] And the lists of Native entities that Assistant Secretary Smith's successors published in 1983, 1985, and 1986 continued to include the "Tlingit & Haida Indians of Alaska."[14]

In 1988 Assistant Secretary of the Interior for Indian Affairs Ross Swimmer published a list that increased the number of Native entities by adding entities to which various statutes, including the Indian Self-Determination Act, authorized the BIA to provide funding and services. In addition to ANCSA regional and village corporations that were "Indian tribes" for the purposes of the Indian Self-Determination Act,[15] the 1988 list for the first time included the "Central Council of Tlingit and Haida Indian Tribes of Alaska."[16]

In 1993 Assistant Secretary of the Interior for Indian Affairs Ada Deer replaced the 1988 list with a new list of Native entities that she said were federally recognized tribes, rather than entities eligible to receive funding and services. Because the attorneys in the Office of the Solicitor who advised the BIA advised her that the members of the Central Council of Tlingit and Haida Indian Tribes of Alaska were not a federally recognized tribe, Assistant Secretary Deer did not include the Central Council on her list.[17]

When he found that out, Ed Thomas, the president of the Central Council, protested to Michael Anderson, the associate solicitor for Indian affairs, that "there is little doubt that my Tribe has conducted itself (and continues to conduct itself) as a Tribe as many other Tribes in the 'Lower 48.'"[18]

When that protest was unavailing, Thomas complained to Alaska Senator Frank Murkowski who was sympathetic to the complaint of a locally prominent constituent about a matter whose legal consequence he did not understand.

Less than a month after Assistant Secretary Deer published her list, the Senate Committee on Indian Affairs reported S. 1654, a bill that amended six Indian-related statutes in various noncontroversial ways. Since he was a member of the committee, prior to the vote to report S. 1654, Senator Murkowski offered an amendment, which the other members accepted, that added a section 7 to the bill that directed the secretary of the interior to add to Assistant Secretary Deer's list of Native entities "the tribe defined and recognized in the Act of June 19, 1935, as amended, relating to the Tlingit and Haida Indians of Alaska."[19] The committee's report on S. 1654 explained that Senator Murkowski's amendment

> simply restores the status quo of October 20, 1993 by placing the Central Council of Tlingit and Haida Indian Tribes of Alaska back on the list and restoring Central Council to the same position it was in before it was deleted from the republished list. The Bureau of Indian Affairs removed the Central Council of Tlingit and Haida Indian Tribes of Alaska from the list without congressional oversight. The Senate Committee on Indian Affairs held no hearings on this matter and the Bureau of Indian Affairs did not formally present any explanation for the removal of the Central Council from the list. This is a significant misuse of federal departmental power. The amendment corrects the deletion.[20]

Before the Senate passed S. 1654, the bill's manager removed section 7,[21] apparently because the BIA threatened to have President Clinton veto the bill had it not been removed.[22]

Senator Murkowski then introduced S. 1784, a bill whose sole provision directed the secretary of the interior to add to Assistant Secretary Deer's list "the tribe defined and recognized in the Act of June 19, 1935, as amended, relating to the Tlingit and Haida Indians of Alaska." That same day and with no explanation of the bill's content, the Senate passed S. 1784 by unanimous consent on a voice vote.[23] After the vote Senator Murkowski inserted a statement into the *Congressional Record* in which he explained that S. 1784 "does not do anything new. The bill makes a technical correction to BIA's list and should not be viewed as setting any precedent for Federal recognition of a tribe. My bill simply restores the status quo of October 20, 1993, by placing the Central Council of Tlingit and Haida Indian Tribes of Alaska back on the list and restores central council to the same position it was in before it was deleted from the republished list."[24]

When S. 1784 reached the U.S. House of Representatives, the Subcommittee on Native American Affairs of the Committee on Natural Resources held a hearing on the bill. The first witness, Debra Maddox, the director of the BIA Office of Tribal Services, told the members of the subcommittee that the Department of the Interior opposed S. 1784 because

> The Central Council of the Tlingit and Haida Indians tribes is not a federally recognized tribe but is a regional organization created for a very specific purpose. The Act of June 19th, 1935, established that the Central Council is the

Alaska Senator Frank Murkowski. Alaska State Library.

> entity under which the Tlingit and Haida Indians could bring suit in Federal Court for the taking of their community property. The Central Council was delegated the responsibility for establishing a roll of Tlingit and Haida Indians entitled to benefit from the judgment funds awarded by the court. Consequent amendments to the 1935 Act gave the council broader responsibilities for the use and distribution of the judgment funds. Thus, the Central Council is recognized by statute for the limited purpose of distributing judgment funds; not as a tribal government exercising general governmental powers over its members and member villages as contemplated by the Federal Register list.[25]

By then Ed Thomas had hired a lobbyist, an attorney named Philip Baker-Shenk, who was a former member of the staff of the Senate Select Committee on Indian Affairs.[26]

After the hearing Baker-Shenk persuaded Tadd Johnson, a member of the Bois Forte Band of Chippewa Indians in northern Minnesota who was the staff director of the subcommittee,[27] to ignore the Department of the Interior's opposition to S. 1784.

In June 1994 Johnson sent other members of the staff of the Committee on Natural Resources an outline that described the content of a new bill that he vouched would "appease the administration, the villages [that were members of the Central Council], and the Central Council." According to the outline, section 2 of the bill would "reaffirm and acknowledge" that "the Central Council of Tlingit and Haida Indians is a federally recognized Indian tribe possessing all the attributes of inherent sovereignty which have not been specifically taken away by Acts of Congress and which are not inconsistent with such tribal status."[28]

A month later, Baker-Shenk gave Johnson a bill text that he urged Johnson to recommend to the members of the Committee on Natural Resources that they report as a substitute for the text of S. 1784.[29] After meeting with Johnson and other staff members, two weeks later Baker-Shenk gave Johnson an amended version of that text,[30] and another month later an amended version of the amended version.[31]

On September 28, 1994, the members of the Committee on Natural Resources met, accepted an amendment in the nature of a substitute for the text of S. 1784 that Representative Bill Richardson, the chairman of the Subcommittee on Native American Affairs, offered, and then voted to report the bill. Representative Richardson's amendment was a rewrite of the bill text that had been written by Tadd Johnson based on the last bill text Philip Baker-Shenk had given to Johnson. The text contained a "finding" that "the United States has acknowledged the Central Council of Tlingit and Haida Indian Tribes of Alaska pursuant to the Act of June 19, 1935 as a federally recognized tribe." And section 3 announced that "Congress reaffirms and acknowledges that the Central Council of Tlingit and Haida Indian Tribes of Alaska is a federally recognized Indian tribe."

Prior to the vote to report S. 1784, Alaska Representative Don Young, the ranking Republican member of the committee, announced that he supported Representative Richardson's amendment because "this is an instance where the Tlingit-Haida Council had been the main council for this group of villages for many years and then were inadvertently left off the list. This is a way we can protect the villages' recognition and recognize the role of the council. This is strongly supported by the people of the Tlingit-Haida region."[32]

Then Wyoming Representative Craig Thomas, the ranking Republican member of the Subcommittee on Native American Affairs, distributed a written statement in which he explained his understanding of the situation as follows: "I found the BIA decision to remove Tlingit-Haida from the list of recognized tribal entities — after almost twelve years of its inclusion thereon — to be highly worrisome. The decision was taken precipitously, with little or no notification to or discussion with the Congress." The statement concluded by asserting that "S. 1784 sets no precedent for the legislative recognition of a native group outside the BIA's Federal Acknowledgment process. S. 1784 would simply restore a previously-recognized group to the BIA's list of recognized tribes, and is therefore only analogous to restoration legislation."[33]

Continuing those mischaracterizations of the Central Council's prior legal status, the committee's report on S. 1784, which Tadd Johnson (and Philip Baker-Shenk?) undoubtedly wrote, asserted that the "Central Council has its legal organizational roots as a Tribe in a 1935 Act which refers to a 'central council' of Tlingit and Haida Indian tribes. The 1935 Act was substantially amended in 1965. The Senate and House committee reports accompanying the 1965 amendments clearly show that Congress intended those amendments to confirm Federal recognition of Central Council as a tribal government."[34] The report pointedly made no mention of the fact that the director of the BIA Office of Tribal Services had testified that the 1935 and 1965 acts said no such thing.

With the One Hundred-third Congress rushing to adjournment, in October Representative Richardson packaged the text of the version of S. 1784 the Committee on Natural Resources had reported and the texts of two other Indian-related bills into a single bill, H.R. 4180. On Representative Richardson's motion, the House then suspended its rules and passed H.R. 4180 by unanimous consent on a voice vote.[35]

Five days later, with no explanation of the bill's content, the Senate passed H.R. 4180 by unanimous consent on another voice vote.[36] The next day Senator Murkowski issued a statement in which he asserted that "we're not setting a precedent for federal recognition of tribes. We are simply restoring the former status by placing the Central Council back on the list."[37]

Since the Senate's passage of the bill text Tadd Johnson had written based on the bill text Philip Baker-Shenk had given to Johnson explicitly designated the Central Council as a federally recognized tribe, the senator either did not read the bill before he issued the statement, or he did read it and did not understand the legal consequences that the One Hundred-third Congress's enactment of H.R. 4180 would bring about.

Because the BIA supported the two other bills Representative Richardson had included in H.R. 4180, on November 2, 1994, President Bill Clinton signed H.R. 4180[38] into law. As a consequence, for more than twenty-five years the members of the Central Council of Tlingit and Haida Indian Tribes of Alaska have been a federally recognized tribe.[39]

Alaska Rural Justice and Law Enforcement Commission

During the August 2003 congressional recess when he was driving to Anchorage on the Glenn Highway, near the intersection with the spur road to Chickaloon, a Native village seventy-four miles northeast of Anchorage, Alaska Senator Ted Stevens saw a sport utility vehicle that had been painted to look like a police car, but with the seal of Chickaloon Village on the doors, parked behind another vehicle on the shoulder of the highway. Standing next to the other vehicle was an individual dressed in a police uniform and wearing a sidearm.[40]

When he returned to Washington, D.C., Stevens learned that the sport utility vehicle, the uniform, the sidearm, and the salary of the "police officer" had been paid for with money the U.S. Department of Justice had given to the Chickaloon village council.

In 1994 the One Hundred-third Congress had enacted the Violent Crime Control and Law Enforcement Act (Crime Control Act).[41] Because it made good on President Bill Clinton's campaign promise to put a hundred thousand additional police officers on the streets, the centerpiece of the act was title I, the Public Safety Partnership and Community Policing Act, which created the Community Oriented Policing Services (COPS) program pursuant to which the attorney general was authorized to give grants to hire, train, and equip new police officers.[42]

As introduced, both H.R. 3355 and S. 1607, the House and Senate versions of the bill the One Hundred-third Congress would enact as the Crime Control Act, limited eligibility for COPS grants to states, local governments, and certain public and private entities. But when the texts were rewritten as the bills moved through the House and Senate Committees on the Judiciary and then were amended during the debates on the House and Senate floors, a reference to "Indian tribal governments" was inserted in order to allow Indian tribes to apply for COPS grants. And most consequently, "Indian tribe" was defined to mean "a tribe, band, pueblo, nation, or other organized group or community of Indians, including an Alaska Native village (as defined in or established under the Alaska Native Claims Settlement Act), that is recognized as eligible for the special programs and services provided by the United States to Indians because of their status as Indians."[43]

Who arranged to include "Alaska Native village" in the "Indian tribe" definition is not known. But in 1995 the Department of Justice began giving COPS grants to Chickaloon and more than forty other Native villages that by 2003, when Alaska Senator Ted Stevens learned about them, totaled more than $10 million.

To prevent the department from continuing to give COPS grants to Native villages in which the village councils had no criminal law enforcement authority, in September 2003 Stevens, who was chairman of the Senate Committee on Appropriations, arranged for the committee to include a rider in the Department of Justice FY 2004 appropriations bill that prohibited the department from giving grants "for courts or police for individual tribes in Alaska (except the Annette Island Indian Reserve)."[44]

When she found out what Stevens had done, NARF attorney Heather Kendall-Miller publicly denounced the rider as "an attack on the tribal community."[45] She then followed up with an editorial in the *Anchorage Daily News* in which she railed that "the Senator's stealth tactic is but another part of his war on tribalism."[46]

A week later Stevens held a press conference during which he told reporters that

> the road they [Kendall-Miller and other members of the tribal sovereignty movement] are on now is the road to destruction of statehood because the

> Native population's increasing at a much much greater rate than the non-Native population. I don't know if you realize that. And they want to have total jurisdiction over anything that happened in a village without regard to state law and without regard to federal law.[47]

In response, Vernita Herdman, a well-known tribal sovereignty activist, publicly accused Stevens of racism.[48] And Kendall-Miller told the *Anchorage Daily News* that she had been as offended by the senator's remarks as Herdman had been because Stevens is "saying that our mere existence is a threat to the state."[49]

Two weeks later in a prerecorded speech that was shown on large video screens at that year's AFN convention, Stevens told the delegates:

> The problem I raised in that press conference ... developed because the former director of BIA, Ada Deer, decreed that every Alaska Native village was a tribe, leading many to assert there are now 231 Alaskan tribes. Some seek to have each Native village declared to be a sovereign tribe.
>
> ...
>
> If those villages are recognized as sovereign nations, the future of Alaska as a state is in jeopardy. Alaska would ultimately encompass a huge collection of independent tribal nations left unconnected by a state government and unprotected by the federal system. The resolution of the sovereignty issue is critical to Alaska's future. A lot is at stake, and there are reasonable differences of opinion. But to be called a "racist" after more than fifty years of dedicated service to Alaskans, particularly Alaska Natives, is something I will not forget. It is a stain on my soul.
>
> ...
>
> I have worked with Alaska Native people for a half century, but I will not be deterred from the cause of helping Alaska Natives by those who seek, not to enhance, but to destroy your future. Tribal sovereignty is not the answer to the problems Alaska Natives face. It merely brings authority to some, power to others, and legal fees to advocates that bring incessant litigation.[50]

While the senator seemingly had held his ground, by then Vernita Herdman and Heather Kendall-Miller playing the racism card had accomplished its purpose. Two days before the beginning of the convention in an interview broadcast on *Native America Calling*, Kendall-Miller told a national public radio audience: "We want him [Stevens] to pull back these riders and acknowledge the existence of tribes in Alaska ... We want him to stop his assault on tribalism."[51] And soon thereafter Stevens signaled that, having been subjected to enough public opprobrium, he would withdraw the rider.

To allow the senator to save face, the AFN convention delegates passed a resolution in which they recommended that the One Hundred-eighth Congress create a commission, an idea that during the discussion of the resolution AFN president Julie Kitka told the delegates "has the backing of Stevens."[52]

A month later Stevens combined the Department of Justice appropriations bill and six other appropriations bills into an omnibus appropriations bill. In the omnibus bill his rider was gone;[53] replaced by a new section 112 that prohibited the Department of Justice from giving out grants to fund tribal courts and tribal law enforcement officers in Alaska only in Native villages that had fewer than twenty-five Native residents or that were located within the Municipality of Anchorage or within the North Slope Borough and the other boroughs that had been organized around the state. Section 112 also directed the attorney general to create an Alaska Rural Justice and Law Enforcement Commission to "review Federal, State, local, and tribal jurisdiction over civil and criminal matters in Alaska," and then submit recommendations to Congress and the Alaska Legislature.[54]

In January 2004 during the discussion in the Senate that preceded the vote to accept the version of the omnibus bill whose content the members of a House-Senate conference committee had negotiated, Stevens rationalized his capitulation as an example of his neutrality policy. Stevens told the Senate:

> Since statehood [Congress] has required Alaska Natives to comply with the same criminal, civil, and regulatory enactments of the Alaska State Legislature to which all other Alaska residents are subject. Like all citizens of my State, Alaska Natives participate in the development of those enactments by electing residents of the communities in which they live to serve in the Alaska State Legislature. In that regard, I am immensely proud that Alaska has a tradition of Native American involvement in the State political system that is unrivaled by that of any other State.
>
> ...
>
> During the Clinton administration, the secretary of the interior, his solicitor and Ada Deer, the Under Secretary (sic) of Indian Affairs, argued that there are more than two hundred sovereign tribal governments in Alaska. Many believe that policy was wrong, as a matter of law, while others assert that tribes have always existed. The provision in this bill creating a rural justice commission does not take sides in that dispute. Rather, it seeks a practical solution to the issue of rural justice and law enforcement.
>
> ...
>
> I want to emphasize that the conference committee does not intend the enactment of section 112(a)(1) to express a view as to whether the 108th Congress believes that either a prior Congress or the secretary of the interior, acting lawfully pursuant to authority he has been delegated by Congress, has created "federally recognized tribes" in Alaska. Nor does the conference committee intend the enactment of section 112(a)(1) to create "federally recognized tribes" in Alaska by implication. The amendment takes no position on the issues which are now pending before the courts.[55]

After Stevens's explanation was printed in the *Congressional Record*, Lisa Sutherland, the member of his staff who had handled the matter for the senator, described her misunderstanding of the law and alluded to the political pressure that had compelled the senator's capitulation as follows:

> If we argue that tribes don't exist in Alaska, we undercut our ability to get federal funding to the tune of about $1 billion a year. Funds cannot be provided to Natives on the basis of race without violating equal protection. Funds must be provided based on the political relationship of Natives with the United States. This has always been a difficult balancing act ... But we did state that this bill is not intended to bolster the argument that there are tribes in Alaska. That is similar to the disclaimer language we did in the 1991 amendments [to ANCSA]. For Senator Stevens to say that as a matter of law there are no tribes in Alaska (except Metlakatla) would have resulted in riots in the streets.[56]

After Stevens arranged for the funds needed to support its activities to be appropriated, in September 2004 United States Attorney General John Ashcroft appointed nine individuals to serve as members of the Alaska Rural Justice and Law Enforcement Commission.[57] The commissioners then recruited forty-eight other individuals to serve as members of working groups, held fifteen hearings, and in 2006 issued a report that contained fifty-three recommendations.

The first recommendation was that the life of the commission be extended indefinitely.[58] After announcing that "[t]here are 229 federally recognized tribes in Alaska and improved communication between them is essential for effective, consistent, and efficient delivery of judicial services," a second recommendation urged that a tribal justice association be formed.[59] A third recommendation urged the State of Alaska to enter into cross-deputization agreements with federally recognized tribes that would authorize tribal police to enforce state criminal laws.[60]

In 2009 Ted Stevens left the Senate. But that year Alaska Senator Lisa Murkowski (whom her father had appointed to his seat in the Senate after he had been elected governor) took Stevens's seat on the Committee on Appropriations.[61] Senator Murkowski arranged for the money needed to support the commission's activities to continue to be appropriated. And the members of the commission continued to hold meetings and issue reports.[62] In 2012 the funding finally ended.[63, *]

The Alaska Rural Justice and Law Enforcement Commission accomplished the objective it had been created to achieve because the Department of Justice continues to give COPS grants to village councils.

For example, as has been described, in 1997 the Yup'ik Eskimo residents of Akiachak, the Native village on the Kuskokwim River in which Willie Kasayulie resides, dissolved their municipal government in order to enable the village council authorized

---

* Between October 2008 and March 2012, the commission's principal staff member was former assistant attorney general and Alaska Inter-Tribal Council executive director Donna Goldsmith.

in the constitution for the Akiachak Native Community (ANC) that Assistant Secretary of the Interior William Warne approved in 1948 pursuant to section 1 of Public Law No. 74-538 and section 16 of the IRA[64] to function as the local government.

In 2006, the year the Alaska Rural Justice and Law Enforcement Commission submitted its first report, the Department of Justice gave the ANC a COPS grant totaling $79,854. A year later the ANC received another COPS grant totaling $157,557.[65]

The money was spent to train five police officers and purchase two sport utility vehicles, four satellite telephones, five computers, ten police dress uniforms, and ten police standard uniforms. The grant application the ANC submitted described the law enforcement situation in Akiachak as follows: "We work with Alaska State Troopers whenever crime requires their intervention but almost all crimes are handled entirely by our own officers. Akiachak has a strong tribal court and most cases are heard in tribal court. Officers are expected to enforce all tribal codes, regulations and local laws."[66] A box on the application form asked, "Do officers have *primary* law enforcement authority for the population to be served?" (emphasis in original). Below that question George Peter, the tribal administrator, circled "yes" without explaining when and how the ANC acquired that authority.

To the present day the Department of Justice has not asked. Instead, in 2009, and then again in 2013, the department awarded the ANC three more COPS grants totaling $463,146.[67]

Six years later, at the behest of Alaska Senator Lisa Murkowski, in May 2019 United States Attorney General William Barr met in Anchorage with thirteen Alaska Natives who represented the AFN and twelve other Native organizations. The purpose of the meeting was to enable those in attendance to complain about the lack of law enforcement in Native villages where domestic violence, child sexual abuse, and other violent crime long had been pervasive.[68]

Two days later Attorney General Barr flew to Bethel and from there he toured Napaskiak, a Native village downriver from Bethel. When he returned to Washington, D.C., the Department of Justice announced that the attorney general had declared a "law enforcement emergency in rural Alaska," a designation that made $6 million available for "hiring, equipping, and training Village Public Safety Officers, Village Police Officers, and Tribal Police Officers working in rural Alaska, as well as for mobile detention facilities." The department also announced that the Office of Community Oriented Policing Services would award Native villages additional COPS grants totaling $4.5 million that the grantees would use to fund "20 officer positions, along with equipment and training."[69]

A month later the Office of Community Oriented Policing Services awarded four Native organizations and sixteen Native villages, including Akiachak and Chickaloon, COPS grants that totaled $1.97 million to purchase new equipment and $3.02 million to hire twenty law enforcement officers.[70]

Violence Against Women Act

In June 1990 Delaware Senator Joe Biden, the chairman of the Senate Committee on the Judiciary, introduced S. 2754, the Violence Against Women Act (VAWA).[71] The bill made grant money available to states and their political subdivisions to fund law enforcement and other activities for the purpose of curtailing domestic and other forms of violence perpetrated against women. The bill also amended various titles in the U.S. Code. One amendment added a new section 2264 to title 18, which read:

> (a) Any protection order[72] issued consistent with the terms of subsection (b) by the court of one State (the issuing State) shall be accorded full faith and credit by the court of another State (the enforcing State) and enforced as if it were the order of the enforcing State.
>
> (b) A protection order made by a State is consistent with the provisions of this section only if—
>
> (1) such court has jurisdiction under the law of such State; and
>
> (2) before the order is issued, reasonable notice and opportunity to be heard is given to the person against whom the order is sought, provided that, in the case of ex parte orders, it shall be sufficient if provision is made in the order for notice and opportunity to be heard as soon as possible after the order is issued, consistent with due process.

The Committee on the Judiciary held three days of hearings on the subject of violence against women[73] and then reported an amendment in the nature of a substitute for the original text of S. 2754.[74] At the hearings no witness representing an Indian tribe testified. And neither the original text of S. 2754 nor the amendment in the nature of a substitute mentioned Indian tribes.

The Senate took no further action on S. 2754 during the One Hundred-first Congress.

When the One Hundred-second Congress convened in January 1991, Senator Biden introduced S. 15,[75] a bill whose text, according to the Committee on the Judiciary, was "substantially similar to legislation introduced in the 101st Congress, S. 2754."[76] But the text was not identical. One difference was the inclusion of a provision that authorized "Indian tribes" to obtain grant money for the purpose of "reduc[ing] the rate of violent crimes against women in Indian country." The committee subsequently explained that the provision had been "drafted in conjunction with the Select Committee on Indian Affairs."[77]

To obtain a grant, an Indian tribe was required to submit an application that contained "a description of the tribes' law enforcement responsibilities for the Indian country described in the application." Because there was no Indian country in Alaska, the grant program had no applicability in Alaska. Nevertheless, the member of the staff of the select committee who wrote the provision included in it the "Indian tribe" definition in the Indian Self-Determination Act. The definition section of the Indian tribe grant provision stated: "The term 'Indian tribe' means any Indian tribe, band, nation, or other organized group or community, including any Alaska Native village or regional or village corporation (as defined in, or established pursuant to, the Alaska Native Claims Settlement Act), which is recognized as eligible for the special services provided by the United States to Indians because of their status as Indians."[78]

The Committee on the Judiciary held a hearing on S. 15 at which no witness representing an Indian tribe and no witness from Alaska testified,[79] and then reported the bill.[80] However, the Senate took no further action on S. 15 during the One Hundred-second Congress.

When the One Hundred-third Congress convened in January 1993, Senator Biden introduced as S. 11 the text of S. 15 that the Committee on the Judiciary had reported during the One Hundred-second Congress,[81] and the committee again reported the bill.[82]

In addition to the VAWA, during the One Hundred-second Congress, Senator Biden had tried, but failed, to pass an omnibus crime control bill. As has been described, in January 1993 the senator began that effort anew by introducing S. 1607, the Violent Crime Control and Law Enforcement Act.[83] During the debate on S. 1607 on the Senate floor, Senator Biden added the text of S. 11 into the bill. The Senate then passed the amended text of S. 1607 as an amendment in the nature of a substitute for the text of H.R. 3355, an omnibus crime control bill that had passed the U.S. House of Representatives.[84]

In March 1994 Representative Jack Brooks, the chairman of the House Committee on the Judiciary, had introduced H.R. 4092, an omnibus crime control bill whose text was an amalgamation of the texts of a number of crime control-related bills the committee had reported.[85] When the Senate sent its amended version of H.R. 3355 back to the House, Representative Brooks arranged for the House to amend the Senate amendment with an amendment whose text was the text of H.R. 4092.[86] A House-Senate conference committee then melded the texts of the Senate and House amendments into the version of H.R. 3355 that President Bill Clinton signed into law as the Violent Crime Control and Law Enforcement Act.[87]

One of the bills whose text Representative Brooks included in the House amendment to the Senate amendment to H.R. 3355 was H.R. 1133, a version of the VAWA that Representative Patricia Schroeder had introduced[88] and in November 1993 the House had passed by a vote of 421 to 0.[89]

The text of H.R. 1133 differed from the text of the version of the VAWA Senator Biden had included in the Senate amendment to H.R. 3355 in a consequential respect. Like the Senate amendment, the text of the section 2265 that would be added to title 18 of the U.S. Code in the version of H.R. 1133 that Representative Schroeder introduced was identical to the text of the section 2265 in the Senate amendment. But before the House Committee on the Judiciary reported H.R. 1133, the text of section

2265 was rewritten to require courts of one state to accord full faith and credit to protection orders issued by courts not only of another state but also of an Indian tribe.[90] Who arranged to insert the term "Indian tribe" into the text of section 2265 is not known.[91]

When the House-Senate conference committee accepted a modified version of the text of section 2265 in the House amendment to the Senate amendment to H.R. 3355 that text became 18 U.S.C. 2265.

Six years later Senator Biden introduced S. 2787, a bill to reauthorize the VAWA. Section 101(b)(4) of S. 2787 added two new provisions to 18 U.S.C. 2265. The first required a state to afford full faith and credit to, and enforce, a protection order issued by another state or by an Indian tribe even though the individual who asked that the order be enforced had not registered or filed the order with a court in the enforcing state. The second provided: "For the purposes of this section, a tribal court shall have full civil jurisdiction to enforce protection orders, including authority to enforce any orders through civil contempt proceedings, exclusion of violators from Indian lands, and other appropriate mechanisms, in matters arising within the authority of the tribe and in which at least 1 of the parties is an Indian."[92]

In 2000 when the One Hundred-sixth Congress enacted a version of the text of S. 2787 as Division B of Public Law No. 106-386, those new provisions were codified as 18 U.S.C. 2265(d)(2) and (e).[93]

While section 2265 did not define the term "Indian tribe," the section provided that an enforcing state was not to accord a protection order full faith and credit unless the issuing court had "jurisdiction over the parties and matter under the law of such State, Indian tribe, or territory."

In 1994 when the One Hundred-third Congress enacted section 2265, no court had suggested that a court that had been created by one of the Native entities that in 1993 Assistant Secretary of the Interior for Indian Affairs Ada Deer said were federally recognized tribes because that was the legal status she intended her publication of her list of Native entities in the *Federal Register* to create had such jurisdiction. So it is reasonable to assume that the One Hundred-sixth Congress did not intend the term "Indian tribe" in section 2265 to include any Native entities within its purview.

But when the VAWA again needed to be reauthorized, in 2005 Senator Biden introduced S. 1197, a bill whose enactment by the One Hundred-ninth Congress would do so.[94] Section 3 of S. 1197 amended the VAWA by adding a definition section that applied throughout the entire act, including 18 U.S.C. 2265.

One definition defined "courts" to mean "any civil or criminal, tribal, and Alaskan village, Federal, State, local or territorial court having jurisdiction to address domestic violence, dating violence, sexual assault or stalking, including immigration, family, juvenile, and dependency courts, and the judicial officers serving in those courts, including judges, magistrate judges, commissioners, justices of the peace, or any other person with decisionmaking authority."

Another definition used the "Indian tribe" definition in the Indian Self-Determination Act as a template to define "Indian tribe" throughout the VAWA, including in 18 U.S.C. 2265, to mean "a tribe, band, pueblo, nation, or other organized group or community of Indians, including any Alaska Native village or regional or village corporation (as defined in, or established pursuant to, the Alaska Native Claims Settlement Act), that is recognized as eligible for the special programs and services provided by the United States to Indians because of their status as Indians."

In 2005 Republicans controlled the Senate. Although he was not a member of the Committee on the Judiciary to which S. 1197 had been referred, Alaska Senator Ted Stevens was Senate president pro tempore and one of the body's most influential Republican members.

In 2002 when Alaska Senator Frank Murkowski had been elected governor of Alaska, he retained John Katz, the longtime director of the office the governor of Alaska maintained in Washington, D.C.[95] Throughout his career as a senator, Governor Murkowski had opposed the tribal sovereignty movement (even though, with no understanding of the legal and policy consequences, in 1994 he had facilitated the One Hundred-third Congress designating the members of the Central Council of Tlingit and Haida Indian Tribes of Alaska as a federally recognized tribe). For that reason, when Senator Biden introduced S. 1197, this author, who had been retained by the Legislative Council of the Alaska Legislature to advise the legislature regarding Alaska Native-related legal and policy issues, brought the "courts" and "Indian tribe" definitions to the attention of John Katz. He then suggested that, since he was Governor Murkowski's representative on Capitol Hill, Katz should ask Senator Stevens to have the Committee on the Judiciary modify the "courts" and "Indian tribe" definitions by removing the references to Alaska.

John Katz said he would do so.

But he did not.

As a consequence, three months later when the Committee on the Judiciary reported S. 1197, the "courts" and "Indian tribe" definitions had not been modified.[96]

In 2005 Elizabeth "Liz" Connell was a senior member of Senator Stevens's staff whose responsibilities included Alaska Native issues.[97] When this author brought the situation regarding the "courts" and "Indian tribe" definitions to her attention, Connell said that if John Katz had brought the matter to his attention before the Committee on the Judiciary reported S. 1197, Senator Stevens could have quietly arranged with Pennsylvania Senator Arlen Specter, the chairman of the committee, to modify the definitions. But now the only way the definitions could be modified was for Senator Stevens to offer an amendment when S. 1197 was debated on the floor of the Senate.

Two years earlier when he had included a rider in the Department of Justice FY 2004 appropriations bill that prohibited the Department of Justice from giving COPS grants to Native villages whose village councils had no criminal jurisdiction, and sovereignty activist Vernita Herdman and NARF attorney Heather Kendall-Miller had publicly accused him of racism, the senator had been subjected to such a barrage of opprobrium from tribal sovereignty activists that he withdrew the rider.

Because Connell believed that if during the debate on S. 1197 on the floor of the Senate, Senator Stevens offered an amendment to remove the references to Alaska Natives in the "courts" and "Indian tribe" definitions he would be subjected to a similar barrage of opprobrium from those same tribal sovereignty activists, she said she would not recommend to the senator that he offer such an amendment.

So during the debate on S. 1197 no amendment was offered, and neither Senator Stevens nor Alaska Senator Lisa Murkowski made any mention of how the One Hundred-ninth Congress's enactment of the bill would affect the tribal sovereignty situation in Alaska. And after Senator Biden and other members of a House-Senate conference committee negotiated a final text, the "courts" and "Indian tribe" definitions were enacted into law in section 3 of Public Law No. 109-162.[98]

Five years later when the VAWA again needed to be reauthorized, in November 2011 Vermont Senator Patrick Leahy, the Democratic chairman of the Committee on the Judiciary, introduced S. 1925, the Violence Against Women Reauthorization Act of 2012.

For Indian tribes whose members resided on reservations in the coterminous states, the policy concern du jour was that the tribes had no authority to prosecute non-Indian men who committed acts of domestic violence on the reservations.* Four months earlier the Department of Justice had sent to Capitol Hill a bill text whose enactment by the One Hundred-twelfth Congress would grant the tribes that authority,[99] and Senator Leahy included that text in S. 1925.[100]

In 1968 the Ninetieth Congress had enacted the Indian Civil Rights Act (ICRA)[101] to require an "Indian tribe," when it exercised "powers of self-government," to comply with some, although not with all, of the provisions in the Bill of Rights in the U.S. Constitution.

Section 904 of S. 1925 added a new section 204 to the ICRA that "recognized and confirmed" that the "power of self-government" of a "participating tribe" included the "inherent" power "to exercise special domestic violence criminal jurisdiction over all persons." And section 905 of S. 1925 amended 18 U.S.C. 2265(e) to read: "For purposes of this section, a court of an Indian tribe shall have full civil jurisdiction to issue and enforce protection orders involving any person, ... to exclude violators from Indian land, and to take other appropriate measures, in matters arising anywhere in the Indian country of the Indian tribe or otherwise within the authority of the Indian tribe."

When the Committee on the Judiciary reported an amendment in the nature of a substitute for the original text of S. 1925, at the request of Alaska Senator Lisa Murkowski, the amendment added language to sections 904 and 905 which stated

* In 1978 in its decision in *Oliphant v. Suquamish Indian* Tribe,[102] the U.S. Supreme Court held that an Indian tribe had no authority to prosecute a non-Indian for a crime allegedly committed on the tribe's reservation. In 1990 in its decision in *Duro v. Reina*,[103] the Court held that a tribe also had no authority to prosecute an Indian who was not a member of the tribe.

that neither section applied "to an Indian tribe in the State of Alaska, except with respect to the Metlakatla Indian Community, Annette Islands Reserve."[104]

Since section 904 defined "participating tribe" in the new section 204 of the ICRA to mean "an Indian tribe that elects to exercise special domestic violence criminal jurisdiction over the Indian country of that Indian tribe," and since the Annette Island reserve was (wrongly) assumed to be the only Indian country in Alaska, the exclusion of "Indian tribes in the State of Alaska" from section 904 had no practical consequence. However, when they discovered that, as a consequence of Senator Murkowski's amendment to section 905, the courts that by then had been created in many Native villages would be prohibited from issuing protective orders that section 905 authorized courts that Indian tribes had established on their reservations in the coterminous states to issue, tribal sovereignty activists were outraged.

At its annual assembly the Central Council of Tlingit and Haida Tribes of Alaska passed a resolution that directed its officers "to consider this an emergency situation and to inform the Alaska Congressional Delegation that the Central Council opposes any language that discriminates against Alaska Native families, the exclusion of Alaska Tribes must be removed from these bills."[105] And in a press release Robert Loescher, one of the authors of the resolution, railed: "We believe the way Congress is addressing the law is a challenge to the sovereignty of our Tribe and all tribes in Alaska."[106]

Two days later the AFN released to the press a letter the organization had sent to Senator Murkowski, Alaska Senator Mark Begich,* and Representative Don Young in which the AFN complained that "it shocks the conscience that an entire state—and home to 45 percent of the tribes in the United States—would be exempt from the entire bill," and asserted that the exemption "cripples the ability of Alaska tribes to intervene even in an emergency."[107]

As Ted Stevens had when Vernita Herdman and Heather Kendall-Miller publicly accused him of racism, Senator Murkowski promptly capitulated.[108] On April 26, 2012, when the Senate voted to pass S. 1925, Senator Murkowski told the Senate:

> Last weekend there was a great deal of concern that arose particularly amongst Alaska tribes that the version of S. 1925 that came out of the Judiciary Committee diminished the ability of the Alaska tribes to issue domestic violence protection orders that would enjoy full faith and credit from the State of Alaska.
>
> The concern we had was the result of an inadvertent technical drafting error that expanded certain tribal powers within Indian Country, but it appeared to repeal other existing tribal powers that are currently held by Alaska tribes. Our state has very little Indian Country. We do not have reservations, with the small exception of one reservation down in southeastern Alaska.

* In the 2008 Senate election in Alaska, Mark Begich, the former Democratic mayor of Anchorage, defeated Ted Stevens by less than 4,000 votes eight days after Stevens had been convicted of violating federal ethics laws.

> So for the past couple of days, I have been working, along with Senator Begich, to address this issue and have worked on a technical correction to address the concern in a way that ensures that Alaska tribes lose none of the jurisdiction or the authority they presently have to issue and to enforce their domestic violence protection orders. It was just this morning that I received a copy of a letter from Ed Thomas, who is president of the Central Council Tlingit and Haida Tribes of the State, and he has come out clearly endorsing the amendment. I would note that Senator Leahy has included these technical corrections in the substitute amendment he intends to bring forward, and I would certainly urge that it be adopted.[109]

Senator Leahy included Senator Murkowski's "technical correction" in his amendment in the nature of a substitute for the version of S. 1925 the Committee on the Judiciary had reported, after which the Senate passed the bill. The correction removed the exclusion of "Indian tribes in the State of Alaska" from sections 904 and 905. However, it added a subsection (b) to section 905 that stated: "Nothing in this Act, including an amendment made by this Act, alters or modifies the jurisdiction or authority of an Indian tribe in the State of Alaska under section 2265(e) of title 18, United States Code (as in effect on the day before the date of enactment of this Act)."[110] And it added a new section 910 that stated: "Nothing in this Act or any amendment made by this Act limits, alters, expands, or diminishes the civil or criminal jurisdiction of the State of Alaska, any subdivision of the State of Alaska, or any Indian tribe in the State of Alaska."[111]

When S. 1925 reached the House of Representatives, which the Republicans controlled, a majority of the members of the Republican caucus objected to section 904, as well as to several other sections of the bill. So Representative Eric Cantor, the majority leader, refused to bring S. 1925 to the floor for a vote before the One Hundred-twelfth Congress adjourned.[112]

In January 2013 when the One Hundred-thirteenth Congress convened, Senator Leahy introduced the text of S. 1925 as S. 47, after which the Senate promptly debated and passed the bill. During the debate, on a voice vote the Senate approved Amendment No. 11, which Senator Murkowski offered at the request of Attorney General Michael Geraghty.[113, *] The amendment rewrote section 910 of the bill to state:

> Sec. 910. Special Rule for the State of Alaska.
>
> (a) Expanded Jurisdiction. — In the State of Alaska, the amendments made by sections 904 and 905 shall only apply to the Indian country (as defined in section 1151 of title 18, United States Code) of the Metlakatla Indian Community, Annette Island Reserve.

* In 2006 Sean Parnell, an attorney and oil company lobbyist who had been a Republican member of the Alaska Legislature, was elected lieutenant governor of Alaska when Sarah Palin was elected governor. In 2009 when Governor Palin resigned in the middle of her term, Lieutenant Governor Parnell became governor. In 2010 he was elected to his own full term. In 2012 he appointed Michael Geraghty, an Anchorage attorney who specialized in commercial litigation, as attorney general.

> (b) Retained Jurisdiction.—The jurisdiction and authority of each Indian tribe in the State of Alaska under section 2265(e) of title 18, United States Code (as in effect on the day before the date of enactment of this Act)—
>
> (1) shall remain in full force and effect; and
>
> (2) are not limited or diminished by this Act or any amendment made by this Act.
>
> (c) Savings Provision.—Nothing in this Act or an amendment made by this Act limits or diminishes the jurisdiction of the State of Alaska, any subdivision of the State of Alaska, or any Indian tribe in the State of Alaska.[114]

When S. 47 was sent to the House, Representative Cantor by then had tired of the national press castigating the members of the Republican caucus for supporting violence against women because they had objected to various provisions in S. 1925. So he brought S. 47 to the floor, where the bill passed on a bipartisan vote. On March 7, 2013, when President Barack Obama signed S. 47 into law, Senator Murkowski's amendment became section 910 of Public Law No. 113-4.[115]

Senator Murkowski touted her amendment as a provision that continued to ensure that "All tribes in Alaska have the power to issue domestic violence protective orders against their members" by "reinforc[ing] the status quo."[116] But that explanation proved unavailing when Natalie Landreth, an attorney who worked with Heather Kendall-Miller in NARF's Anchorage office, issued a press release in which she charged that

> Senator Lisa Murkowski, who authored the Alaska exclusion apparently at the urging of the Alaska Attorney General's office, rebuffed all requests to remove the exclusion ... We are tired of the separate but equal treatment that Alaska tribes receive from the courts and Congress. They are tribes just like tribes in the Lower 48 and they are entitled to be treated like all other tribes. These exclusions, which have found their way into numerous bills over the years, say to Alaska's tribes that they are different and lesser than other tribes. In the case of VAWA, it means that Alaska Native women are less deserving of protection, less important. I find that unconscionable.[117]

Senator Murkowski pushed back by telling the Alaska Public Radio Network: "It was very clear that [section 904 of Public Law No. 113-4] was designed to be implemented in Indian country. In Alaska, the only Indian country, the only reservation, is Metlakatla. So I wanted to make sure that Metlakatla was going to be treated similarly to all other reservations, to all other land in Indian country."[118]

But when tribal sovereignty activists continued to complain, as she had in 2012, the senator capitulated. In August 2014 the *Washington Post* reported that "[a]fter pressure from Alaska Natives, Murkowski is reversing her position and trying to repeal the provision she inserted."[119]

Alaska Senator Lisa Murkowski.
Krysti Sshallenberger/KYUK.

In October 2014 the delegates who attended that year's AFN convention passed a resolution that demanded "the repeal of the Special Rule on Alaska contained in section 910 of VAWA 2013."[120]

Three weeks later Senator Murkowski introduced S. 2945, a bill Alaska Senator Mark Begich co-sponsored[121] whose single sentence stated: "Section 910 of the Violence Against Women Reauthorization Act of 2013 is repealed."[122]

Another three weeks later, on the floor of the Senate, Senator Begich called up S. 1474, a bill he had introduced and the Committee on Indian Affairs had reported. He then amended the bill by substituting the text of S. 2945. With no explanation by Senators Begich or Murkowski of the amended bill's purpose or legal consequence, the Senate passed S. 1474 on a voice vote,[123] after which Senator Murkowski issued a press release in which she explained that "Alaska tribes asked me to repeal Section 910 of VAWA, and I heard them loud and clear."[124]

Two days later Alaska Representative Don Young arranged for the House, also without any explanation of the bill's purpose or legal consequence, to pass S. 1474 on another voice vote,[125] after which he touted his accomplishment by explaining:

"In the many conversations I have had with Alaska Native leaders and families since the reauthorization of VAWA last year, I heard a consistent, clear, and powerful message: that Section 910 was an error and must be repealed."[126] A week later President Obama signed S. 1474 into law.[127]

The new section 204, which section 904 of S. 47 added to the ICRA, granted a "participating tribe" authority "to exercise special domestic violence criminal jurisdiction over all persons."[128] But since section 204 defined a "participating tribe" as an "an Indian tribe that elects to exercise special domestic violence criminal jurisdiction over the Indian country of that Indian tribe," and since there is no Indian country in Alaska, no "Indian tribe" in Alaska was a "participating tribe." As a consequence, while, pursuant to 18 U.S.C. 2265(a) and (e), an "Indian tribe" in Alaska had authority to issue a protection order, the individual who is the subject of the order must be a member of the tribe.

In addition, 18 U.S.C. 2265(b) provided that Alaska Dstrict and Superior Courts and state law enforcement personnel must accord full faith and credit to, and enforce, a protection order that a court of an "Indian tribe" in Alaska has issued only if the court gave the individual who is the subject of the order "reasonable notice and opportunity to be heard," or, if the order was issued *ex parte*, afforded that individual notice and an opportunity to be heard "within a reasonable time after the order is issued, sufficient to protect the respondent's due process rights."

How were Alaska Dstrict and Superior Court judges and Alaska State Troopers to determine whether a protection order had been issued by the court of an "Indian tribe" that had jurisdiction over the individual who was the subject of the order because the individual was a member of the tribe and whether the order had been issued in a manner that satisfied the due process requirements in 18 U.S.C. 2265(b)?

Alaska Statute 18.66.140 provided:

(a) A certified copy of an unexpired protective order issued in another jurisdiction may be filed with the clerk of court in any judicial district in this state.

(b) A protective order filed in accordance with (a) of this section has the same effect and must be enforced in the same manner as a protective order issued by a court of this state.

(c) When a protective order is filed with the court under this section, the court shall have the order delivered to the appropriate local law enforcement agency for entry into the central registry of protective orders under AS 18.65.540.

Nine months after the One Hundred-thirteenth Congress enacted S. 47 as Public Law No. 113-4, in December 2013 Attorney General Geraghty informed Troy Eid, the chairman of the Indian Law and Order Commission,* that "the Alaska State

* In 2010 the One Hundred-eleventh Congress created the Indian Law and Order Commission to study "law enforcement and criminal justice in tribal communities," and then submit a report on

Troopers ... enforce tribal court protective orders. They are required to be registered in state court but Commissioner [of Public Safety Joe] Masters assured me on more than one occasion that, if confronted with an emergency or tense situation, the troopers enforce the orders without the formality of state court registration."[129] In July 2014 United States Associate Attorney General Tony West admonished Attorney General Geraghty that 18 U.S.C. 2265(d)(2) directs that "[a]ny protection order that is otherwise consistent with this section shall be accorded full faith and credit, notwithstanding failure to comply with any requirement that the order be registered or filed in the enforcing State, tribal, or territorial jurisdiction."[130]

Four months later Alaska Governor Sean Parnell ran for a second full term in the November 2014 gubernatorial election and was defeated by Bill Walker, a Republican who had run as an independent candidate. When he was sworn into office, Governor Walker appointed his former law partner, an Anchorage attorney named Craig Richards, to succeed Michael Geraghty as attorney general.

In July 2015 Attorney General Richards issued an Attorney General's Opinion in which he advised that "Alaska's statutes requiring registration of tribal and foreign protection orders before enforcement are void and without effect" because the VAWA "expressly preempts state registration laws by requiring states to give full faith and credit to protection orders 'notwithstanding failure to comply with any requirement that the order be registered or filed.'" However, the opinion also advised that

> VAWA requires the State to enforce only tribal and foreign protection orders that are "consistent" with VAWA. An order is consistent with VAWA if the issuing "court has jurisdiction over the parties and matter under the law of such State, Indian tribe, or territory," and "reasonable notice and opportunity to be heard is given" to the offender "sufficient to protect that person's right to due process." Because only consistent orders are entitled to full faith and credit, the State may review a tribal order for jurisdiction and due process before giving it full faith and credit.[133]

Alaska Statute A.S. 18.65.540 requires the Department of Public Safety to "maintain a central registry of protective orders." Before it adds a protection order that has been issued by the court of an "Indian tribe" to the registry, how is the department—as Attorney General Richards in his Attorney General's Opinion directed it to do—to review the order to determine whether that court had jurisdiction over the indi-

---

that subject.[131] The report the commission submitted in 2013[132] contained a chapter devoted to criminal justice in Native villages in Alaska. In that chapter the commission recommended that Congress "repeal Section 910 of Title IX of the Violence Against Women Reauthorization Act of 2013 and thereby permit Alaska Native communities and their courts to address domestic violence and sexual assault, committed by Tribal members and non-Natives, the same as now will be done in the lower 48," and "affirm the inherent criminal jurisdiction of Alaska Native tribal governments over their members within the external boundaries of their villages." With respect to those recommendations it merits mention that the commission's advisory committee included Wilson Justin and Georgianna Lincoln, both prominent members of tribal sovereignty movement.

vidual who was the subject of the order because he or she was a member of the tribe that had created the court and had provided that individual reasonable notice and an opportunity to be heard?

In June 2016 Craig Richards resigned and Governor Walker appointed Anchorage attorney Jahna Lindemuth to succeed Richards as attorney general. Two months after she assumed office, Attorney General Lindemuth announced that "the Department of Public Safety, in consultation with the Department of Law, instructs state law enforcement officers to put the safety of citizens first and enforce any tribal court protective order that appears valid on its face. Any challenge to the tribal protective order can be addressed later in a court proceeding."[134]

In other words, with the knowledge and approval of the attorney general the Department of Public Safety would add to its central registry protection orders that had been issued by courts that had been created in Native villages without determining that an order had been issued lawfully.

In 2017 the Alaska Legislature would codify that procedure.

The Attorney General's Opinion that Attorney General Richards had issued concluded by recommending that the State of Alaska "resolve the conflict between its statutes and [the VAWA] with legislative amendments that bring Alaska's statutes into compliance with federal law."

In January 2016 Representative Bryce Edgmon, an Alaska Native who had been the longtime chairman of Choggiung Limited, the ANCSA village corporation headquartered in Dillingham, introduced HB 221 in the Alaska House of Representatives.

Section 6 of HB 221 amended subsection (b) of Alaska Statute 18.66.140 to eliminate the requirement that a protection order that had been issued in another jurisdiction be filed with the clerk of a district or superior court before the Alaska State Troopers could enforce the order. Section 6 also stated that a "protective order issued in another jurisdiction" was an order that had been "issued by a court of the United States, a court of another state or territory, a United States military tribunal, or a tribal court" and that was "entitled to full faith and credit under 18 U.S.C. 2265."

HB 221 did not define the term "tribal court." But when the House Judiciary Committee held a hearing on the bill, Representative Edgmon told the committee that he intended "tribal court" to mean a court that had been created in a Native village. Representative Edgmon also told the committee that he was a "strong proponent of tribal courts," that "tribal courts have a growing role in terms of providing justice and other services out in the local areas," and that "the purpose of the bill is motivated (sic) by allowing tribal courts to take an additional step under Alaska law to increase their duties."[135]

Pursuant to Alaska Statute 11.56.740, violating a protection order is a misdemeanor. How was an Alaska State Trooper to determine whether a protection order that had been issued by a tribal court was "entitled to full faith and credit under 18 U.S.C. 2265" before the trooper enforced the order by arresting the individual who was the subject of the order for having violated it?

Not only did HB 221 establish no procedure for making that determination, section 7 of the bill added a subsection (d) to Alaska Statute 18.66.140 that provided: "A protective order issued in another jurisdiction that appears authentic on its face is presumed valid."

In other words, if an Alaska State Trooper determined that an individual had violated a directive that had been written on a piece of paper that purported to be a protection order that had been issued by a tribal court and that piece of paper appeared "authentic on its face," subsection (d) directed the trooper to arrest that individual without investigating whether, because he was not a member of the "Indian tribe" that had created the court that had issued the order, the court had no jurisdiction over that individual, or, if the individual was a member of the "Indian tribe" that had created the court, the court had not afforded the individual the notice and opportunity to be heard that 18 U.S.C. 2265 required.

When he testified at the hearing the House Judiciary Committee held on HB 221, Representative Edgmon indicated that he had no idea what in its legal particulars his bill did other than amend the Alaska Statutes to comply with the requirements of the VAWA, whatever those requirements were. However, when Tim Clark, the member of his staff who was handling HB 221 for Representative Edgmon, testified, he explained that section 7 had been included in the bill in order to add "a presumption of validity on the part of law enforcement so that they're encouraged to enforce a protective order issued by another jurisdiction so long as it appears authentic on its face. We kind of think of that as an error on the side of caution. That presumption of validity does exist in other states who've (sic) addressed these matters."[136]

Who made the decision to include section 7 in HB 221 even though the VAWA did not require a "presumption of validity"? According to Clark, "While drafting the bill I looked at the implementation of VAWA in other states and came across the presumption of validity in Washington state law." So Clark decided on his own to include section 7 in the bill, after which, according to Clark, Representative Edgmon signed off and "[t]he Department of Law never had a problem with us including it."[137]

While the Judiciary Committee reported HB 221 to the Alaska House of Representatives,[138] no further action on the bill was taken prior to the adjournment of the Alaska Legislature.

In January 2017 when the first session of the new legislature began, Representative Edgmon reintroduced HB 221 as HB 8. When the House Judiciary Committee held a hearing on the bill, Assistant Attorney General Mary Lundquist was asked to explain how it would be determined that a protection order was entitled to full faith and credit. She answered:

> Although we don't look at those issues up front, the person against whom the proceeding is — the violation of the protection order is — being brought they have an opportunity to object in court as to whether there was jurisdiction in the issuing court, personal jurisdiction, subject matter jurisdiction, whether they were given due process. So there will be an opportunity to challenge a protection order once it's in court.[139]

That was the end of the discussion of the matter. And no further mention was made when the members of the Alaska House of Representatives discussed HB 8 before passing the bill by a vote of 38 to 2. Nor was any mention made when on the last day of the legislative session the text of HB 8 was included in an amendment in the nature of a substitute for the text of SB 55, an omnibus crime control bill that had passed the Alaska Senate. Nor was any mention made when the Alaska Senate, by a vote of 17 to 0, accepted the House substitute.

The number of protection orders the Department of Public Safety lists on its central registry fluctuates day to day. To pick a day, on March 26, 2019, the registry contained 1,583 orders.[140]

How many of those orders had been issued by a tribal court?

When he was asked, Department of Public Safety spokesman Trooper Captain Daniel Lowden explained that "[w]e do not track tribal orders as a separate category," and "the registry does not have a field for the name of the court or the court case number." Instead, the names of the parties and the conditions the judge who signed the order imposed on the individual who is the subject of the order are the only information contained in the registry.[141] As a consequence, when a trooper consults the registry, not only is there no way for the trooper to know whether a protection order had been issued by a tribal court, there is no way the trooper can determine whether the order "appears authentic on its face."[142]

In the November 2018 elections, Democratic candidates won a majority of the seats in the U.S. House of Representatives in the One Hundred-sixteenth Congress that convened in January 2019.

On March 7, 2019, California Representative Karen Bass, the chair of the Subcommittee on Crime, Terrorism, and Homeland Security of the House Committee on the Judiciary, introduced H.R. 1585, the Violence Against Women Reauthorization Act of 2019.

Title IX of the bill, entitled "Safety for Indian Women," began with section 901, which contained fifteen findings of fact. Finding no. 3 stated: "The vast majority of Native victims — 96% of women and 89% of male victims — report being victimized by a non-Indian." And finding no. 15 stated:

> In States with restrictive land settlement acts such as Alaska, "Indian country" is limited, resources for local tribal responses either nonexistent or insufficient to meet the needs, jurisdiction unnecessarily complicated and increases the

> already high levels of victimization of American Indian and Alaska Native women. According to the Tribal Law and Order Act Commission report, Alaska Native women are overrepresented in the domestic violence victim population by 250 percent; they comprise 19 percent of the State population, but are 47 percent of reported rape victims. And among other Indian Tribes, Alaska Native women suffer the highest rates of domestic and sexual violence in the country.

How Representative Bass determined the factual validity of those findings was not explained.

To address finding no. 15, section 903 of title IX contained a provision that amended section 204 of the ICRA "to create a pilot project to allow up to five Indian tribes in Alaska to implement special tribal criminal jurisdiction" over non-Indians accused of domestic, dating, or sexual violence, stalking, sex trafficking, violating a protection order, obstructing justice, or assaulting a law enforcement or correctional officer within a tribe's "Indian country," which a companion provision defined as "Alaska Native-owned Townsites, Allotments, and former reservation lands acquired in fee by Alaska Native Village Corporations pursuant to the Alaska Native Claims Settlement Act and other lands transferred in fee to Native villages."

Who arranged to have Representative Bass include section 903 in H.R. 1585? When asked, all Milagros Cisneros, an attorney on the staff of the Subcommittee on Crime, Terrorism, and Homeland Security who had been involved in writing the bill, would say was that the "pilot project idea came from a broad group of advocates that work on the issues addressed by VAWA, and that have been working on these issues for many years."[143]

However it happened, six days after Representative Bass introduced H.R. 1585, the Committee on the Judiciary convened to enable the members to mark-up and then report an amendment in the nature of a substitute for the original text of H.R. 1585 that Representative Jerrold Nadler, the chairman of the committee, offered.[144]

During the mark-up Representative James Sensenbrenner, a former Republican chairman of the committee, offered an amendment whose adoption would repeal section 204 of the ICRA in its entirety. Representative Sensenbrenner explained that in 2013 he had voted against S. 47 because it added section 204 to the ICRA, a provision he considered "constitutionally problematic." He then argued:

> Tribal courts do not necessarily adhere to the same constitutional provisions that protect the rights of all defendants in Federal and State courts. This sets us down the road to a dangerous path.
>
> In other words, some tribal courts say that if you are tried before a tribal court, the protections of the U.S. Constitution, of which there are many, particularly in the Fourth, Fifth, and Fourteenth Amendments, do not apply. They apply for someone who is accused of the same type of crime, either in a Federal or a State court. This committee has not looked at this question,

> and, in effect, the 2013 reauthorization ended up taking away the constitutional rights of someone who happens to cross a reservation line and ends up being accused of domestic violence.
>
> What this amendment does is to strip the special domestic violence criminal jurisdiction for Indian tribes provision. Congress has a right to be concerned about spousal abuse, and I think every member of this committee is concerned about spousal abuse, and our voting records and our public and private statements have indicated it. On other forms of domestic violence on Indian reservations, this issue should be addressed in a constitutionally sound manner.
>
> I have been on this committee for 40 years. We have never had a hearing on whether we should take away the constitutional rights of non-Indians who end up being charged in tribal courts. That is why this amendment should be adopted. And I think that those who are in support of the amendment should be allowed to talk about it, and those who are in support of continuing the current provision in law, you know, should have more than the debate on an amendment on an important reauthorization bill (sic) the 5-minute rule.[145]

When Representative Sennsenbrenner finished explaining the rationale for his amendment, Representative Nadler instructed the Democratic members of the committee to vote no because

> the 2013 VAWA reauthorization included a provision, and, therefore, it is included in current law, included a provision that reaffirmed the inherent sovereign authority of Indian tribal governments to exercise criminal jurisdiction over certain non-Indians. The provision was limited to crimes of domestic violence, dating violence, and criminal violations of protection orders.
>
> By exercising this jurisdiction, tribal communities have increased safety and justice for some victims. There are no constitutional concerns with this provision. This amendment seeks to do away with all of this that we have had operating in the law since 2013. It is a salutary provision of the law. It should not be abolished, and, therefore, I oppose the amendment.[146]

Representative Sennsenbrenner's amendment then was voted down on a party-line vote, after which, on another party-line vote, the committee reported H.R. 1585.

A week later when H.R. 1585 was debated on the House floor, Alaska Representative Don Young offered an amendment that added to the four categories of land in the "Indian country" definition in the pilot project provision a fifth category: "All lands within any Alaska Native village with a population that is at least 75 percent Native."

The House accepted the amendment by unanimous consent on a voice vote.

Prior to that vote Representative Young, reading from a script his staff had written, explained that "the bill would create an Alaska Native jurisdiction pilot program for five villages, but only covers Native lands that are largely outside the villages. These lands are not where people live and, therefore, not where crimes are committed. My amendment would add jurisdiction for all lands inside Alaska Native villages to cover where the majority of violence actually occurs." Representative Young concluded by telling the House that "the National Congress of American Indians, Alaska Federation of Natives, the Tanana Chiefs Conference, and Bristol Bay Native Corporation" supported his amendment.[147]

The next afternoon the House passed H.R. 1585 and sent the bill to the Senate.

Because the bill contained a number of provisions, including a "boyfriend" provision that prohibited individuals who had subjected their domestic partners or paramours to domestic violence from possessing a firearm to which most, if not all, Republican senators objected, in the Senate, H.R. 1585 was politically dead on arrival. Because it was, Iowa Senator Joni Ernst, a Republican member of the Committee on the Judiciary who had been both a rape victim and a victim of domestic violence, arranged with California Senator Dianne Feinstein, the ranking Democratic member of the committee, to jointly write a new bill to reauthorize the VAWA that would contain only those provisions that senators from both parties could support.

The senators and their staffs began meeting. But in November, according to Senator Ernst, "after months of work and mountains of effort toward a bipartisan bill, it all came to a screeching halt" because in the run-up to the 2020 election the members of the Democratic caucus "decided to move forward on the House-passed VAWA bill," which Ernst disparaged as "chalk full of partisan political talking points."[148]

Two weeks later, on November 13, 2019, Senator Feinstein introduced S. 2843, whose text was a modified version of the text of H.R. 1585 and which all Democratic senators co-sponsored. S. 2843 contained provisions relating to Indian tribes and Indian country, including a section 903 that amended section 204 of the ICRA to require the attorney general to "establish a pilot program for Native villages in Alaska to exercise special tribal criminal jurisdiction [over non-Natives] in village areas" and defined "village area" to mean "the Alaska Native Village Statistical Area [ANVSA] covering all or any portion of a Native village."

An ANVSA is an intellectual construct the Bureau of the Census invented to facilitate the analysis of data obtained during the decennial census. The boundaries of ANVSAs are not marked on the ground and exist only on maps that are not easily obtainable. For those reasons, in 2008 the Bureau cautioned that "[r]epresentation of ANVSA boundaries in Census Bureau products is solely for the purpose of data collection, tabulation, and presentation and does not convey or confer any rights to land ownership, governmental authority, or jurisdictional status."[149] Nevertheless, in S. 2843 Senator Feinstein employed ANVSAs for a purpose — the conferral of governmental authority and jurisdictional status — for which the concept had explicitly not been intended.

The week after Senator Feinstein introduced S. 2843, Senator Ernst introduced her own bill, S. 2920, which South Carolina Senator Lindsey Graham, the Republican chairman of the Committee on the Judiciary, and nine other Republican senators, including Alaska Senator Dan Sullivan,* co-sponsored. Like S. 2843, S. 2920 contained provisions relating to Indian tribes and Indian country, including a provision that amended section 204 of the ICRA. But that amendment did not contain a pilot program to enable "Indian tribes in Alaska" to exercise criminal jurisdiction over non-Natives.

When Senator Feinstein stopped meeting with Senator Ernst and Senator Ernst then decided to write her own bill, Alaska Senator Lisa Murkowski apparently learned that Ernst's bill would not contain a provision authorizing a pilot program. As a consequence, the month before Senator Feinstein introduced S. 2843, Senator Murkowski introduced S. 2616, the Alaska Tribal Public Safety Empowerment Act, which she touted as a bill that "builds upon the Alaska pilot (sic) championed by Congressman Young in H.R. 1585 that the House passed in April of this year." She also said she had introduced the bill at the request of the AFN, the Association of Village Council Presidents, and the Central Council of Tlingit Haida Indian Tribes of Alaska.[150]

S. 2616 expanded the pilot project from five "Indian tribes in Alaska" to thirty. Section 4(a) of the bill provided:

> Subject to title II of the [Indian] Civil Rights Act of 1968, and regardless of the holder of title in and to any applicable land, Congress recognizes and affirms that any Indian tribe in the State [of Alaska] occupying a village may exercise, as part of the inherent authority of the Indian tribe —
>
> (1) criminal and civil jurisdiction over all Alaska Natives present in the village; and
>
> (2) full civil jurisdiction within the village —
>
> (A) to issue and enforce protection orders involving any individual, including the authority to enforce such an order through a civil contempt proceeding;
>
> (B) to exclude violators from the village; and

* The scion of a wealthy Republican family in Ohio, after graduating from military boarding school, Harvard, and Georgetown Law School, Sullivan married Julie Fate, a member of Alaska Senator Ted Stevens's staff who is of Athabascan Indian descent and the daughter of a locally prominent family in Fairbanks. In 2009 Alaska Governor Sarah Palin appointed Sullivan, who had been working for the Bush administration in Washington, D.C., and as a consequence was unemployed, to succeed Talis Colberg as attorney general. In the 2014 Alaska Senate election Sullivan narrowly defeated Mark Begich, the incumbent Democratic senator who in the 2008 Alaska Senate election had narrowly defeated Ted Stevens. In 2020 Sullivan was elected to a second term.

(C) to use other appropriate mechanisms to address matters arising anywhere in the village that are subject of protection orders.

And section 3(4) of the bill defined "village" to mean the "Alaska Native Village Statistical Area covering all or any portion of a Native village," which undoubtedly is where the member of Senator Feinstein's staff who wrote S. 2843 came across the idea of using ANVSAs as a substitute for the "Indian country" definition in H.R. 1585.

No senator, Republican or Democrat, wanted to be accused of being opposed to preventing violence from being perpetrated against women. So in concept a bill to reauthorize the VAWA had bipartisan support. But with control of the Senate during the One Hundred-seventeenth Congress to be decided by the outcome of the 2020 election contests in which twenty Republican and eleven Democratic senators were running for reelection, to prevent the other party from gaining partisan advantage, Kentucky Senator Mitch McConnell, the Republican majority leader, refused to allow the Senate to vote on H.R. 1585 or S. 2843 and New York Senator Chuck Schumer, the Democratic minority leader, refused to allow the Senate to vote on S. 2920. As a consequence, on January 3, 2021, when the One Hundred-sixteenth Congress adjourned the bills died.

In the November 2020 elections former Delaware Senator Joe Biden, who in 1990 had been the sponsor of the VAWA, was elected president, and Democratic candidates won a majority of the seats in the House of Representatives and fifty seats in the Senate that, when Vice President Kamala Harris voted whenever her vote was needed, gave Democratic senators control of that body as well during the One Hundred-seventeenth Congress.

On March 8, 2021, Texas Representative Sheila Jackson Lee, who had succeeded Representative Karen Bass as chair of the Subcommittee on Crime, Terrorism, and Homeland Security of the House Committee on the Judiciary, introduced H.R. 1620, the Violence Against Women Reauthorization Act of 2021.

Although H.R. 1620 was referred to seven committees, President Biden urged "swift passage,"[151] and nine days after it was introduced Representative Jerrold Nadler, the chairman of the Committee on the Judiciary, brought the bill to the floor, where after an hour of cursory debate the House passed H.R. 1620 on a mostly party-line vote.[152]

Since the text of H.R. 1620 was based on the text of the version of H.R. 1585 that the House had passed in 2019, section 903 of H.R. 1620 contained the pilot program that delegated five "Indian tribes in Alaska" the authority to jail, and in the tribes' courts prosecute, non-Natives, as well as the "Indian country" definition Alaska Representative Don Young had amended during the debate on H.R. 1585.[153]

In the Senate, as H.R. 1585 had been during the previous Congress, H.R. 1620 was politically dead on arrival because ten Republican senators needed to be willing to vote to end the filibuster that Senator Schumer, who was now the Democratic majority leader, would provoke if he tried to bring the bill to the floor. But because they objected to the boyfriend provision, as well as to several other provisions in H.R. 1620, no Republican senator supported the bill.

To demonstrate that, while they opposed H.R. 1620, the members of the Republican caucus supported reauthorizing the VAWA, Senator McConnell, the Republican minority leader, asked Senator Ernst, who had led the Republican effort to reauthorize the VAWA during the previous Congress, to write a new bill that Republican senators could support. Senator Ernst agreed, and during an impromptu news conference when she was asked about the VAWA reauthorization she confirmed that "we are working on a bill again, taking what we worked on in the last Congress."[154]

At the beginning of the One Hundred-seventeenth Congress, Alaska Senator Lisa Murkowski, who had been a member of the Committee on Indian Affairs since 2003, became the Republican vice chair of the committee. So Senator Ernst asked Senator Murkowski to write the sections of the new bill dealing with Indian tribes. Senator Murkowski agreed, and during that same impromptu news conference Senator Ernst announced that "we have Lisa Murkowski now, who is working on the tribal portion."

S. 2920, the bill Senator Ernst wrote during the One Hundred-sixteenth Congress, had not included a pilot project for "Indian tribes in Alaska," which may have been why Senator Murkowski introduced S. 2616, her bill whose enactment would have created a pilot project and expanded eligibility to participate from five "Indian tribes in Alaska" to thirty.

In October 2019 when Senator Murkowski introduced S. 2616, the bill was referred to the Committee on Indian Affairs. But during the fourteen months that remained of the One Hundred-sixteenth Congress, the committee did not hold a hearing on the bill. Since she was a member of the committee, the fact that no hearing was held suggests that Senator Murkowski did not ask North Dakota Senator John Hoeven, the Republican chairman, to schedule one.

If she did not, her failure to do so would suggest that, while Senator Murkowski introduced S. 2616 at the request of the AFN, the Association of Village Council Presidents, and the Central Council of Tlingit Haida Indian Tribes of Alaska in order to curry favor with Native organizations whose support she will need when she runs for reelection in 2022, privately she was not supportive of Congress delegating "Indian tribes in Alaska" authority to jail, and for their courts to prosecute, non-Natives.

If that is not the reason the committee did not hold a hearing, now that she is writing the "tribal portion" of Senator Ernst's new bill, Senator Murkowski is well-positioned to arrange for the bill to include the text of S. 2616. Whether she will or not is, as of this writing, not known. However, on June 14, 2021 Senator Murkowski published an editorial in the *Anchorage Daily News* in which she touted her efforts to persuade the One Hundred-seventeenth Congress to enact legislation that would address the "on-going crisis of sexual assault and domestic violence in Alaska." She concluded the editorial by announcing that, "I am engaging in bipartisan discussions on the reauthorization of VAWA. I'm pushing for strong tribal provisions, which would empower Alaska Natives to obtain protection under Special Domestic Violence Criminal Jurisdiction."[155]

Sixteen

Section 5 of the Indian Reorganization Act, which the Seventy-third Congress enacted in 1934, authorizes the secretary of the interior to acquire any land he wishes at any location he considers appropriate as long as he acquires the land "for the purpose of providing land for Indians." Section 5 also provides that "title to lands or rights acquired pursuant to this Act shall be taken in the name of the United States in trust for the Indian tribe or individual Indian for which the land is acquired, and such lands or rights shall be exempt from State and local taxation." For the purposes of section 5, as well as for the purposes of all other sections of the IRA, section 19 of the IRA defines "Indian" to mean:

(1) persons of Indian descent who are members of any recognized Indian tribe now under Federal jurisdiction,

(2) persons who are descendants of such members who were, on June 1, 1934, residing within the present boundaries of any Indian reservation, and

(3) all other persons of one-half or more Indian blood.

The authority to acquire land that section 5 delegates to the secretary of the interior is so unfettered that in 1995 Judge James Loken of the U.S. Court of Appeals for the Eighth Circuit concluded that section 5 "permits the secretary to purchase a factory, an office building, a residential subdivision, or a golf course in trust for an Indian tribe, thereby removing these properties from state and local tax rolls. Indeed, it would permit the secretary to purchase the Empire State Building in trust for a tribal chieftain as a wedding present."[1]

Section 5 was one of the sections of the IRA that section 13 of the IRA did not apply in the Territory of Alaska. But at the request of Alaska Delegate Anthony Dimond in 1935, Felix Cohen, the assistant solicitor at the Department of the Interior who had written the bill that in amended form the Seventy-third Congress enacted as the IRA, wrote the bill that in 1936 Dimond introduced in the Seventy-fourth Congress as H.R. 9866.

Section 1 of H.R. 9866 included section 5 as one of the sections of the IRA that "shall hereafter apply to the Territory of Alaska."

Secretary of the Interior Harold Ickes explained to the members of the House Committee on Indian Affairs to which the bill had been referred that section 1 of H.R. 9866 extended the application of section 5 to the Territory of Alaska because doing so was "necessary in the establishment and the administration of [the reservations that section 2 of the bill authorized the secretary of the interior to designate]."[2] In other words, Felix Cohen and Secretary Ickes intended the secretary to use the authority section 5 delegated for the singular purpose of acquiring privately owned land that was located within the boundaries of the Indian reservations that section 2 of H.R. 9866 authorized the secretary to designate in the future. However, if that was their intent, Felix Cohen and William Paul, whom the Alaska Native Brotherhood had sent to Washington, D.C., to work with Cohen on the bill, made a drafting error when they wrote an amendment to H.R. 9866 that the members of the Committee on Indian Affairs adopted before they reported the bill to the U.S. House of Representatives.

The amendment authorized the secretary of the interior to issue "groups of Indians in Alaska not heretofore recognized as bands or tribes, but having a common bond of occupation, or association, or residence within a well-defined neighborhood, community, or rural district" constitutions pursuant to section 16 of the IRA and corporate charters pursuant to section 17 of the IRA. But the amendment did not amend the "Indian" definition in section 19 of the IRA to include those groups.

The legal consequence was that section 5 of the IRA delegated the secretary of the interior authority to acquire land in Alaska for a group of Alaska Natives only if the members of the group could qualify as section 19 "Indians" by demonstrating that they were members of a "recognized Indian tribe" that on June 18, 1934, (the date President Franklin Roosevelt signed the IRA into law) had been "under Federal jurisdiction." But there were no such groups.

Because there were not, between 1936 when the Seventy-fourth Congress enacted H.R. 9866 as Public Law No. 74-538 and 1971 when the Ninety-second Congress enacted ANCSA, with a single ambiguous possible exception,* the secretary of the interior did not exercise the authority section 5 delegated and acquire any land in Alaska.

---

* Between 1947 and 1950 the BIA acquired land for three corporations whose charters had been approved by the secretary of the interior pursuant to section 1 of Public Law No. 74-538 and section 17 of the IRA. In 1938 Assistant Secretary of the Interior Oscar Chapman approved a charter for the Klawock Cooperative Association, which "a group of Indians having a common bond of occupation in the fishing industry in Klawock" had submitted. In 1939 Assistant Secretary Chapman approved a charter for the Angoon Community Association, which "a group of Indians having a common bond of residence in the neighborhood of Angoon" had submitted. And in 1947 Assistant Secretary of the Interior William Warne approved a charter for the Organized Village of Kake, which, according to the charter, "the Kake Indians of Alaska, an Indian band or tribe," had submitted.[3] In 1939, by which time the secretary of the interior had approved charters that the Tlingit and Haida Indian residents of four other communities in southeast Alaska had submitted, the BIA began loaning money to the corporations from the revolving fund that section 10 of the IRA had established.[4] In 1947 and 1949 the BIA loaned the corporations in Angoon, Klawock, and Kake several hundred thousand dollars each to purchase salmon canneries that were being operated in those communities.[5] The BIA had the sellers convey the title to the land on which the cannery buildings were located to the United States.[6] The deed, dated February 15, 1950, in which P.E. Harris & Co. conveyed its title to the land under the cannery it owned in Kake states that the title was conveyed "to the United States of America in trust for the Organized Village of Kake." And the deed, dated March 29, 1950, in which three Tlingit Indian residents of Klawock conveyed their title to the land under the cannery they owned in Klawock states that the title was conveyed "to the United States of America in trust for the Klawock Cooperative Association." The deed for the cannery in Kake does not identify the statute that authorized the United States to accept the deed. However, the deed for the cannery in Klawock states: "This

As has been described, pursuant to section 1 of Public Law No. 74-538 and section 16 of the IRA, in 1939 Assistant Secretary of the Interior Oscar Chapman approved a constitution for an organization called the Native Village of Venetie (NVV). Then exercising the authority section 2 of Public Law No. 74-538 delegated, in 1943 Assistant Secretary Chapman designated 1.8 million acres of public land within and surrounding Venetie and the nearby community of Arctic Village as the Venetie reserve.

In 1971 in section 19(a) of ANCSA, the Ninety-second Congress revoked the Venetie reserve and all other reserves (other than the Annette Island reserve) that had been set aside "for Native use or for the administration of Native affairs."

After the Venetie reserve was revoked, pursuant to section 8 of ANCSA the Gwitch'in Indian residents of Venetie and Arctic Village incorporated the Venetie Indian Corporation and the Neets'ai Corporation. The corporations then elected for the secretary of the interior to convey to the corporations fee title to the 1.8 million acres of public land that had been within the boundaries of the reserve.

In 1976 Donald Wright, a Fairbanks resident of Athabascan Indian descent whom the village council that the NVV constitution had authorized the residents of Venetie to elect had hired as an advisor, informed Commissioner of Indian Affairs Morris Thompson that when the Venetie Indian Corporation and the Neets'ai Corporation received their fee titles to the 1.8 million acres, the corporations intended to convey their titles to Secretary of the Interior Thomas Kleppe and then request Commissioner Thompson to recommend to the secretary that he accept the deeds and take the title to the land into trust in the name of the United States pursuant to section 5 of the IRA.

When Commissioner Thompson passed Wright's communication up through the Department of the Interior bureaucracy, Under Secretary of the Interior Kent Frizzell investigated the matter. After doing so, he informed Commissioner Thompson "that the Alaska Native Claims Settlement Act precludes the secretary from restoring land held in fee by Alaska Natives to trust status pursuant to Section 5 of the Indian Reorganization Act."[8]

A year later when Jimmy Carter became president and appointed Idaho Governor Cecil Andrus to succeed Thomas Kleppe as secretary, Donald Wright tried again by

---

conveyance is made pursuant to the provisions of the Act of June 18, 1934 [IRA], as amended by the Act of May 1, 1936 [Public Law No. 74-538]. But contrary to that assertion, Public Law No. 74-538 did not amend the IRA, and the sentence does not identify the provisions of the IRA to which it refers. And while someone at the BIA wrote the deed,[7] there is no evidence that before he or she did so the solicitor of the Department of the Interior conducted a legal analysis in which he concluded that, as sections 5 and 19 of the IRA required them to be, the members of the Klawock Cooperative Association were members of an "Indian tribe" that on June 18, 1934 had been both "recognized" and "under Federal jurisdiction."

asking Secretary Andrus to agree to take the corporations' fee titles to the land within the boundaries of the revoked Venetie reserve into trust.[9]

Associate Solicitor for Indian Affairs Thomas Fredericks researched the issue and in 1978 issued a legal opinion in which he advised that his research had "reaffirm[ed] the conclusion of the former under secretary" because "the intent of Congress [in section 2(b) of ANCSA] to permanently remove all Native lands in Alaska from trust status is unmistakable." Fredericks also explained that

> the structure and legislative history of Section 19 [of ANCSA] itself precludes the restoration of former reservations to trust status ... It is clear from alternatives to Section 19 in earlier proposed settlement legislation that Congress did not exclude the alternative of continued trust status by oversight .. the Councils of Venetie and Arctic Village proposed an amendment to Section 15 of H.R. 10193 (an earlier version of Section 19) which would have permitted the retention of trust status. The proposal was never incorporated into ANCSA.[10]

Based on that legal opinion, the solicitor of the Department of the Interior informed Donald Wright that Secretary Andrus "simply does not have the authority to ignore the policy and statutory provisions of the Alaska Native Claims Settlement Act and restore the former Venetie reserve to trust status."[11]

As a consequence, instead of to Secretary Andrus, in 1979 when the Venetie Indian Corporation and the Neets'ai Corporation received their fee titles to the 1.8 million acres, the corporations conveyed their titles to the NVV.[12]

Two months before Associate Solicitor Fredericks advised that "the intent of Congress [in section 2(b) of ANCSA] to permanently remove all Native lands in Alaska from trust status is unmistakable," in July 1978, Assistant Secretary of the Interior for Indian Affairs Forrest Gerard published in the *Federal Register* a proposed rule that, if published as a final rule, would promulgate regulations that would establish the procedure the secretary of the interior henceforth would follow to acquire land for Indians pursuant to section 5 of the IRA.[13]

In 1980 when he published the final rule, Thomas Fredericks, who now was deputy assistant secretary of the interior for Indian affairs, explained in the supplementary information section of the rule that during the public comment period it had been

> pointed out that the Alaska Native Claims Settlement Act does not contemplate the further acquisition of land in trust status, or the holding of land in such status, in the State of Alaska, with the exception of acquisitions for the Metlakatla Indian Community; consequently a sentence has been added to section 120a.1 to specify that the regulations do not apply, except for Metlakatla, in the State of Alaska.[14]

The sentence stated, "These regulations do not cover the acquisition of land in trust status in the State of Alaska, except acquisitions for the Metlakatla Indian Community of the Annette Island Reserve or its members."[15]

In the legal opinion he wrote in 1978, Fredericks had assumed, albeit without deciding, that the Gwich'in Athabascan Indian residents of Venetie and Arctic Village were "Indians" as section 19 of the IRA defines that term.

But were they?

As above described, section 19 defines "Indian" to mean:

1) persons of Indian descent who are members of any recognized Indian tribe now under Federal jurisdiction,
2) persons who are descendants of such members who were, on June 1, 1934, residing within the present boundaries of any Indian reservation, and
3) all other persons of one-half or more Indian blood.

In 1978 most, if not all, of the Gwich'in Athabascan Indian residents of Venetie and Arctic Village were "persons of one-half or more Indian blood." So section 5 of the IRA authorized the secretary of the interior to acquire land for those individuals and to take the title to that land into trust in the name of the United States for the benefit of those individuals as individuals. But were the Gwich'in Athabascan Indian residents of Venetie and Arctic Village members of an "Indian tribe" that on June 18, 1934, had been both "recognized" and "under Federal jurisdiction" within the meaning of that word and phrase in the first prong of the section 19 "Indian" definition?

In 1976 Under Secretary Frizzell and in 1978 Associate Solicitor Fredericks did not consider that question. Nor for the next sixteen years was any mention made of it until the year after Assistant Secretary of the Interior for Indian Affairs Ada Deer attempted to create more than two hundred federally recognized tribes in Alaska by publishing her list of Native entities in the *Federal Register*.

In 1994 NARF attorneys Lare Aschenbrenner, Robert Anderson, and Heather Kendall filed a petition on behalf of three of those entities — the Chilkoot Indian Association, the Native Village of Larsen Bay, and the Kenaitze Indian Tribe — that requested Assistant Secretary Deer to "(1) remove the portion of the existing regulation that prohibits the acquisition of land in trust status in the State of Alaska for Alaska Native villages other than Metlakatla and (2) include in the definition of 'tribe' those Alaska Native villages listed on the Department of the Interior's list of federally recognized tribes."[16] In their petition the NARF attorneys argued:

> On October 21, 1993 the Department of the Interior, Bureau of Indian Affairs, published a new list of federally recognized tribes in Alaska. Through this publication, the Department expressly recognized the sovereign tribal status of Alaska Native villages . . . The Department of the Interior's express recognition that Alaska Native tribes share the same tribal status as other federally recognized tribes makes the present regulation with respect to acquisition of restricted or trust lands internally inconsistent. There is no basis in law for the exclusion of Alaska Native tribes from the regulations governing acquisition of trust lands.[17]

Assistant Secretary Deer took no action on the petition. But in 1999 Kevin Gover, who in 1997 had replaced Deer as assistant secretary,[18,*] released for public comment a proposed rule whose promulgation as a final rule would rewrite the regulations that established the process the secretary of the interior employed to acquire land for Indians pursuant to section 5 of the IRA.[19]

Section 151.3(c) of the proposed regulations continued to state that the secretary "will not accept title to land in trust in the State of Alaska, except for the Metlakatla Indian Community of the Annette Island Reserve of Alaska or its members."[20] However, in the preamble in which he explained the proposed regulations, Assistant Secretary Gover cited the petition the NARF attorneys had filed, and then opined that there was a "credible legal argument that ANCSA did not supercede the secretary's authority to take land into trust in Alaska under the IRA." He then invited "comment on the continued validity of the associate solicitor's opinion and issues raised by the petition ... in light of the Supreme Court's ruling in the *Venetie* case."[22]

Ten months later and four days before he and all other Clinton administration political appointees departed the Department of the Interior, on January 16, 2001, Assistant Secretary Gover published in the *Federal Register* a modified version of his proposed regulations as a final rule.[23]

According to John Leshy, who at the time was solicitor of the Department of the Interior, Secretary of the Interior Bruce Babbitt personally made the decision to retain in the modified regulations the sentence that prohibited the secretary from acquiring land in Alaska pursuant to section 5 of the IRA other than land on Annette Island.[24] However, on the same day Assistant Secretary Gover issued his final rule, Solicitor Leshy rescinded the legal opinion Associate Solicitor Fredericks had issued in 1978 because

> the 1978 Opinion gave little weight to the fact that Congress had not repealed section 5 of the IRA, which is the generic authority by which the Secretary takes Indian land into trust, and which Congress expressly extended to Alaska in 1936. The failure of Congress to repeal that section, when it was repealing others affecting Indian status in Alaska, five years after Congress enacted the Alaska Native Claims Settlement Act in 1971, raises a serious question as to whether the authority to take land into trust in Alaska still exists.[25]

That rationale ignored the fact that in 1971 the Ninety-second Congress that enacted ANCSA and in 1976 the Ninety-fourth Congress that enacted the Federal Land Policy and Management Act[26] (the statute Solicitor Leshy referenced without naming), had no reason to repeal the applicability of section 5 of the IRA to Alaska. First, because no secretary of the interior had ever exercised the authority that section 5 del-

* During his confirmation hearing, Gover told Alaska Senator Frank Murkowski that "the position of the administration ... is that the federally recognized Alaska tribes and villages share an equal status with federally recognized Indian tribal governments in the lower 48 states ... I share this view."[21]

egated. And second, because in 1971 and 1976 there were no Alaska Native groups whose members were members of an "Indian tribe" that on June 18, 1934, had been "recognized" and "under Federal jurisdiction" and hence were "Indians" as the first prong of the "Indian" definition in section 19 of the IRA defines that term.

Nevertheless, in the preamble to his rewrite of the section 5 regulations, after announcing his agreement with the legal conclusion Solicitor Leshy had announced, Assistant Secretary Gover explained that

> the position of the Department [of the Interior] has long been, as a matter of law and policy, that Alaska Native lands (sic) ought not to be taken in trust. Therefore, the Department has determined that the prohibition in the existing regulations on taking Alaska lands into trust (other than Metlakatla) ought to remain in place for a period of three years during which time the Department will consider the legal and policy issues involved in determining whether the Department ought to remove the prohibition on taking Alaska lands into trust. If the Department determines that the prohibition on taking lands into trust in Alaska should be lifted, notice and comment will be provided.[27]

The new regulations were to take effect three weeks after George W. Bush was inaugurated as president. However, immediately after the inauguration, President Bush's chief of staff directed the heads of executive branch departments to postpone the effective date of all regulations that had not yet taken effect in order to afford the new president's political appointees an opportunity to review their content.[28] That directive was the first of a series of postponements of the effective date of the regulations Assistant Secretary Gover had promulgated,[29] until November 2001 when Neal McCaleb, whom President Bush appointed to succeed Gover as assistant secretary, withdrew the regulations.[30]

Five years later, in 2006, in the U.S. District Court for the District of Columbia NARF attorney Heather Kendall-Miller, representing three Native villages and the Chilkoot Indian Association, filed *Akiachak Native Community v. Department of the Interior*,[31] a lawsuit in which the plaintiffs sought "declaratory and injunctive relief preventing the Department of the Interior from excluding federally recognized Alaska Tribes from the regulation's land into trust petition process," as well as an order directing the Department "to implement the acquisition of land into trust procedures without regard to the bar against Alaska tribes as currently contained." In their consolidated complaint, each plaintiff alleged that it was "a federally recognized tribe recognized by the United States as a sovereign government with legal rights and responsibilities."

Since in 1993 Assistant Secretary Deer had attempted to create exactly that legal status, in the answer its attorneys at the U.S. Department of Justice filed in response to the consolidated complaint, the Department of the Interior admitted those allegations.[32] Nor is it a surprise that, when the district court granted the motion the

State of Alaska filed in which it asked the court for leave to intervene as a defendant, in the answer to the consolidated complaint he filed, Attorney General Talis Colberg, who throughout his tenure as attorney general did not challenge assertions of tribal status, admitted that each plaintiff "is a federally recognized tribe."[33]

But by gratuitously making that admission, Attorney General Colberg conceded the merit of the first cause of action in the consolidated complaint, which alleged that the sentence in the regulations that prohibited the secretary of the interior from acquiring land in Alaska (other than land on Annette Island) pursuant to section 5 of the IRA violated 25 U.S.C. 476(g).[34]

In 1936 the solicitor of the Department of the Interior issued a legal opinion in which he concluded that the secretary of the interior had authority pursuant to section 16 of the IRA to approve constitutions for two groups of Indians whose members were living on federally-owned public land in Minnesota. But the solicitor concluded that, because their members were not a "historical tribe," the groups did not possess "inherent" powers of self-government. Specifically, the solicitor advised that, rather than those "powers as rest upon the sovereign capacity of the tribe," each group possessed only those "powers which are incidental to its ownership of property and to its carrying on of business," as well as "those which may be delegated by the secretary of the interior."[35]

In 1993 that division of Indian tribes into "historic" tribes and "created" tribes became an issue when a bill regarding the Yaqui Indians was introduced in the U.S. House of Representatives.

Beginning in the seventeenth century, Indians who lived along the Yaqui River, which flows into the Gulf of California in northern Mexico, had resisted, first Spanish and then Mexican, encroachments on the land they occupied. To end further resistance, in 1885 Mexican president Porfino Diaz ordered the Mexican army to clear the Yaqui River Valley of Yaquis. In a series of military engagements, thousands of Yaquis were killed.[36]

Several thousand other Yaquis fled north. By 1930 Yaqui refugees had established seven settlements in Arizona, one of which was Old Pascua, a thirty-two-acre tract of desert on the outskirts of Tucson. In 1930 Tucson had a population of 32,000. But by 1960 the population was 213,000 and the city had encircled Old Pasqua within whose over-crowded neighborhood four hundred Yaqui Indians lived in shacks they had constructed from railroad ties, discarded corrugated sheet metal, and cardboard.

In 1964 Representative Morris Udall, whose congressional district included Tucson, persuaded the Eighty-eighth Congress to enact a statute that gave the Pascua Yaqui Association, a nonprofit corporation the Yaquis at Old Pascua had incorporated, title to a 202-acre tract of federally-owned public land ten miles south of Tucson. However, because the Yaquis were Indians from Mexico who were "in no way associated with or under the jurisdiction of the Bureau of Indian Affairs,"[37] the statute made clear that "none of the statutes of the United States which affect Indians because of their status as Indians shall be applicable to the Yaqui Indians."[38]

Half the residents of Old Pascua moved onto the 202-acre tract, which the Yaquis named Pascua Pueblo.

Fourteen years later no members serving in the Ninety-fifth Congress knew (or if they did know, cared) that the Yaquis were not American Indians. As a consequence of the disinterest, in 1978 Representative Udall and Arizona Senator Dennis DeConcini arranged for, first the Senate, and then the House to pass, with no discussion or debate in either body, S. 1633, a bill Senator DeConcini had introduced whose text announced that henceforth the members of the Pascua Yaqui Association would be known as the Pascua Yaqui Tribe and would be eligible "for the services and assistance provided to Indians because of their status as Indians by or through any department or agency, or instrumentality of the United States, or under any statute of the United States." The bill also extended the provisions of the IRA to the new tribe.[39]

After the Ninety-fifth Congress enacted S. 1633 as Public Law No. 95-375, the BIA took the position that the Pascua Yaqui Tribe did not have "all the powers of a sovereign tribal government" because it was a "created" tribe, rather than a "historic" tribe.[40]

In 1993 members of the Pascua Yaqui Tribe complained about their legal status to Representative Edward Pastor, who in 1991 when Morris Udall resigned due to ill health had been elected to Udall's seat in the U.S. House of Representatives.

In February of that year, Representative Pastor introduced H.R. 734, a bill whose enactment by the One Hundred-third Congress would amend the 1978 statute by adding a sentence that stated: "The Pascua Yaqui Tribe, a historic Indian tribe, is acknowledged as a federally recognized Indian tribe possessing all the attributes of inherent sovereignty which have not been specifically taken away by Acts of Congress and which are not inconsistent with such tribal status."[41] When the Subcommittee on Native American Affairs of the House Committee on Natural Resources held a hearing on H.R. 734, the BIA opposed the bill because

> while the Pascua Yaqui may have had some status to justify Congress' extension of Federal Indian benefits to them in the exercise of Congress' power over Indians, the Pascua Yaqui cannot meet the criteria for a historic tribe. We see no justification for the change in the status of the Pascua Yaqui Tribe. There are numerous other Indian tribes that are eligible for Federal services and benefits but, like the Pascua Yaqui Indian Tribe, are not historic tribes with all the attributes of inherent sovereignty. Therefore, we urge the committee to consider the precedent that would be set by enactment of H.R. 734.[42]

When members of the Pascua Yaqui Tribe then complained about the BIA's intransigence to Arizona Senator John McCain, in April 1994 he introduced S. 2017, a bill whose enactment by the One Hundred-third Congress would add two subsections to section 16 of the IRA. The first, subsection (f), stated: "Departments or agencies of the United States shall not promulgate any regulation or make any decision or determination pursuant to the Act of June 18, 1934, as amended or any other Act of Congress with respect to a federally recognized Indian tribe that classifies, enhances, or diminishes the privileges and immunities available to the Indian tribe relative to other federally recognized tribes by virtue of their status as Indian tribes." The second, subsection (g), stated: "Any regulation or administrative decision or determination of a department or agency of the United States that is in existence or effect on the date of enactment of this Act and that classifies, enhances, or diminishes the privileges and immunities available to a federally recognized Indian tribe relative to the privileges and immunities available to other federally recognized tribes by virtue of their status as Indian tribes shall have no force or effect."

The same day he introduced S. 2017, Senator McCain had a statement printed in the *Congressional Record* in which he explained the need for the bill. The senator was neither an attorney nor a historian. Nevertheless, in that statement, which likely had been written by a member of the staff of the Committee on Indian Affairs of which he was vice chairman, McCain lectured:

> I find absolutely no basis in law or policy for the manner in which section 16 has been interpreted by the Department of the Interior ... Neither the Congress nor the Secretary [of the Interior] can create a tribe where none previously existed. Not only is this simple common sense, it is also the law as enunciated by the Federal courts. Section 16 of the IRA did not authorize the Secretary to create Indian tribes. Congress itself cannot create Indian tribes, so there is no authority for the Congress to delegate to the Secretary in this regard. The recognition of a tribe by the Federal Government is just that—the recognition that there is a sovereign entity with governmental authority which predates the U.S. Constitution and with which the Federal Government has established formal relations. All that section 16 was intended to do was to provide authority and procedures for the adoption, amendment, and approval of tribal constitutions for those tribes that choose to employ its provisions ... On its face, section 16 does not authorize or require the Secretary of the Interior to draw distinctions between tribes or to categorize them based on their powers of governance.[43]

Senator McCain could have had the Committee on Indian Affairs hold a hearing on S. 2017 so that the legal and policy consequences that would result if the One Hundred-third Congress enacted the bill could have been considered. Instead, five weeks after he introduced S. 2017, when the Senate took up S. 1654, a bill that amended five Indian-related statutes, the senator added the text of S. 2017 as another amendment, after which the Senate passed S. 1654 by unanimous consent on a voice vote.[44] Four days later the House passed S. 1654 on another voice vote.[45] When President Bill Clinton signed S. 1654 into law as Public Law No. 103-263, the McCain amendment to S. 1654 was codified as 25 U.S.C. 476(f) and (g).

If, as Attorney General Colberg conceded in the answer to the consolidated complaint the State of Alaska filed in the *Akiachak Native Community* lawsuit, the plaintiffs were federally recognized tribes, pursuant to 25 U.S.C. 476(g) the regulation that since 1980 had prohibited the secretary of the interior from acquiring land in Alaska (other than land on Annette Island) and taking the title to that land into trust in the name of the United States had "no force or effect."

To try to avoid that outcome, in the motion for summary judgment he filed on behalf of the State, Attorney General Colberg pointed out that in section 19(a) of ANCSA, the Ninety-second Congress had revoked all reserves in Alaska (other than the Annette Island reserve) that had been set aside "for Native use or for administration of Native affairs," and in section 2(b) of ANCSA had directed that the ANCSA settlement be accomplished "without establishing any permanent racially defined institutions, rights, privileges, or obligations, without creating a reservation system or lengthy wardship or trusteeship, and without adding to the categories of property and institutions enjoying special tax privileges." He then argued that "[t]aking land into trust in Alaska would, by definition, create a trusteeship in violation of Congress's intent."[46]

Attorney General Colberg then attempted to explain away NARF attorney Heather Kendall-Miller's arguments regarding 25 U.S.C. 476(g) as "largely red herrings that distract from the central legal issue in this case, which is whether ANCSA precludes the secretary from taking land into trust in Alaska."[47] Continuing on in the same vein, he then asserted that "[t]he ANCSA ban does not discriminate between Alaska tribes and other tribes 'by virtue of their status as tribes.' The ban distinguishes Alaska tribes from other tribes by virtue of their status as tribes subject to the ANCSA land claims settlement."[48]

That attempt to persuade the district court to disregard the plain meaning of the text of 25 U.S.C. 476(g) proved unavailing when in a decision he issued in March 2013, District Judge Rudolph Contreras concluded:

> The Secretary [of the Interior] does not deny that his regulation diminishes the privileges available to tribes of Alaska Natives (except for the Metlakatlans) relative to the "privileges ... available to all other federally recognized tribes by virtue of their status as Indian tribes." 25 U.S.C. 476(g). Instead he asks the court to adopt limiting constructions that have no basis in the statutory text. But a law "is not susceptible to a limiting construction" when "its language is plain and its meaning unambiguous." The Secretary offers no other arguments, and the challenged regulation shall therefore "have no force of effect." 25 U.S.C. 476(g).[49]

Judge Contreras then issued a second decision in which he severed the sentence "These regulations do not cover the acquisition of land in trust status in the State of Alaska, except acquisitions for the Metlakatla Indian Community of the Annette

Island Reserve or its members" from the regulation in which it had been included for more than thirty years.[50]

When Judge Contreras issued a final judgment, the Department of the Interior and the State of Alaska each appealed the judgment to the U.S. Court of Appeals for the District of Columbia Circuit.

Two years after the *Akiachak Native Community* lawsuit had been filed, in 2008 the Department of the Interior had informed Judge Contreras that even though the department continued to contest the validity of the causes of action NARF attorney Heather Kendall-Miller had alleged in the plaintiffs' consolidated complaint, the department agreed with her central contention, which was that the secretary of the interior had authority pursuant to section 5 of the IRA to acquire land in Alaska. The department told Judge Contreras that

> front and center in this litigation is the apparent agreement of the parties now that the secretary of the United States Department of the Interior has discretionary authority to take Indian lands (sic) into trust status in Alaska. The secretary's discretionary authority to do so is through 25 U.S.C. 465, enacted as Section 5 of the Indian Reorganization Act of 1934, which was made applicable to Alaska in the 1936 IRA amendments. Subsequent laws—the Alaska Native Claims Settlement Act of 1971, and the Federal Land Policy and Management Act, have not removed the secretary's discretionary authority to take Indian lands (sic) into trust status in Alaska.[51]

The year before Judge Contreras entered his final judgment, in August 2012 President Barack Obama appointed Kevin Washburn, a professor at the University of New Mexico School of Law who specialized in federal Indian law and who is a member of the Chickasaw Nation in Oklahoma and a nationally known tribal sovereignty advocate,[52] as assistant secretary of the interior for Indian affairs.[53]

From the outset of the *Akiachak Native Community* lawsuit, career civil service employees in the BIA bureaucracy; the Bush, and later Obama, administration political appointees who supervised them; and the attorneys in the Office of the Solicitor who advised them, had agreed with Kendall-Miller that, notwithstanding the Ninety-second Congress's enactment of ANCSA, section 5 of the IRA continued to delegate the secretary of the interior authority to acquire land in Alaska and take the title to that land into trust in the name of the United States for the federally recognized tribes that Assistant Secretary Deer had created.

Since he was of the same mind, five months after the Department of the Interior appealed the final judgment Judge Contreras had issued, Assistant Secretary Washburn published in the *Federal Register* a proposed rule whose promulgation as a final rule would remove the sentence in 25 C.F.R. 151.1 that prohibited the secretary from acquiring land in Alaska (other than land on Annette Island) and taking the title to that land into trust in the name of the United States.[54] In his explanation of the purpose of the rule-making, Assistant Secretary Washburn perorated:

> The categorical exclusion of Alaska from the regulations is particularly unwarranted because ... it was added to the regulations based on a mistaken legal interpretation of ANCSA, not because of public policy concerns. Congressional policy has remained constant since 1934 with the enactment of Section 5 of the IRA. By providing authority to take land into trust—an authority that was not revoked by ANCSA—Congress recognized that restoring tribal lands to trust status was important to tribal self-governance by providing a physical space where tribal governments may exercise sovereign powers to provide for their citizens. Restoring tribal homelands also supports the Federal trust responsibility to Indian nations because it supports the ability of tribal governments to provide for their people, thus making them more self-sufficient. Therefore, given that the authority in Section 5 remains intact for lands in Alaska, it is unnecessary and inappropriate to categorically exclude all Alaska lands from the land-into-trust regulations.
>
> ...
>
> For more than 25 years, Alaska Native Tribal governments have been at the forefront of Federal policies supporting tribal self-determination and self-governance. The tribal governments in Alaska have made tremendous use of various Federal self-governance policies, thereby increasing self-sufficiency and better quality of life for Alaska Natives ... For all the reasons mentioned above, the Department reconsiders its past approach barring land into trust in Alaska and proposes to amend its regulations by removing the Alaska Exception.[55]

The month after Assistant Secretary Washburn published his proposed rule, at his direction the Department of the Interior filed a motion in the U.S. Court of Appeals for the District of Columbia Circuit in which it requested the court to dismiss the appeal the department had filed, and the court granted the motion.[56]

In December 2014 Assistant Secretary Washburn issued a final rule that amended 25 C.F.R. 151.1 by removing the sentence "These regulations do not cover the acquisition of land in trust status in the State of Alaska, except acquisitions for the Metlakatla Indian Community of the Annette Island Reserve or its members."[57] When he did so he baldly asserted that the secretary of the interior acquiring land in Alaska pursuant to section 5 of the IRA and taking the title to that land into trust in the name of the United States would not contravene the policy objectives the Ninety-second Congress intended its enactment of ANCSA to achieve because

> it is important to remember that Alaska Native land and history did not commence with ANCSA, and that ANCSA did not terminate Alaska Native tribal governments ... [W]hile ANCSA revoked existing reservations in Alaska and established a separate statutory scheme in Alaska for the settlement of land claims, it did not repeal the Secretary's authority to take land into trust in Alaska under the IRA. There is nothing precluding the settlement

> codified in ANCSA and the Department's land-into-trust authority under the IRA from coexisting in Alaska.[58]

The month before Assistant Secretary Washburn issued his final rule, in November 2014 Bill Walker, a Republican who had changed his party registration to Independent, was elected governor of Alaska by defeating Sean Parnell, the incumbent Republican governor, by 6,223 votes in an election in which 280,000 votes had been cast.[59] Walker won only because Byron Mallott, the Democratic Party's gubernatorial candidate, who had received 42,327 votes in the primary election,[60] ended his campaign in order to become Walker's running mate.

The son of a Tlingit Indian mother and Caucasian father, Mallott had been raised in Yakutat, a community on the northern coast of the southeast Alaska panhandle. Because in 1970 a majority of the community's residents were of Tlingit Indian descent, the secretary of the interior designated Yakutat as a Native village for the purposes of ANCSA. And in 1993 Assistant Secretary Deer included "Yakutat Tlingit Tribe" on the list of Native entities she published in the *Federal Register*.

In 1965 when he was twenty-two years old, Mallott had been elected mayor of Yakutat, which in 1948 had incorporated a municipal government under the laws of the Territory of Alaska. As has been described, in 1970 Alaska Governor Bill Egan appointed Mallott director of the Rural Affairs Agency, and two years later he appointed Mallott commissioner of a new Department of Community and Regional Affairs that the governor had had the legislature create. In both of those positions Mallott's job was to encourage residents of communities that would be designated as Native villages for the purposes of ANCSA to incorporate municipal governments.

But by 2013 when he began his campaign for governor, Mallott had become an outspoken tribal sovereignty advocate who, as the *Alaska Journal of Commerce* reported, during a campaign event in Bethel told voters in the most populous Yup'ik Eskimo community in western Alaska "that he agreed completely with the notion of tribal sovereignty."[61] And in December 2014 when he became lieutenant governor, Mallott took the oath of office while wearing traditional Tlingit regalia.

Six weeks after Governor Walker and Lieutenant Governor Mallott assumed office, in January 2015 the State of Alaska asked the members of the three-judge panel of the U.S. Court of Appeals for the District of Columbia Circuit who had been assigned to decide the State's appeal in the *Akiachak Native Community* lawsuit to postpone briefing for six months because "Governor Walker has directed Lieutenant Governor Byron Mallott and Attorney General Craig Richards and other cabinet members to establish a working group to gather stakeholder input and explore a range of policy options on [the land into trust] issue and related tribal issues in Alaska, including potential alternatives to continuing this litigation."[62]

When it learned of the State's request, the *Alaska Dispatch News* reported that "Gov. Bill Walker said during his campaign that the way to improve State-Native re-

Bill Walker and Byron Mallott Inaugurated Governor and Lieutenant Governor of Alaska, December 1, 2014. Merrick Peirce.

lations is to stop suing each other," and it quoted the governor's press secretary saying, "We are looking at ways to improve the State's relationship with tribes, while still protecting the State's interest."[63]

In April when he appeared at the annual convention of the Central Council of the Tlingit and Haida Indian Tribes of Alaska and was asked, "What your position is on land into trust in Alaska," Governor Walker answered: "It's not anything that I'm personally opposed to. I want to make sure we do it in the right way and that it gets done as soon as we can, but there's a few nuances we have to address along the way."[64]

In August the *Alaska Journal of Commerce* described Lieutenant Governor Mallott, who was chairing the working group Governor Walker had established to address those nuances, as "a longtime backer of giving tribes the right to put land into trust."[65]

In the end, the effort to appease the working group's chairman and other tribal sovereignty advocates while at the same time "protecting the State's interest" proved to be a circle that could not be squared.

When the working group's effort ended in failure and the State finally filed its brief, less than three of the brief's sixty-one pages addressed the legal issue on which Judge Contreras had based his decisions, which was that the sentence in 25 C.F.R. 151.1 whose validity was at issue violated 25 U.S.C. 476(g). The other fifty-eight pages contained a rehash of the arguments about the intent of the Ninety-second Congress embodied in ANCSA that Judge Contreras had concluded were legally irrelevant.

A year later, on July 1, 2016, two of the members of the three-judge panel that had been assigned to decide it dismissed the State's appeal. As the two deciding judges explained their reasoning: "Unfortunately for Alaska, which intervened in the district court as a defendant and brought no independent claim for relief, the controversy between the tribes and the Department [of the Interior] is now moot"[66] because

> even assuming, as Alaska argues, that the district court's interpretation of ANCSA injured the State, such injury cannot extend our jurisdiction by creating a new controversy on appeal. In essence, Alaska urges us to "entertain the appeal so as to advise the parties of what their rights would be in what is essentially a new legal controversy"—whether Interior's 2014 rule correctly interprets ANCSA. We are without jurisdiction to provide such an advisory opinion. Assuming Alaska's claim is ripe, we see no barrier to the State raising it directly under the A[dministrative] P[rocedure] A[ct], or if and when Interior attempts to take any land into trust in Alaska.[67]

After the appeal was dismissed, the State had ninety days to petition the U.S. Supreme Court to issue a writ of certiorari and review the dismissal.

But instead of doing so, on August 15 Jahna Lindemuth, whom two months earlier Governor Walker had appointed to succeed Craig Richards as attorney general, announced that the State was conceding defeat because "I don't see any need to use our limited resources in pursuing dead-end litigation" and "it seems more productive to come back to the table and see if the State's concerns can be addressed outside of litigation."[68] That same day NARF attorney Heather Kendall-Miller issued a press release in which she celebrated Attorney General Lindemuth's capitulation as a "historic victory for Alaska tribes."[69]

A week later Attorney General Lindemuth explained her understanding of what the state of the law now was regarding the authority of the secretary of the interior to acquire land in Alaska and take the title to that land into trust in the name of the United States pursuant to section 5 of the IRA:

> The way that case came down, it was mooted out by federal regulation, so basically the legal issues didn't exist anymore. We weren't going to win that issue, so it's as if that case never existed. So it's kind of fortuitous that the timing of that happened as it did, because it gives us some breathing room to deal with this issue of switching from litigation to diplomatic efforts.
>
> I'm going to meet with all the different people who have concerns about land into trust. And then I gather all those concerns and understand what all the issues are and see if as a state we can narrow down the issues and resolve the concerns that are left. I think this might be easier than we're all envisioning right now. The end result may be a set of federal regulations unique to Alaska. We could end up with a set of standards the Department of Law

uses to evaluate trust applications, so we'd object to this particular instance, but not to that situation—here's our concerns and how we'll deal with them.[70]

Since 25 U.S.C. 476(f) prohibits the secretary of the interior from adopting a regulation "that classifies, enhances, or diminishes the privileges and immunities available to [an] Indian tribe relative to other federally recognized tribes by virtue of their status as Indian tribes," Attorney General Lindemuth's assertion that "a set of federal regulations unique to Alaska" might alleviate the State's concerns reflected a startling lack of understanding of both a plain meaning reading of the text of 25 U.S.C. 476(f) and of Judge Contreras's decisions.

By the time the State's appeal of Judge Contreras's decision was dismissed, six Native groups had submitted applications to the BIA that requested the secretary of the interior to acquire land in Alaska for the groups pursuant to section 5 of the IRA. One of those groups was the Craig Tribal Association.

Craig is a community located on the west side of Prince of Wales Island in southeast Alaska that had grown up around a salmon cannery that began operating in 1908. In 1922 the two hundred residents of Craig incorporated a municipal government under the laws of the Territory of Alaska.[71] In 1938 Assistant Secretary of the Interior Oscar Chapman approved a constitution for the Craig Community Association that "a group of Indians having a common bond of residence in the neighborhood of Craig" had submitted pursuant to section 1 of Public Law No. 74-538 and section 16 of the IRA.[72]

In 1971 section 16 of ANCSA designated Craig as a Native village, authorized residents of Craig who had one-quarter or more Tlingit or Haida Indian blood to incorporate a village corporation, and authorized the secretary of the interior to convey to the corporation fee title to the surface estate of 23,040 acres of federally-owned public land located within and around the community.

In 1982 when Assistant Secretary of the Interior for Indian Affairs Ken Smith published in the *Federal Register* the first list of "Alaska Native Entities Recognized and Eligible to Receive Services From the United States Bureau of Indian Affairs," he included the "Craig Community Association" on the list.[73] When the list was republished in 1983, 1985, 1986, and 1988, the Craig Community Association remained listed.

In 1993 when Assistant Secretary of the Interior for Indian Affairs Ada Deer published her list of Native entities that she said was a list of "villages and regional tribes" that, because of their appearance on the list, henceforth would have "the same status as tribes in the contiguous 48 states," she included the Craig Community Association on her list.[74] When Assistant Secretary Deer's list was republished in 1995, 1998, 2000, 2002, 2005, 2009, and 2010, the Craig Community Association remained listed.

Then in 2011 Eugene Virden, the director of the BIA Alaska regional office, approved a constitution that had been submitted by "a group of Alaska Natives and American Indians having a common bond of residence in the neighborhood of Craig."

The principal difference between the new constitution and the constitution Assistant Secretary Chapman had approved in 1938 was that the Craig Community Association had been renamed the Craig Tribal Association (CTA).[75]

A year later when acting Assistant Secretary of the Interior for Indian Affairs Michael Black again republished the list of Native entities, it now included "Craig Tribal Association (previously listed as the Craig Community Association)."[76]

Five months after Assistant Secretary of the Interior for Indian Affairs Kevin Washburn published in the *Federal Register* a proposed rule whose promulgation as a final rule would remove from 25 C.F.R. 151.1 the sentence "These regulations do not cover the acquisition of land in trust status in the State of Alaska, except acquisitions for the Metlakatla Indian Community of the Annette Island Reserve or its members," in September 2014 the CTA submitted an application to the BIA in which it requested the secretary of the interior to take into trust in the name of the United States pursuant to section 5 of the IRA the title to two parcels of land located within the city limits of the city of Craig. On October 6, 2016, the CTA submitted a separate application for each parcel, one of which was 1.08 acres of land the Craig Community Association had purchased in 1996 and on which it had constructed a building the CTA used as its headquarters and also leased to commercial users.

On October 7, 2016, the director of the BIA Alaska regional office notified the State of Alaska and the City of Craig that they had thirty days to submit comments regarding the application for the 1.08 acres.[77]

Consistent with what Governor Walker had promised when he appeared at the annual convention of the Central Council of Tlingit and Haida Indian Tribes of Alaska, on December 9, 2016, Attorney General Lindemuth informed the director that "the State does not object to placing this particular parcel into trust."[78] And the Craig city council also had no objection.

On January 10, 2017, Lawrence Roberts, the principal deputy assistant secretary of the interior for Indian affairs, approved the CTA's application and directed the director of the BIA Alaska regional office to acquire in the name of the United States in trust for the CTA the title to the 1.08 acres.[79] In a letter he sent to the president of the CTA in which he announced that decision, Assistant Secretary Roberts stated:

> Craig Tribal Association is a federally recognized tribe with Tribal headquarters located in the City of Craig, Alaska. The Tribe is organized under the IRA and has a constitution and by-laws approved by the secretary of the interior on July 13, 1938 and ratified by members of the Tribe on October 8, 1938. The Tribe is included on the list of federally recognized tribes.[80]

That description of the legal status of the CTA ignored the facts that the "groups of Indians in Alaska" for which section 1 of Public Law No. 74-538 authorized the secretary to approve a constitution pursuant to section 16 of the IRA were groups that had "not heretofore [been] recognized as bands or tribes," that the Tlingit and Haida Indians in Craig who in 1938 submitted their constitution to the secretary had done so not as a federally recognized tribe but as "a group of Indians having a common bond of residence in the neighborhood of Craig," and that the constitution Assistant Secretary Chapman approved was for the Craig Community Association—rather than the CTA.

But even if Assistant Secretary Roberts's assertion that the members of the CTA were a federally recognized tribe had been legally correct, there was another, equally legally consequential, consideration regarding whether his approval of the CTA's application had been lawful.

In 2009 in its decision in *Carcieri v.* Salazar,[81] the U.S. Supreme Court announced that the Seventy-third Congress that enacted the IRA intended the word "now" in the phrase "recognized Indian tribe now under Federal jurisdiction" in the first prong of the "Indian" definition in section 19 of the IRA to mean June 18, 1934, the date President Franklin Roosevelt signed the IRA into law.

The *Carcieri* decision was problematical because if the Tlingit and Haida Indian residents of Craig did not become a "recognized Indian tribe" until 1938 when Assistant Secretary Chapman approved a constitution for the Craig Community Association, the tribe could not have been "recognized" and "under Federal jurisdiction" on June 18, 1934. And the situation was even more problematical if the Tlingit and Haida Indian residents of Craig did not become a "recognized Indian tribe" until 1993 when Assistant Secretary Deer published her list of Native entities.*

---

* In *Carcieri v. Salazar*, Rhode Island Governor Donald Carcieri challenged the validity of a decision the secretary of the interior had made to take into trust pursuant to section 5 of the IRA the title to thirty-one acres of land in Rhode Island that the Narragansett Indian Tribe had purchased. Because at the beginning of the lawsuit the Department of the Interior admitted that on June 18, 1934, the Narragansett Indian Tribe had not been "under Federal jurisdiction," the U.S. Supreme Court reasoned to the result it announced in its decision without deciding whether the Seventy-third Congress intended the phrase "recognized Indian tribe now under Federal jurisdiction" in the first prong of the "Indian" definition in section 19 of the IRA to require an "Indian tribe" to have been both "recognized" and "under Federal jurisdiction" on June 18, 1934. In 2014 Hilary Tompkins, whom President Barack Obama had appointed solicitor of the Department of the Interior, issued Solicitor Opinion M-37029, entitled "The Meaning of 'Under Federal Jurisdiction' for Purposes of the Indian Reorganization Act." At the end of the opinion Solicitor Tompkins gratuitously expressed her view that "the IRA does not require that the agency determine whether a tribe was a 'recognized Indian tribe' in 1934; a tribe need only be 'recognized' at the time the statute is applied (e.g., at the time the secretary decides to take land into trust)." In 2018 Daniel Jorjani, whom President Donald Trump had appointed to succeed Tomkins as solicitor, began a review of Solicitor Opinion M-37029. After doing so, in 2020 Solicitor Jorjani issued Solicitor Opinion M-37055 in which he withdrew Solicitor Opinion M-37029 because, in his view, Solicitor Tompkins's conclusion regarding the intent of the Seventy-third Congress embodied in the text of the first prong of the "Indian" definition in section 19 of the IRA was "not consistent with the ordinary meaning, statutory context, legislative history, or contemporary administrative understanding of the phrase 'recognized Indian tribe now under federal jurisdiction.'" On January 20, 2021 President Joe Biden appointed former NARF attorney Robert Anderson as principal deputy solicitor of the Department of the Interior. On April 27, 2021 Principal Deputy Solicitor Anderson issued Solicitor Opinion M-37070 in which he withdrew Solicitor Opinion M-37055 and reinstated Solicitor Opinion M-37029.

To rid himself of those problems, in his letter to the president of the CTA, Assistant Secretary Roberts announced that

> after carefully examining the language of the Indian Reorganization Act ("IRA") and the 1936 Amendments to the IRA ("Alaska IRA"), as well as both statutes' purposes and legislative histories, and in accordance with the guidance provided by the Office of the Solicitor, I have determined that Congress's extension of Section 5 of the IRA (the provision authorizing the secretary to acquire land in trust for Indians) to Alaska through the Alaska IRA provides specific authority for the secretary to place land in trust for Federally recognized tribes in Alaska. That authority is not constrained by the Supreme Court's decision in *Carcieri v. Salazar*. Moreover, neither the Alaska Native Claims Settlement Act, nor the Federal Land Policy and Management Act, expressly or impliedly repeal that authority. I therefore conclude that the Department has authority to acquire land in trust for the Tribe. The Solicitor will be issuing a new opinion in the near future that sets out the supporting legal analysis of the underlying authorities upon which this decision has been made.[82]

The solicitor to whom Assistant Secretary Roberts referred in his letter was Hilary Tompkins. Although she had been raised from birth by Caucasian adoptive parents in New Jersey, Tompkins is of Navajo descent[83] and by the time President Obama appointed her solicitor, she considered herself a "Proud Navajo."

Two days before President Trump assumed office and she departed the Department of the Interior, in an interview with *Indian Country Today*, Solicitor Tompkins touted as one of her most important accomplishments her involvement in the rule-making in which Assistant Secretary Washburn removed the sentence "These regulations do not cover the acquisition of land in trust status in the State of Alaska, except acquisitions for the Metlakatla Indian Community of the Annette Island Reserve or its members" from 25 C.F.R. 151.1.[84] Of equal consequence, seven days before she departed and three days after Assistant Secretary Roberts approved the CTA's application for the 1.08-acre parcel of land the CTA owned in Craig, on January 13, 2017, Solicitor Tompkins issued Solicitor Opinion M-37043, entitled "Authority to Acquire Land into Trust in Alaska," which was the "new opinion" to which Assistant Secretary Roberts had alluded in his letter to the president of the CTA.

In its decision in *Carcieri v. Salazar*, the U.S. Supreme Court had noted in passing that in statutes other than the IRA, "Congress chose to expand the Secretary's authority to particular Indian tribes not necessarily encompassed within the definitions of 'Indian' set forth in [section 19 of the IRA]."[85] In a footnote the Court listed four such statutes, one of which was Public Law No. 74-538.[86]

That statement was a dictum that was of no legal consequence. However, transforming that dictum into a holding, after noting that "the *Carcieri* Court expressly cited to the Alaska IRA [Public Law No. 74-538]," in Solicitor Opinion M-37043 Solicitor Thompkins announced that "the Secretary, therefore, possesses the requisite authority to acquire land in trust for Alaska Natives under the Alaska IRA and Interior need not render a determination whether Alaska Native tribes fit within any of the other definitions of 'Indian' in Section 19 of the IRA, including the first definition that was at issue in the *Carcieri* decision."

Solicitor Tompkins further opined that the Seventy-third Congress intended its inclusion of the sentence "For the purposes of this Act, Eskimos and other aboriginal people of Alaska shall be considered Indians" in the "Indian" definition in section 19 to create "a separate category of 'Indians' under the IRA." She then explained that she had reasoned to that conclusion because

> if Congress had intended to require Alaska Natives to meet one of the first three definitions of "Indian" in the first sentence of Section 19, then the reference to Alaska Natives in the next sentence of Section 19 would be surplusage, as eligible Alaska Natives would have already met one of the other three definitions. Instead, the use of the word "considered" in Section 19 suggests that Alaska Natives were to be regarded as "Indians" in the appropriate sections of the IRA, regardless of whether they meet one of the other definitions.[87]

There is a difference between a good faith, but wrong, reading of the text of a statute and intellectual dishonesty. And in Solicitor Opinion M-37043 Solicitor Tompkins crossed that line.

The IRA is composed of eighteen sections, plus the "Indian" definition in section 19. In those eighteen sections the words "Indian" and "Indians" appear thirty-eight times. For that reason, the sentence "For the purposes of this Act, Eskimos and other aboriginal peoples of Alaska shall be considered Indians" was included in section 19 to make clear that each time the word "Indian" or "Indians" appears in the eighteen other sections those words include within their purviews, not only Indians in the coterminous states, but also Indians, Eskimos, and Aleuts in the Territory of Alaska. The inclusion of that sentence in section 19 allowed Indians, Eskimos, and Aleuts of "one-half or more" Indian, Eskimo, or Aleut blood to borrow money that section 11 of the IRA made available for "the payment of tuition and other expenses in recognized vocational and trade schools," and to benefit from the preference for employment with the BIA that section 12 of the IRA established.

To reason to the conclusion regarding the intent of the Seventy-third Congress embodied in the sentence "For the purposes of this Act, Eskimos and other aboriginal peoples of Alaska shall be considered Indians" that she announced in Solicitor Opinion M-37043 also required Solicitor Tompkins to disregard the contrary view of Felix Cohen, the assistant solicitor at the Department of the Interior who wrote the texts of both section 19 of the IRA and H.R. 9866.

After the Seventy-third Congress enacted the IRA, Cohen sent Fred Daiker, a senior member of the staff of Commissioner of Indian Affairs John Collier, a memorandum in which he stated: "It seems to me that sec. 19 puts Eskimos on the same basis as Indians. To qualify for the benefits of the [IRA] they must meet one of 3 criteria: tribal affiliation, tribal descent plus residence on a reservation, or the half-blood test."[88]

In Solicitor Opinion M-37043, Solicitor Tompkins dismissed Cohen's understanding, as well as other contemporaneous statements that are consistent with Cohen's understanding, as "statements [that] fall short of the official legal position for Interior" and that also are "conclusionary" and lack "any thorough legal explanation or analysis of the legislative history of the IRA."[89] Solicitor Tompkins did so even though Cohen's and the other statements are the type of evidence of the intent of the Seventy-third Congress embodied in the text of section 19 of the IRA that in its decision in *Carcieri v. Salazar* the U.S. Supreme Court found probative.

Four days after President Trump was inaugurated, his chief of staff directed the heads of executive branch departments to suspend regulatory actions that had been taken at the end of the Obama administration, including the issuance of statements that set forth interpretations of a "statutory or regulatory issue," in order to provide the new president's political appointees an opportunity to review them.

Implementing that directive, in June 2018 Daniel Jorjani, whom President Trump had appointed principal deputy solicitor of the Department of the Interior and who, because the president had not nominated anyone to serve as solicitor, was the acting solicitor, issued Solicitor Opinion M-37053 in which he withdrew Solicitor Opinion M-37043 in order to provide the Office of the Solicitor an opportunity to review the legal analysis contained therein, which Solicitor Opinion M-37053 characterized as "incomplete and unbalanced." At the conclusion of Solicitor Opinion M-37053, Principal Deputy Solicitor Jorjani announced that "a minimum of six months would seem appropriate to provide adequate notice and a meaningful opportunity to comment on the secretary's exercise of his authority to take off-reservation land into trust in Alaska and the issues left unresolved by Sol. Op. M-37043, followed by a further six months to allow the Department to conduct a considered review of any and all comments received."

Five months after Principal Deputy Solicitor Jorjani withdrew Solicitor Opinion M-37043, in November 2018 Mike Dunleavy, a right of conservative Republican, was elected to succeed Bill Walker as governor of Alaska. When he assumed office Governor Dunleavy appointed an equally conservative Anchorage attorney named Kevin Clarkson to succeed Jahna Lindemuth as attorney general.

In January 2019 Attorney General Clarkson submitted to the Office of the Solicitor comments on behalf of the State of Alaska regarding Solicitor Opinion M-37043 in which he requested that the opinion not be reinstated and that the Department of the Interior "amend its trust land regulations to reinstate the Alaska exclusion" because "acquiring new lands in trust in Alaska was foreclosed by ANCSA and is not in Alaska's best interests."

In those comments Attorney General Clarkson did not argue that there were no groups in Alaska that qualified as "Indians" within the meaning of that term in section

19 of the IRA. He also did not argue that Solicitor Tompkins was wrong that the Seventy-fourth Congress had intended its inclusion of the reference to section 5 of the IRA in section 1 of Public Law No. 74-538 to authorize the secretary of the interior to acquire land for a group whose membership was composed of Alaska Natives even though those individuals did not qualify as "Indians" within the meaning of the definition of that term in section 19 of the IRA.

Instead, Attorney General Clarkson made the same argument regarding the intent of the Ninety-second Congress embodied in sections 2(b) and 19(a) of ANCSA that Attorneys General Colberg and Richards had made in the *Akiachak Native Community* lawsuit and that District Judge Contreras had found legally irrelevant. And in making that argument Attorney General Clarkson gratuitously conceded that there were "229 federally recognized tribes" in Alaska.[90]

When he withdrew Solicitor Opinion M-37043, Principal Deputy Solicitor Jorjani did not void the acceptance by the director of the BIA Alaska regional office of the deed to the 1.08-acre parcel of land in Craig whose title the CTA had conveyed to the United States.

As has been described, the U.S. Supreme Court has decided that a state has no jurisdiction to enforce its criminal and civil laws within the boundaries of Indian country located within the state's borders. And in 1948 in section 1151 of title 18 of the U.S. Code, the Eightieth Congress created three categories of Indian country: Indian reservations, dependent Indian communities, and Indian allotments.

Section 7 of the IRA authorizes the secretary of the interior "to proclaim new Indian reservations on lands acquired pursuant to any authority conferred by this Act." And in 1936 in section 1 of Public Law No. 74-538, the Seventy-fourth Congress applied section 7 of the IRA to the Territory (later State) of Alaska.

Land whose title the secretary of the interior has acquired pursuant to section 5 of the IRA is not an Indian reservation until and unless the secretary proclaims it to be such pursuant to section 7 of the IRA. Nevertheless, in 2014 when he removed the sentence "These regulations do not cover the acquisition of land in trust status in Alaska" from the regulations that create the procedure the BIA employs to decide whether the secretary will acquire land for a recognized Indian tribe pursuant to section 5 of the IRA, Assistant Secretary of the Interior for Indian Affairs Kevin Washburn announced that "The department's position has been that land held in trust by the United States on behalf of a federally recognized Indian tribe is 'Indian country.' As a legal matter, an Alaska tribe possessing trust lands would be able to exercise jurisdiction over such land consistent with the manner in which Indian tribes exercise authority over trust lands located in the rest of the country."[91]

Assistant Secretary Washburn did not explain the legal analysis on which he based that pronouncement of purported law. But consistent with that pronouncement, after the acceptance by the director of the BIA Alaska regional office of the CTA's deed to the 1.08-acre parcel of land it owned in Craig, the CTA opened a smoke shop in the building it had built on the parcel in which it began selling cigarettes without collecting the State of Alaska's $2 per pack tobacco tax.

In addition, as has been described, section 1156 of title 18 of the U.S. Code imposes criminal penalties for the possession of "intoxicating liquors in the Indian country." However, in 1953 the Eighty-third Congress added section 1161 to title 18, which exempts from the section 1156 prohibition the possession and sale of intoxicating liquor within the boundaries of a tract of Indian country if the liquor is possessed or sold in conformity with both "the laws of the State" in which the Indian country is located and "an ordinance duly adopted by the tribe having jurisdiction over such area of Indian country." Section 1161 also provides that an ordinance becomes effective when the secretary of the interior publishes a notice in the *Federal Register* that announces that he has certified the ordinance.

In November 2017 the CTA adopted an alcohol control ordinance. In September 2018 Assistant Secretary of the Interior for Indian Affairs Tara Sweeny published a notice in the *Federal Register* in which she announced that she had certified the ordinance.[92]

The ordinance purports to regulate the introduction, distribution, possession, sale, and consumption of liquor, beer, spirits, and wine "within or upon Tribal lands" by authorizing the "duly elected legislative body of the Craig Tribal Association" to issue licenses that authorize the licensees to sell alcoholic beverages for personal consumption. The ordinance defines "Tribal lands" to mean "all land within the definition of 'Indian country' as established and described by federal law and that is under the jurisdiction of the Craig Tribal Association, including, but not limited to all lands held in trust by the federal government, located within the same, as are now in existence or may hereafter be added to."

To certify the ordinance required Assistant Secretary Sweeny to conclude that the members of the CTA were a "tribe" within the meaning of that undefined word in section 1161 and that the 1.08-acre parcel of land in Craig whose title the United States held in trust for the CTA was Indian country, even though the secretary of the interior had not, pursuant to section 7 of the IRA, proclaimed the parcel to be an Indian reservation. However, Assistant Secretary Sweeny did not explain the legal analysis on which she relied to reason to those conclusions.

In April 2019 President Trump nominated Daniel Jorjani, who since 2017 had been serving as principal deputy solicitor, to be solicitor of the Department of the Interior.[93] The nomination coincided with the expiration of the twelve-month consultation and analysis period that Jorjani had announced in Solicitor Opinion M-37053. But during the hearing the Senate Committee on Energy and Natural Resources held on his nomination, which Alaska Senator Lisa Murkowski chaired, he was not asked what the outcome of his analysis was regarding the authority of the secretary of the interior to acquire land in Alaska pursuant to section 5 of the IRA.[94]

Another year-and-a-half later, on the last day of the Trump administration, January 19, 2021, Solicitor Jorjani answered the question that Senator Murkowski had not asked by issuing Solicitor Opinion M-37064 in which he permanently withdrew Solicitor Opinion M-37043 because he had concluded that there was "substantial doubt" that the legal conclusions Solicitor Tompkins had announced in Solicitor Opinion M-37043 were correct.[95]

Solicitor Jorjani attached to Solicitor Opinion M-37064 a legal memorandum entitled "Authority to Acquire Land in Trust in Alaska" that described the analysis that had led him to that conclusion.

The analysis was a rehash of the analysis that in more summary form had been contained in the legal opinion Associate Solicitor for Indian Affairs Thomas Fredericks had issued in 1978, which in 2001 Solicitor John Leshy had rescinded four days before he and all other Clinton administration political appointees departed the Department of the Interior.

In his opinion Associate Solicitor Fredericks assumed that the Native Village of Venetie was the governing body of a "recognized Indian tribe" that on June 18, 1934, had been "under Federal jurisdiction" for which section 5 of the IRA authorized the secretary of the interior to acquire land, but that it would be an abuse of discretion if the secretary of the interior acquired land for the NVV pursuant to section 5 because in 1971 in section 2(b) of ANCSA the Ninety-second Congress had directed the secretary to implement the ANCSA land settlement "without creating a reservation system or lengthy wardship or trusteeship" and "without adding to the categories of property and institutions enjoying special tax privileges."

Solicitor Jorjani concluded his analysis as follows:

> A departure from the original policy of the Department that the Secretary not exercise his or her discretionary authority to accept land in trust in Alaska should be strongly supported by weighty legal analysis, informed by legislative history, the Department's contemporaneous interpretations of the scope of the Secretary's authority, and the views of Alaska Native leadership in the period immediately surrounding ANCSA's enactment, none of which Sol. Op. M-37043 clearly provided.
>
> Ultimately, the legal uncertainty and questions of appropriate Department policy with regard to land in trust in Alaska are best answered by the constitutional branch that enacted the IRA, the Alaska IRA, the [Alaska] Statehood Act, ANCSA and FLPMA: the United States Congress. Absent such clear direction, a determination by the Secretary to accept land in trust in Alaska would likely be subject to protracted litigation and a credible A[dministrative] P[rocedure] A[ct] challenge asserting that the Department's actions were "arbitrary, capricious, an abuse of discretion, or otherwise not in accordance with the law."

To try and attract the support of Native American voters, the month prior to the November 2020 presidential election the Biden-Harris campaign issued a fifteen-page Plan for Tribal Nations that, in pertinent part, promised that if candidate Biden became President Biden, he would "end Trump's reversal of the Obama-Biden policy that affirmed that Alaska Native tribes are rightfully able to place land into trust."[96]

Solicitor Opinion M-37064 prevented that promise from being kept.

On the same day, January 20, 2021, that Solicitor Jorjani departed the Department of the Interior, President Joe Biden appointed former NARF attorney Robert Anderson to serve as the new principal deputy solicitor. And three months later the president nominated Anderson to serve as solicitor. By a vote of 53 to 43, with Alaska Senator Lisa Murkowski one of only three Republican senators who voted in the affirmative, on September 29, 2021 the Senate confirmed the nomination.[97]

Section 2635.101(b)(8) and (14) of title 5 of the Code of Federal Regulations requires every federal employee, not only to act impartially, but to also not take any action that "a reasonable person with knowledge of the relevant facts" would conclude creates the appearance that the employee may not have acted impartially.

As has been described, when he had been employed by NARF in its office in Anchorage, in 1993 Anderson had been instrumental behind the scenes in persuading Assistant Secretary of the Interior for Indian Affairs Ada Deer to try and create more than two hundred federally recognized tribes in Alaska by publishing a list of Native entities and a preamble in the *Federal Register*. And in 1994 Anderson (and NARF attorneys Lare Aschenbrenner and Heather Kendall) had filed a petition that requested Assistant Secretary Deer to amend the regulations that govern the exercise by the secretary of the interior of the authority section 5 of the IRA delegates to the secretary to acquire land for Indians by removing the sentence that prohibited the secretary from acquiring land in Alaska.

Notwithstanding NARF attorney Anderson's prior involvement with the Alaska tribal status and land in Alaska into trust issues, on April 27, 2021, Principal Deputy Solicitor Anderson issued Solicitor Opinion M-37069 in which he withdrew Solicitor Opinion M-37064 and instructed the BIA to, ninety days after the end of a consultation period, resume processing applications that request the secretary of the interior to acquire land in Alaska pursuant to section 5 of the IRA.

Seventeen

Traditionally, gambling is an activity state legislatures regulate. That is why in Hawaii all forms of gambling are prohibited and in Nevada casinos are ubiquitous.

In Alaska, section 135 of the criminal code the Fifty-fifth Congress created for the District of Alaska in 1899 prohibited lotteries, and section 152 prohibited poker, craps, roulette, and all other forms of gambling.[1] In 1912 the Sixty-second Congress enacted the Third Alaska Organic Act, which designated the District of Alaska as the Territory of Alaska and provided that all laws then in force would remain in force until a particular law was amended or repealed by the legislature that the act authorized the "male citizens of the United States" who resided in Alaska to elect.[2]

For the next thirty-seven years, the Territorial Legislature allowed the prohibition on gambling in the 1899 criminal code to remain in force,[3] although in Anchorage, Fairbanks, Juneau, and the other major towns the prohibition was only occasionally enforced.

That changed in 1959 when Alaska became a state and in 1960 the commissioner of the new Department of Public Safety announced that Alaska State Troopers would begin enforcing section 135 of the 1899 criminal code by shutting down the Nenana Ice Classic and other raffles and lotteries that had operated, in the case of the Ice Classic, for more than forty years.[4]

The Alaska Legislature responded by enacting a statute that authorized nonprofit organizations to annually purchase a permit that authorized an organization to operate raffles and lotteries, bingo games, fishing derbies, and certain contests of skill.[5] The statute delegated the commissioner of revenue authority to regulate the methods and manner pursuant to which those forms of gambling could be conducted, and required the nonprofit organizations to spend the money they earned on "educational, civic, public, charitable, patriotic, or religious uses in the state."

In many communities that would be designated as Native villages for the purposes of ANCSA, village councils began purchasing permits to operate bingo games that provided a popular recreational activity and generated money that was used for community purposes. In 2019 Native villages to which the Department of Revenue issued permits earned $3.69 million operating bingo games and selling pull-tab cards.[6, *]

* A pull-tab card is a card with a tab that can be pulled back to reveal a row of symbols. If the symbols on the card match, the owner wins a cash prize.

In 1959 in its decision in *Williams v. Lee*[7] the U.S. Supreme Court ruled that states have no authority to enforce their laws inside the boundaries of Indian reservations except to the extent Congress grants a state that authority.

In 1964 Leonard Tonasket, an Indian who lived on the Colville reservation in the state of Washington, decided to test the *Williams v. Lee* rule by opening a smoke shop on the reservation in which he sold cigarettes to non-Indians without collecting the State's cigarette tax. When Tonasket and Indians who opened smoke shops on other reservations in the state of Washington initially prevailed in the lawsuits the Washington attorney general filed to force the shops to collect the tax, other Indians opened smoke shops on reservations in other states, including in 1977 on the Seminole reservation in Hollywood, Florida, west of Fort Lauderdale.[8]

The success of that venture set into motion a series of events that in 1979 resulted in Howard Tommie, the former chairman of the Seminole Indian Tribe of Florida, and Jack Cooper, an associate of the legendary organized crime figure Meyer Lansky, opening a bingo hall on the Seminole reservation in which games were played in violation of the State of Florida's charitable bingo law that, among other provisions, limited the amount of money that could be paid out in jackpots and required the profits to be spent exclusively for charitable purposes.[9]

The business model Howard Tommie and Jack Cooper pioneered quickly spread and by 1986 112 bingo halls were being operated on Indian reservations in twenty states.[10]

As has been described, Northway is a Native village in the Alaska interior forty-two miles west of the Canadian border. In 1986 Sally Smith, the director of the Public Services Division of the Alaska Department of Revenue, learned that the village council in Northway was conducting bingo games and selling pull-tab cards without having purchased a charitable gaming permit. When she asked the Department of Law for advice, without analyzing whether the Athabascan Indian residents of Northway were a federally recognized tribe, Assistant Attorney General Douglas Mertz advised Smith that Northway was not located within the boundaries of an Indian reservation and "outside of reservations, the legal presumption is that state authority controls and Natives are fully subject to it." Mertz then advised that "the village of Northway is not insulated from state law by any federal statute or regulation, so Alaska's gaming laws apply to the same extent as they would everywhere else in the state."[11]

A year later in the decision it issued in *California v. Cabazon and Morongo Bands of Mission* Indians,[12] the U.S. Supreme Court held that the State of California had no authority to enforce its charitable bingo and local option poker room statutes on the bands' reservations. The *Cabazon and Morongo Bands* decision was the final event in a series of events that had begun with the opening of the bingo hall on the Seminole reservation that in 1988 resulted in the One Hundredth Congress enacting the Indian Gaming Regulatory Act (IGRA),[13] which established the terms and conditions pursuant to which an "Indian tribe" can operate a gambling facility on the tribe's "Indian lands."

The IGRA divided gambling — which the IGRA calls "gaming" — into three classes: class I (social games played for prizes of minimal value and games played in connection with religious ceremonies and celebrations), class II (bingo, some types of non-banked card games, and the sale of pull-tab cards), class III (all other forms of gambling). The IGRA required a tribe that wanted to engage in class II or class III gaming to submit a gaming ordinance to the chairman of the three-member National Indian Gaming Commission (NIGC) that the IGRA created. If the chairman approved its ordinance and a tribe wanted to offer class III gaming, the IGRA required the tribe to negotiate a Tribal-State Compact with the state in which its "Indian lands" were located that would describe how the class III gaming would be regulated.

Section 4(5) of the IGRA defined "Indian tribe" to mean an "Indian tribe, band, nation, or other organized group or community of Indians which (A) is recognized as eligible by the secretary [of the interior] for the special programs and services provided by the United States to Indians because of their status as Indians, and (B) is recognized as possessing powers of self-government." And section 4(4) of the IGRA defined "Indian lands" to mean "(A) all lands within the limits of any Indian reservation; and (B) any lands title to which is either held in trust by the United States for the benefit of any Indian tribe or individual or held by any Indian tribe or individual subject to restriction by the United States against alienation and over which an Indian tribe exercises governmental power."

In 1804 the Russian American Company opened a trading post at a location on Baranof Island in southeast Alaska that would become the community known as Sitka. After its founding Tlingit Indians, whom the Russians called Kolosh, began settling outside the log palisade that ringed the trading post. When he visited Sitka in 1860, the Russian naval officer Pavel Golovin reported that "there is a wooden wall which separates the Russian settlement from the Kolosh. At one place the Kolosh settlement comes almost up to the wall, and continues along the shore."[14]

By 1880 when Alexander Militich enumerated the first census in southeast Alaska, the palisade was gone and Militich recorded that 540 Indians lived in the "Sitka Indian village" and 376 Caucasians and Creoles (the offspring of Caucasian fathers and Indian mothers) lived in the town that the Russian American Company trading post by then had become.[15] In 1910 500 Indians lived in the Indian village and 539 Caucasians and Creoles lived in the town. In 1913 when the Caucasian and Creole residents incorporated a municipal government, the Indian village became a neighborhood inside the city limits. In 1930 the city of Sitka had 1,056 residents whose racial composition likely was similar to what the racial composition had been in 1910.

In 1938 "a group of Indians having a common bond of residence in the neighborhood of Sitka, Territory of Alaska" submitted to the secretary of the interior a constitution for an organization called the Sitka Community Association that Assistant Secretary of the Interior Oscar Chapman approved pursuant to section 1 of Public Law No. 74-538 and section 16 of the IRA.[16]

By 1971 the population of Sitka had tripled to more than 3,300 residents, a substantial majority of whom were non-Natives. As a consequence, Sitka could not qualify as a Native village for the purposes of ANCSA. Instead, in section 14(h)(3) of ANCSA, the Ninety-second Congress authorized Natives living in Sitka to incorporate a corporation under the laws of the State of Alaska and authorized the secretary of the interior to convey to the corporation the title to the surface estate of not more than 23,040 acres of federally-owned public land located within "reasonable proximity" of Sitka.

In 1982 when Assistant Secretary of the Interior for Indian Affairs Ken Smith published in the *Federal Register* the first list of "Alaska Native Entities Recognized and Eligible to Receive Services From the United States Bureau of Indian Affairs," he included the Sitka Community Association on the list.[17] When the list was republished in 1983, 1985, 1986, and 1988, the Sitka Community Association remained listed.

In 1991, by which time the tribal sovereignty movement was sweeping through the Native community, the members of the Sitka Community Association submitted to the secretary of the interior a new constitution for the organization "formerly known as the Sitka Community Association" that henceforth would be known as "the 'Sitka Tribe of Alaska' [STA] a federally recognized tribe." Article II of the constitution provided:

> The jurisdiction of the Sitka Tribe of Alaska shall extend to all lands constituting the Native Village of Sitka and the areas formerly known as "Indian Possessions" and "Cottage Settlement", and to all surrounding areas of Indian Country, if any, including all customary and traditional use and access areas in the vicinity of Baranof Island, Chichagof and surrounding islands, and all fee lands and allotments and lands owned by Sealaska, Inc. or Shee Atika, Inc. located therein, to the fullest extent permitted by federal and tribal law.[18]

Without explaining how the members of the Sitka Community Association could transform themselves into a federally recognized tribe by simply renaming their organization, in 1992 Assistant Secretary of the Interior for Indian Affairs Eddie Brown approved the new constitution. But he did so with a caveat that he printed above his signature, which read:

> This approval shall not be construed to validate any assertion that the Sitka Tribe of Alaska has governmental authority over lands (including management of, or regulation of, the taking of fish and wildlife) or persons who are not members of the tribe, absent a ruling by a court of competent jurisdiction, an opinion of the Solicitor of the Department of the Interior or an Act of Congress subsequent to the date of the certification which indicates the existence of such authority over lands or non-members. This Constitution is

effective as of this date; *Provided*, That nothing in this approval shall be construed as authorizing any action under this document that would be contrary to Federal law.[19]

After the constitution was approved, the STA submitted a gaming ordinance to the chairman of the NIGC. In response, in April 1993 Michael Cox, the NIGC's general counsel, asked the solicitor of the Department of the Interior for advice as to whether the members of the STA were an "Indian tribe," as section 4(5) of the IGRA defined that term, and, if they were, whether there were "Indian lands," as section 4(4) of the IGRA defined that term, in or around Sitka on which the tribe could conduct bingo games and sell pull-tab cards.

In a letter dated June 23, 1993, John Trezise, the acting associate solicitor for Indian affairs, advised Cox that five months earlier Solicitor Thomas Sansonetti had issued Solicitor Opinion M-36975 (Governmental Jurisdiction of Alaska Native Villages Over Land and Nonmembers) in which he had concluded that "there are Native entities in Alaska that have inherent sovereign governmental authority." Trezise then opined that "such entities, in our view, are within the IGRA definition of 'tribe.'" He then noted that Solicitor Sansonetti had not identified the entities that possessed such governmental authority. However, it was not necessary to decide whether the STA was such an entity because, even if it was, despite the description in article II of the constitution of the geographical expanse of the STA's jurisdiction, there was no land in or around Sitka that qualified as "Indian lands."[20]

Klawock is a community on Prince of Wales Island in southeast Alaska that had grown up around a trading post and salmon saltery that had begun operating in 1868. In 1929 the 437 residents of Klawock incorporated a municipal government. In 1938 Assistant Secretary of the Interior Oscar Chapman approved, pursuant to section 1 of Public Law No. 74-538 and section 16 of the IRA, a constitution for an organization called the Klawock Cooperative Association (KCA) that had been submitted by "a group of Indians having a common bond of occupation in the fishing industry, including the catching, processing, and selling of fish and building of fishing boats and equipment, in Klawock, Territory of Alaska."[21]

In 1982 when Assistant Secretary of the Interior for Indian Affairs Ken Smith published in the *Federal Register* the first list of "Alaska Native Entities Recognized and Eligible to Receive Services From the United States Bureau of Indian Affairs," he included the KCA on his list.[22] In October 1993 when Assistant Secretary of the Interior for Indian Affairs Ada Deer published her list of Native entities and announced that, as a consequence of the publication, the listed entities henceforth had "the same governmental status as other federally acknowledged Indian tribes," she included the KCA on her list.[23]

Two months earlier the KCA had submitted a gaming ordinance to the chairman of the NIGC. The ordinance had been written by Bert Hirsch, the attorney from New York who in 1982 had represented the Tyonek village council in *Native Village of*

Tyonek v. Puckett, the lawsuit whose filing was one of the events that began the tribal sovereignty movement.

When the chairman of the NIGC received the ordinance, as he had when the STA submitted its ordinance, Michael Cox, the NIGC's general counsel, asked the solicitor of the Department of the Interior for advice. In a letter dated November 15, 1993, Michael Anderson, the associate solicitor for Indian affairs, advised Cox that "we conclude that the KCA falls within the Indian tribe definition [in section 4(5) of the IGRA] because it is organized under the Indian Reorganization Act; its constitution contains a broad statement of powers of the tribal government and it is listed as a federally-recognized tribe in the Department's official listing of tribes." In the latter regard, Anderson found determinative the fact that "most recently, the KCA was included in the October 21, 1993, list of Alaska tribal entities published at 58 Fed. Reg. 54364."

Insofar as whether there was land in Klawock that qualified as "Indian lands" was concerned, as has been described, in 1949 the BIA loaned the KCA several hundred thousand dollars to purchase a salmon cannery in Klawock, and the BIA had the seller convey to the United States a deed to the cannery buildings and the land under the buildings. Anderson advised Cox that the site of the long defunct cannery qualified as "Indian lands" because the land was a "dependent Indian community," and hence was "Indian country" as in 1948 the Eightieth Congress had defined the latter term in 18 U.S.C. 1151.

Anderson concluded that the site was a dependent Indian community (a term that in section 1151 the Eightieth Congress did not define) because the United States held title to the land, the KCA was renting buildings that had housed the cannery to its members, was operating a smoke shop in another of the buildings, and was using a building to house the KCA's offices.[24, *] The day after Michael Cox received Anderson's letter the chairman of the NIGC approved the KCA's gaming ordinance.[25]

A day later the *Anchorage Daily News* reported that "the Klawock decision came as a surprise to some state officials and people in Alaska Native legal circles who weren't even aware the tribal council there had applied for a permit."[26]

Two of the state officials who were surprised were Governor Walter Hickel and Attorney General Charles Cole who, as has been described, both strongly opposed

---

* In 1998 in the decision it issued in *State of Alaska v. Native Village of Venetie Tribal Government*, the U.S. Supreme Court identified the standards the Eightieth Congress intended be applied to determine whether a parcel of land is a dependent Indian community. The application of those standards to the cannery site at Klawock results in the conclusion that Associate Solicitor Anderson's determination that the site was a dependent Indian community, and hence section 1151 Indian country, and hence section 4(4) of the IGRA "Indian lands," was clearly erroneous. Nevertheless, no governor of Alaska has requested the secretary of the interior or the chairman of the NIGC to correct the error. As a consequence, until the COVID-19 pandemic, in a sixty-five seat hall in one of the cannery buildings, the KCA operated bingo games on Tuesday and Thursday evenings and Saturday afternoons, as well as video gaming machines whose software had been programmed to mimic pull-tab cards.[29]

the tribal sovereignty movement. And Hickel objected to gambling in general because he did not think it was a "socially productive activity."[27] Nevertheless, when she was asked what the governor's position was regarding the KCA's gaming ordinance, Assistant Attorney General Elizabeth Barry, who was advising Attorney General Cole regarding Alaska Native-related legal issues, answered: "I know we're looking into it, but I don't know what our position will be. This is the first time we've really had to deal with it."[28]

After she looked into it, Barry apparently not only advised Attorney General Cole to advise Governor Hickel to do nothing, she also apparently advised that she agreed with Associate Solicitor Anderson that the KCA was an IGRA section 4(5) "Indian tribe," and, because it was, the State was obligated to negotiate a Tribal-State Compact with the KCA that would authorize the KCA to offer class III gaming.

As has been described, Akiachak is a community on the Kuskokwim River whose residents are of Yup'ik Eskimo descent. In 1948 Assistant Secretary of the Interior William Warne approved, pursuant to section 1 of Public Law No. 74-538 and section 16 of the IRA, a constitution for an organization called the Akiachak Native Community (ANC) that had been submitted by "a group of Eskimos having the common bond of living together in Akiachak, Territory of Alaska." In 1971 the townsite trustee at the Bureau of Land Management surveyed a townsite at Akiachak that subdivided the land within the townsite into blocks, streets, and house lots.

At the instigation of Willie Kasayulie, the future president of the Alaska Native Coalition and founder of the Yupiit Nation, in 1977 the residents of Akiachak incorporated a municipal government that, also at the instigation of Willie Kasayulie, in 1990 they voted to dissolve. In 1993 when Assistant Secretary of the Interior for Indian Affairs Ada Deer published her list of Native entities and announced that, as a consequence of the publication, the listed entities henceforth would have "the same governmental status as other federally acknowledged Indian tribes," she included the ANC on her list.[30]

Represented by Bert Hirsch, the attorney who also was representing the KCA, in October 1994 the ANC submitted a gaming ordinance to the chairman of the NIGC to conduct class II gaming in a building located on Lot 10 within the Akiachak townsite.

In January 1995 the ANC amended its ordinance to add class III gaming. Five months later John Leshy, the solicitor of the Department of the Interior, advised the chairman of the NIGC that Lot 10 did not qualify as "Indian lands." After the chairman then denied the ordinance, the ANC informed the chairman that it had identified another lot within the Akiachak townsite, designated Lot 1, on which it would conduct class II and class III gaming.

Although the chairman of the NIGC had not decided whether Lot 1 qualified as "Indian lands," in October 1996 the ANC filed a lawsuit against the chairman in the U.S. District Court for the District of Columbia in which the ANC sought a declaratory judgment that Lot 10 and Lot 1 both qualified as "Indian lands."[31] In its complaint the ANC alleged that it was an Indian tribe "recognized by the secretary of the interior" and that the ANC had a "government-to-government relationship" with the United States.

Kenai is a town on the Kenai Peninsula 158 road miles south of Anchorage. In 1970 "a group of Kenaitze Indians residing principally within the Kenai Peninsula Borough" submitted to the secretary of the interior, pursuant to section 1 of Public Law No. 74-538 and section 16 of the IRA, a constitution for an organization called the Kenaitze Indian Tribe (KIT), which the secretary approved in 1971. In 1982 when Assistant Secretary of the Interior for Indian Affairs Ken Smith published in the *Federal Register* the first list of "Alaska Native Entities Recognized and Eligible to Receive Services From the United States Bureau of Indian Affairs," he included the KIT on his list.[32] In 1993 when Assistant Secretary of the Interior for Indian Affairs Ada Deer published her list of Native entities and announced that, as a consequence of the publication, the listed entities henceforth had "the same governmental status as other federally acknowledged Indian tribes," she included the KIT on her list.[33]

Represented by Bert Hirsch, in January 1995 the KIT submitted a gaming ordinance to the chairman of the NIGC. A month later the KIT informed the chairman that if he approved the ordinance, the KIT would open a class II gaming facility on ten acres of land in Kenai, designated Lot 16, that was part of an Alaska Native allotment that the KIT was in the process of purchasing from the owner.

Michael Cox, the NIGC's general counsel, asked John Leshy, the solicitor of the Department of the Interior, for advice as to whether "a restricted Native allotment held by a member of the Kenaitze Indian Tribe fits within the 'Indian lands' definition of the Indian Gaming Regulatory Act."

As has been described, in 1993 Thomas Sansonetti, the solicitor of the Department of the Interior, had issued Solicitor Opinion M-36975. In that opinion he announced that in 1948 the Eightieth Congress had intended the undefined term "Indian allotments" in the 18 U.S.C. 1151 definition of the term "Indian country" to include Alaska Native allotments. But he then announced that he was "not convinced that any specific villages or groups can claim jurisdictional authority over allotment parcels ... particularly in the absence of a tribal territorial base (e.g., a reservation), there is little to no basis for an Alaska village claiming *territorial* jurisdiction over an Alaska Native allotment" (emphasis in original).[34]

Citing that portion of Solicitor Opinion M-36975, in a letter dated May 12, 1995, former NARF attorney Robert Anderson, whom Solicitor Leshy had recently arranged for Secretary of the Interior Bruce Babbitt to appoint as the associate solicitor for Indian affairs, advised Cox that Lot 16 did not qualify as "Indian lands" because "we are not convinced, based on the information before us, that the Kenaitze Indian Tribe exercises governmental power over the land."[35]

Relying on that legal advice, three days later the chairman of the NIGC disapproved the KIT's gaming ordinance.[36]

In response, in October 1996 the KIT joined the ANC as a plaintiff in the lawsuit the ANC had filed. In their joint complaint the KIT alleged that it was an Indian tribe "recognized by the secretary of the interior" and that the KIT had a "government-to-government relationship" with the United States. The complaint also alleged that if its gaming ordinance was approved, the KIT would open a class II gaming facility on a forty-acre parcel of land, designated as Lot 1, which was part of the same Alaska Native allotment within whose boundaries Lot 16 was located.

Barrow (in 2016 renamed Utqiagvik), on the windswept coast of the Arctic Ocean, is the northernmost community in Alaska. Most Barrow residents are of Inupiat Eskimo descent. In 1939 Assistant Secretary of the Interior Oscar Chapman approved, pursuant to section 1 of Public Law No. 74-538 and section 16 of the IRA, a constitution for an organization called the Native Village of Barrow (NVB) that had been submitted by "a group of Eskimos having the common bond of living together in the Village of Barrow, Territory of Alaska."[37]

In 1958 the residents of Barrow incorporated a municipal government. They then petitioned the townsite trustee at the Bureau of Land Management for a townsite. In 1964 a townsite was surveyed that contained more than two hundred house lots. The townsite trustee then conveyed the title to each lot to the individual who occupied it with a restriction in the deed that prohibited the lot from being sold without the permission of the BIA.

In 1971 the Ninety-second Congress designated Barrow as a Native village for the purposes of ANCSA. In 1993 when Assistant Secretary of the Interior for Indian Affairs Ada Deer published her list of Native entities and announced that, as a consequence of the publication, the listed entities henceforth would have the "the same governmental status as other federally acknowledged Indian tribes," she included the NVB on her list.[38]

During the 1990s the NVB initially annually purchased a permit from the Alaska Department of Revenue that authorized the NVB to sell pull-tab cards pursuant to the terms and conditions in the State's charitable gaming statute. But in December 1994 an investigator from the Department of Revenue visited Barrow and discovered that the NVB was selling pull-tab cards that it had purchased unlawfully from Spokane Punchboards, a vendor in the state of Washington, and was paying the purchasers of winning cards $1,000 when $500 was the limit in the State's charitable gaming statute. The investigator also discovered that the NVB was selling pull-tab cards after the NVB had reached the limit on the annual total pay-out that the State's charitable gaming statute established.

When the investigator reported those violations to Dennis Parker, the chief of the police department for the North Slope Borough in which the city of Barrow was located, according to the investigator, Parker said he was taking a "hands-off position" "based on how hot the issue had become in reference to Native sovereignty issues. He informed me that, if he became involved in confiscating pull-tab games and/or citing individuals for conducting illegal gaming, the whole matter would escalate."

The investigator then met with Arnold Brower, the president of the NVB. During the meeting Brower told the investigator that the NVB had the legal right to sell pull-tab cards in violation of the State's charitable gaming statute because the NVB was "sovereign." Brower also said he "had been in touch with most of the other villages throughout the state concerning sovereignty issues" and "had confided with Roseann Demmert [the chairperson of the KCA] from Klawock." At the conclusion of the meeting, the investigator told Brower that the NVB needed to "cease gaming until this matter could be cleared up."[39]

The week before the investigator visited Barrow, Tony Knowles was sworn into office to succeed Walter Hickel as governor of Alaska. As has been described, Governor Knowles retained Bruce Botelho, whom after Attorney General Charles Cole resigned Governor Hickel had appointed to succeed Cole as attorney general, as his attorney general.

When Arnold Brower ignored the investigator's order that the NVB stop its illegal sales of pull-tab cards, Attorney General Botelho took no action against Brower and the NVB. Instead, in April 1995 the Department of Law informed Patricia Johnson, the owner of Spokane Punchboards, that she would be prosecuted if she continued selling pull-tab cards to the NVB.

When Johnson expressed her concern about being prosecuted to the NVB, in January 1996 Hans Walker, the attorney in Washington, D.C., who represented the NVB and who in 1980 had been the associate solicitor for Indian affairs at the Department of the Interior, demanded that Attorney General Botelho "cease interfering with the contracts between our client and Spokane Punchboards or any other pull-tab distributor" because the interference was an "unwarranted intrusion" on the NVB's "sovereign rights to engage in economic development."

Walker's legal rationale for that demand was that—because the members of the NVB were a federally recognized tribe and the building in which the NVB was selling pull-tab cards was located on a lot in the Barrow townsite that was Indian country—the State of Alaska had no authority to require the NVB and Spokane Punchboards to comply with the State's charitable gaming statute.[40]

In making that argument, Walker did not mention that the month after the investigator told Arnold Brower that the NVB needed to stop violating the State's charitable gaming statute, in January 1995 the NVB had submitted a gaming ordinance to the chairman of the NIGC. Nor did he mention that in April 1995 the chairman disapproved the ordinance because John Leshy, the solicitor of the Department of the Interior, had concluded that the lot in the Barrow townsite on which the building in which the NVB was selling pull-tab cards was located did not qualify as "Indian lands" because the NVB did not exercise governmental power over the lot as the "Indian lands" definition in section 4(4) of the IGRA required.

Three months later, in April 1996 Dennis Poshard, the director of the Charitable Gaming Division of the Alaska Department of Revenue, made an unannounced visit to Barrow. After observing that the NVB was continuing to sell pull-tab cards in violation of the State's charitable gaming statute, he told Arnold Brower that "he either stop the illegal gambling with pull-tabs or his organization would be prosecuted." When Brower assured Poshard that the NVB would do so, the director took him at his word, and the Department of Revenue issued the NVB a new permit whose terms and conditions the NVB continued to ignore.

In February 1999 Senator Robin Taylor, the Republican chairman of the Judiciary Committee of the Alaska Senate, learned that, rather than $500, the NVB was paying purchasers of winning pull-tab cards $5,000.[41]

When Taylor brought the matter to the attention of Larry Meyers, the director of the Audit Division of the Alaska Department of Revenue, Meyers asked the North Slope Borough police department to investigate. A week later Meyers informed Taylor that the police department had "reported back to us that they did observe evidence that at least one game that offers prizes in excess of the limit exists at one of the location (sic) that currently holds a state permit to conduct charitable gaming." Meyers also assured Taylor that "if our own investigation proves that in fact that our statutes are being violated we will take prompt steps to issue a notice of violation and follow up accordingly."[42]

Several weeks later Gary Dodson, the chief of compliance and investigations in the Audit Division, sent the NVB a notice that informed the NVB that its unlawful sale of pull-tab cards had "once again been referred to the Attorney General's Office."

When the Department of Law received the referral Assistant Attorney General Vince Usera wrote Hans Walker that if within ten days the NVB did not stop selling pull-tab cards in violation of its charitable gaming statute, the State "will take appropriate civil and criminal action."

In response, Walker indignantly told Usera that the lot in the Barrow townsite on which the building in which the NVB was selling pull-tab cards was located "is restricted fee land and, as Indian country, is land over which the State of Alaska has no jurisdiction." Walker also told Usera that "the Tribe has been attempting to obtain federal approval of its tribal gaming ordinance which is needed to govern class II gaming," and that because the chairman of the NIGC had disapproved the ordinance, "the Tribe, having exhausted administrative remedies, is preparing to file a suit in the U.S. district court." He then requested that "the State of Alaska not initiate criminal action pending resolution of the Indian country issue in U.S. district court."[43]

A month later, in April 1999 the NVB filed a lawsuit against the NIGC in the U.S. District Court for the District of Columbia. In its complaint the NVB alleged that it was a federally recognized tribe, and then informed the court that

> lack of an approved gaming ordinance has resulted in NVB being subject to threats of enforcement action by the State of Alaska for NVB failing to comply with state law regarding the sale of pull tabs. While it is NVB's position that

> the state has no jurisdiction over the townsite lot or tribal gaming, the state continues to threaten the tribe and its employees with fines and other punishment if NVB does not stop its class II activities.
>
> Due to these threats, because NVB believes it is being treated differently than tribes in the lower 48 states and because NVB believes it is entitled to engage in class II gaming under the IGRA, NVB seeks review of the NIGC's disapproval of its tribal gaming ordinance as well as the underlying opinion of the Department of the Interior.[44]

In the answer to the NVB's complaint that they filed the attorneys at the U.S. Department of Justice who represented the NIGC admitted that the members of the NVB were a federally recognized tribe and denied that the lot in the Barrow townsite on which the building in which the NVB was selling pull-tab cards was located qualified as "Indian lands."

Section 11(d)(1)(B) of the IGRA authorizes an "Indian tribe" to operate a gaming facility on its "Indian lands" that offers any form of gambling that the state in which the "Indian lands" are located permits any person, organization, or entity to engage in "for any purpose."

In 1983 the Alaska Legislature amended the State's charitable gaming statute to add a provision that authorized the Alaska Department of Revenue to issue permits to nonprofit organizations to hold "Monte Carlo Night" fund-raising events at which attendees could play blackjack and other card games, craps, and roulette for noncash prizes.[45] In 1994 the American Cancer Society, the Kodiak Lions Club, and more than sixty other nonprofit organizations held Monte Carlo Night fund-raising events that collectively raised more than $100,000.[46]

In November 1993 when he orchestrated the approval by the chairman of the NIGC of the KCA's gaming ordinance, Bert Hirsch, the KCA's attorney, explained to Roseann Demmert, the president of the KCA, that because the State had a Monte Carlo Night provision in its charitable gaming statute, the IGRA required the State to negotiate a Tribal-State Compact with the KCA that would authorize the KCA to offer the same games that could be played at Monte Carlo Night fund-raising events.

In April 1994 the negotiations began when Hirsch and several representatives of the KCA met with Assistant Attorney General Vincent Usera. Rather than questioning the validity of the determination of the chairman of the NIGC that the members of the KCA were an "Indian tribe" and the site of the cannery in Klawock qualified as "Indian lands," prior to the meeting Usera explained that, "We are approaching this to help [Roseann Demmert and the other members of the KCA] make a go of this thing. We don't see a point in making life difficult for everybody."[47]

After the meeting, the negotiations stayed on "square one" until September when the KCA gave the State a draft compact to which Usera responded by informing

Hirsch that no further negotiations could take place until the governor who would be elected to succeed Walter Hickel in the November election assumed office.

In November Tony Knowles won the election, and in December when he was sworn into office his spokesperson announced that what Governor Knowles would do about the negotiations with the KCA "hasn't been discussed and probably won't be until sometime next year when the new administration is up and running."[48]

What Governor Knowles soon thereafter decided to do was resume the negotiations. At the next meeting in February, Bert Hirsch represented the KCA and Tim Towarak and Albert Kookesh, from Governor Knowles's office, and Assistant Attorneys General Vincent Usera and Barbara Ritchie from the Department of Law, represented the State.

By April the major issues had been resolved, and on May 7 the *Anchorage Daily News* reported: "For the past year, tribal officials and lawyers in the Hickel and Knowles administrations have been negotiating a compact covering the kinds of games allowed and their regulation, including background checks of employees and any management companies hired by the tribe. They also agreed to state audits of the casino's books. Both the lawyer for the tribe and state officials said this week that the two sides were close to signing the compact."[49]

But before the compact could be signed, the negotiations between Bert Hirsch and the members of Governor Knowles's negotiating team were derailed by two Republican members of the Alaska Senate, Mike Miller and Robin Taylor, who before the *Anchorage Daily News* published its news report had discovered that the governor was on the verge of signing a Tribal-State Compact that would authorize the KCA to open a casino that would offer blackjack, craps, and roulette because the Monte Carlo Night provision in the State's charitable gaming statute required that outcome.

On April 28 Senator Miller arranged for the Rules Committee, which he chaired, to introduce SB 172, a bill whose enactment would repeal the Monte Carlo Night provision because, as Senator Taylor explained, "Before anyone takes advantage of our existing laws and creates casinos, we ought to close that loophole now."[50]

Over the objections of the nonprofit organizations that raised money by holding Monte Carlo Night fund-raising events, the Alaska Senate passed SB 172 four days after it was introduced. After the vote his press secretary said Governor Knowles opposed "trying to ramrod any bill through the legislature." Instead, he wanted a Commission on Gaming and Gambling that he had persuaded the legislature to create to study "gaming in all its forms."

But a week later Governor Knowles abruptly reversed course. Prior to the vote on SB 172 in the Alaska House of Representatives, he sent the House a letter in which he announced that he now supported the bill, which only days earlier he had opposed, stating: "I am concerned about any possible expansion of casino gaming and gambling in Alaska, especially in the absence of public debate. State laws permitting Monte Carlo nights create a right for the tribe to operate a casino, without being subject to the restrictions state laws impose on charities."[51]

If he was as concerned as he now said he was, Governor Knowles could have directed Attorney General Botelho to file a lawsuit that challenged the validity of the decision of the chairman of the NIGC that the members of the KCA were an "Indian tribe" and that the site of the cannery in Klawock was "Indian lands" as those terms were defined in the IGRA.

Only he knows why he did not. But as previously described, seven months earlier Tony Knowles had been elected governor by 583 votes in an election he would have lost if during the 1994 AFN convention the delegates had not endorsed his candidacy in part because candidate Knowles promised that Governor Knowles would drop the State's opposition to the idea that the Native residents of Klawock and all other Native villages were members of federally recognized tribes. And six months after the Alaska Legislature repealed the Monte Carlo Night provision, he made good on that campaign promise by in November 1995 directing Attorney General Botelho not to appeal to the U.S. Court of Appeals for the Ninth Circuit the decision District Judge H. Russel Holland had issued in the consolidated *Native Village of Venetie I.R.A. Council* and *State of Alaska v. Native Village of Venetie Tribal Government* lawsuits in which Judge Holland had held that the Gwitch'in Indian members of the Native Village of Venetie were a federally recognized tribe.

In the U.S. District Court for the District of Columbia, the *Akiachak Native Community and Kenaitze Indian Tribe* and *Native Village of Barrow* lawsuits were assigned to Judge Richard Roberts. After the usual delays, by May 2000 the parties had filed their briefs in the *Akiachak Native Community and Kenaitze Indian Tribe* lawsuit and had filed almost all their briefs in the *Native Village of Barrow* lawsuit.

Then on May 8 Attorney General Bruce Botelho filed motions in which he asked Judge Roberts to grant the State of Alaska leave to intervene as a defendant in both lawsuits. The answers to the complaints Attorney General Botelho filed with his motions admitted the validity of the plaintiffs' assertions that their members were federally recognized tribes and therefore were "Indian tribes" as section 4(5) of the IGRA defined that term.

That admission limited the State to arguing that John Leshy, the solicitor of the Department of the Interior, and Robert Anderson, the associate solicitor for Indian affairs, had been correct when they advised Michael Cox, the NIGC's general counsel, who then advised the chairman of the NIGC, that the townsite lots and Alaska Native allotment parcel on which the ANC, the KIT, and the NVB wanted to operate gaming facilities did not qualify as "Indian lands," which was the legal argument the attorneys at the U.S. Department of Justice already were making.

So why, with the briefing almost completed, did the governor decide in the eleventh hour that the State needed to intervene? When he was asked that question, Attorney General Botelho answered, "The Knowles administration doesn't want to see substantial expansion of gaming and another battle over Indian country."[52]

But the ANC filed its lawsuit more than three years earlier, and the NVB filed its lawsuit more than a year earlier. So a more likely reason may have been that members of the Republican-controlled legislature had become aware of the lawsuits and of the governor's inaction.

In a letter to Governor Knowles written after Attorney General Botelho filed the State's motions to intervene, after noting that "these lawsuits raise questions of which the answers are of profound importance to the Alaska Legislature's ability to continue to assert its regulatory jurisdiction in Native villages," Senator Mike Miller, who now was chairman of the Legislative Council, which functions in the legislature's stead between legislative sessions, asked the governor when he "first became aware that Akiachak, Barrow, and the Kenaitzes had filed lawsuits in the U.S. District Court for the District of Columbia," and why "the attorney general [did] not attempt to intervene in the lawsuits until May 8, 2000, by which time the cross-motions for summary judgment had been fully briefed?"[53]

In the letter in which he responded, Governor Knowles did not answer either question. Instead, he simply vouched that "as with the 1995 legislation [that repealed the Monte Carlo Night provision], I continue to oppose efforts to expand gaming in Alaska."[54]

In January and February 2001 when he issued decisions in both lawsuits, Judge Roberts denied the State's motions to intervene.*

In his decision in the *Akiachak Native Community and Kenaitze Indian Tribe* lawsuit, Judge Roberts remanded the disputes between the parties to the NIGC and directed the chairman of the NIGC to decide whether the two parcels of land that had not been included in the gaming ordinances he had disapproved but on which the ANC and the KIT subsequently said they wanted to operate gaming facilities qualified as "Indian lands."[55] In his decision in the *Native Village of Barrow* lawsuit, Judge Roberts affirmed the decision of the NIGC that the townsite lot in Barrow on which the building in which the NVB was selling pull-tab cards was located did not qualify as "Indian lands."[56]

After Judge Roberts issued his decision in the *Native Village of Barrow* lawsuit, the NVB announced that it would appeal the decision. When their gaming ordinances were sent back to the NIGC, the ANC and the KIT asked the chairman of the NIGC not to decide whether the townsite lot and allotment parcel on which they wanted to operate gaming facilities qualified as "Indian lands" until the circuit court decided the NVB's appeal. But when the NVB then decided not to file an appeal after all, rather than asking the chairman to decide whether the townsite lot and allotment

* After Attorney General Botelho filed his motions, the Legislative Council filed motions to intervene in order to argue to Judge Roberts that the members of the ANC, the KIT, and the NVB were not "Indian tribes" as section 4(5) of the IGRA defines that term because they were not members of federally recognized tribes, which they had to be in order to possess the "powers of self-government" that the "Indian tribe" definition required than to possess. After the Legislative Council filed its motions, represented by former NARF attorney Lare Aschenbrenner, the Alaska Inter-Tribal Council filed motions to intervene in order to defend the ANC's, the KIT's, and the NVB's tribal status. When he denied the State's motions to intervene, Judge Roberts also denied the Legislative Council's and the AITC's motions to intervene.

parcel qualified as "Indian lands," in 2003 the ANC and the KIT withdrew their gaming ordinances.[57]

The reason NVB did not file an appeal was that Arnold Brower and other members of the NVB had realized that Governor Knowles had no interest in further confrontation.

A year later, in May 2002 Senator Rick Halford, the Republican president of the Alaska Senate, sent Governor Knowles a letter in which he asked whether the NVB had applied to the Alaska Department of Revenue for a charitable gaming permit and, if it had not, whether the NVB was again selling pull-tab cards in violation of the State's charitable gaming statute, and, if it was, how the governor intended to respond to that flaunting of state law. In response, an underling at the Department of Revenue, rather than the governor, told the senator that the NVB had not applied for a permit, that the Department of Revenue had no new information about the NVB's sale of pull-tab cards, and that "although we have concerns about any illegal gaming activity, we have not been able to expend significant resources on illegal gaming in villages."[58]

Three months later, in November 2002, Alaska Senator Frank Murkowski was elected to succeed Tony Knowles as governor. When Knowles was asked the month after he departed office why his administration had not prosecuted the NVB, he said he had had more important things to worry about than illegal gambling in Barrow, and then tried to obfuscate by lecturing: "I don't know if prosecuting a minor violation of a gaming law rises to the same level as other crimes, like child abuse or violence."[59] But when he was asked the same question, former Attorney General Botelho more candidly explained that "early on, the prevailing view of the [Knowles] administration was that to pursue criminal action against Barrow would be to unduly antagonize state and tribal relations."[60]

Gregg Renkes, whom Governor Murkowski appointed attorney general, had a decidedly different view of his responsibilities as the State's chief law enforcement officer than his predecessor had had. Attorney General Renkes's response to the efforts of ICWA "Indian tribes" in Alaska to initiate child custody proceedings and his response to Superior Court Judge Peter Michalski's enforcement of the village council order banishing John Tague from Perryville have been described.

Insofar as the NVB was concerned, at Attorney General Renkes's direction, in May 2003 the Department of Law provided the NVB a last chance to purchase a permit from the Alaska Department of Revenue and conform the NVB's sale of pull-tab cards to the requirements of, and the limitations contained in, the State's charitable gaming statute. When the NVB did not purchase a permit, in June Alaska State Troopers raided the building in which the NVB was selling pull-tab cards, seized $2,500 in cash, a cash register and the office furniture, and confiscated the NVB's inventory of unsold cards.[61]

Negotiations then began that in April 2004 resulted in an agreement: the NVB agreed that it henceforth would purchase a permit and comply with the State's charitable gaming statute and Attorney General Renkes agreed that he would not prosecute Arnold Brower and other members and employees of the NVB for the years of illegal gambling in which the NVB had engaged. "We are pleased that the Native Village of Barrow has now obtained a permit from the State of Alaska," Renkes announced after hands were shaken. "We want to encourage charitable gaming, but in accordance with state laws and regulations, so that all charitable gaming operators are abiding by the same rules and the playing field is level."[62]

The Eklutna River empties into Cook Inlet twenty-two miles north of downtown Anchorage.

Early in the nineteenth century, several Dena'ina Indian families may have lived at the mouth of the river. But if they did, by 1897 they had moved on when ten Dena'ina Indian families relocated from Knik, the bustling supply center for miners who had stampeded into the area to prospect for gold, to a location two miles above the mouth of the river. In 1918 the Alaska Railroad, which was being constructed from Seward north to Fairbanks, ran its track across the river and established a train stop near the cluster of cabins that would become known as the community of Eklutna.

At the train stop, in 1924 the Bureau of Education, which inside the Department of the Interior administered education and other programs for Alaska Natives, opened an orphanage and in 1926 a boarding school.

When the orphanage was being built, in August 1924 B.B. Mozee, the superintendent of the central district of the Bureau of Education's Alaska Division, reported that

> believing implicitly in the possibilities of Eklutna, I have filed upon a large area for a reserve. Though over nineteen hundred acres comprise the tract, a great deal of it is tideland, some is high land, and much is level or gently sloping. Included within this filing is the deserted native village of Eklutna; owners of some of the cabins may wish to return. By having the old village site within our confines we shall be able to prevent the unscrupulous from exercising "squatter's rights" and thereby forcing themselves upon former native holdings.[63, *]

* In 1927 President Calvin Coolidge reserved 1,819 acres of public land at Eklutna "for the use of the United States Bureau of Education for educational purposes."[65] Five months after the Seventy-fourth Congress enacted Public Law No. 74-538, on the recommendation of the BIA, in October 1936 Secretary of the Interior Harold Ickes issued an order in which he temporarily withdrew 328,000 acres of public land within and surrounding Eklutna for possible designation as a reservation pursuant to section 2 of Public Law No. 74-538. In 1942 Secretary Ickes revoked that order except as to 9,200 acres. In 1961 the reserve for the boarding school that had been established in 1927 was revoked and 1,800 acres of public land surrounding Eklutna was withdrawn for use by the BIA "in connection with administration of Native affairs in the vicinity of Eklutna." In 1971 in section 19(a) of ANCSA the Ninety-second Congress revoked that withdrawal.

Actually, the village only appeared deserted because, as they did every summer, the Indians who lived in the cabins were camped on the beach at Cook Inlet at the locations at which they fished for salmon. As the Bureau of Education's annual report on the Eklutna boarding school more accurately reported in 1930: "An old native village is located about a mile north of the school. There are at present about eight good houses where the villagers come at certain times. They travel in and out and are never very long at the village."[64]

Also in 1930 the census for the first time listed "Eklutna village" and recorded that 158 individuals lived at that location. Since that number included ninety-two children at the boarding school and ten teachers and staff members, fifty-six individuals lived in the village.

In 1946 the BIA closed the boarding school, and by 1960 only fifty individuals, half of whom were children, lived at Eklutna.

By then the community was riven with discord that had divided the two dozen adults into what Nancy Yaw Davis, an anthropologist who spent time in Eklutna, described as Faction A, led by a Dena'ina Indian named Mike Alex who considered himself the titular head of the village, and Faction B, whose members included Mike Alex's brother and who referred to themselves as the Community Hall Organization. According to Davis,

> An established pattern of contention between the two groups had existed for a long period, but formal organization of [Faction B, the Community Hall Organization] was instigated in 1961 by a letter from the State Governor's office. This letter requested the names of the chief, treasurer, secretary, marshal, and village members. At that time Eklutna had none of these elected officials since there was no organization of this type. The young men laughed at the idea of a "chief", saying, "What do they think we are—savages?" However, despite these feelings, the letter was used as an excuse for taking steps toward formal organization. The possibility of acquiring funds for village improvement gave added stimulus to the idea.
>
> The Community Hall Organization held its first meeting on December 12, 1961. At the meeting the group decided elections should be held "sometime." Six months later, on May 5, 1962, the elections were held. A young man 26 years old was elected president. Another man, who lives near but not in the village, was elected vice-president. The step-father of the president and brother of Faction A's chief [Mike Alex] was elected treasurer. The president's sister was elected secretary. The president's parallel cousin (father's brother's son) was elected marshal. Thus, all but one of the officers were directly related to the president. The one non-villager may have been elected to the position of vice-president because he had the use of a bull-dozer and a gas saw which were needed to build the [community] hall.[66]

While it now had officers, the Community Hall Organization was an informal association of like-minded individuals. The organization had no local governmental or any other authority. A year later that fact became apparent when the Alaska Legislature enacted the Mandatory Borough Act, which directed the residents of Election District No. 8, whose boundaries included both the town of Anchorage and the community of Eklutna, to organize a borough that would be governed by members of an elected assembly.[67]

In September 1963 thirty-seven Eklutna residents voted in the election in which voters in Election District No. 8 and voters in Election District No. 7, which ran from Talkeetna south through the Matanuska-Susitna Valley to the town of Palmer, rejected the idea of organizing a borough that would have included both districts.[68] Three months later Eklutna residents voted in a second election in which voters in Election District No. 8 approved the organization of the Greater Anchorage Area Borough and elected a borough assembly, one of whose members represented Eklutna, as well as the nearby communities of Birchwood, Chugiak, and Eagle River south of Eklutna.

Like all residents of the Greater Anchorage Area Borough, Eklutna residents were required to comply with the ordinances the borough assembly adopted. However, because the community of Eklutna was not of a "modern and urban character" and a majority of the residents had one-quarter or more Dena'ina Indian blood, in 1971 the Ninety-second Congress designated Eklutna as a Native village for the purposes of ANCSA.

In 1982 when Assistant Secretary of the Interior for Indian Affairs Ken Smith published in the *Federal Register* the first list of "Alaska Native Entities Recognized and Eligible to Receive Services From the United States Bureau of Indian Affairs" he included "Eklutna Native Village" on his list.[69] In October 1993 when Assistant Secretary of the Interior for Indian Affairs Ada Deer published her list of Native entities and announced that, as a consequence of the publication, the listed entities henceforth had the "the same governmental status as other federally acknowledged Indian tribes," she included "Eklutna Native Village" on her list.

A month later the chairman of the NIGC approved the gaming ordinance the Klawock Cooperative Association had submitted.

Having been educated by the KCA, in 1995 the Native Village of Eklutna (NVE), as the Community Hall Organization by then had been renamed, submitted a gaming ordinance to the chairman of the NIGC. The ordinance stated that the NVE would operate a class II gaming facility on eight acres of land located five miles south of Eklutna and a mile west of the North Birchwood exit of the Glenn Highway, the freeway that begins in Anchorage and then runs north past Eklutna to the town of Palmer in the Matanuska-Susitna Valley. The eight acres were an Alaska Native allotment that in 1963 the BIA had given to Mike Alex's sister, Olga Ondola, at which she had lived until her death, after which her son George Ondola moved onto the property.[70]

As has been described, section 4(4) of the IGRA defines "Indian lands" to include land whose title is held by an "Indian individual" subject to a restriction by the United States against alienation, if the "Indian tribe" that the individual is a member of "exercises governmental power" over the land. As has also been described, in 1993 in Solicitor Opinion M-36975 Thomas Sansonetti, the solicitor of the Department of the Interior, had announced that in 1948 the Eightieth Congress that enacted the "Indian country" definition in 18 U.S.C. 1151 had intended the undefined term "Indian allotments" in the definition to include Alaska Native allotments. But Solicitor Sansonetti then announced that he was "not convinced that any specific villages or groups can claim jurisdictional authority over allotment parcels ... particularly in the absence of a tribal territorial base (e.g., a reservation), there is little to no basis for an Alaska village claiming *territorial* jurisdiction over an Alaska Native allotment" (emphasis in original).[71]

Relying on that legal conclusion, five days after he sent a similar letter regarding the Alaska Native allotment on which the Kenaitze Indian Tribe wanted to operate a class II gaming facility, in a letter dated May 17, 1995, Robert Anderson, the associate solicitor for Indian affairs, advised Michael Cox, the NIGC's general counsel, that "we are not convinced, based on the information before us, that the Eklutna Indian Tribe exercises government power over the [Ondola allotment]. Therefore, we cannot conclude that the land in question is 'Indian land' as defined in the IGRA."[72]

Lloyd Miller, the attorney who in 1984 had opened the Anchorage office of the Sonosky law firm, represented the NVE. In 1993 Miller had been a member of the group of attorneys who behind the scenes had orchestrated Assistant Secretary of the Interior for Indian Affairs Ada Deer's publication in the *Federal Register* of her list of Native entities that she said henceforth would have "the same status as tribes in the contiguous 48 states." Another member of that group was Robert Anderson, who in 1984 had opened NARF's office in Anchorage and who early in 1995 John Leshy, the solicitor of the Department of the Interior, had arranged for Secretary of the Interior Bruce Babbitt to appoint as associate solicitor for Indian affairs.

Anderson apparently told Lloyd Miller about the letter he had sent to Michael Cox because on May 19 the *Anchorage Daily News* reported that "lawyers for the Eklutna tribe withdrew their proposed gambling ordinance—the same day the [National Indian Gaming Commission] was expected to rule on it."[73] To assist Miller in avoiding having the letter be a binding legal determination by the Office of the Solicitor, in a letter dated May 18 that he sent to Cox, Anderson described the May 17 letter as a "draft," which it was not. He then told Cox:

> After we sent the draft to your office, we received correspondence from the Eklutna Tribe dated May 16, 1995, withdrawing their request for your office's review of your ordinance. Accordingly, since the issue was no longer ripe for decision in your office, our opinion was not finalized and will not be issued. If your office transmitted copies of the draft opinion to other entities, we request that you notify each entity that the opinion was never issued and that the draft opinion is not binding.

Eight months after Lloyd Miller withdrew the NVE's gaming ordinance, on January 27, 1996 the members of the NVE adopted a constitution that declared that the NVE was a "federally recognized tribal government" and described the land over which the tribe purported to assert its jurisdiction to include "all fee and allotment lands within the traditional lands of Eklutna, notwithstanding the issuance of any patent or unrestricted fee title to such lands." When the constitution was adopted, the chairman of the "Traditional Tribal Council" the constitution created was George Ondola, who was living on his mother's allotment.[74]

Eleven years later, on April 3, 2007, the NVE submitted a new gaming ordinance to the chairman of the NIGC. The ordinance described the land on which the NVE would operate a class II gaming facility as land that was "subject to restriction by the United States against alienation" and "subject to the governmental authority of the NVE Tribal Council."[75] Without saying so explicitly, that description described the Ondola allotment.

On April 11 the general counsel of the NIGC invited interested parties to submit written comments on the NVE's gaming ordinance, and on May 17 Attorney General Talis Colberg did so, as did Senator Lyda Green, the president of the Alaska Senate, and Representative John Harris, the speaker of the Alaska House of Representatives.

In his comments Attorney General Colberg conceded that the members of the NVE were a federally recognized tribe (and therefore were an "Indian tribe" as section 4(5) of the IGRA defines that term). But he then argued that the Ondola allotment did not qualify as "Indian lands" because in 1993 in Solicitor Opinion M-36975 Thomas Sansonetti, the solicitor of the Department of the Interior, had determined that federally recognized tribes in Alaska did not "exercise governmental power" over Alaska Native allotments and in his letter dated May 17, 1995, Associate Solicitor Anderson had advised Michael Cox, the NIGC's general counsel, that the Ondola allotment did not qualify as "Indian lands" for that reason.

In their comments Senator Green and Representative Harris made similar arguments regarding the "Indian lands" issue, but they also argued that the members of the NVE were not a federally recognized tribe and therefore were not an "Indian tribe" as section 4(5) of the IGRA defines that term.

In 2001 Senator Rick Halford, the president of the Alaska Senate, and Representative Brian Porter, the speaker of the Alaska House of Representatives, had asked Secretary of the Interior Gale Norton to "undertake a *de novo* legal and policy review of the Department of the Interior's position regarding the existence of 'federally recognized tribes' in Alaska."[76] But because David Bernhardt, the solicitor of the Department of the Interior, objected, Secretary Norton refused to do so.

In their comments on the NVE's gaming ordinance, Senator Green and Representative Harris renewed the request for a *de novo* review. They also asked Secretary Norton's successor, Secretary of the Interior Dirk Kempthorne, to "direct the chairman of the NIGC to take no action on the NVE ordinance until the legal and policy review that we are requesting has been completed."[77]

In 2001 Senator Halford and Representative Porter had submitted their request for a *de novo* review with the knowledge and approval of Alaska Senators Ted Stevens and Frank Murkowski. Both senators had been in office in 1982 when the tribal sovereignty movement began, and from its inception they both had opposed the movement (notwithstanding Senator Murkowski's involvement in 1994 in the enactment by the One Hundred-third Congress of the Tlingit and Haida Status Clarification Act).[78] But in 2002 when Senator Murkowski appointed his daughter Lisa Murkowski to his seat in the Senate after he was elected governor, the politics inside the Alaska congressional delegation changed. After Senator Green and Representative Harris submitted their comments on the NVE's gaming ordinance and in those comments renewed Senator Halford and Representative Porter's request for a *de novo* review of Alaska Native tribal status, *Indian Country Today* reported that

> off-record sources in Alaska and Washington, speaking on condition of anonymity due to the tenor of debate in Alaska on Native issues generally, said Interior shows no appetite for heeding the Alaska Legislature's contentious request [for a *de novo* legal and policy review of Alaska Native tribal status] in the last year and a half of President George W. Bush's administration. Interior did not respond to a request for Kempthorne's reaction. Press Secretary Kevin Sweeney provided a response from Sen. Lisa Murkowski, R-Alaska: "This is not the first time that several Alaska state legislators have asked the Secretary of the Interior to determine whether Alaska Native villages were appropriately included on the list of federally recognized tribes. On all prior occasions the secretary of the interior has declined to reopen the matter. The decisions of Secretary Kempthorne's predecessors were legally supportable and we don't see Secretary Kempthorne reversing course, nor is Senator Murkowski encouraging him to do so."[79]

While Secretary Kempthorne did not authorize the review, someone at the Department of the Interior apparently informed Lloyd Miller that, as Associate Solicitor Anderson had in 1995, the present associate solicitor for Indian affairs had concluded that the Ondola allotment did not qualify as "Indian lands" because the NVE did not "exercise governmental power" over the land within the boundaries of the allotment. To prevent the chairman of the NIGC from issuing a decision denying the NVE's gaming ordinance for that reason, in a letter dated June 25, 2007, Marissa Flannery, an attorney who worked for Miller, informed the chairman that the NVE was withdrawing "the Tribe's Amended and Restated Gaming Ordinance and the Indian land determination that was submitted for your approval on April 2, 2007," and that "the Tribe will be resubmitting a substitute ordinance shortly."[80]

In fact, the NVE would not submit anything for another nine years.

Rather than another gaming ordinance, in June 2016 the NVE, represented as it had been since 1995 by attorneys in the Sonosky law firm, submitted a request to the Department of the Interior in which it asked the department to issue a determination that the Ondola allotment qualified as "Indian lands."

Over the next three years members of the NVE and attorneys from the Sonosky firm met with attorneys in the Office of the Solicitor, the acting assistant secretary of the interior for Indian affairs, and Associate Deputy Secretary of the Interior James Cason to whom the assistant secretary reported. During those meetings the NVE members revealed that Marnell Gaming, a casino design and management company headquartered in Las Vegas, had agreed to loan the NVE $10 million to construct a 35,000 square foot casino on the Ondola allotment whose gaming floor would contain five hundred class II video gaming machines.

While whether the Ondola allotment qualified as "Indian lands" was a question of law, at a meeting held in August 2017 Associate Deputy Secretary Cason suggested that the NVE needed Alaska Senators Lisa Murkowski and Dan Sullivan and Alaska Representative Don Young to support the idea of the NVE opening a gaming facility on the allotment.

Following up on the suggestion, in November members of the NVE met with Representative Young, after which he sent Associate Deputy Secretary Cason a letter in which he expressed his "strong support for the Native Village of Eklutna's proposed tribal gaming project and NVE's Indian lands determination request pending before the Department" because "the project will support as many as 150 new full-time equivalent positions, plus as many as 500 indirect new jobs."[81]

Two months later Ethan Berkowitz, the mayor of the Municipality of Anchorage within whose boundaries Eklutna and the Ondola allotment are located, met with Aaron Leggett, the president of the NVE. After the meeting Mayor Berkowitz sent Associate Deputy Secretary Cason a letter in which he announced that "the Municipality of Anchorage supports the Tribe's goals of economic self-determination and believes both the Tribe and the surrounding community will benefit from the jobs and related economic development the project will bring."[82] However, Mayor Berkowitz did not consult the members of the community councils in the surrounding communities — Birchwood, Chugiak, Eagle River — before he sent his letter. Nor did the mayor and Representative Young release their letters to the press.

Five months after Mayor Berkowitz sent his letter, in June 2018 John Tahsuda, the principal deputy assistant secretary of the interior for Indian affairs, announced that, as it had in 1995 and 2007, the Department of the Interior had determined that the Ondola allotment did not qualify as "Indian lands."[83]

In August 2019 the NVE filed a lawsuit in the U.S. District Court for the District of Columbia against the Department of the Interior. The complaint alleged that the members of the NVE are a "federally recognized tribe" and requested the court to issue "a declaratory judgment reversing the Department's negative Indian lands determination and declaring that the [Ondola] Allotment constitutes 'Indian lands' within the meaning of [the 'Indian lands' definition in section 4(4) of the IGRA]."

In September 2021 District Judge Dabney Friedrich issued a memorandum decision in which she announced that the Department of the Interior's "conclusion that the Ondola Allotment did not meet the requirements of the Indian lands test was rational. Though the Tribe may not agree with Interior's application of law to the facts at hand, the record shows that Interior made a reasoned judgment which the Court will not second-guess. Thus, the Tribe's claim that Interior acted arbitrarily and capriciously in applying the Indian lands test set forth in the Sansonetti Opinion must fail."[84] Judge Friedrich then issued an order in which she directed the Clerk of Court to close the case.

Conclusion

With no understanding of the legal or policy consequences that would have resulted had the Ninety-fifth Congress enacted it, in 1977 Alaska Senators Ted Stevens and Mike Gravel introduced S. 2046, the bill that designated the Native associations listed in section 7(a) of the Alaska Native Claims Settlement Act as "Indian tribes" that would have had "all rights, prerogatives, and duties held by federally recognized tribes in the contiguous States of the United States."

Over the next forty-four years: in 1993 Assistant Secretary of the Interior for Indian Affairs Ada Deer purported to create more than two hundred federally recognized tribes in Alaska by publishing a list of Native entities and a preamble in the *Federal Register*; in 1999 in its decision in the *John v. Baker* lawsuit the Alaska Supreme Court accepted the legal validity of Assistant Secretary Deer's action; in 2001 the Alaska Supreme Court announced that the Native residents of a community who qualify as an "Indian tribe" for the purposes of the Indian Child Welfare Act have authority to create courts that have jurisdiction to involve themselves in child custody matters without having to petition the secretary of the interior pursuant to section 108 of the ICWA to grant that jurisdiction; in 2006 when it reauthorized the Violence Against Women Act, the One Hundred-ninth Congress designated the Native residents of those communities as "Indian tribes" for the purpose of creating courts that have authority to enforce protection orders; in 2013 when it again reauthorized the VAWA, the One Hundred-thirteenth Congress authorized those courts to also issue protection orders; in 2015 Alaska Governor Bill Walker announced that he supported the secretary of the interior acquiring land in Alaska and taking the title to that land into trust pursuant to section 5 of the Indian Reorganization Act; and in 2017 Attorney General Jahna Lindemuth announced that the State's attorneys and law enforcement officers would not intervene in banishments in Native villages, even when the individual who has been banished is a non-Native.

Those and the tribal sovereignty movement's other achievements were accomplished by astute lawyering and lobbying by attorneys employed in the Anchorage office of the Native American Rights Fund, as well as by other members of the small group of attorneys who beginning in 1978 when David Case wrote *The Special Relationship of Alaska Natives to the Federal Government* staffed the movement; lawyering by attorneys at the Alaska Department of Law and Office of Public Advocacy that ranged from analytically incoherent to duplicitous; the complicity of Assistant Secretary Deer and her successors, as well as other members of the Department of the Interior bureaucracy; and, most consequentially, decisions made by a succession of governors and members of Alaska's congressional delegation, who did not understand the legal and policy consequences of many of those decisions or who did understand and decided to subordinate the future of Alaska as a socially cohesive multi-ethnic polity to personal political ambition.

In 2016 former NARF attorney Robert Anderson, who since 2001 had been a professor of Indian law at the University of Washington Law School, triumphantly announced that "the books are rightfully closed on the question[] of [Alaska Native] tribal status" and "the basic structure of tribal governance is firmly established as a matter of federal law."[1]

But the books are not closed until the U.S. Supreme Court settles the question or Congress enacts a statute that does so.

In 1997 the U.S. Supreme Court likely would not have granted the petition for a writ of certiorari that the State of Alaska filed in the *State of Alaska v. Native Village of Venetie Tribal Government* lawsuit had now-Chief Justice John Roberts not represented the State and had Alaska Senator Ted Stevens not filed a brief in which he asked his lifelong friend Chief Justice William Rehnquist to have the Court grant the petition. So it is unlikely the Court will grant another petition that will require it to settle the question of Alaska Native tribal status, particularly if the petition is filed by a petitioner other than the State of Alaska.[2]

But even if someday the U.S. Supreme Court is willing to grant another petition, whether it is a good result or a bad one for there to be more than two hundred federally recognized tribes in Alaska whose governing bodies possess governmental authority and sovereign immunity is a policy question that—as the Indian Commerce Clause of the U.S. Constitution commands—Congress, rather than the Court, should decide.

Since the answer to that question would affect only one state, there is no reason for Congress to legislate unless the members of Alaska's congressional delegation ask Congress to. But since 1982 when Alaska Senator Ted Stevens settled on "neutrality" as his response to the tribal sovereignty movement, not only has no member been willing to ask, but in 2019 Alaska Senator Lisa Murkowski and Alaska Representative Don Young urged the One Hundred-sixteenth Congress to grant courts that have been created in Native villages whose Native residents, since 2006, have been members of "Indian tribes" for the purposes of the Violence Against Women Act the authority to prosecute and, if they decide that doing so is appropriate, incarcerate non-Natives.

Given those judicial and political realities, Robert Anderson is almost correct. The books are almost closed on the question of Alaska Native tribal status, and the tribalization of federal Indian policy in Alaska in contravention of the policy choice on which the Forty-eighth Congress settled in 1884 and that the Ninety-second Congress codified in 1971 in the Alaska Native Claims Settlement Act seemingly is on the cusp of being achieved. As this history of the tribal sovereignty movement to the present date has described, how that happened has been quite a story.

Notes

Introduction

1. Pub. L. No. 92-203, 85 Stat. 688 (codified as amended at 43 U.S.C. 1601 *et seq.*).

2. Oswalt, *Historic Settlements Along the Kuskokwim River, Alaska*, at 26 ("Reinhold Separe (Sipary), a pioneer United States-era trader at Kolmakovsky [the trading post a hundred miles upriver], appears to have established the first trading post at Bethel"); Oswalt, *Mission of Change in Alaska*, at 23–25, 30–32, 35 (establishment of Moravian mission at Bethel described).

3. "Calista Holds Historic Meeting," *Tundra Drums*, Sept. 21, 1974.

4. H.R. 39, 95th Cong. (as introduced, Jan. 4, 1977).

5. *Inclusion of Alaska Lands in National Park, Forest, Wildlife Refuge, and Wild and Scenic Rivers Systems: Hearings on H.R. 39 Before the Subcomm. on General Oversight and Alaska Lands of the H. Comm. on Interior and Insular Affairs*, 95th Cong. Part XI, 398–411 (1977) (statement of Donald C. Mitchell on behalf of Alaska Legal Services Corporation).

6. *Id.* at 153–158.

7. Donald Mitchell, *Sold American*; Donald Mitchell, *Take My Land Take My Life*.

8. "Tyonek Lawsuit Raises 'Sovereignty' Issue," *Anchorage Daily Times*, Dec. 15, 1982 (preliminary injunction hearing in *Native Village of Tyonek v. Puckett* lawsuit described).

9. *Native Village of Stevens v. Alaska Management & Planning*, 757 P.2d 32, 37 (Alaska 1988) ("Federal-Native relationships were examined in detail by a task force appointed to study the subject by the Governor of Alaska. The task force issued a report of impressive scholarship").

10. *Id.* at 41.

Chapter One

1. Cohen, *Handbook of Federal Indian Law*, at 268.

2. *Montoya v. United States*, 180 U.S. 261, 266 (1901).

3. H.R. Rep. No. 103-781, at 2–3 (1994). *Accord* Newton (ed.), *Cohen's Handbook of Federal Indian Law*, at 133–134.

4. Donald Mitchell, *Sold American*, at 65–99 (Sheldon Jackson's involvement in Alaska and as the principal lobbyist for the organization of a civil government described). *See also* Stewart, *Sheldon Jackson*, at 319–320 ("From the date of his first visit [to Alaska in 1877] he [Sheldon Jackson] sought interviews with members of Congress and wrote letters to influential men of the nation, as well as appeals in the public press, urging the establishment of public schools and the formation of a provisional government for the administration of justice and the protection of life and property").

5. *See generally* Hoxie, *A Final Promise*.

6. Statement of Rev. Sheldon Jackson, D.D., Feb. 3, 1880, *printed at* S. Rep. No. 47-454, at 13 (1882).

7. 23 Stat. 24 (1884).

8. *In re Sah Quah*, 31 F. 327, 329 (D. Alaska 1886).

9. Address of Dr. Jackson, Oct. 9, 1895, *printed in 1895 Report of the Board of Indian Commissioners*, at 25.

10. *Condition of Natives of Alaska*, S. Doc. No. 60-257, at 2, 1908.

11. *United States v. Kes-tu-ish (alias Moses)*, U.S. District Court for the District of Alaska, Division No. 1, No. 344-B (1902). Court file at Alaska State Archives, Juneau, Alaska. *See also* William R. Hunt, *Distant Justice*, at 304–305.

12. Letter from Ray Lyman Wilbur, Secretary of the Interior, to the Hon. Edgar Howard, Chairman, House Committee on Indian Affairs, March 14, 1932, *reprinted at Authorizing the Tlingit and Haida Indians to Bring Suit in the United States Court of Claims: Hearing on S. 1196 Before the S. Comm. on Indian Affairs*, 72d Cong. 16 (1932).

13. Pub. L. No. 62-334, 37 Stat. 512 (1912).

14. Ch. 11 SLA 1915. In 1917 the Alaska Territorial Legislature amended the 1915 statute by adding a section that read: "That nothing contained in the Act shall be construed or interpreted as in any way giving to the village organizations, provided for herein any right, authority, or jurisdiction over the property of white residents residing within the corporate limits of the village; it being the purpose of this act to provide governments for the Indian residents of such villages only. Provided, however, that if any white person violates any lawful ordinance of such village he shall be deemed guilty of a misdemeanor an d tried before a United States Commissioner." Ch. 25 SLA 1917.

15. Ch. 23 SLA 1929.

16. *Annual Report to the Commissioner of Indian Affairs of the School at Noatak, Alaska, for the Year Ending June 30, 1933*, Alaska School Service, Office of Indian Affairs, U.S. Department of the Interior.

17. Wilkins, *On the Drafting of Tribal Constitutions*, at xv and xxi ("[In 1933] he [Felix Cohen] received a one-year appointment from Nathan Margold, solicitor for the Department of the Interior, as an assistant solicitor, expressly to help draft the basic legislation that came to be known as the Wheeler-Howard bill, or the Indian Reorganization Act" and "Cohen ... did not work alone in drafting the IRA, although it appears that he was its principal author"); Dalia Tusk Mitchell, *Architect of Justice: Felix S. Cohen and the Founding of American Legal Pluralism*, at 81 ("In retrospect, Collier recalled that the act [the IRA] was drafted by the Solicitor's Office, 'particularly' by Felix Cohen").

18. The history of the development of the content of and the drafting of S. 2755 is described in Rusco, *A Fateful Time*, at 176–208.

19. S. 2755 is printed in *To Grant to Indians Living Under Federal Tutelage the Freedom to Organize for Purposes of Local Self-Government and Economic Enterprise: Hearing on S. 2755 Before the S. Comm. on Indian Affairs*, 73d Cong. 1–15 (1934) [hereinafter "Senate IRA Hearings"].

20. Secretarial Order No. 494 (March 14, 1931).

21. Senator Wheeler's meeting with Assistant Commissioner Zimmerman is described in Rusco, *A Fateful Time*, at 249–251.

22. Senate IRA Hearings, at 237.

23. S. 3645 is printed at *id.* at 234–234.

24. *Id.* at 265.

25. S. Rep. No. 73-1080, at 3 (1934) (explaining that section 15 of S. 3645 "makes the provisions dealing with Indian corporations and Indian education applicable to Alaska"). Section 15 exempted

from application in the Territory of Alaska section 5 of H.R. 3645, which authorized the Secretary of the Interior to acquire land "for the purpose of providing land for Indians."

26. 78 *Cong. Rec.* 9268 (1934) (Representative Isabella Greenway, who was a member of the Committee on Indian Affairs, explaining, "Last night many of us redrafted the bill, leaving nothing in it but the title"). The bill the Committee reported is printed at H. Rep. No. 73-1804, at 1–5 (1934), and 78 *Cong. Rec.* 11724–11726 (1934).

27. *American Petroleum Institute v. Knecht*, 456 F. Supp. 889, 931 (C.D. Cal. 1978).

Chapter Two

1. Pub. L. No. 59-147, 34 Stat. 169 (1906).

2. Letter from Anthony J. Dimond, Delegate, to Dear Sir, March 5, 1935. Anthony J. Dimond Papers.

3. *Ibid.* ("This matter [i.e., the problem with section 17] has engaged the attention of the Indian Office here and today the bill, of which a copy is enclosed, was submitted to me").

4. Donald Mitchell, *Sold American*, at 295–296, 306–309 (involvement of Felix Cohen in drafting H.R. 9866 described).

5. Letter from Harold L. Ickes, Secretary of the Interior, to the Hon. Will Rogers, Chairman, Committee on Indian Affairs, U.S. House of Representatives, March 14, 1936, *reprinted at* H.R. Rep. No. 74-2244, at 4 (1936).

6. After Congress enacted H.R. 9866, in the May 15, 1936, issue of the BIA newsletter *Indians at Work*, Commissioner Collier reported that "[t]he principal credit for the enactment of the legislation is due to Delegate Anthony J. Dimond of Alaska and to William L. Paul, representative of the Alaska Native Brotherhood."

7. Donald Mitchell, *Sold American*, at 221–223, 238–239 (organization of the Alaska Native Brotherhood and William Paul's election as Grand Secretary described).

8. Letter from William Paul to Delegate Anthony Dimond, Feb. 27, 1934, printed at *Readjustment of Indian Affairs: Hearings on H.R. 7902 Before the H. Comm. on Indian Affairs*, 73d Cong. 498 (1934).

9. *See generally* Murray, *The Devil and Mr. Duncan.*

10. 21 *Cong. Rec.* 10092 (1890) (statement of Senator Dawes).

11. 26 Stat. 1095, 1101 (1891).

12. Constitution of the Metlakatla Indian Community Annette Islands Reserve, Alaska, available at https://thorpe.law.ou.edu/IRA/metlacons.html.

13. *United States v. Booth*, 161 F. Supp. 269 (D. Alaska 1958).

14. 83 *Fed. Reg.* 34867 (2018) ("Metlakatla Indian Community, Annette Island Reserve" listed as a "Native Entity Within the State of Alaska Recognized and Eligible to Receive Services From the United States Bureau of Indian Affairs").

15. Memorandum from William L. Paul, Felix S. Cohen, and Paul W. Gordon to Commissioner Collier, Jan. 22, 1936, *printed in* Donald Mitchell, *Sold American*, at 309.

16. Hoxie, *A Final Promise*, at 32–33.

17. Section 1, H.R. 9866, 74th Cong. (as reported by H. Comm. on Indian Affairs, March 26, 1936); H.R. Rep. No. 74-2244, at 1 (1936).

18. H.R. Rep. 74-2244, at 1–2 (1936).

19. Instructions for Organization in Alaska Under the Reorganization Act of June 18, 1934, and the Alaska Act of May 1, 1936, and the Amendments Thereto, Dec. 7, 1937 [hereinafter "Zimmerman Instructions"].

20. *Id.* at 9.

21. Letter from William L. Paul, Grand Secretary, Alaska Native Brotherhood, to the Hon. Oscar L. Chapman, Aug. 18, 1940 (quoting letter dated July 6, 1940, from Assistant Secretary Chapman). William Lewis Paul Papers.

22. The communities for which the Secretary of the Interior approved constitutions and corporate charters, and the date each constitution and charter was approved, are listed in Appendix A, Report of the Governor of Alaska's Task Force on Federal-State-Tribal Relations, 1986.

23. *See e.g.*, Article IV, Section 1, Constitution of the Organized Village of Kwethluk (approved May 11, 1938); Article 4, Section 1, Constitution of the Native Village of Kotzebue (approved May 23, 1939); Article IV, Section 1, Constitution of the Native Village of Stevens (approved Dec. 30, 1939); Article IV, Section 1, Constitution of the Akiachak Native Community (approved Aug. 6, 1948), available at https://thorpe.law.ou.edu/IRA.html.

24. *Repeal Act Authorizing Secretary of the Interior to Create Indian Reservations in Alaska: Hearings on S. 2037 and S.J. Res. 162 Before the Subcomm. of the S. Comm. on Interior and Insular Affairs*, 80th Cong. 13 (1948) (list of reservations designated pursuant to section 2) [hereinafter "1948 Hearings"].

25. *Ibid.*

26. *Nomination of Oscar L. Chapman to be Secretary of the Interior: Hearing Before the S. Comm. on Interior and Insular Affairs*, 81st Cong. (1950).

27. Confidential Memorandum from Anthony Dimond to E.L. "Bob" Bartlett, Nov. 20, 1947. Edward Lewis "Bob" Bartlett Papers.

28. Donald Mitchell, *Sold American*, at 339.

29. "Alaskan Indian Bill Introduced by Sen. Butler," *Daily Alaska Empire*, Jan. 21, 1948.

30. 94 *Cong. Rec.* 9095–9097 (1948).

31. Federal Land Policy and Management Act, Section 704(a), Pub. L. No. 94-579, 90 Stat. 2743 (1976).

32. Memorandum entitled "Incorporation of Native villages" from Dale M. Belcher, Credit Officer, BIA Alaska Regional Office, to Robert L. Bennett, Director, BIA Alaska Regional Office, Feb. 23, 1951. Copy in administrative record for Solicitor's Opinion M—36975, Governmental Jurisdiction of Alaska Native Villages Over Land and Nonmembers, 1993.

33. *See generally* Naske, *An Interpretative History of Alaskan Statehood.*

34. *Alaska Statehood: Hearings on H.R. 331 and S. 2036 Before the S. Comm. on Interior and Insular Affairs*, 81st Cong. 206–223 (1950).

35. *Id.* at 325–326, 328–355; *Hawaii-Alaska Statehood: Hearings on H.R. 2535, et al., Before the H. Comm. on Interior and Insular Affairs*, 84th Cong. 105–106, 129–135, 265–268, 358–360 (1955).

36. *Id.* at 234.

37. *Statehood for Alaska: Hearings on H.R. 50, et al., Before the Subcomm. on Territorial and Insular Affairs of the H. Comm. on Interior and Insular Affairs*, 85th Cong. 130 (1957).

38. Letter from Roger Ernst, Assistant Secretary of the Interior, to the Hon. Emanuel Celler, Chairman, House Committee on the Judiciary, Feb. 25, 1958, reprinted in S. Rep. No. 85-1872, at 2–3 (1958). The single anomalous exception to Congress's consistent understanding subsequent to 1867 that Alaska Natives had not been recognized as "tribes" in a political sense is the enactment by Congress in 1958 of Public Law No. 85-615 in response to *In re McCord*, 151 F. Supp. 132 (D. Alaska 1957). The circumstances that resulted in the *McCord* decision and the enactment of Public Law No. 85-615 are described in Donald Mitchell, "*Alaska v. Native Village of Venetie*: Statutory Construction or Judicial Usurpation? Why History Counts" [hereinafter "Why History Counts"].

Chapter Three

1. H.R. 4388, 82d Cong. (as introduced, June 11, 1951). The circumstances that motivated Delegate Bartlett to introduce H.R. 4388 are described in Donald Mitchell, *Sold American* 398–399.

2. *Hearing on H.R. 4388 Before the Subcomm. on Indian Affairs of the H. Comm. on Interior and Insular Affairs*, 82d Cong. 31–32 (1951). The Subcommittee did not publish the transcript of its hearing. A copy of the transcript is in the H.R. 4388 bill file at the Center for Legislative Archives, National Archives, Washington, D.C.

3. Field Committee, *Alaska Natives and the Land*, at 47–48.

4. *Alaska Native Land Claims: Hearings on S. 2906, et al., Before the S. Comm. on Interior and Insular Affairs*, 90th Cong. (1968) [hereinafter "1968 Senate Hearing"]; *Alaska Native Land Claims: Hearing on H.R. 11213, et al., Before the Subcomm. on Indian Affairs of the H. Comm. on Interior and Insular Affairs*, 90th Cong. (1968); *Alaska Native Land Claims: Hearing on S. 1830 Before the S. Comm. on Interior and Insular Affairs*, 91st Cong. (1969); *Alaska Native Land Claims: Hearings on H.R. 13142, et al., Before the Subcomm. on Indian Affairs of the H. Comm. on Interior and Insular Affairs*, 91st Cong., Parts I and II (1969); *Alaska Native Land Claims: Hearings on S. 35 and S. 835 Before the S. Comm. on Interior and Insular Affairs*, 92d Cong. (1971); *Alaska Native Land Claims: Hearings on H.R. 3100, et al., Before the Subcomm. on Indian Affairs of the H. Comm. on Interior and Insular Affairs*, 92d Cong. (1971).

5. In 1967 the leaders of Native organizations active in the Native land claims movement created the Alaska Federation of Natives (AFN) as a statewide organization whose mission was to lobby Congress to settle Native land claims on fair terms. In 1970 the AFN was incorporated under the Alaska Nonprofit Corporation Act to "promote the physical, economic, and social well-being of the natives of Alaska."

6. 1968 Senate Hearing, at 62–63.

7. "Profiles of the North: Willie Hensley," *Alaska Journal*, Spring 1979.

8. The American Indians — Message from the President of the United States, 116 *Cong. Rec.* 23131, 23133 (1970).

9. "Agreement Signed T-H Take Over of Programs," *Tundra Times*, March 3, 1971. *See also Indian Self-Determination and Education Assistance Act: Hearings on S. 1017 and Related Bills Before the Subcomm. on Indian Affairs of the H. Comm. on Interior and Insular Affairs*, 93d Cong. 115–119 (1974) (statement of Joseph Wilson) [hereinafter "1974 House hearing"].

10. The Forgotten American — Message From the President of the United States, 114 *Cong. Rec. 5394* (1968).

11. *See* Kvasnicka and Viola (eds.), *The Commissioners of Indian Affairs, 1824–1977*, at 327 1979.

12. Sec. 23, ch. 431, 36 Stat. 855, 861 (1910).

13. 1974 House Hearing, at 118.

14. The staff member was Frank Ducheneaux. *See id.*, at II. *See also Impact of Supreme Court's Ruling in Duro v. Reina: Hearing on S. 962 and S. 963 Before the S. Select Comm. on Indian Affairs*, 102d Cong. 73 (1991) (statement of Frank Ducheneaux) ("I was for eighteen years Counsel on Indian Affairs to the House Committee on Interior and Insular Affairs"); "Indian Lawyer Cites 'Hostile' Atmosphere in Washington," *Indianz.com*, April 15, 2005 ("Ducheneaux was the first Native American to serve as legal counsel to the House committee that oversees Indian affairs. From 1973 until 1990, he helped pass major pieces of legislation that heralded a new era in federal Indian policy"); "Frank Ducheneaux, Reid Chambers, and Harry Sachse Honored for Lifetime Achievement in Federal Indian Law," *Indian Country Today*, March 25, 2019 ("From 1970 (sic) to 1990, Frank [Ducheneaux] served as Counsel on Indian Affairs to the House Committee on Interior and Insular Affairs ... During those decades comprising 'the Golden Age' of federal Indian law, he played a prominent role in every major

piece of Indian legislation to come before the Committee, including the Indian Self-Determination and Education Assistance Act....").

15. H.R. Rep. No. 93-1600, at 2 (1974).

16. Pub. L. No. 93-638, 88 Stat. 2203 (1975).

17. *Cook Inlet Native Association v. Bowen*, 810 F.2d 1471 (9th Cir. 1987) (holding that the term "Indian tribe" in the Indian Self-Determination and Education Assistance Act does not include within its purview the regional associations listed in section 7(a) of the Alaska Native Claims Settlement Act).

18. *Implementation of Public Law 93-638, the Indian Self-Determination and Education Assistance Act: Hearings Before the Subcomm. on Indian Affairs of the H. Comm. on Interior and Insular Affairs*, 94th Cong. 266 (1975).

19. Proposed resolution pertaining to the Indian Self-Determination and Education Assistance Act printed in *Problems of Definition of Tribe in Alaska Relating to Public Law 93-638: Hearings Before the Subcomm. on Indian Affairs of the S. Comm. on Interior and Insular Affairs*, 94th Cong. 324–325 (1976).

20. *Ibid.*

21. 122 *Cong. Rec.* 29473 (1976).

22. Amendment No. 436, S. 522, 94th Cong., *printed at* 122 *Cong. Rec.* 29480 (1976).

23. *Ibid.*

24. *Ibid.*

25. Pub. L. No. 94-437, 90 Stat. 1400 (1976).

26. "Non-Profit Native Corporations Hope for Relief on Contracting," *Tundra Times*, June 15, 1977 ("Representatives from state and federal agencies, congressional staffs, and the Native corporations met on June 1, 2, and 3 for the first in a series of conferences addressing the problems and future role of Native non-profit corporations ... A tentative meeting has also been scheduled for mid-July in Washington, D.C. to meet with state and national leaders and to recommend legislative solutions for consideration by Congress").

27. Memorandum from Francis Williamson, Commissioner, Alaska Department of Health and Social Services, to the Honorable Jay S. Hammond, Governor of Alaska, July 28, 1977 ("the proposed act was unanimously adopted by representatives of the regional non-profit corporations on July 8, 1977"). Executive Director's Subject Files, Ruralcap Records, Elmer E. Rasmusen Library, University of Alaska Fairbanks.

28. 123 *Cong. Rec.* 27509–27510 (1977) (statement of Alaska Senator Mike Gravel explaining that S. 2046 had been introduced "at the request of the Alaska Native Regional Non-Profit Corporations").

29. At the beginning of the Ninety-fifth Congress, in January 1977 the Senate reorganized its Committee system. The Committee on Interior and Insular Affairs was renamed the Committee on Energy and Natural Resources and, at the instigation of Senator James Abourezk, who had been chairman of the committee's Subcommittee on Indian Affairs, the committee's jurisdiction over Indian-related legislation was transferred to a Select Committee on Indian Affairs that Senator Abourezk would chair. Senator Abourezk agreed that, as a condition of its creation, the select committee would terminate at the end of the Ninety-fifth Congress. However, the life of the select committee was periodically extended until 1984 when the Senate voted to make the select committee a permanent committee.

30. *Pueblo Lands and Alaska Natives Governing Bodies: Hearing on S. 1789 and S. 2046 Before the S. Select Comm. on Indian Affairs*, 95th Cong. (1977) [hereinafter "First S. 2046 Hearing"].

31. *Consolidating Alaska Native Governing Bodies: Hearings on S. 1920 and S. 2046 Before the S. Select Comm. on Indian Affairs*, 95th Cong. (1977) [hereinafter "Second S. 2046 Hearing"].

32. Hess, *Taking Control.*

33. Second S. 2046 Hearing, at 373–77 (letter from Avrum Gross, Attorney General of Alaska, to the Senate Select Committee on Indian Affairs, Nov. 9, 1977).

34. First S. 2046 Hearing, at 59 (statement of Eben Hopson, Mayor, North Slope Borough, Barrow, Alaska).

35. Pub. L. No. 96-487, 94 Stat. 2371 (1980).

36. *Inclusion of Alaska Lands in National Park, Forest, Wildlife Refuge, and Wild and Scenic Rivers Systems: Hearings on H.R. 39, et al., Before the Subcomm. on General Oversight and Alaska Lands of the H. Comm. on Interior and Insular Affairs*, 95th Cong., Parts I–XVI (1977); *Alaska National Interest Lands Conservation Act of 1979: Hearings on H.R. 39 Before the H. Comm. on Interior and Insular Affairs*, 96th Cong. (1979); *Alaska Lands: Hearings on H.R. 39 Before the Subcomm. on Fisheries and Wildlife Conservation and the Environment of the H. Comm. on Merchant Marine and Fisheries*, 95th Cong., Parts I and II (1977–1978); *Alaska National Interest Lands: Hearings on H.R. 39, et al., Before the Subcomm. on Fisheries and Wildlife Conservation and the Environment of the H. Comm. on Merchant Marine and Fisheries*, 96th Cong., Parts I and II (1979); *Alaska Natural Resource Issues and Alaska National Interest Lands Legislation: Hearings on S. 499, et al., Before the S. Comm. on Energy and Natural Resources*, 95th Cong., Parts I–III (1978); *Committee Print: Alaska Village Workshops on Alaska National Interest Lands Legislation Before the S. Comm. on Energy and Natural Resources*, 95th Cong. (1978).

Chapter Four

1. 25 C.F.R. 54.6(b) (1978).

2. 44 *Fed. Reg.* 7231 (1979).

3. 47 *Fed. Reg.* 53133 (1982).

4. *Id.* at 53133–53134.

5. Corporate Charter of the Ketchikan Indian Corporation Alaska, ratified Dec. 20, 1939, available at https://thorpe.law.ou.edu/IRA/ketchrtr.html.

6. 666 P.2d 1015 (Alaska 1983).

7. *Id.* at 1020.

8. *Id.* at 1024 n. 2.

9. Case, *Special Relationship*, at iii (David Case acknowledging that Scott Keep "provided helpful insights on the Federal 'trust responsibility'").

10. Donald Mitchell, "Why History Counts," at 403–404 (*Board of Equalization v. Alaska Native Brotherhood* decision and David Case letter discussed).

11. Personal communication from David Case to Author, Feb. 25, 2018.

12. 48 *Fed. Reg.* 56865 (1983). *See also* 58 *Fed. Reg.* 54364 (1993) (admission that in response to *Board of Equalization v. Alaska Native Brotherhood* "[a] number of Alaska Native organizations complained that the preamble was ambiguous and cast doubt on the tribal status of Alaska Native villages and regional tribes").

13. "Tribal Reservation Status Questioned by Hammond," *Tundra Times*, Dec. 16, 1981.

14. "Interior Oks IRA Status for Circle," *Fairbanks Daily News-Miner*, Oct. 15, 1981.

15. Letter from Jay S. Hammond, Governor of Alaska, to the Honorable James G. Watt, Nov. 5, 1981.

16. "Tribal Reservation Status Questioned by Hammond," *Tundra Times*, Dec. 16, 1981.

17. Executive Order No. 2141 (1915). *See also* Donald Mitchell, *Take My Land Take My Life*, at 67–75 (history of Tyonek and Moquawkie reserve described).

18. Constitution and By-Laws of the Native Village of Tyonek, ratified Nov. 27, 1939, available at https://thorpe.law.ou.edu/IRA/tyocons.html.

19. Report of the First Regular Meeting of the Members of Native Village of Tyonek, Dec. 1, 1939.

20. Memorandum entitled "Enforcement of Native Village of Tyonek Rule No. 4 — Excluding 'White Men' from the Village" from Alaska Regional Solicitor to BIA Alaska Area Director, Jan. 20, 1983 (validity of the legal analysis regarding Rule No. 4 in the 1978 memorandum reaffirmed)

21. "Village May Vote to Ban Whites," *Anchorage Daily News*, Aug. 11, 1982).

22. *Native Village of Tyonek v. Puckett*, U.S. District Court for the District of Alaska No. A82-369 Civil, Reporter's Transcript, Findings of Fact Conclusions of Law and Decision, Dec. 3, 1986.

23. 890 F.2d 1054. See also "Federal Court May Rehear Tyonek Suit," *Tundra Times*, Aug. 21, 1989 (commentator reporting that "This is the first ninth circuit case to confirm that Alaska villages enjoy the same sovereign immunity from suit that all other tribal governments enjoy").

24. 957 F.2d 631.

25. *Native Village of Tyonek v. Puckett*, U.S. District Court for the District of Alaska No. A82-369 Civil, Order: Tribal Status/Sovereign Immunity, Oct. 29, 1996.

26. *Native Village of Tyonek v. Puckett*, 133 F.3d 928 (9th Cir. 1997), 1997 WL 801472, at 1

27. "Villagers Denounce 'Nebulous' IRA Language," *Tundra Times*, Oct. 27, 1982; "Villages Threaten to Bolt AFN," *Anchorage Daily Times*, Oct. 22, 1982.

28. "Villagers Denounce 'Nebulous' IRA Language," *Tundra Times*, Oct. 27, 1982.

29. *Ibid.*

30. "Native Convention Closes With List of Resolutions," *Anchorage Daily Times*, Oct. 23, 1982.

31. "Natives Told to Use Sovereignty," *Anchorage Daily Times*, March 10, 1983; "Sparks Fly at IRA Meeting in Anchorage," *Tundra Times*, March 23, 1983.

32. The Indian Reorganization Act: Transcript of a Conference Sponsored by the Alaska Federation of Natives, March 8–9, 1983, at 47.

33. "Villages Threaten to Bolt AFN," *Anchorage Daily Times*, Oct. 22, 1982.

34. "Statewide IRA Group Begun," *Tundra Times*, March 16, 1983; United Tribes of Alaska New IRA Federation," *Tundra Times*, May 11, 1983.

35. "Native Leaders to Discuss Powers of Tribes," *Anchorage Daily Times*, Oct. 16, 1983; "AFN Refuses Floor to Dissidents," *Anchorage Daily Times*, Oct. 19, 1983; Agenda: United Tribes of Alaska General Assembly," *Tundra Times*, Oct. 19, 1983.

36. "Tanana Chiefs President Says Sovereignty Move Not Takeover," *Anchorage Daily Times*, Oct. 26, 1984.

37. "Speaker Criticizes Land Settlement Act," *Anchorage Daily Times*, Oct. 27, 1984.

38. "UTA Congress Puts Sovereignty on the Map," *Tundra Times*, Sept. 23, 1985.

39. "UTA Congress Elects Charlie 'K' New Chairman," *Tundra Times*, Sept. 23, 1985.

40. "Can Sovereignty Survive the UTA?," *Tundra Times*, Oct. 14, 1985.

41. *Ibid.*

Chapter Five

1. "Inuit Circumpolar Conference Underway," *Tundra Times*, June 15, 1977.

2. "Berger: A Lifetime Devoted to Native Justice," *Tundra Times*, Oct. 19, 1983. *And see* Berger, *One Man's Justice*.

3. Agreement Made as of August 29, 1983, Between Thomas R. Berger and Inuit Circumpolar Conference and Revised Terms of Reference, *printed in* David Case, "Listen to the Canary: A Reply to Professor Branson," 4 *Alaska Law Review* 209, 220–221 (1987).

4. Berger, *Village Journey*. *See also* "Berger Report Released at Long Last," *Tundra Times*, Sept. 16, 1985; "Clash Avoided Over Study of Settlement Act," *Anchorage Daily Times*, Sept. 17, 1985.

5. Berger, *Village Journey*, at 140.

6. *Id.* at 141.

7. *Id.* at 154.

8. Letter from Thomas R. Berger to Author, July 2, 2015.

9. Berger, *Village Journey*, at 170–171.

10. *Alaska Native Claims Settlement Act: Hearing on H.R. 4162 Before the H. Comm. on Interior and Insular Affairs*, 99th Cong. 261–270 (1986) (statement of Hon. Thomas Berger, Commissioner, Alaska Native Review Commission) [hereinafter "1986 House Hearing"].

11. *Id.* at 262.

12. *Id.* at 264.

13. "UTA Won't Discuss Sovereignty," *Tundra Times*, Sept. 21, 1983; "Agenda, United Tribes of Alaska, General Assembly," *Tundra Times*, Oct. 19, 1983.

14. "Berger Urges Sovereignty," *Anchorage Daily Times*, Sept. 21, 1985.

15. "8 Amendments Seek to Protect Lands," *Anchorage Daily Times*, Oct. 27, 1985.

16. "AFN Winds Up Convention With Compromises," *Anchorage Daily Times*, Oct. 27, 1985.

17. "Alaska Native Sovereignty Backers Present Proposals in Washington," *Anchorage Daily Times*, April 18, 1986 (Alaska Native Coalition described as "a new organization of some 25 tribal governments and village councils ... that is apparent successor to the debt-crippled United Tribes of Alaska"); "ANC Speaks for Villagers in 1991 Issue," *Tundra Times*, March 23, 1987 (reporting that "[i]n March 1986, well over 20 people gathered in Sitka to discuss the formation of a statewide coalition to represent the concerns of villages and tribes" and that "[t]he ANC embraces the findings of the Alaska Native Review Commission and intends to bring those findings to Congress").

18. 1986 House Hearing, at 138.

19. *Id.* at 139.

20. 426 U.S. 373 (1976).

21. 151 F. Supp. 132 (D. Alaska 1957).

22. For the circumstances that led to the *In re McCord* decision, *see* Donald Mitchell, "Why History Counts," at 382–385.

23. *Id.* at 384–385.

24. 1986 House Hearing, at 159–178.

25. *Id.* at 164–165.

26. *Id.* at 165–166.

27. H.R. Rep. No. 99-712 (1986).

28. 132 *Cong. Rec.* 17798–17805 (1986).

29. *Amendments to the Alaska Native Claims Settlement Act and the Alaska National Interest Lands Conservation Act and to Establish a Memorial in the District of Columbia: Hearing on S. 485, S. 1330, S. 2065, and S. 2370 Before the Subcomm. on Public Lands, Reserved Water and Resource Conservation of the S. Comm. on Energy and Natural Resources*, 99th Cong. (1986) [hereinafter "1986 Senate Hearing"].

30. *Id.* at 3.

31. *Id.* at 76.

32. Senate Pulls 1991 Bill at Natives' Request," *Anchorage Daily Times*, Sept. 25, 1986.

33. "Native Group Opposes Senate Claims Amendments, Stops Bill," *Anchorage Daily News* Sept. 26, 1986.

34. 132 *Cong. Rec.* 29049–29060 (1986).

35. *Id.* at 29059.

36. "AFN Decides to Try Again on Claims Bill," *Anchorage Daily News*, Oct. 19, 1986.

37. Alaska Federation of Natives Resolution No. 86-02 (Oct. 18, 1986).

38. "AFN Decides to Try Again on Claims Bill," *Anchorage Daily News*, Oct. 19, 1986.

39. 133 *Cong. Rec.* 860 (1987).

40. H.R. Rep. No. 100-31 (1987).

41. 133 *Cong. Rec.* 7376–7382 (1987).

42. Memorandum entitled "1991 Strategies in U.S. House" from Morris Thompson to Alaska Federation of Natives 1991 Steering Committee, Dec. 19, 1986.

43. 133 *Cong. Rec.* 11516 (1987).

44. 133 *Cong. Rec.* 11525 (1987).

45. *Alaska Native Claims Settlement Act Amendments of 1987: Hearing on S. 1145 and H.R. 287 Before the S. Comm. on Energy and Natural Resources*, 100th Cong. (1987) [hereinafter "1987 Senate Hearing"].

46. *Id.* at 2.

47. *Id.* at 114.

48. *Id.* at 249.

49. *See* Motions Passed at the Alaska Federation of Natives 1991 Steering Committee Meeting, May 7, 1987.

50. 1987 Senate Hearing, at 249.

51. "'1991' Moves Ahead," *Anchorage Daily News*, Sept. 24, 1987.

52. S. Rep. No. 100-201, at 23 (1987).

53. "Senate Panel Delays Action on 1991 Bill," *Tundra Times*, Sept. 21, 1987.

54. Alaska Federation of Natives Convention Resolution No. 87-01. *See also* "AFN Votes Yes on 1991 Proposals," *Anchorage Daily Times*, Oct. 24, 1987.

55. 133 *Cong. Rec.* 29803–29812 (1987). *See also* "1991 Land Bill Clears Senate," *Anchorage Daily News*, Oct. 30, 1987.

56. 133 *Cong. Rec.* 36727–36744 and 37713–37728 (1987).

57. Pub. L. No. 100-241, 101 Stat. 1788 (1988). *And see* "Reagan Oks Extension of Alaska Stock Sales Ban," *Anchorage Daily News*, Feb. 4, 1988.

58. 133 *Cong. Rec.* 37722 (1987).

Chapter Six

1. State of Alaska, Official Returns by Election Precinct, General Election, Nov. 2, 1982, available at https://www.elections.alaska.gov/Core/Archive/82GENR/82genr.pdf.

2. Resolution, Rural Alaska Village Participation Conference, March 29–31, 1983.

3. "Sheffield Declines Sovereignty Credit," *Anchorage Daily News*, April 9, 1983. *See also* "UTA to Governor: Deal Directly with Tribes," *Tundra Times*, Nov. 2, 1983.

4. Letter from Alaska Senators Ted Stevens and Frank Murkowski and Alaska Representative Don Young to the Hon. Bill Sheffield, April 21, 1983. Alaska State Archives.

5. "Governor to Meet with Native Tribes," *Anchorage Daily Times*, July 8, 1983; Letter from William C. "Spud" Williams, President, Tanana Chiefs Conference, to the Hon. Bill Sheffield, Oct. 6, 1983.

6. "Governor to Meet with Native Tribes," *Anchorage Daily Times*, July 8, 1983.

7. "Sheffield, Watt Settle Oil Dispute," *Anchorage Daily News*, Aug. 24, 1983. *And see* "Watt, Sheffield to Address Native Sovereignty Issue," *Anchorage Daily Times*, Aug. 23, 1983.

8. "Sheffield Talks of Native Sovereignty," *Tundra Times*, March 21, 1984.

9. *Ibid.*

10. "New United Tribes Groups Sets (sic) Session," *Daily Sentinel*, Oct. 7, 1983 (Willie Goodwin described as "head of United Tribes"); "Native Sovereignty Task Force Appointed," *Tundra Times*, May 30, 1984.

11. Letter from Governor Bill Sheffield to Ronald Somerville, Executive Director, Alaska Outdoor Council, May 8, 1984. Alaska State Archives.

12. "Task Force Hears Two Sides," *Tundra Times*, Dec. 17, 1984.

13. "How Stevens Village Came to Be," *Alaska Sportsman Magazine*, Sept. 1959.

14. Table 5, Sixteenth Census of the United States, at 1197 (1942).

15. Constitution and By-Laws of the Native Village of Stevens Alaska, *available at* https://thorpe.law.ou.edu/IRA/stevcons.html.

16. 757 P.2d 32 (Alaska 1988).

17. *Id.* at 41.

18. "Rulings Raise Sovereignty Issues," *Tundra Times*, May 30, 1988.

19. "Native Groups Seek Rehearing in Sovereignty," *Tundra Times*, June 13, 1988.

20. Alaska Supreme Court No. S-1345, Order (Aug. 25, 1988); "Supreme Court Rejects Petition for Sovereignty," *Tundra Times*, Aug. 29, 1988.

21. 826 P.2d 751 (Alaska 1992).

Chapter Seven

1. *See* http://www.narf.org/.

2. Native American Rights Fund, 1984 Annual Report, at 3.

3. Memorandum from Lare Aschenbrenner and Bob Anderson (with attached Proposed Legislation) to AVCP and Calista Corporation, Aug. 22, 1985. Alaska State Archives.

4. "United Tribes Aims to Establish Rights of Villages," *Anchorage Daily News*, Sept. 18, 1985 (reporting that "Anderson believes that Native sovereignty rights transcend [the Alaska Native Claims Settlement Act]. But proposed legislation being considered by representatives of 89 villages at the United Tribes convention would make those rights clear").

5. "Native Sovereignty Backers Seek Amendments to Settlement Act," *Anchorage Daily News*, April 18, 1986 (reporting that "[Robert Anderson] and attorney Lare Aschenbrenner, also of the Native American fund, are primary legal counsel for the coalition"). *See also* 1986 Senate Hearing, at 283–284 (statement of Bob Anderson, staff attorney, Native American Rights Fund).

6. 47 *Fed. Reg.* 53133–53135 (1982).

7. 48 *Fed. Reg.* 56865–56866 (1983); 50 *Fed. Reg.* 6058–6059 (1985); 51 *Fed. Reg.* 25118–25119 (1986).

8. 53 *Fed. Reg.* 52832–52835 (1988).

9. *Id.* at 52832–52833.

10. *Ibid.*

11. "Interior's List Called a Blow to Sovereignty," *Tundra Times*, Jan. 2, 1989.

12. Letter from Lare Aschenbrenner and fourteen other attorneys to Eddie Brown, Assistant Secretary for Indian Affairs, and William Lavell, Feb. 27, 1990. A copy of this letter and the letters, memoranda, and other documents cited in endnotes 24, 26–27, 55–57, 61, and 68 are in the appendix to Donald Craig Mitchell, Comments Regarding Solicitor Opinion M-37043, Dec. 13, 2018, *available at* https://www.bia.gov/sites/bia.gov/files/assets/as-ia/raca/pdf/22-FTT_Mitchell-Don.pdf.

13. Ch. 155 SLA 1980.

14. Informal Opinion of the Attorney General of Alaska No. J-66-829-81 (State Financial Aid to Benefit Unincorporated Communities), Sept. 2, 1981.

15. U.S. District Court for the District of Alaska No. 85-503 Civil.

16. 339 F.2d 360 (9th Cir. 1964).

17. S. Rep. No. 89-1507, at 5 (1966) (Deputy Attorney General Ramsey Clark explaining, "One of the purposes of the bill apparently is to overcome the effect of the decision in the case of *Yoder v. Assiniboine and Sioux Tribes*").

18. 112 *Cong. Rec.* 20768, 22883, and 24827 (1966).

19. *Native Village of Akiachak v. Hoffman*, U.S. District Court for the District of Alaska No. A85-503 Civil, Transcript of Oral Decision Granting Defendants' Motion to Dismiss, Oct. 28, 1987.

20. 872 F.2d 1384 (9th Cir. 1989), decision withdrawn and replaced, 896 F.2d 1157 (9th Cir. 1990).

21. 896 F.2d at 1160. In 1939 Assistant Secretary of the Interior Oscar Chapman approved a constitution for the Native Village of Noatak pursuant to section 1 of Pub. L. No. 74-538 and section 16 of the Indian Reorganization Act. Constitution and By-Laws of the Native Village of Noatak, *available at* https://thorpe.law.ou.edu/IRA/noacons.html.

22. 896 F.2d at 1160.

23. *Hoffman v. Native Village of Noatak*, U.S. Supreme Court, Petition for a Writ of Certiorari No. 89-1782.

24. Letter from Lare Aschenbrenner, Lloyd Miller, David Case, Reid Chambers, Eric Smith, and Fran Ayer to William Lavell, June 15, 1990.

25. 498 U.S. 807 (1990).

26. Letter from Lare Aschenbrenner, Lloyd Miller, David Case, Michael Walleri, Bertram Hirsch, and nine other attorneys to Lynn Forcia, Chief, BIA Branch of Acknowledgment and Research, Jan. 14, 1992.

27. Memorandum entitled "United States Supreme Court Action Threatens Tribal Status of Alaska Villages," from Sonosky, Chambers, Sachse & Miller to General Counsel Clients, Oct. 5, 1990.

28. 501 U.S. 775 (1991).

29. "Court Backs State; Native Sovereignty in Limbo," *Anchorage Daily News*, June 25, 1991.

30. "Villages Lose Fight to Sue Government: Top Court Doesn't Rule on Tribal Status," *Anchorage Daily Times*, June 25, 1991.

31. Memorandum entitled "Priorities for Alaska Issues" from Secretary Manuel Lujan to Solicitor, Assistant Secretaries, Bureau Directors, Assistant to the Secretary for Alaska, June 19, 1991.

32. *Copy available at* https://www.doi.gov/sites/doi.gov/files/uploads/m-36975.pdf.

33. Solicitor's Opinion M-36975, Governmental Jurisdiction of Alaska Native Villages Over Land and Nonmembers, Jan. 11, 1993 [hereinafter "Sansonetti opinion"], at 47.

34. *Id.* at 27. *And see* Solicitor's Opinion M—26915 (Feb. 24, 1932).

35. Secretarial Order No. 494 (March 14, 1931).

36. Pub. L. No. 67-85, 42 Stat. 208 (1921).

37. Donald Mitchell, *Sold American*, at 288–289 (circumstances that resulted in Secretary Wilbur's decision and Solicitor Finney's opinion described).

38. Sansonetti opinion, at 27 n. 82.

39. *Authorizing the Tlingit and Haida Indians to Bring Suit in the United States Court of Claims: Hearing on S. 1196 Before the S. Comm. on Indian Affairs*, 72d Cong. 16 (1932) (Wilbur letter reprinted).

40. Sansonetti opinion, at 31–33.

41. Zimmerman Instructions, at 9.

42. Letter from Assistant Commissioner William Zimmerman to Claude M. Hirst, General Superintendent, Juneau, Alaska, June 26, 1940. The letter indicates that the content of the letter had been approved by Assistant Commissioner Zimmerman's superior, Assistant Secretary of the Interior Oscar Chapman.

43. Sansonetti opinion, at 132.

44. *Id.* at 113–122, 132.

45. Memorandum entitled "Liquor Ordinance, Village of Allakaket, Alaska," from Associate Solicitor, Division of Indian Affairs, to Commissioner of Indian Affairs, Oct. 1, 1980.

46. *Mutual Agreements and Compacts Respecting Jurisdiction and Governmental Operations: Hearing on S. 563 Before the S. Select Comm. on Indian Affairs*, 97th Cong. 17 (1981).

47. "Village of Chalkyitsik, Alaska; Ordinance Prohibiting the Introduction, Possession, and Sale of Intoxicating Beverages," 48 *Fed. Reg.* 21378 (1983).

48. "Village of Minto Liquor Ordinance," 51 *Fed. Reg.* 28779 (1986).

49. "Sheffield Questions Ordinance for Minto," *Tundra Times*, Oct. 13, 1986.

50. Sansonetti opinion, at 122.

51. Pub. L. No. 59-171, 34 Stat. 197 (1906).

52. Sansonetti opinion, at 129.

53. Letter from Daniel K. Inouye, Chairman, Select Committee on Indian Affairs, to the Hon. Manuel Lujan, Secretary, U.S. Department of the Interior, Nov. 9, 1992. *See also* Letter from Daniel K. Inouye, Chairman, Select Committee on Indian Affairs, to the Hon. Warren Christopher and Vernon Jordan, Co-Chairman, President-Elect Clinton's Transition Board, Dec. 11, 1992 (reporting that "[i]n November, I met with Interior Secretary Lujan for the purpose of encouraging him not to allow the issuance of a Solicitor's opinion of the status of tribal governments in Alaska, in order to provide the new Interior Secretary with the opportunity to make a determination as to whether such an opinion is warranted or necessary. I enclose a copy of the letter that I delivered to Secretary Lujan at the time of our meeting").

54. "Ruling Gives Natives Tribal Status But Still Rejects Self-Government," *Anchorage Daily News*, Jan. 13, 1993.

55. Letter from Lare Aschenbrenner, Robert Anderson, and other attorneys to the Hon. Bruce Babbitt, Secretary, United States Department of the Interior, Feb. 12, 1993.

56. Memorandum entitled "New List of Federally Recognized Tribes" from "Lare A & Bob A." to attorneys, March 20, 1993.

57. Facsimile Transmittal Cover Sheet from Lare A. To Scott Keep, March 22, 1993.

58. 139 *Cong. Rec.* 14839 (1993).

59. *Nomination of Ada Deer: Hearing Before the S. Comm. on Indian Affairs*, 103d Cong. 9 (1993) (statement of Ada Deer).

60. 139 *Cong. Rec.* 15999 (1993).

61. Letter from Lawrence Aschenbrenner and Robert Anderson to John Trezise, Acting Associate Solicitor, Indian Affairs Division, and Scott Keep, Assistant Solicitor, Aug. 4, 1993.

62. "Looking Back on Babbitt's Visit," *Anchorage Daily News*, Aug. 30, 1993.

63. "What Babbitt Sees, Hears Will Affect Alaska Policies," *Fairbanks Daily News-Miner*, Aug. 9, 1993 (reporting that "[a]mong those most delighted by the secretary's trip are Native leaders. Babbitt will tour Native villages with Ada Deer, assistant secretary for Indian affairs, who, like Babbitt, is a strong advocate of Native self-government"); "Babbitt Hears Whalers Woes," *Fairbanks Daily News-Miner*, Aug. 14, 1993 ("Also joining Babbitt in Kaktovik was Ada Deer, newly appointed director of the BIA, who will travel with the secretary for part of his trip").

64. In December 1992 many of the same individuals who had created first the United Tribes of Alaska and then the Alaska Native Coalition organized the Alaska Inter-Tribal Council "to act as a unified voice of Alaska Native tribes and represent them on issues and initiatives of importance to their interests." *See* "New Group Links Governments," *Anchorage Daily News*, Dec. 11, 1992; "Alaska Inter-Tribal Council: United Nations for State's Tribes," *Tundra Times*, Jan. 7, 1993; "Alaska Inter-Tribal Council to Host Convention," *Tundra Times*, Nov. 2, 1994.

65. "Babbitt Says Solve Subsistence First," *Tundra Times*, Aug. 25, 1993.

66. "Babbitt in for a Whirlwind Visit," *Bristol Bay Times*, Aug. 20, 1993.

67. "Tribal Power: What Will Babbitt Hear in Dillingham," *Anchorage Daily News*, Aug. 19, 1993.

68. Facsimile Transmission entitled "Alaska List," from Lloyd B. Miller to John D. Trezise, Deputy Associate Solicitor—Indians, Sept. 30, 1993.

69. "Deer Announces Tribal Regulations at AFN Meet: Shock, Anger for Tribes Missing from New List," *Tundra Times*, Oct. 20, 1993.

70. 58 *Fed. Reg.* 54364–54369 (1993).

71. *Id.* at 54364.

72. 4 Stat. 564.

73. 2 Stat. 402.

74. Viola & Herman, *Thomas L. McKenney*, at 4–5.

75. Prucha, *American Indian Policy in the Formative Years*, at 57.

76. *Id.* at 58–59.

77. 8 *Gales & Seaton's Register of Debates in Congress*, at 988 (1832).

78. *J.W. Hampton, Jr. & Company v. United States*, 276 U.S. 394, 409 (1928); *Yakus v. United States*, 321 U.S. 414, 426 (1944). *And see Louisiana Public Service Commission v. FCC*, 476 U.S. 355, 374 (1986) (reiterating that "[a]n agency may not confer power on itself").

Chapter Eight

1. 564 P.2d 53 (Alaska 1977).

2. American Indian Policy Review Commission, *Final Report*, at 423.

3. Pub. L. No. 95-608, 92 Stat. 3069 (1978) (codified at 25 U.S.C. 1901 *et seq.*).

4. H.R. Rep. No. 95-1386, at 25 (1978).

5. Informal Opinion of Alaska Attorney General (State Recognition of Native Council Adoption Orders), April 16, 1986.

6. Personal Communication from Douglas Mertz to Author, Aug. 5, 2020.

7. 687 F. Supp. 1380, 1381–1382 (D. Alaska 1988).

8. *Id.* at 1393.

9. 151 F. Supp. 132 (D. Alaska 1957).

10. 918 F.2d 797 (9th Cir. 1990).

11. *Id.* at 807.

12. Solicitor's Opinion, Powers of Indian Tribes, Oct. 25, 1934. Felix Cohen's authorship of the opinion is described in Dalia Tusk Mitchell, *Architect of Justice*, at 112–115. Cohen's invention of the doctrine of "inherent" tribal sovereignty is described in Deloria and Lytle, *The Nations Within*, at 158–160.

13. Deloria and Lytle, *The Nations Within*, at 160.

14. 918 F.2d at 811.

15. *Ibid.* In June 1991 the U.S. Supreme Court issued its decision in *Blatchford v. Native Village of Noatak*, 501 U.S. 775, in which the Court held that the Eleventh Amendment to the U.S. Constitution barred the Native Village of Noatak and Circle Village from filing a lawsuit against the State of Alaska to try and obtain a money judgment. In September 1991 the three-judge panel that ten months earlier had issued its decision in *Native Village of Venetie I.R.A. Council* withdrew the decision and issued a new decision. That decision referenced the *Blatchford* decision in the panel's analysis of why the Eleventh Amendment did not bar the Native Village of Venetie and Native Village of Fort Yukon from filing their lawsuit against the State of Alaska to try and obtain prospective injunctive relief. *See Native Village of Venetie I.R.A. Council v. State*, 944 F.2d 548 (9th Cir. 1991).

16. Constitution of the Native Village of Venetie, Alaska (approved May 15, 1939), *available at* https://thorpe.law.ou.edu/IRA/vencons.html.

17. *State of Alaska v. Native Village of Venetie Tribal Government*, 101 F.3d 1286, 1289 (1996) ("In 1976, the Native Village of Venetie restructured its council to include formal representation from Arctic Village (another community comprised of Neets'aii Gwichin)").

18. No. F87-051. The preceding description of the events that resulted in the filing of the lawsuit is based on documents in the file of the U.S. District Court.

19. 856 F.2d 1384 (9th Cir. 1988).

20. *Id.* at 1391.

21. 944 F.2d at 558–559.

22. 856 F.2d at 1387.

23. *Native Village of Venetie I.R.A. Council v. State of Alaska* and *State of Alaska v. Native Village of Venetie Tribal Government*, 1994 WL 730893 (D. Alaska, Dec. 23, 1994).

24. *State of Alaska v. Native Village of Venetie Tribal Government*, 1995 WL 462232 (D. Alaska, Aug. 9, 1995).

25. *Id.* at 11.

26. *Id.* at 16.

27. *Id.* at 20.

28. *Ibid.*

29. "Secretary Babbitt Selects Robert T. Anderson to be Counselor to the Secretary," *Press Release: U.S. Department of the Interior*, Dec. 18, 1997.

30. "Laying Down the Law." *First Alaskans*, June 2010.

31. Donald Mitchell, "Why History Counts," at 421 (Attorney General Botelho's explanation of why he did not file an appeal described).

32. 1994 Alaska General Election Official Results Statewide Summary, *available at* https://www.elections.alaska.gov/Core/Archive/94GENR/result94.php.

33. "Tundra Times Exclusive Interview: Gubernatorial Candidate Steve Cowper," *Tundra Times*, June 16, 1986.

34. Alaska Administrative Order No. 123 (Sept. 10, 1990).

35. Personal Communication from Steve Cowper to Author, May 4, 2017.

36. *Ibid.*

37. *Ibid.*

38. "Hickel Revises State Policy on Tribal Powers," *Press Release: Office of the Governor of Alaska*, Aug. 16, 1991.

39. Alaska Administrative Order No. 125 (Aug. 16, 1991).

40. "Questions of Native Sovereignty Claims Never Get 'Settled' in Court," *Anchorage Daily Times*, March 8, 1992.

41. "Upset Cole Quits as Top Lawyer," *Anchorage Daily News*, Jan. 6, 1994.

42. "Botelho Named Attorney General," *Anchorage Daily News*, Jan. 13, 1994.

43. "Subsistence, Tribal Rights Top AFN Debate," *Anchorage Daily News*, Oct. 27, 1990.

44. "Election '94," *Tundra Drums*, Aug. 18, 1994.

45. "AFN Abandons Neutrality, Endorses Knowles," *Tundra Times*, Oct. 19, 1994.

46. *See* 1994 Alaska General Election Official Results By Precinct, *see* Endnote 32.

47. "Botelho Holds on to Job," *Anchorage Daily News*, Jan. 6, 1995.

48. "Candidates Court Natives' Favor," *Anchorage Daily News*, Oct. 16, 1998.

49. 101 F.3d 1286 (9th Cir. 1996).

50. *Id.* at 1294.

51. 101 F.3d at 1295.

52. *Id.* at 1296.

53. *Id.* at 1297.

54. *Id.* at 1299–1300.

55. *Id.* at 1302–1303.

56. Pub. L. No. 85-615. *And see* Donald Mitchell, "Why History Counts," at 382–385 (circumstances that motivated Congress to add the Territory of Alaska to the list of states in 28 U.S.C. 1360 described).

57. 426 U.S. 373 (1976).

58. 480 U.S. 202 (1987).

59. "State to Seek Quick Appeal of Sovereignty Ruling," *Anchorage Daily News*, Nov. 22, 1996.

60. "Court Sticks with Ruling on Villages," *Anchorage Daily News*, Jan. 10, 1997.

61. U.S. Supreme Court Journal, 1996 Term, *available at* http://www.supremecourt.gov/orders/journal/jnl96.pdf.

62. "State Hires Help in Indian Country Case," *Anchorage Daily News*, Jan. 24, 1997.

63. *State of Alaska v. Native Village of Venetie Tribal Government*, No. 96-1577, Brief of Amici Curiae States of California, et al., in Support of Petitioner State of Alaska, at 3.

64. Donald Mitchell, *Take My Land Take My Life*, at 220–236 (Ted Stevens biography prior to his appointment to the Senate described).

65. 107 *Cong. Rec.* 944 (1961) (Colorado Republican Senator Gordon Allott on January 17, 1961, telling the Senate, "Another of the brilliant young men with whom I have enjoyed working is Ted Stevens, Solicitor of the Department of the Interior"). *See also ibid.* 532 (Ten days before he departed office, on January 10, 1961, President Dwight Eisenhower nominated "Theodore F. Stevens of Alaska to be Solicitor for the Department of the Interior").

66. 400 U.S. 423 (1971).

67. Section 4(a), S. 2502, 95th Cong. (1978).

68. *Tribal-State Compact Act of 1978: Hearings on S. 2502 Before the S. Select Comm. on Indian Affairs*, 95th Cong. iii–iv (1978).

69. S. Rep. No. 95-1178, at 12 (1978).

70. 124 *Cong. Rec.* 34458–34461 (1978).

71. Section 3(a), S. 1181, 96th Cong. (1979).

72. *Jurisdiction on Indian Reservations: Hearings on S. 1181, S. 1722, and S. 2832 Before the S. Select Comm. on Indian Affairs*, 96th Cong. iii–iv (1980).

73. S. Rep. No. 96-759, at 1 (1980).

74. *Id.* at 7.

75. 126 *Cong. Rec.* 12813–12815 (1980).

76. *Id.* at 12815. *And see Mutual Agreements and Compacts Respecting Jurisdiction and Governmental Operations: Hearing on S. 563 Before the S. Select Comm. on Indian Affairs*, 97th Cong. 17 (1981) (Senator DeConcini noting, "Under the last Congress, the committee was asked by Senator Stevens to delete any reference to Alaskan villages from the definition").

77. Title II, Pub. L. No. 97-473, 96 Stat. 2605, 2607 (1983).

78. *1981–82 Miscellaneous Tax Bills XVI: Hearing on S. 1298, S. 2197, and S. 2498 Before the Subcomm. on Taxation and Debt Management of the S. Comm. on Finance*, 97th Cong. 58 (1982) (statement of Deputy Assistant Secretary of the Interior for Indian Affairs Roy Sampsel).

79. Section 4, S. 1298, 97th Cong. 1st Sess. (as introduced, June 2, 1981).

80. 128 *Cong. Rec.* 26901 (1982).

81. H. Con. Res. 439, 97th Cong. (Dec. 21, 1982). *See also* 128 *Cong. Rec.* 33309–33310 and 33572–33573 (1982).

82. Remarks of the Honorable Ted Stevens before the Alaska State Legislature, Senate and House Joint Journal Supplement No. 5 (Feb. 8, 1983).

83. *State of Alaska v. Native Village of Venetie Tribal Government*, U.S. Supreme Court No. 96-1577, Brief of the Honorable Theodore F. (Ted) Stevens as Amicus Curiae in Support of Petitioner, at 1–2.

84. 151 *Cong. Rec.* 19600 (2005).

85. 521 U.S. 1103 (1997).

86. "Justices to Rule on Indian Country," *Anchorage Daily News*, June 24, 1997.

87. 522 U.S. 520 (1998).

88. *Id.* at 532.

89. 522 U.S. at 532–533.

90. "Laying Down the Law," *First Alaskans*, June 2010 ("[Lloyd Miller] and Kendall-Miller were married in 1996").

91. *Id.* at 533–534.

Chapter Nine

1. Community Information Northway Village, Alaska Department of Commerce, Community, and Economic Development ("Residence at the new site provided Native workers with construction jobs on the Alaska Highway and at the Northway airfield during World War II."), *available at* https://www.commerce.alaska.gov/dcra/DCRAExternal/community/Details/b6650fff-672c-46af-90c1-3f157a4ab13e.

2. 58 *Fed. Reg.* 54369 (1993). Because the Secretary of the Interior has not approved a constitution for the Athabascan Indian residents of Northway pursuant to section 1 of Public Law No. 74-538 and section 16 of the IRA, in 1976 the village council in Northway adopted its own articles of incorporation and by-laws. In 2004 forty-three Northway residents voted to adopt a constitution "as a federally recognized Indian tribe and under the inherent sovereign authority of our Tribe." *See* Constitution of the Northway Tribe, available at http://www.aptalaska.net/~nicholr/Constitution%20of%20NVC.pdf.

3. *Baker v. John*, Alaska Superior Court No. 4FA-95-3103 Civil, Complaint and Petition for Child Custody, Dec. 28, 1995.

4. *Baker v. John*, Alaska Superior Court No. 4FA-95-3103 Civil, Findings of Fact, Conclusions of Law, and Judgment, April 1, 1997, at 3.

5. *John v. Baker*, Alaska Supreme Court No. S-08099, Appellant's Brief, at 40–41.

6. While John Franich signed several, all the briefs were written Deborah Niedermeyer. Personal Communications from John Franich to Author, April 6, 2016, and Deborah Niedermeyer, April 6, 2016.

7. Personal Communication from Deborah Niedermeyer to Author, April 8, 2016.

8. *John v. Baker*, Alaska Supreme Court No. S-08099, Brief of Appellee, at 9.

9. *John v. Baker*, Alaska Supreme Court No. S-08099, Supplemental Brief of Appellee, at 12.

10. *John v. Baker*, Alaska Supreme Court No. S-08099, Oral Argument June 19, 1998, Audio tape AP 916, Tape Position 1048–1055. NARF attorney Heather Kendall Miller filed a brief on behalf of *amici curiae* Native Village of Venetie and the Alaska Inter-Tribal Council in support of Anita John.

11. "Natives Challenge Governor," *Fairbanks Daily News Miner*, March 20, 1997.

12. "Rain, Protest Mark Governor's Picnic," *Anchorage Daily News*, Aug. 10, 1997.

13. "AFN Gives Knowles Cool Response," *Anchorage Daily News*, Oct. 24, 1997.

14. "Indian Country Claim Falls," *Anchorage Daily News*, Feb. 26, 1998.

15. Alaska Administrative Order No. 174 (Feb. 20, 1998).

16. "Knowles Names Mallott Campaign Chair," *Tundra Drums*, March 22, 1990.

17. "Tribal Groups Critical," *Anchorage Daily News*, March 7, 1998; "Native Leaders Pick 4 Nominees for Task Force," *Anchorage Daily News*, March 14, 1998. *And see* Final Report to the Governor, Alaska Commission on Rural Government and Empowerment, at 116–124 (1999).

18. "Knowles Offers Tribes Joint Court Jurisdiction," *Anchorage Daily News*, April 22, 1998; "State Weighs in for Tribal Courts' Role," *Anchorage Daily News*, May 5, 1998.

19. Title I, Pub. L. No. 103-454, 108 Stat. 4791 (1994).

20. *John v. Baker*, Alaska Supreme Court No. S-08099, Amicus Brief of the State of Alaska, at 6.

21. *Id.* at 45.

22. *John v. Baker*, Alaska Supreme Court No. S-08099, Brief of the United States as Amicus Curiae, at 33.

23. "Johnny on the Spot," *Juneau Empire*, 1998, *available at* http://www.icepeople.net/mark/lindauer.html.

24. *John v. Baker*, Alaska Supreme Court No. S-08099, Brief of the United States as Amicus Curiae, at 47–48.

25. *Flast v. Cohen*, 392 U.S. 83, 101 (1968).

26. *Baker v. Carr*, 369 U.S. 186, 204 (1962).

27. In addition to the U.S. Department of Justice and the State of Alaska, the Native Village of Northway, the Native Village of Venetie Tribal Government, the Alaska Inter-Tribal Council, the Paskenta Band of Nomlaki Indians, the Scotts Valley Band of Pomo Indians, and the Death Valley Timbisha Shoshone Tribe filed *amicus* briefs.

28. "Secretary Babbitt Selects Robert T. Anderson to be Counselor to the Secretary," *Press Release: Department of the Interior*, Dec. 18, 1997.

29. Personal communication from Deborah Niedermeyer to Author, April 6, 2016.

30. 982 P.2d 738 (Alaska 1999).

31. While they did not question the conclusion of the majority that, as a consequence of Assistant Secretary Deer's publication in 1993 in the *Federal Register* of her list of Native entities, the Athabascan Indian residents of Northway were a federally recognized tribe that possessed "the same sovereign powers as recognized tribes in other states," see *id.* at 776 n. 75, two justices contended that the tribe at Northway could not exercise its sovereign powers outside the boundaries of "Indian country" unless Congress enacted a statute that authorized the tribe to do so. *Id.* at 765–805.

32. *Id.* at 749.

33. *Id.* at 749–750.

34. *Id.* at 759.

35. *Id.* at 765.

36. Articles of Incorporation of the Association of Village Council Presidents, available at https://www.commerce.alaska.gov/cbp/main/search/entities.

37. 58 *Fed. Reg.* 54368 (1993).

38. 30 P.3d 68 (Alaska 2001).

39. In 1940 in *United States v. United States Fidelity & Guaranty* Co., 309 U.S. 506, the U.S. Supreme Court announced the Court-invented rule that "Indian Nations are exempt from suit without Congressional authorization." In 1998 in *Kiowa Tribe of Oklahoma v. Manufacturing Technologies, Inc.*, 523 U.S. 751, a majority of the members of the Court declined to revisit that holding even though, as Justice Anthony Kennedy acknowledged in the decision he wrote for a majority of the members of the Court, the Court's rule that a federally recognized tribe possesses sovereign immunity "can be challenged as inapposite to modern, wide-ranging tribal enterprises extending well beyond traditional tribal customs and activities." In 2014 in *Michigan v. Bay Mills Indian Community*, 572 U.S. 782, the Court again declined to "revisit our prior decisions holding that, absent ... an abrogation [of tribal sovereign immunity by Congress] (or a waiver), Indian tribes have immunity even when a suit arises from off-reservation commercial activity."

40. *Runyon v. Association of Village Council Presidents*, Alaska Supreme Court Nos. S-10772 and S-10838, Brief for the Legislative Council of the Alaska Legislature as Amicus Curiae in Support of Appellants, at 21.

41. *Louisiana Public Service Commission v. F.C.C.*, 476 U.S. 355, 374 (1986). *Accord State of Alaska v. Native Village of Venetie Tribal Government*, 522 U.S. at 531 n. 6 (holding that federal Alaska

Native policy can be established only by "some explicit action by Congress" or by the Department of the Interior "acting under delegated authority").

42. 140 *Cong. Rec.* 27,244 (1994) (statement of Representative Craig Thomas, the principal sponsor of the bill Congress enacted as the Federally Recognized Indian Tribe List Act, explaining that the bill's "findings are not legally binding").

43. H.R. Rep. No. 103-781, at 6 (1994).

44. *Id.* at 4–5.

45. 84 P.3d 437 (Alaska 2004).

46. *Id.* at 439 n. 3. After refusing to revisit its decision in *John v. Baker I*, the court held: "Any judgment against AVCP will be paid out of the Association's coffers alone. Even if they fall short, the villages' assets will be safe from execution. This legal insulation makes clear that AVCP is not an arm of the villages. The villages therefore are not the real parties in interest to this lawsuit. And AVCP is not entitled to the protection of the villages' tribal sovereign immunity." *Id.* at 441.

47. 58 *Fed. Reg.* 54369 (1993).

48. *McCrary v. Ivanoff Bay Village*, Alaska Superior Court No. 3AN-09-10267.

49. *McCrary v. Ivanoff Bay Village*, Memorandum in Support of Motion to Dismiss, at 5.

50. *McCrary v. Ivanoff Bay Village*, Alaska Supreme Court No. S-13972, Brief of Appellant, at 8.

51. 265 P.3d 337 (Alaska 2011).

52. *Id.* at 340.

Chapter Ten

1. 25 U.S.C. 1903(8).

2. 25 U.S.C. 1903(4).

3. *In the Matter of J.M.*, Alaska Supreme Court No. S-0943, Brief of Appellant, at x.

4. 25 U.S.C. 1911(c).

5. 25 U.S.C. 1911(a).

6. *In the Matter of J.M.*, Alaska Supreme Court No. S-0943, Brief of Appellant, at xi.

7. H.R. Rep. No. 95-1386, at 21 (1978).

8. Personal Communication from Rebecca Snowe to Author, June 17, 2016.

9. 718 P.2d 150 (Alaska 1986).

10. 722 P.2d 219 (Alaska 1986).

11. 25 U.S.C. 1911(b).

12. 25 U.S.C. 1918.

13. H.R. Rep. No. 95-1386, at 25 (1978).

14. 722 P.2d at 222.

15. 744 P.2d 1173 (Alaska 1987).

16. 843 P.2d 1214 (Alaska 1992).

17. 58 *Fed. Reg.* 54369 (1993).

18. *Amendments to the Indian Child Welfare Act: Hearing Before the S. Comm. on Indian Affairs*, 104th Cong. 250 (1996).

19. "Rule of Self-Law: Tribal Courts Tackle Cases with Traditional Values," *Anchorage Daily News*, Sept. 23, 2003 ("AITC executive director Donna Goldsmith said tribal courts meet a need in rural Alaska and benefit the state by providing legal aid at little expense"); "Alaska Tribes Want to Handle Child Abuse Cases on Their Own, but the State Thinks It Might Do a Better Job," *Anchorage Press*, Sept. 9, 2004 ("While Alaska's more than 230 federally recognized tribes don't necessarily live in 'Indian Country' like tribes in the Lower 48, the Alaska Supreme Court has decided their courts have a right to hear child custody cases in most circumstances. Donna Goldsmith, a tribal advocate who is executive director for the Alaska Inter-Tribal Council, tackled one of these recent cases as a special assistant to the attorney general").

20. *In the Matter of C.R.H.*, Alaska Supreme Court No. S-9677, Appellee State of Alaska's Brief, at 6. When asked whether the position of the State of Alaska that Donna Goldsmith had announced in her brief accurately described the policy of the administration of Governor Tony Knowles, or whether Goldsmith decided on her own what the position of the State of Alaska would be, former Attorney General Bruce Botelho answered: "I don't recall speaking to Tony about the case before it was argued (or, for that matter, afterwards)." Personal communication from Bruce Botelho to Author, May 24, 2016.

21. *In the Matter of C.R.H.*, Alaska Supreme Court No. S-9677, Audiotape of Oral Argument, May 16, 2001.

22. 29 P.3d at 852.

23. *United States v. Wise*, 370 U.S. 405, 411 (1962). *Accord Carcieri v. Salazar*, 555 U.S. 379 (2009) (phrase "now under Federal jurisdiction" in section 19 of the IRA means what the Seventy-Third Congress that enacted the IRA in 1934 intended it to mean); *MCI Telecommunications Corp. v. AT&T Co.*, 512 U.S. 218, 228 (1994) (the date Congress enacted a statute is "the most relevant time" for interpreting the meaning of a term contained therein); *United States v. Champlin Refining Co.*, 341 U.S. 290, 297 (1951) (a "statute cannot be divorced from the circumstances existing at the time it was passed").

24. *Indian Child Welfare Act of 1977: Hearing on S. 1214 Before the S. Select Comm. on Indian Affairs*, 95th Cong. 237 (1977) (letter from Daniel Branch, Alaska Legal Services Corporation, Bethel, Alaska, to Senator James Abourezk, Aug. 10, 1977).

25. *Id.* at 241 (letter from Michael Jeffrey, Alaska Legal Services Corporation, Barrow, Alaska, to Senator James Abourezk, Aug. 3, 1977). *And see Indian Child Welfare Act of 1978: Hearings on S. 1214 Before the Subcomm. on Indian Affairs and Public Lands of the H. Comm. on Interior and Insular Affairs*, 95th Cong. 94 (1978) (statement of Donald Mitchell, attorney representing the Rural Alaska Community Action Program, informing the Subcommittee that "in Alaska, ... you have villages that have never been part of the reservation system, they don't have a tribal organization per se.").

26. 982 P.2d at 761.

27. *Id.* at 766.

28. *Id.* at 766–767.

29. Memorandum entitled "In the Matter of C.R.H.," from Donna J. Goldsmith, Assistant Attorney General, to Jay Livey, Commissioner, Department of Health and Social Services, March 29, 2002.

30. *McDaniel v. Cory*, 631 P.2d 82, 88 (Alaska 1981).

31. *Sitton v. Felix*, Alaska Superior Court No. FA-03-1395 CI.

32. *Sitton v. Native Village of Northway*, U.S. District Court for the District of Alaska No. A03-0134 CV. The description of the dispute between Andrea Sitton and Darrel Felix regarding the custody of H.F. set out herein is based on the facts to which Ms. Sitton attested in *Sitton v. Native Village of Northway*, Affidavit of Andrea Sitton in Support of Plaintiffs Motion for Summary Judgment, Jan. 5, 2004.

33. *Sitton v. Native Village of Northway*, U.S. District Court for the District of Alaska No. A03-0134-CV, Order: Motion to Dismiss or Stay, April 20, 2004.

34. *Sitton v. Native Village of Northway*, U.S. Court of Appeals for the Ninth Circuit No. 04-35461, Order, Jan. 19, 2005.

35. *Baker v. Native Village of Northway*, U.S. District Court for the District of Alaska No. A01-377 CIV; *McCrary v. Ivanof Bay Village*, U.S. District Court for the District of Alaska No. 3:03-cv-259; *S.P. v. Native Village of Minto*, U.S. District Court for the District of Alaska No. 3:09-cv-92.

Chapter Eleven

1. Alaska Commission on Rural Governance and Empowerment, Final Report to the Governor (June 1999), at 11.

2. *Id.* at 60.

3. "AFN Welcomes Knowles Stance at Convention," *Anchorage Daily News*, Oct. 21, 1999.

4. "State, Tribes to Negotiate Accord," *Anchorage Daily News*, Dec. 7, 1999.

5. "227 Tribes Pick Delegates for Talks," *Anchorage Daily News*, Feb. 18, 2000.

6. "State, Tribes Seek Path to Balance of Power," *Anchorage Daily News*, May 18, 2000.

7. Alaska Administrative Order No. 186, Sept. 29, 2000.

8. Letter from Ted Stevens and Frank Murkowski, United States senators, and Don Young, Congressman for All Alaska, to the Honorable Tony Knowles, Sept. 28, 2000.

9. Letter from Governor Tony Knowles to the Honorable Ted Stevens, Frank Murkowski, and Don Young, Sept. 29, 2000.

10. "State 'Recognizes' Alaska Tribes," *Anchorage Daily News*, Sept. 30, 2000.

11. "Tribal Relations Team to Meet," *Anchorage Daily News*, Nov. 30, 2000; "One Word Cripples State-Tribal Talks," *Anchorage Daily News*, Dec. 3, 2002.

12. "Natives, Knowles Ink Millennium Agreement," *Anchorage Daily News*, April 12, 2001

13. "Tribes in Alaska," *Anchorage Daily News*, April 13, 2001.

14. Personal Communication from Bruce Botelho to Author, April 30, 2020.

15. *Ibid.*

16. Letter from Gregg D. Renkes, Attorney General, to Joel Gilbertson, Commissioner, Department of Health and Social Services, regarding "Jurisdiction of State and Tribal Courts in Child Protection Matters," Oct. 1, 2004.

17. *Id.* at 2 n. 3.

18. In the opinion letter, Attorney General Renkes also advised that "[i]n the event the state receives and investigates a report of harm on a child who is properly within the jurisdiction of a tribal court, the state may release this otherwise confidential information to the tribe pursuant to A.S. 47.10.093(f)" because "A tribe is a 'person' under A.S. 01.10.060(8)." However, that advice appears to have been erroneous. Notwithstanding A.S. 47.17.040, A.S. 47.10.093(f) authorizes the DFYS to release information pertaining to a child who is subject to A.S. 47.17.010 *et seq.* to any "person with a legitimate interest." In turn, A.S. 01.10.060(8) defines "person" to include "a corporation, company, partnership, firm, association, organization, business trust, or society, as well as a natural person." Attorney General Renkes advised Commissioner Gilbertson that federally recognized tribes in Alaska "fit well" within the common definitions of the terms "association" and "organization." While in A.S. 01.10.060 the terms "association" and "organization" are not defined, the Second Alaska State Legislature enacted that statute in 1962. Ch. 62 SLA 1962. It stretches credulity to believe that in 1962 the members of the Second Alaska State Legislature intended either term to include within its purview federally recognized tribes that in her opinion in *John v. Baker* Alaska Supreme Court Justice Dana Fabe acknowledged did not exist prior to 1993.

19. Heather Kendall-Miller, "*State of Alaska v. Native Village of Tanana*: Enhancing Tribal Power by Affirming Concurrent Tribal Jurisdiction to Initiate ICWA-Defined Child Custody Proceedings, Both Inside and Outside of Indian Country," 28 *Alaska Law Review* 217, 235 (2011) (amendments to Child Protective Services Manual described).

20. *Id.* at 237–238 (procedural history of *State v. Native Village of Tanana* lawsuit described).

21. *State v. Native Village of Tanana*, Alaska Supreme Court No. S-13333, Brief of Appellant State of Alaska, at 44.

22. 249 P.3d 734 (Alaska 2011).

23. *Id.* at 750.

24. *Id.* at 751.

25. *Id.* at 752.

26. Constitution and By-Laws of the Native Village of Minto Alaska, *available at* https://thorpe.law.ou.edu/IRA/mintocons.html.

27. 58 *Fed. Reg.* 54369 (1993).

28. Alaska Superior Court No. 4FA-09-2508 CI.

29. 25 U.S.C. 1911(d).

30. 175 P.3d 50 (Alaska 2008).

31. *Parks v. Simmonds*, Alaska Superior Court No. 4FA-09-2508 CI, Decision Denying Motion to Dismiss, Nov. 12, 2010.

32. *Ibid.*

33. 982 P.2d at 761.

34. 329 P.3d 995 (Alaska 2014).

35. *Id.* at 1008.

36. *Id.* at 1015.

37. 520 U.S. 438 (1997).

38. *Id.* at 459 n. 14.

39. 329 P.3d at 1022.

40. 58 *Fed. Reg.* 54369 (1993).

41. U.S. District Court for the District of Alaska No. 3:06-cv-211.

42. 62 *Fed. Reg.* 1470 (1997) and 63 *Fed. Reg.* 59574 (1998).

43. 64 *Fed. Reg.* 36391 (1999).

44. *Kaltag Tribal Council v. Jackson*, Complaint, at 5.

45. *Kaltag Tribal Council v. Jackson*, Defendants' Memorandum of Points and Authorities in Support of Motion for Summary Judgment, at 11.

46. 944 F.2d 548 (9th Cir. 1991).

47. 2008 WL 9434481, at 11–12.

48. 344 Fed. Appx. 324 (9th Cir. 2009).

49. *Hogan v. Kaltag Tribal Council*, U.S. Supreme Court No. 09-960, Petition for Writ of Certiorari, at i.

50. H.R. Rep. No. 103-781, at 2–3 (1994). *Accord* Newton, *Cohen's Handbook of Federal Indian Law*, at 133–134.

51. *Native Village of Venetie I.R.A. Council v. State*, 1994 WL 730893 (Dec. 23, 1994), at 21.

52. *Hogan v. Kaltag Tribal Council*, U.S. Supreme Court No. 09-960, Petition for Writ of Certiorari, at 2.

53. 562 U.S. 827 (2010).

Chapter Twelve

1. Angell, *Public Safety and the Justice System in Alaskan Native Villages*, at 15–16, 18.

2. *Consolidating Alaska Natives Governing Bodies: Hearings on S. 1920 and S. 2046 Before the S. Select Comm. on Indian Affairs*, 95th Cong. 332–333 (1977).

3. Wood, *Turnover Among Alaska Village Public Safety Officers*, at 19.

4. Ch. 131 SLA 1980 (codified at A.S. 4.11.496).

5. Personal Communication from Alaska Department of Public Safety to Author, Sept. 20, 2020. And see "Can Alaska's VPSO Program Be Saved? A Task Force Suggests Big Changes," *Anchorage Daily News*, Jan. 24, 2020.

6. *See* "Tununak Woman Sentenced in Booze Import Case," *Tundra Drums*, Sept. 9, 1982; "Booze Due to Dry Village Stopped," *Tundra Drums*, Sept. 17, 1987 (Alaska State Troopers order airplane chartered by Pilot Station resident to transport alcohol into Pilot Station to return to Bethel after which resident arrested); "2 Arrested While Trying to Ship Booze to Hooper Bay," *Tundra Drums*, Sept. 24, 1987.

7. Letter from Paul J. Longpre, Village Public Safety Officer, Sleetmute, Alaska, to Joint Special Committee on Local Option Laws, Alaska State Legislature, Dec. 6, 1985. Records of the Joint Special Committee on Local Option Laws, Alaska State Law Library.

8. "Liquor Question Fails in Aniak, Succeeds in Kipnik and Iliamna," *Tundra Drums*, Oct. 14, 1982.

9. "Editor's Note," *Tundra Drums*, Nov. 25, 1987.

10. "LKSD Employees Given Option Not to Travel to Kipnuk," *Tundra Drums*, Nov. 5, 1987.

11. Letter from Rosita Worl, Special Assistant to Governor of Alaska, to Jimmy Paul, Chairman, Kipnuk Traditional Council, and Isaac Mute, Chairman, Kipnuk Elders Council, Feb. 25, 1987, *quoted in* "Says State of Alaska: Kipnuk Searches Illegal," *Tundra Drums*, March 3, 1988.

12. "Native Sovereignty: Quiet Revolution in the Bush," *Anchorage Daily News*, July 10, 1988; "Payment of $100 for Waiver of Searches Is 'Cost of Doing Business in Kipnik," *Tundra Drums*, May 5, 1988 (reporting that the Kipnuk traditional council had fined a school district employee $100 for refusing to be subjected to a search).

13. "State Explores Limits of Native Sovereignty," *Anchorage Daily News*, July 11, 1988.

14. "Cowper Speech Sparks Mixed Reaction," *Juneau Empire*, Oct. 24, 1988.

15. Constitution and By-Laws of the Native Village of Tununak, *available at* https// thorpe.law.ou.edu/IRA/tunucons.html.

16. "Village Defies Troopers," *Anchorage Daily News*, April 16, 1989; "Taking a Stand: Tununak Elders Claim Sovereignty, Defy State's Efforts to Arrest, Prosecute Villagers," *Anchorage Daily News*, May 21, 1989.

Chapter Thirteen

1. 4 Alaska Constitutional Convention Proceedings, at 2611.

2. Constitution and By-Laws of the Native Village of Kotzebue, Alaska, and Constitution and By-Laws of the Native Village of Unalakleet, *available at* https://thorpe.law.ou.edu/IRA/kotzcons.html and https://thorpe.law.ou.edu/IRA/unacons.html.

3. Ch. 150 SLA 1957.

4. Marston, *Men of the Tundra*, at 140.

5. Ch. 150 SLA 1957.

6. Ch. 79 SLA 1959.

7. Division of Community and Regional Affairs, Alaska Department of Commerce, Community, and Economic Development, List of Incorporated Alaska Cities, Community Database Online.

8. Community Database Online.

9. Constitution and By-Laws of the Akiachak Native Community, *available at* https://thorpe.law.ou.edu/IRA/akiacons.html.

10. Willie Kasayulie Biography, Alaska Division of Elections, 1996 Election Pamphlet; Willie Kasayulie Interview Tape No. H2004-07-35, University of Alaska Fairbanks Oral History Collection, available at http://jukebox.uaf.edu/yupiit/akiachak/htm/williekasayulie.htm.

11. "State, Tribal Ways Often Differ," *Tundra Times*, Nov. 16, 1983.

12. *Ibid.*

13. "Lewis to Akiachak: Here's How You Dissolve," *Tundra Drums*, Nov. 3, 1983.

14. "Akiachak Seeks IRA Status," *Tundra Times*, Nov. 9, 1983.

15. "Dissolution of Akiachak City Moves Forward," *Tundra Drums*, March 7, 1985.

16. "Akiachak Dissolution Denied by State," *Tundra Drums*, May 23, 1985.

17. "Akiachak Residents Pursuing Dissolution Issue in Court," *Anchorage Daily News*, Jan. 2, 1986.

18. *Kasayulie v. Alaska Local Boundary Commission*, Alaska Superior Court No. 4BE-85-00441 Civil.

19. Letter entitled "CSCB 50 (Finance) (Dissolution of Municipalities)" from Grace Berg Schaible, Attorney General, to the Honorable Jan Faiks, April 20, 1987.

20. Memorandum entitled "Committee Substitute for Senate Bill 50 (Rules) am," from David Hoffman, Commissioner, Department of Community & Regional Affairs, Jan. 26, 1988.

21. Ch. 35 SLA 1988.

22. "Native Sovereignty: Quiet Revolution in the Bush," *Anchorage Daily News*, July 10, 1988.

23. "Sovereignty Means Local Control," *Tundra Times*, Oct. 17, 1988.

24. "Akiachak Nears Hearing Stage of Dissolution," *Tundra Drums*, Feb. 16, 1989.

25. "State Verifies Akiachak's Tribal Vote," *Tundra Times*, Feb. 12, 1990.

26. 1987 Alaska Senate Journal, at 1433.

27. *Id.* at 847 (Letter of Intent CSSB 50 (FIN)).

28. "Akiachak Tribal Effort Takes Six Years," *Tundra Times*, March 26, 1990.

29. Ch. 200 SLA 1972.

30. Affairs of State Message by Governor William A. Egan, Senate and House Journal Supplement No. 1, Jan. 11, 1972.

31. "Villagers Form New Government," *Anchorage Daily Times*, July 7, 1984; "Yup'iks Want Sovereignty," *Tundra Times*, July 11, 1984.

32. "Push for Self-Determination Now, AFN Told," *Tundra Times*, Jan. 27, 1986.

33. *Ibid.*; "Kasayulie and Yupiit Nation to Lobby Congress," *Tundra Drums*, Feb. 6, 1986. *And see* Kizzia, *The Wake of the Unseen Object*, at 209–228 (Yupiit Nation meeting described).

34. "Yupiit Nation Is Growing," *Tundra Times*, Feb. 24, 1986.

35. "Yupiit Nation Adds Three Villages," *Tundra Drums*, March 13, 1986.

36. "By 1990, Yupiit Nation Looks to Have in Place Its Own Tribal Courts," *Tundra Drums*, Dec. 31, 1987.

37. "19-Member Yupiit Nation Awarded Federal Grant," *Tundra Drums*, Sept. 24, 1987; "Yupiit Nation Hires Staff," *Tundra Drums*, Dec. 3, 1987.

38. "Kasayulie Resigns," *Tundra Drums*, Dec. 16, 1990.

39. "Atmautluak Tribal Court Fines Fish & Wildlife Boss," *Tundra Drums*, Dec. 10, 1987; "*State v. Berlin* Brings Sovereignty Issue to State Court," *Tundra Drums*, Dec. 24, 1987.

40. Constitution and By-Laws of the Native Village of Kwinhagak, *available at* https://thorpe.law.ou.edu/IRA/kwincons.html.

41. "Poaching Probe Riles Villagers," *Anchorage Daily News*, March 24, 1989.

42. *Ibid.*

43. Williams, *Alaska State Troopers*, at 235.

44. "State Law Enforcement Officials Say It's Time to Clear the Air with Villagers," *Tundra Drums*, April 20, 1989.

45. "Taking a Stand," *Alaska Daily News*, May 21, 1989.

46. "Troopers Arrest Five Tununak Men This Week," *Tundra Drums*, Sept. 28, 1989.

47. "Tununak Activists Halt Arrest," *Anchorage Daily News*, Sept. 28, 1994.

48. "Troopers Arrest Ostrosky," *Anchorage Daily News*, Oct. 3, 1994; "Activist Jailed After Tununak Confrontation," *Tundra Drums*, Oct. 6, 1994; "Troopers Arrest Tununak Leaders, *Anchorage Daily News*, Oct. 7, 1994; "Troopers Make Tununak Arrest," *Tundra Drums*, Oct. 13, 1994.

49. "Tables Turn on Trooper Serving Warrant on Elusive Tribal Official," *Anchorage Daily News*, June 22, 1995.

50. *State of Alaska v. Pitka*, Alaska District Court No. 4BE-94-01163 CR; *State of Alaska v. Kanrilak*, Alaska District Court No. 4BE-94-01165 CR.

Chapter Fourteen

1. Miller, "Banishment," at 365–366; Snider, "Banishment: The History of Its Use and a Proposal for Its Abolition Under the First Amendment," at 459–465.

2. *Id.* at 460.

3. Zuckerman, *Peaceable Kingdoms*, at 113.

4. *Cooper v. Telfair*, 4 U.S. 14 (1800).

5. Shinn, *Mining Camps*, at 181–182.

6. "Town Meet Insists on Tighter Liquor Law Control Here: Overflowing School Auditorium Lays Crime Wave to Drink," *Anchorage Daily Times*, Oct. 30, 1945.

7. "Twelve Get Ouster Orders by City Police," *Anchorage Daily Times*, Nov. 3, 1945.

8. "Seattle Protests Bums Sent From Anchorage," *Anchorage Daily Times*, Nov. 16, 1945.

9. Personal Communication from Richard Burton to Author, Sept. 13, 2017.

10. *Edison v. State*, 709 P.2d 510 (Alaska Ct. App. 1985).

11. *Adolph Rivers v. State of Alaska*, Memorandum Opinion No. 6604, 2018 WL 1357352 (Alaska Ct. App. March 14, 2018).

12. Williams, *Alaska State Troopers*, at 192.

13. *Ibid.*

14. Personal Communication from Richard Burton to Author, Sept. 13, 2017.

15. "The Ever-Vigilant Venetie," *Anchorage Daily News*, Jan. 10, 1988.

16. "Get Out of Town," *Anchorage Daily News*, July 2, 1997.

17. *Native Village of Perryville v. Tague*, Alaska Superior Court No. 3AN-00-12245 CI, Affidavit of Gerald Kosbruk, para. Nos. 8–15, at 3–5; "Trouble in Perryville," *Anchorage Daily News*, Nov. 2, 2003.

18. "Togiak Tribe Banishes Dillingham Man for Ten Years," *Alaska Dispatch News*, April 13, 2016.

19. "Young Man Blamed for Three Arson Deaths in Alaska Village Gets Traditional Justice: Banishment," *Alaska Dispatch News*, Sept. 12, 2016.

20. "Alaska Village Banishes Six Over Drug and Alcohol Suspicions," *Alaska Dispatch News*, Sept. 15, 2016.

21. "Allakaket Banishes Four People Over Meth," *Fairbanks Daily News-Miner*, Feb. 24, 2017; "Allakaket Tribe Banishes Four Amid Claims of Meth Use," *Alaska Dispatch News*, Feb. 24, 2017; "Meth Dealers Banished from Alaska Village," *Associated Press*, Feb. 25, 2017.

22. 495 U.S. 676, 696–697 (1990).

23. 1913 Annual Report of the Revenue-Cutter Service, at 93–94.

24. Constitution and By-Laws of the Native Village of Perryville Alaska, *available at* https://thorpe.law.ou.edu/IRA/percons.html.

25. Act of March 3, 1891, 20 Stat. 1095, 1099.

26. Alaskan Townsites—Status and Rights of Indian Occupants, 37 Decisions of the Department of the Interior Pertaining to Public Lands, Dec. 29, 1908.

27. Act of May 25, 1926, 44 Stat. 629.

28. U.S. Survey No. 4993, Perryville Townsite Alaska, Alaska State Office, Bureau of Land Management, Department of the Interior, July 10, 1969.

29. Tract Book, Perryville Townsite, U.S. Survey No. 4993, Alaska State Office, Bureau of Land Management, Department of the Interior.

30. *Native Village of Perryville v. Tague*, Alaska Superior Court No. 3AN-00-12245 CI, Native Village of Perryville IRA Council Resolution No. 99-07, March 25, 1999.

31. *Native Village of Perryville v. Tague*, Alaska Superior Court No. 3AN-00-12245 CI, Complaint for Permanent Injunction, Nov. 20, 2000.

32. *Native Village of Perryville v. Tague*, Alaska Superior Court No. 3AN-00-12245 CI, Permanent Injunction Against Defendant John W. Tague, March 10, 2001.

33. *Native Village of Perryville v. Tague*, Alaska Superior Court No. 3AN-00-12245 CI, Motion for Writ of Assistance, Jan. 10, 2003.

34. *Native Village of Perryville v. Tague*, Alaska Superior Court No. 3AN-00-12245 CI, Writ of Assistance, Jan. 10, 2003.

35. Letter from Gregg D. Renkes, Attorney General, to the Hon. Peter Michalski, March 18, 2003 ("The trooper immediately contacted the Anchorage Attorney General's Office, which was also unaware of the injunction or the writ of assistance. The trooper was advised to enforce the writ, but to make no arrests on the basis of that order. The trooper thereupon contacted the individual in Perryville and reminded him of the injunction, and the man left the village voluntarily").

36. *Ibid.*

37. *Native Village of Perryville v. Tague*, Alaska Superior Court No. 3AN-00-12245 CI, State's Memorandum as *Amicus Curiae*, Not in Support of Either Party, but in Support of the Alaska State Troopers and the State of Alaska, at 3–4, May 6, 2003.

38. *Native Village of Perryville v. Tague*, Alaska Superior Court No. 3AN-00-12245 CI, Order, Nov. 19, 2003.

39. "Miller: Sarah Palin's Hostile Record on Alaska Native Subsistence," *Indian Country Today*, Sept. 12, 2008; "Palin's Opposition to Native Rights," *Tundra Drums*, Oct. 9, 2008.

40. Petroff, *Report on the Population, Industries, and Resources of Alaska*, at 17.

41. *Id.* at 15.

42. Report of W.T. Lopp, Superintendent of the Northern District, November 1908 ("At the mouth of the Togiak River, ... we found a white trader, by the name of Johnny Owens, whose hospitality was enjoyed for two sunny days"), *printed at* Bureau of Education, *Report on Education in Alaska, 1909*, Chapter XXX, Appendix at LIV (1910).

43. Bureau of Indian Affairs, *Togiak, Alaska — Village Study*, Aug. 1966.

44. U.S. Survey 4905, Alaska, Togiak Townsite, Alaska State Office, Bureau of Land Management, Department of the Interior, June 12, 1969; Tract Book, Togiak Townsite, U.S. Survey 4905, Alaska State Office, Bureau of Land Management, Department of the Interior, June 23, 1973.

45. Letter of Agreement and Intent Between the City of Togiak and Togiak Natives Limited Addressing the Identification of ANCSA, Section 14(c)(3) Lands, March 26, 1998.

46. Affidavit of Robert Beasley, Director, Alaska Alcoholic Beverage Control Board, June 23, 2014.

47. Pub. L. No. 96-487, Section 1405, 94 Stat. 2494 (1980).

48. Alaska Police Standards Council, Training History Report: Parker, Aaron Andrew, Nov. 8, 2017.

49. "Monegan to Mediate Togiak Dispute," *Bristol Bay Times*, May 29, 2008.

50. "Togiak Residents Organize to Recall Mayor, Chief," *Bristol Bay Times*, June 7, 2007; "Togiak Officials Refute Residents Charges," *Bristol Bay Times*, June 14, 2007.

51. "Togiak Gets Three New City Council Members," *Bristol Bay Times*, Oct. 18, 2007.

52. "Togiak Torn by Turmoil," *Bristol Bay Times*, Dec. 6, 2007.

53. "Police Issue Warning to Bootleggers," *Bristol Bay Times*, Feb. 14, 2008; "Crackdown on Bootleggers Part of Substance-Abuse Solution," *Bristol Bay Times*, Feb. 21, 2008.

54. "Togiak Group Claims Rights Violation," *Bristol Bay Times*, March 13, 2008.

55. *State of Alaska v. Coopchiak*, No. 3DI-08-00064 CR.

56. "Togiak Group Claims Rights Violation," *Bristol Bay Times*, March 13, 2008.

57. Traditional Council of Togiak, Togiak Tribal Court Order Regarding: Complaint and Demand for Aaron A. Parker to Vacate the Tribal Community of Togiak, April 8, 2008.

58. Letter from Monica Jenicek, Assistant Attorney General, to Chief Aaron A. Parker, April 9, 2008.

59. "Leadership to Change After Vote in Togiak," *Bristol Bay Times*, Oct. 16, 2008.

60. In the Matter of Aaron Andrew Parker, Alaska Police Standards Council No. 2016-05, *Accusation*, para. Nos. 8–9 at 3 ("[Parker] stated he had been suspended from his position as Chief in Togiak and denied access to any city property" and "was terminated from the Togiak Police Department on or about December 5, 2008").

61. COPS Program, U.S. Department of Justice, *available at* https://cops.usdoj.gov/aboutcops.

62. Traditional Council of Togiak Grant Application, Bureau of Justice Assistance, Office of Justice Programs, U.S. Department of Justice, Tribal Community and Justice Profile Part B, at 6 (2016) ("In 2015, the Traditional Council of Togiak was awarded a COPS grant. This grant allowed the Tribe to hire one Tribal police officer (TPO). The TPO, under the authority of the Traditional Council of Togiak, enforce (sic) tribal laws and ordinances").

63. "Troubles for Togiak After Banishing Suspected Bootlegger," *KDLG Dillingham*, April 7, 2017 [hereinafter "Troubles for Togiak"].

64. *Ibid.*

65. This account of Ronald Oertwich's incarceration in Togiak is based on the facts alleged in the complaint Oertwich filed in *Oertwich v. Traditional Village of Togiak*, U.S. District Court for the District of Alaska No. 3:19-cv-00082, as well as the accounts described in the opening and response briefs that were filed in *Oertwich v. Traditional Village of Togiak*, U.S. Court of Appeals for the Ninth Circuit No. 19-36029.

66. *State of Alaska v. Oertwich*, No. 3DI-10-00205 CR. *See* also "Troopers Report Incidents in Four Bristol Bay Communities," *Bristol Bay Times*, May 6, 2011.

67. "Tribal Banishment of Togiak non-Native Draws State Investigation," *Alaska Dispatch News*, April 3, 2017.

68. Troubles for Togiak.

69. Personal Communication from Richard Burton to Author, April 4, 2017.

70. Troubles for Togiak.

71. "State Won't Interfere With Tribal Banishments Despite Civil Rights Issues, AG Says," *Alaska Dispatch News*, Oct. 7, 2017.

72. Letter entitled "Legal Status of Tribal Governments in Alaska" from Jahna Lindemuth, Attorney General, to the Hon. Bill Walker, Oct. 19, 2017.

73. Attorney General Jahna Lindemuth, Keynote Address, Alaska Native Law Conference, Oct. 17, 2017, video recording available at Alaska Bar Association. *See also* "Alaska AG Outlines State Position on Tribal Banishment," *Associated Press*, Oct. 18, 2017.

74. "Brother of Trooper in Charge of Northwest Arctic Drug Crimes Banished from Kiana for Alleged Meth Dealing," *KOTZ Kotzebue*, Sept. 20, 2019; "Trooper's Brother Banished from Kiana for Alleged Meth Dealing," *Arctic Sounder*, Oct. 7, 2019.

75. "Kiana Tribe Banishes Suspected Meth Dealer from Village," *Anchorage Daily News*, Oct. 6, 2019.

76. Personal Communication from Assistant Attorney General Maria Bahr to Author, May 22, 2020.

Chapter Fifteen

1. Pub. L. No. 74-152, 49 Stat. 388 (1935).

2. Donald Mitchell, *Sold American*, at 355 ("[Assistant Secretary of the Interior Oscar] Chapman instructed Claude Hirst, the Bureau of Indian Affairs Alaska superintendent in Juneau, to order bureau schoolteachers to hold an election in each southeast Alaska village to select a Tlingit-Haida Central Council"); Letter from John Carver, Under Secretary of the Interior, to the Hon. Henry Jackson, Chairman, Senate Committee on Interior and Insular Affairs, March 16, 1965, *printed in* S. Rep. No. 89-159, at 4–5 (1965) ("The present body calling itself the central council grew out of a meeting organized at Wrangell in 1941 for the purpose of selecting a claims attorney").

3. Donald Mitchell, *Sold American*, at 262–286, 360–364 (history of statute authorizing Tlingit-Haida land claims lawsuit to be filed and organization of Tlingit-Haida Central Council described).

4. Pub. L. No. 89-130, 79 Stat. 543 (1965).

5. *Tlingit and Haida Indians of Alaska v. United States*, 389 F.2d 778 (Ct. Cl. 1968).

6. Pub. L. 91-335, 84 Stat. 431 (1970).

7. "Native Area Director," *Tundra Times*, Feb. 10, 1971.

8. "Agreement Signed T-H Take Over Programs," *Tundra Times*, March 3, 1971. The BIA relied on the Buy Indian Act, Ch. 431, Section 23, 36 Stat. 855, 861 (1910) (codified as amended at 25 U.S.C. 47), as the statute in which Congress purportedly granted the BIA authority to enter into the contract. However, the Buy Indian Act simply authorizes the secretary of the interior to employ "Indian labor" and to purchase the products of "Indian industry."

9. *Cogo v. Central Council of the Tlingit and Haida Indians of Alaska*, 465 F. Supp. 1286 1290 (D. Alaska 1979) (adoption of THCC Constitution described).

10. Kvasnicka and Viola, *The Commissioners of Indian Affairs*, at 341–346.

11. Letter from Morris Thompson, Commissioner of Indian Affairs, to BIA Alaska Area Director, July 24, 1975, *printed in Cogo v. Central Council of the Tlingit and Haida Indians of Alaska*, *supra* at 1289–1290.

12. *Consolidating Alaska Natives Governing Bodies: Hearings on S. 1920 and S. 2046 Before the S. Select Comm. on Indian Affairs*, 95th Cong. 23 (1977) (statement of Ray Paddock, Jr., president, Central Council, Tlingit and Haida Indians of Alaska).

13. 47 *Fed. Reg.* 53130, 53135 (1982).

14. 48 *Fed. Reg.* 56862, 56866 (1983); 50 *Fed. Reg.* 6055, 6059 (1985); 51 *Fed. Reg.* 25115, 29119 (1986).

15. 53 *Fed. Reg.* 52829, 52833–5285 (1988).

16. *Id.* at 52833.

17. 58 *Fed. Reg.* 54364, 54368–54369 (1993).

18. Letter from Edward Thomas, President, Central Council, Tlingit and Haida Indian Tribes of Alaska, to Michael Anderson, Associate Solicitor for Indian Affairs, Sept. 29, 1993. Legislative Bill Files (S. 1675—S. 1784), House Committee on Natural Resources, 103d Congress, Record Group 233, Center for Legislative Archives, National Archives and Records Administration [hereinafter "S. 1784 House Records"].

19. Section 7, S. 1654, 103d Cong. (as reported by S. Comm. on Indian Affairs, Nov. 19, 1993).

20. S. Rep. No. 103-191, at 6 (1993). The text of the Murkowski amendment and the description of the amendment in the committee's report were disingenuous in that they describe the Tlingit and Haida Indians as a "tribe," even though the 1935 act and the amendments to the act the Eighty-ninth and Ninety-first Congresses enacted in 1965 and 1970 did not do so.

21. 139 *Cong. Rec.* 32429 (1993).

22. Letter from Ada Deer, Assistant Secretary for Indian affairs, to the Hon. George Miller, Chairman, House Committee on Natural Resources, March 10, 1994 (explaining that the BIA "support[ed] the removal of the former section 7 from [S. 1654]. The removed portion has since been separately introduced as a bill, S. 1784. We have provided separately in testimony to this Committee views on S. 1784, which we do not support"), *printed at* H.R. Rep. No. 103-479, Part 1, at 17–21 (1994).

23. 139 *Cong. Rec.* 32428 (1993).

24. *Ibid.* In the *Congressional Record* Senator Murkowski appears to have been present on the floor and to have spoken to the Senate. However, the C-Span video recording of the floor session demonstrates that he was not and his statement was inserted into the *Congressional Record* after the unrecorded voice vote to pass S. 1784. *See* http://www.c-span.org/video/?52585-1/senate-session, at 50:40–51:23 (Senate floor session, Nov. 24, 1993).

25. *Central Council Tlingit and Haida Status Clarification: Hearing on S. 1784 Before the Subcomm. on Native American Affairs of the H. Comm. on Natural Resources*, 103d Cong. 5–6 (1994) (statement of Debra Maddox, Acting Director, BIA Office of Tribal Services).

26. In 1994 Philip Baker-Shenk was a member of Pirtle, Morisset, Schlosser & Ayer, a law firm in Washington, D.C., that specialized in representing Native American clients.

27. 1993–1994 *Congressional Directory*, at 457. *See also* https://cla.d.umn.edu/american-indian-studies/faculty-staff/tadd-johnson ("From 1990–1995, [Tadd Johnson] served as counsel and staff director to the United States House of Representatives Committee on Natural Resources in the Office of Indian Affairs and the Subcommittee on Native American Affairs").

28. Memorandum entitled "Central Council of Tlingit and Haida," from Tadd Johnson to Jeff Petrich and Julie Petro, June 14, 1994. S. 1784 House Records.

29. Memorandum entitled "S. 1784," from Philip Baker-Shenk to Tadd Johnson, July 12, 1994. *Ibid.*

30. Letter entitled "Revisions as Discussed During our July 22, 1994 Meeting on S. 1784," from Philip Baker-Shenk to Jeffrey Petrich, Deputy General Counsel, Committee on Natural Resources, July 23, 1994. *Ibid.*

31. Memorandum entitled "Central Council," from Tadd Johnson to Jeff Petrich, Sept. 22, 1994. *Ibid.*

32. Transcript of Proceedings, Mark-Up of S. 1784. *Ibid.*

33. *Ibid.*

34. H.R. Rep. No. 103-800, at 2 (1994).

35. 140 *Cong. Rec.* 27244–27246 (1994).

36. *Id.* at 29537. *See also id.* at 28832–28833.

37. "Tribal Status Restored," *Anchorage Daily News*, Oct. 9, 1994.

38. Pub. L. No. 103-454, 108 Stat. 4791 (1994).

39. *See most recently State v. Central Council of Tlingit and Haida Indian Tribes of Alaska*, 371 P.3d 255, 259 (Alaska 2016) ("The Central Council of Tlingit and Haida Indian Tribes of Alaska is a federally recognized Indian tribe based in southeast Alaska. Central Council has established a tribal court system asserting jurisdiction over civil, criminal, probate, and juvenile law matters").

40. Personal Communication from Ted Stevens to Author, Sept. 3, 2003.

41. Pub. L. No. 103-322, 108 Stat. 1796 (1994).

42. Section 10003, Title I, Pub. L. No. 103-322, 108 Stat. 1807–1815 (1994).

43. *Ibid.*

44. Section 109, Title I, S. 1585, 108th Cong. (as reported by Committee on Appropriations, Sept. 5, 2003). *And see* S. Rep. No. 108-144, at 49–50, 68 (2003).

45. "Tribal Courts, Officers Get No Funding in Bill," *Anchorage Daily News*, Sept. 3, 2003.

46. "Stevens Continues War of Tribalism," *Anchorage Daily News*, Sept. 24, 2003.

47. "Stevens Remarks Called Racist," *Anchorage Daily News*, Oct. 9, 2003.

48. *Ibid.*

49. *Ibid.*

50. "Stevens Airs 50 Years of Dedication to Natives," *Anchorage Daily News*, Oct. 25, 2003.

51. "Alaska Natives Confront Debates Over Legal Status," *Indianz.com*, Oct. 21, 2003.

52. "AFN Votes to Endorse New Commission," *Anchorage Daily News*, Oct. 26, 2003.

53. "Senators Leave With Work to Do," *Anchorage Daily News*, Nov. 26, 2003; "Stevens Backs Off Plan to End Tribal Justice Grants," *Anchorage Daily News*, Dec. 1, 2003.

54. Division B, Title I, Section 112, Pub. L. No. 108-1999, 118 Stat. 3, 62–63 (2004).

55. 150 *Cong. Rec.* 290 (2004).

56. Personal Communication from Lisa Sutherland, Deputy Staff Director, Senate Committee on Appropriations, to Author, Jan. 24, 2004.

57. "Attorney General John Ashcroft Appoints the Alaska Rural Justice and Law Enforcement Commission," *Press Release: U.S. Department of Justice*, Sept. 2, 2004.

58. Alaska Rural Justice and Law Enforcement Commission, *Initial Report and Recommendations*, at 80.

59. *Id.* at 85.

60. *Id.* at 87.

61. 2009–2010 *Congressional Directory*, at 339.

62. Alaska Rural Justice and Law Enforcement Commission, *Report to the United States Congress and the Alaska State Legislature.*

63. According to James Torgerson, who was a member of the commission, in 2012 "we ran out of money." Personal Communication from James Torgerson to Author, Sept. 17, 2016. In 2013 Senator Murkowski arranged for the One Hundred-thirteenth Congress to direct "[t]he Attorney General, in consultation with the Attorney General of the State of Alaska, the Commissioner of Public Safety of the State of Alaska, the Alaska Federation of Natives and Federally recognized Indian tribes in the State of Alaska" to report to Congress within one year "with respect to whether the Alaska Rural Justice and Law Enforcement Commission established under Section 112(a)(1) of the Consolidated Appropriations Act, 2004, should be continued and appropriations authorized for the continued work of the commission." *See* Section 909(b), Pub. L. No. 113-4, 127 Stat. 54, 126. The Department of Justice ignored the directive, no report was submitted, and no additional money was appropriated.

64. *See* Chapter thirteen, note 9.

65. Letter from Carl Reed, Director, Office of Community Oriented Policing Services, Department of Justice, to George Peter, Tribal Administrator, Akiachak Native Community, Sept. 5, 2007.

66. U.S. Department of Justice, Community Oriented Policing Services, Tribal Resources Program Grant No. 2007HEWX0007, Project Description Narrative, at 8.

67. Personal Communication from Chaun Eason, FOIA Officer, Office of Community Oriented Policing Services, U.S. Department of Justice, to Author, April 25, 2019.

68. "Alaska Native Leaders Call on Attorney General Barr for Help, Tribal Authority to Make Up for Lack of Police," *Anchorage Daily News*, May 30, 2019.

69. "Attorney General William P. Barr Announces Emergency Funding to Address Public Safety Crisis in Rural Alaska," *Press Release: U.S. Department of Justice*, June 28, 2019.

70. "Justice Department Awards Nearly $5 Million for Equipment and Public Safety Officers in Alaska Native Villages," *Press Release: Office of Community Oriented Policing Services, U.S. Department of Justice*, July 30, 2019.

71. S. 2754, 101st Cong. (as introduced, June 19, 1990). The text of the bill is printed at 136 *Cong. Rec.* 14564–14569 (1990).

72. 18 U.S.C. 2266(5) defines "protection order" to mean

> (A) any injunction, restraining order, or any other order issued by a civil or criminal court for the purpose of preventing violent or threatening acts or harassment against, sexual violence, or contact or communication with or physical proximity to, another person, including any temporary or final order issued by a civil or criminal court whether obtained by filing an independent action or as a pendente lite order in another proceeding so long as any civil or criminal order was issued in response to a complaint, petition, or motion filed by or on behalf of a person seeking protection; and
>
> (B) any support, child custody or visitation provisions, orders, remedies or relief issued as part of a protection order, restraining order, or injunction pursuant to State, tribal, territorial, or local law authorizing the issuance of protection orders, restraining orders, or injunctions for the protection of victims of domestic violence, sexual

73. *Women and Violence: Hearings on Legislation to Reduce the Growing Problem of Violent Crime Against Women Before the S. Comm. on the Judiciary*, 101st Cong., Parts 1 and 2 (1994).

74. S. Rep. No. 101-545 (1990).

75. S. 15, 102d Cong. (as introduced, Jan. 14, 1991). The text of the bill is printed at 137 *Cong. Rec.* 1302–1314 (1991).

76. S. Rep. No. 101-197, at 35 (1991).

77. *Id.* at 56.

78. *See* "Indian tribe" definition in 25 U.S.C. 5304(e).

79. *Violence Against Women: Victims of the System: Hearing on S. 15 Before the S. Comm. on the Judiciary*, 102d Cong. (1991).

80. S. Rep. No. 102-197 (1991).

81. S. 11, 103d Cong. (as introduced, Jan. 21, 1993). The text of the bill is printed at 139 *Cong. Rec.* 740–752 (1993).

82. S. Rep. No. 103-138 (1993).

83. 139 *Cong. Rec.* 26979 (1993).

84. Title XXXII, H.R. 3355, 103d Cong. 566–622 (as passed by U.S. House of Representatives, Nov. 19, 1993).

85. 140 *Cong. Rec.* 5468 (1994).

86. *Id.* at 8142. The text of the House amendment to the Senate amendment is printed at *id.* at 8142–8197.

87. Pub. L. No. 103-322, 108 Stat. 1796 (1994). The convoluted actions in the Senate and House that culminated in Congress's enactment of the Violent Crime Control and Law Enforcement Act are discussed at 1993 *Congressional Quarterly Almanac*, at 293–300; 1994 *Congressional Quarterly Almanac*, at 273–294.

88. H.R. 1133, 103d Cong. (as introduced, Feb. 24, 1993).

89. 139 *Cong. Rec.* 31337 (1993).

90. *Compare* the text of section 2265 in H.R. 1133, 103d Cong. 49–50 (as introduced, Feb. 24, 1993) *with* the text of section 2265 in H.R. 1133, 103d Cong. 38–39 (as reported by Committee on the Judiciary, Nov. 20, 1993). *See also* H.R. Rep. No. 103-395, at 35–36 (1993) (Committee on the Judiciary explaining that its version of section 2265 "provides that a protection order issued by one State or Indian tribe shall be accorded full faith and credit by the courts of another State or Indian tribe and enforced as if it were the order of the enforcing State or tribe").

91. During the One Hundred-third Congress no member of the Subcommittee on Native American Affairs of the Committee on Natural Resources was a member of the Committee on the Judiciary. 1993–1994 *Congressional Directory*, at 449 and 456. Representative Elton Gallegly was the only member of the Committee on Natural Resources who was a member of the Committee on the Judiciary. *Id.* at 449 and 455. But Gallegly, who represented Ventura County in southern California had no Indian tribes in his congressional district.

92. Section 101(b)(4), S. 2787, 106th Cong. 9–10 (as introduced, June 26, 2000). The text of section 101 is printed at 146 *Cong. Rec.* 12260 (2000).

93. Pub. L. No. 106-386, 114 Stat. 1464, 1494 (2000). A House-Senate conference committee whose members negotiated the final text of H.R. 3244, a bill that sought to remedy the problem of human trafficking, included the text of S. 2787 in that bill. Significantly, the conference committee's version of 18 U.S.C. 2265(e) omitted the phrase "and in which at least 1 of the parties is an Indian." The conference report on H.R. 3244 makes no mention of that change and states only that the new

18 U.S.C. 2265(e) was intended to "clarif[y] that tribal courts have full civil jurisdiction to enforce protection orders in matters arising within the authority of the tribe." H.R. Rep. No. 106-935, at 104 (2000).

94. S. 1197, 109th Cong. (as introduced, June 8, 2005).

95. Alaska Directory of State Officials (February 2005), at 28.

96. S. 1197, 109th Cong. 269 and 273 (as reported by S. Committee on the Judiciary, Sept. 12, 2005).

97. "Alaska Native Health Board Holds MEGA Meeting," *Anchorage Native News*, July/Aug. 2007 ("Those attending included ... Alaska Sen. Ted Stevens and Legislative Assistant and Senior Health Advisor Elizabeth Connell").

98. Pub. L. No. 109-162, 119 Stat. 2960, 2964–2966 (2006). The definitions are codified at 42 U.S.C. 13925(a)(2) and (16), but they have not been codified in 18 U.S.C. 2266, the section that defines the terms in 18 U.S.C. 2265.

99. Letter from Ronald Weich, Assistant Attorney General, to the Hon. Joseph R. Biden, Jr. (with attachments), July 21, 2011.

100. Sections 901–908, S. 1925, 112th Cong. 164–182 (as introduced, Nov. 30, 2011).

101. Pub. L. No. 90-284 Title II, 82 Stat. 73, 77 (1968) (codified as amended at 25 U.S.C. 1301 *et seq.*).

102. 435 U.S. 191 (1978).

103. 495 U.S. 676 (1990).

104. Sections 904 and 905, S. 1925, 112th Cong. 364, 370–371 (as reported by the S. Comm. on the Judiciary, Feb. 7, 2012).

105. Opposition to Any Language Excluding Alaska Native Tribes from the Violence Against Women Act, Resolution TA/ 12-58, Seventy-seventh Annual Tribal Assembly, Central Council of Tlingit and Haida Indian Tribes of Alaska, April 21, 2012.

106. "Tribe Strongly Opposes Exclusion from Violence Against Women Act," *Press Release: Central Council of Tlingit and Haida Indian Tribes of Alaska*, April 23, 2012.

107. "Alaska Tribes Say Violence Against Women Act Could Harm Their People," *McClatchy*, April 24, 2012.

108. *Ibid.* ("Alaska Sens. Lisa Murkowski, a Republican, and Mark Begich, a Democrat, said Tuesday they would introduce amendments to try to allow Alaska tribes to continue having protective orders respected").

109. 158 *Cong. Rec.* 5738 (2012).

110. Section 905, S. 1925, 112th Cong. 190 (as passed by Senate, April 26, 2012). *See also* "Amendment Lets Alaska Tribes Keep Restraining-Order Powers," *Anchorage Daily News*, April 26, 2012 ("The U.S. Senate passed the Violence Against Women reauthorization act Thursday with a last-minute amendment that lets Alaska tribes continue to issue domestic violence protective orders but excludes them from powers given to Lower 48 tribes to criminally prosecute offenders").

111. Section 910, S. 1925, 112th Cong. 197 (as passed by Senate, April 26, 2012).

112. "House GOP Lets Violence Against Women Act Passed by Senate Die Without a Vote," *Huffington Post*, Jan. 2, 2013 ("Despite the late-stage intervention by Vice President Joe Biden, House Republican leaders failed to advance the Senate's 2012 reauthorization of the Violence Against Women Act").

113. Letter from Michael Geraghty, Attorney General, to Troy Eid, Chairman, Indian Law and Order Commission, Dec. 3, 2013 (Section 910 had been "sought by the State" in order to clarify "that the [Violence Against Women Reauthorization] Act, while expanding the jurisdiction of tribal courts in the lower 48 to issue protective orders, did not expand or retract tribal court jurisdiction in Alaska")

[hereinafter "Geraghty 2013 letter"], *reprinted in* "Attorney General Geraghty's Response Letter to Chairman Troy Eid Regarding the ILOC," *Press Release: Alaska Department of Law*, Dec. 6, 2013.

114. 159 *Cong. Rec.* 1204 (2013).

115. Pub. L. No. 113-4, 127 Stat. 54, 126 (2013).

116. "Obama Signs Revised VAWA, Aid for Vulnerable Alaskans," *Alaska Dispatch*, March 7, 2013.

117. "Violence Against Women Act No Victory for Alaska's Tribes," *Press Release: Native American Rights Fund*, March 10, 2013.

118. "Murkowski Clarifies VAWA Dispute," *Alaska Public Radio Network*, March 22, 2013.

119. "Senator Tries to Repeal Divisive Provision She Inserted in Violence Against Women Act," *Washington Post*, Aug. 2, 2014.

120. Resolution No. 14-45, 2014 Alaska Federation of Natives Convention, Oct. 25, 2014.

121. 160 *Cong. Rec.* 16102 (2014).

122. S. 2945, 113th Cong. (as introduced, Nov. 19, 2014).

123. 160 *Cong. Rec.* 17327–17329 (2014).

124. "Senate Passes VAWA Amendment Repeal," *Press Release: Office of United States Senator Lisa Murkowski*, Dec. 9, 2014.

125. 160 *Cong. Rec.* 18706–18707 (2014).

126. "Murkowski, Young Assure VAWA Amendment Repeal: Duo's Efforts Solidified Support to Remove Provision as Congress Adjourns," *Press Release: Office of Representative Don Young*, Dec. 12, 2014.

127. Pub. L. No. 113-275, 128 Stat. 2988 (2014).

128. 25 U.S.C. 1304(b)(1).

129. Geraghty 2013 Letter.

130. Letter from Tony West, Associate Attorney General, to Michael Geraghty, Attorney General, July 28, 2014.

131. Sec. 235, Pub. L. No. 111-211, 124 Stat. 2258, 2282.

132. Indian Law & Order Commission, *A Roadmap for Making Native America Safer: Report to the President & Congress of the United States* (November 2013), *available at* http://www.aisc.ucla.edu/iloc/report/index.html.

133. Violence Against Women Act and Tribal Protection Orders, Alaska Attorney General Opinion No. AN2013102606, July 30, 2015.

134. Letter from Jahna Lindemuth, Attorney General, to Author, Aug. 29, 2016.

135. Hearing on House Bill 221, Judiciary Committee, Alaska House of Representatives, Jan. 29, 2016, *available at* https://www.360north.org/gavel/video/?clientID=2147483647&eventID=2016011118.

136. *Ibid.*

137. Personal Communication from Tim Clark to Author, April 8, 2019.

138. Alaska House Journal, at 1562 (Feb. 3, 2016).

139. Hearing on House Bill 8, Judiciary Committee, Alaska House of Representatives, Feb. 8, 2017, *available at* https://www.360north.org/gavel/video/?clientID=2147483647& eventID=2017021093.

140. Personal Communication from Capt. Daniel Lowden, Alaska State Troopers, to Author, March 29, 2019.

141. *Ibid.*

142. Personal Communication from Capt. Daniel Lowden, Alaska State Troopers, to Author, April 5, 2019.

143. Personal Communication from Milagros Cisneros, Subcommittee on Crime, Terrorism, and Homeland Security, Committee on the Judiciary, U.S. House of Representatives, to Author, July 29, 2019.

144. Transcript, Markup of H.R. 1585, House Committee on the Judiciary, 116th Congress, March 13, 2019.

145. *Id.* at 21–22.

146. *Id.* at 23.

147. 165 *Cong. Rec.* H3034 (daily ed. April 3, 2019).

148. 165 *Cong. Rec.* S6467 (daily ed. Nov. 7, 2019).

149. Alaska Native Areas Program for the 2010 Census — Notice of Final Criteria and Guidelines, 73 *Fed. Reg.* 65572, 65574 (2008).

150. "Murkowski Introduces Legislation to Address Alaska's Rural Public Safety Crisis," *Press Release: Office of Senator Lisa Murkowski*, Oct. 17, 2019.

151. "Statement by President Biden on the Introduction of the Violence Against Women Reauthorization Act of 2021," *The White House*, March 8, 2021.

152. 167 *Cong. Rec.* H1432–H1479 (daily ed. March 17, 2021).

153. *Id.* at H1449.

154. "House Votes to Reauthorize the Violence Against Women Act," *Gwinnett Daily Post*, March 17, 2021.

155. "We Must Address Gender-Based Violence and Domestic Violence in Alaska," *Anchorage Daily News*, June 13, 2021.

Chapter Sixteen

1. *State of South Dakota v. United States Department of the Interior*, 69 F.3d 878, 882 (8th Cir. 1995).

2. Letter from Harold L. Ickes, Secretary of the Interior, to the Hon. Will Rogers, Chairman, Committee on Indian Affairs, U.S. House of Representatives, March 14, 1936, *printed in* H.R. Rep. No. 74-2244, at 4 (1936).

3. The corporate charters are available at http://thorpe.law.ou.edu/IRA.html.

4. Annual Report of the Governor of Alaska to the Secretary of the Interior for the Fiscal Year Ending June 30, 1948, at 60 ("Since the credit program started in 1939 a total of 65 corporate loans have been made to the various native villages organized in Alaska").

5. Annual Report of the Governor of Alaska to the Secretary of the Interior for the Fiscal Year Ending June 30, 1948, at 61 ("The Angoon Community Association purchased the Hood Bay Salmon Co. Cannery this year"); Annual Report of the Governor of Alaska to the Secretary of the Interior for the Fiscal Year Ending June 30, 1950, at 60 ("The Keku Cannery [was] purchased by Organized Village of Kake from the P.E. Harris Co. this year" and "The Klawock Cooperative Association purchased the Charlie Demmert Cannery which was still under lease in 1950 but should be in operation in 1951"). *And see* de Laguna, *The Story of a Tlingit Community*, at 198–199 (1960) (reporting that the corporation in Angoon purchased "the salmon cannery at Hood Bay in November 1947" and "the loan from the Government to buy the cannery amounted to $258,000, with 20 years allowed in which to liquidate it").

6. Sansonetti Opinion, at 112 n. 277. Kake deed, dated Feb. 15, 1950, available at Recorder's Office, Alaska Department of Natural Resources, Anchorage, Alaska. Klawock deed, dated March 29, 1950, available at Land Titles & Records Department, Alaska Regional Office, Bureau of Indian Affairs.

7. Scherer, at 53 (deed conveying the Klawock cannery "was prepared on Department [of the Interior] letterhead for signature before a notary public").

8. "Trust Land for the Natives of Venetie and Arctic Village," Memorandum to Assistant Secretary—Indian Affairs from Associate Solicitor—Indian Affairs, Thomas W. Fredericks, Sept. 15, 1978 [hereinafter "Fredericks Memorandum"].

9. Second S. 2046 Hearing, at 264 (statement of Donald Wright that "we petitioned the last administration and we have petitioned this administration [to have the Secretary of the Interior "hold the former reservation in trust status"]).

10. Fredericks Memorandum.

11. Letter from Solicitor of the Department of the Interior to Donald R. Wright, Sept. 20, 1978.

12. *State of Alaska v. Native Village of Venetie Tribal Government*, U.S. District Court for the District of Alaska No. F87-0051 CV, Unpublished Order (Decision—Indian Country), Aug. 2, 1995, at 30 ("In 1979, as part of a settlement of Alaska Native land claims, a United States patent was issued conveying the former Chandalar Reservation to Neets'ai Corporation and Venetie Indian Corporation ... This same area was conveyed by warranty deeds dated September 1, 1979 (sic), from the two village corporations to the Tribal Government").

13. 43 *Fed. Reg.* 32311 (1978).

14. 45 *Fed. Reg.* 62034 (1980).

15. 25 C.F.R. 120a.1 (1980). In 1982 25 C.F.R. 120a.1 was renumbered 25 C.F.R. 151.1. *See* 47 *Fed. Reg.* 13326 (1982).

16. 60 *Fed. Reg.* 1956 (1995).

17. Petition for Rule-Making to the Secretary of Interior to Revise 25 C.F.R. 151.1 to Bring Federally Recognized Alaska Native Tribes Within the Scope of Federal Regulations Authorizing the Acquisition of Land in Trust Status, at 13–14, Oct. 11, 1994.

18. 143 *Cong. Rec.* 25690–25691 (1997) (Kevin Gover confirmed as Assistant Secretary of the Interior for Indian Affairs).

19. Acquisition of Title to Land in Trust, 64 *Fed. Reg.* 17574 (1999).

20. *Id.* at 17583.

21. *Nomination of Kevin Gover: Hearing Before the S. Comm. on Indian Affairs*, 105th Cong. 51 (1997). *And see also id.* at 60–61 (Gover refuses to publish a new list of Native entities that includes the ANCSA regional and village corporations that had been included on the list of Native Entities Within the State of Alaska Recognized and Eligible to Receive Services From the United States Bureau of Indian Affairs that Assistant Secretary Ross Swimmer had published in 1988, but which Assistant Secretary Ada Deer had excluded from the list of Native Entities she published in 1993).

22. Acquisition of Title to Land in Trust, 64 *Fed. Reg.* 17578 (1999). Fourteen months earlier in its decision in *State of Alaska v. Native Village of Venetie Tribal Government*, the U.S. Supreme Court held that the land within the boundaries of the revoked Venetie reserve that the Native Village of Venetie owned in fee was not a "dependent Indian community," and hence was not "Indian country."

23. Acquisition of Title to Land in Trust, 66 *Fed. Reg.* 3452 (2001).

24. Personal Communication from John Leshy to Author, Aug. 30, 2016.

25. Memorandum entitled "Rescinding the September 15, 1978, Opinion of the Associate Solicitor for Indian Affairs entitled 'Trust Land for the Natives of Venetie and Arctic Village,'" from John Leshy, Solicitor, to Assistant Secretary—Indian Affairs, Jan. 16, 2001.

26. Pub. L. No. 94-579, 90 Stat. 2743, 2792 (1976). Section 704 repealed twenty-nine statutes Congress enacted between 1888 and 1952 that authorized the withdrawal of public land for various purposes. One of those statutes was section 2 of Public Law No. 74-538, which authorized the Secretary of the Interior to withdraw public land in Alaska as "Indian reservations."

27. 66 *Fed. Reg.* 3454 (2001).

28. Memorandum for the Heads and Acting Heads of Executive Departments and Agencies, 66 *Fed. Reg.* 7702 (2001).

29. *See, e.g.*, Acquisition of Title to Land in Trust; Delay of Effective Date, 66 *Fed. Reg.* 8899 and 19403 (2001).

30. Acquisition of Title to Land in Trust; Withdrawal of Final Rule, 66 *Fed. Reg.* 56608 (2001).

31. U.S. District Court for the District of Columbia No. 1:06-cv-0069.

32. *Ibid.* Answer of the United States to Plaintiffs' Complaint, para. nos. 5–8, at 2.

33. *Ibid.* Intervenor-Defendant Answer, para. nos. 5–8, at 2–3.

34. *Ibid.* Consolidated Complaint, para. no. 54, at 14 ("The regulatory bar which prohibits plaintiffs from having the defendant take property in trust or restricted status, while other federally recognized tribes and their members are allowed to do so, is a violation of 25 U.S.C. 476(f)&(g)").

35. Solicitor's Opinion, Sioux — Elections on Constitutions, April 15, 1936; Solicitor's Opinion, Powers of Indian Group Organized Under IRA But Not as Historical Tribe, April 15, 1938.

36. *See generally* Hu-DeHardt, *Yaqui Resistance and Survival: The Struggle for Land and Autonomy, 1821–1910* (1984).

37. H.R. Rep. No. 88-1805, at 2 (1964).

38. Pub. L. No. 88-350, 78 Stat. 1196 (1964).

39. Pub. L No. 95-375, 92 Stat. 712 (1978).

40. H.R. Rep. No. 103-204, at 1–2 (1993).

41. H.R. 734, 103d Cong. (as introduced, Feb. 2, 1993).

42. *Pascua Yaqui Status Clarification Act: Hearing on H.R. 734 Before the Subcomm. on Native American Affairs of the H. Comm. on Natural Resources*, 103d Cong. 12–13 (1993) (statement of Carol A. Bagon, Director, Office of Tribal Services, Bureau of Indian Affairs).

43. 140 *Cong. Rec.* 7552 (1994).

44. *Id.* at 11232–11235.

45. *Id.* at 11376–11378.

46. *Akiachak Native Community v. Department of the Interior*, U.S. District Court for the District of Columbia No. 1:06-cv-00969 [hereinafter "*Akiachak Native Community*"], State of Alaska's Opposition to Plaintiffs' Motion for Summary Judgment and Cross-Motion for Summary Judgment, at 12.

47. *Id.* at 27.

48. *Id.* at 29.

49. *Akiachak Native Community v. Salazar*, 935 F. Supp. 2d 195, 211 (D.D.C. 2013).

50. *Akiachak Native Community v. Jewell*, 995 F. Supp. 2d 1 (D.D.C. 2013).

51. *Akiachak Native Community*, Defendants' Reply in Support of Defendants' Cross-Motion for Summary Judgment, at 1–2.

52. *Nomination of Kevin Washburn to Be Assistant Secretary for Indian Affairs, U.S. Department of the Interior: Hearing Before the S. Comm. on Indian Affairs*, 112th Cong. 7–9 (2012) (statement of Kevin Washburn).

53. "President Obama Announces More Key Administration Posts," *Press Release: White House*, Aug. 2, 2012.

54. Land Acquisitions in the State of Alaska, 79 *Fed. Reg.* 24648 (2014).

55. *Id.* at 24651–24652.

56. *Department of the Interior v. Akiachak Native Community*, U.S. Court of Appeals for the District of Columbia Circuit No. 13-5361 [hereinafter "*Akiachak Native Community* Appeal"], Motion for Voluntary Dismissal Pursuant to Rule 42(b), and Order (June 12, 2014).

57. Land Acquisitions in the State of Alaska, 79 *Fed. Reg.* 76888 (2014).

58. *Id.* at 76890.

59. State of Alaska, Division of Elections, Nov. 4, 2014, Official General Election Results.

60. State of Alaska, Division of Elections, Aug. 19, 2014, Official Primary Election Results.

61. "Appeal in Akiachak Case Revives Tribal Sovereignty Fight," *Alaska Journal of Commerce*, Aug. 26, 2015.

62. *Akiachak Native Community* Appeal, Motion to Suspend Briefing for Six Months, at 2.

63. "State Holds Up Effort to Expand Indian Country in Alaska," *Alaska Dispatch News*, Feb. 5, 2015.

64. Video: Governor Walker on Land Into Trust, Central Council of the Tlingit and Haida Indian Tribes of Alaska, April 15–17, 2015, *available at* http://www.ccthita.org/government/president/media/index.html.

65. "Appeal in Akiachak Case Revives Tribal Sovereignty Fight," *Alaska Journal of Commerce*, Aug. 26, 2015.

66. *Akiachak Native Community v. Department of the Interior*, 827 F.3d 100, 102 (D.C. Cir. 2016).

67. *Ibid.* 113.

68. "Alaska Attorney General Not Appealing Lands Into Trust Case," *Press Release: Alaska Department of Law*, Aug. 15, 2016.

69. "Land Into Trust Litigation Ends — Historic Victory for Alaska Tribes, *Press Release: Native American Rights Fund*, Aug. 15, 2016.

70. "Alaska's Attorney General Looks for Creative Solutions to Address Crime Amid Budget Cuts," *Alaska Dispatch News*, Aug. 23, 2016.

71. Alaska Department of Commerce, Community and Economic Development, Division of Community and Regional Affairs, Community Information: Craig.

72. Constitution and By-Laws of the Craig Community Association of Craig, Alaska, *available at* https://thorpe.law.ou.edu/IRA.craigcons.html.

73. 47 *Fed. Reg.* 53130, 53134 (1982).

74. 58 *Fed. Reg.* 54364, 54369 (1993).

75. Section 2, Article I, Constitution and By-Laws of the Craig Tribal Association of Craig, Alaska, ratified July 9, 2011 ("The Craig Tribal Association of Craig, Alaska, is a continuation in existence of the same tribal entity formerly known as the Craig Community Association."

76. 77 *Fed. Reg.* 47868, 47872 (2012).

77. Notice of (Non-Gaming) Trust Land Acquisition Application, Bureau of Indian Affairs, Alaska Region, *Alaska Department of Law*, Oct. 7, 2016.

78. Letter captioned "State of Alaska's Comments on the Craig Tribal Association's Trust Land Acquisition Application," from Jahna Lindemuth, Attorney General, to Kathy Cline, Acting Regional Director, BIA Alaska Region, Dec. 9, 2016.

79. Land Acquisitions; Craig Tribal Association, Craig, Alaska, 82 *Fed. Reg.* 4915 (2017).

80. Letter from Lawrence S. Roberts, Principal Deputy Assistant Secretary — Indian Affairs, to Clinton Cook, Sr., Tribal President, Craig Tribal Association, Jan. 12, 2017 [hereinafter "Roberts Decision Document"].

81. 555 U.S. 379 (2009).

82. Roberts Decision Document, at 5–6.

83. "Hilary Tompkins Shares Legal Hopes for Federal-Tribal Relations," *Indian Country Today Media Network*, Jan. 18, 2017 (Interview in which Tompkins explains, "I was born on the Navajo reservation into a family that was burdened with the social ills of alcoholism and poverty." After having been adopted by a Caucasian family, "As a young adult I reconnected with my roots and lived on the Navajo Reservation. I learned about my Navajo culture which at its core stresses the importance of living in harmony with the Earth").

84. *Ibid.*

85. 555 U.S. at 392.

86. *Ibid.* n. 6.

87. Solicitor's Opinion M-37043, Authority to Acquire Land into Trust in Alaska, Jan. 13, 2017 [hereinafter "Tompkins Opinion"], at 13–14.

88. Memorandum from Felix S. Cohen, Assistant Solicitor, to Fred H. Daiker, Assistant to the Commissioner of Indian Affairs, n.d., *cited in* Tompkin's Opinion, at 19.

89. Tompkins Opinion, at 20.

90. Letter from Kevin G. Clarkson, Attorney General, to Principal Deputy Solicitor Daniel Jorjani, captioned "Objection to Solicitor Opinion M-37043, 'Authority to Acquire Land into Trust in Alaska' Pending Review," Jan. 25, 2019.

91. Land Acquisitions in the State of Alaska, 79 *Fed. Reg.* 76888, 76893 (2014).

92. Craig Tribal Association of Craig, Alaska's Alcohol Control Ordinance, 83 *Fed. Reg.* 45960 (2018).

93. 165 *Cong. Rec.* S2161 (daily ed. April 1, 2019).

94. *See Greenblatt and Jorjani Nominations: Hearing Before the S. Comm. on Energy and Natural Resources*, 116th Cong. (2019).

95. Solicitor Opinion M-37064 (Permanent Withdrawal of Solicitor Opinion M-37043, "Authority to Acquire Land into Trust in Alaska"), Jan. 19, 2021.

96. "Biden-Harris Campaign Announces Tribal Nations Plan," *Indian Country Today*, Oct. 8, 2020. Biden-Harris Plan for Tribal Nations available at https://joebiden.com/tribalnations/.

97. 167 *Cong. Rec.* S6770 (daily ed. Sept. 29, 2012).

Chapter Seventeen

1. Sections 135 and 152, 30 Stat. 1253, 1273, 1275 (1899).

2. Section 3, Pub. L. No. 62-333, 37 Stat. 512 (1912).

3. Sections 1 and 15, Chapter 13, Title 65, Alaska Compiled Laws Annotated 1949.

4. "Senate Approves Restrictive Gambling Bill, 18-2," *Daily Alaska Empire*, Feb. 7, 1960 (reporting that "[s]torm warnings were up this year that the new state Department of Public Safety planned to enforce anti-gambling laws now on the books, unless the Legislature indicated otherwise").

5. Ch. 27 SLA (1960).

6. Charitable Gaming 2019 Annual Report, Tax Division, Alaska Department of Revenue, at 6.

7. 358 U.S. 217 (1959).

8. Donald Mitchell, *Wampum*, at 11–35.

9. *Id.* at 36–58.

10. Survey of Indian Bingo Activity, July 1, 1987, *printed in Gaming Activities on Indian Reservations and Lands: Hearing on S. 555 and S. 1303 Before the S. Select Committee on Indian Affairs*, 100th Cong. 237–251 (1987).

11. Memorandum entitled "Gambling Activities of Native Councils," from Douglas Mertz, Assistant Attorney General, to Sally Smith, Director, Public Services Division, Alaska Department of Revenue, April 25, 1986, *printed in* Informal Opinions of the Attorney General of Alaska.

12. 480 U.S. 202 (1987).

13. Pub. L. No. 100-497, 102 Stat. 2467 (1988).

14. Golovin, *Encounters*, at 81.

15. Petroff, *Report on the Population, Industries, and Resources of Alaska*, at 32.

16. "Constitution and By-Laws of the Sitka Community Association," *available at* https://thorpe.law.ou.edu/IRA/sitkacons.html.

17. 47 *Fed. Reg.* 53130, 53135 (1982).

18. Article II, Constitution of the Sitka Tribe of Alaska, November 26, 1991, *available at* https://www.sitkatribe.org/uploads/cms/19911126-STA-Constitution.pdf.

19. Certificate of Approval, Constitution of the Sitka Tribe of Alaska, available at *ibid.*

20. Letter from John Trezise, Acting Associate Solicitor for Indian Affairs, to Michael Cox, General Counsel, National Indian Gaming Commission, June 23, 1993.

21. Constitution and By-Laws of the Klawock Cooperative Association Alaska, *available at* https://thorpe.law.ou.edu/IRA/klawockcons.html.

22. 47 *Fed. Reg.* 53130, 53134 (1982).

23. 58 *Fed. Reg.* 54364, 54369 (1993).

24. Letter from Michael Anderson, Associate Solicitor for Indian Affairs, to Michael Cox, General Counsel, National Indian Gaming Commission, Nov. 15, 1993.

25. Letter from Andrew Hope, Chairman, National Indian Gaming Commission, to Roseann Demmert, President, Klawock Cooperative Association, Nov. 16, 1993.

26. "Tlingits in Klawock Win Gaming Permit," *Anchorage Daily News*, Nov. 17, 1993.

27. Message Vetoing SB 370, an Act providing an exemption from gambling laws for gambling conducted by cruise ships for their ticketed passengers in the offshore water of the state, June 9, 1994. 1994 Alaska Senate Journal, at 4818–4819.

28. "Tlingits in Klawock Win Gaming Permit," *Anchorage Daily News*, Nov. 17, 1993.

29. *See* NIGC Gaming Tribe Report (Sorted by State), Jan. 13, 2020. *See also* Klawock Bingo, Five Hundred Nations, July 30, 2020.

30. 58 *Fed. Reg.* 54364, 54369 (1993).

31. *Akiachak Native Community v. Monteau*, U.S. District Court for the District of Columbia No. 1:96-cv-02302.

32. 47 *Fed. Reg.* 53130, 53134 (1982).

33. 58 *Fed. Reg.* 54364, 54369 (1993).

34. Sansonetti Opinion, at 129.

35. Letter from Robert Anderson, Associate Solicitor for Indian Affairs, to Michael Cox, General Counsel, National Indian Gaming Commission, May 12, 1995.

36. "Natives' Casinos Faltering," *Anchorage Daily News*, May 19, 1995 ("The Kenaitze Indian Tribe's proposal to open a casino on the Kenai Peninsula has been tentatively rejected by the National Indian Gaming Commission ... The commission acted against the Kenaitze on Monday, turning down the tribe's bid for a gambling casino and tribal bingo hall near its Kenai offices and clinic").

37. Constitution and By-Laws of the Native Village of Barrow, *available at* https://thorpe.law.ou.edu/IRA/barcons.html.

38. 58 *Fed. Reg.* 54364, 54369 (1993).

39. Native Village of Barrow (Permit 940886), Investigative Report, Division of Charitable Gaming, Alaska Department of Revenue (Dec. 14, 1994).

40. Letter entitled "Native Village of Barrow. Spokane Punchboards," from Hans Walker, Jr., Hobbs, Straus, Dean & Walker, to Bruce Botelho, Attorney General, Jan. 5, 1996.

41. Memorandum entitled "Pull-Tabs," from Robin Taylor, Chairman, Judiciary Committee, Alaska Senate, to Larry Meyers, Director, Income & Excise Audit Division, Alaska Department of Revenue, Feb. 18, 1999.

42. Letter entitled "Pull-Tab Inquiry Dated, 2-18-99," from Larry Meyers, Director, Income & Excise Audit Division, Alaska Department of Revenue, to the Hon. Robin Taylor, Feb. 26, 1999.

43. Letter entitled "Native Village of Barrow," from Hans Walker, Jr., Hobbs, Straus, Dean & Walker, to Vince Usera, Assistant Attorney General, March 8, 1999.

44. Paragraph Nos. 24 and 25, Complaint, *Native Village of Barrow v. National Indian Gaming Commission*, U.S. District Court for the District of Columbia No. 1:99-cv-00886.

45. Ch. 59 SLA 1983.

46. "Senate Passes Anti-Gaming Bill," *Anchorage Daily News*, May 3, 1995.

47. "State Ready to Talk Gambling with Klawock," *Anchorage Daily News*, April 6, 1994.

48. "Election Further Delays Casino Gambling in Klawock," *Anchorage Daily News*, Dec. 5, 1994.

49. "Tribes Pursue Gambling," *Anchorage Daily News*, May 7, 1995; "New Law Imperils Alaskan Indian Casinos," *Gaming & Wagering Business*, Aug. 1, 1995 ("Until the introduction of the Monte Carlo bill in late April, the Klawock Band had virtually completed negotiations for a compact with Gov. Knowles. The compact called for the operation of all manner of casino games except slot machines, which are specifically prohibited by state law").

50. *Ibid.*

51. "House Passes Bill to Ban Monte Carlo Nights," *Anchorage Daily News*, May 11, 1995.

52. "State Battles Bid to Expand Tribal Powers," *Anchorage Daily News*, June 20, 2000.

53. Letter from Senator Mike Miller, Chairman, Legislative Council, Alaska Legislature, to the Hon. Tony Knowles, June 15, 2000.

54. Letter from Tony Knowles, Governor of Alaska, to the Hon. Mike Miller, June 29, 2000.

55. *Akiachak Native Community v. Monteau*, U.S. District Court for the District of Columbia No. 96-cv-2302, Memorandum Opinion, Jan. 18, 2001.

56. *Native Village of Barrow v. National Indian Gaming Commission*, U.S. District Court for the District of Columbia No. 99-cv-886, Memorandum Opinion and Order, Feb. 28, 2001.

57. Final Order: In re Class II Gaming Ordinance of the Akiachak Native Community, National Indian Gaming Commission, March 18, 2004; Final Order: In re Class II Gaming Ordinance of the Kenaitze Indian Tribe, National Indian Gaming Commission, March 18, 2004.

58. Letter from Neil Slotnick, Deputy Commissioner, Alaska Department of Revenue, to the Hon. Rick Halford, Aug. 9, 2002.

59. "Ripping It Up," *Anchorage Press*, Jan. 16–22, 2003.

60. *Ibid.*

61. "Troopers Shut Down Pulltab Operation," *Arctic Sounder*, July 10, 2003.

62. Untitled, *Press Release: Alaska Department of Law*, Alaska Department of Law, April 23, 2004; "State of Alaska, Native Village of Barrow Settle Pull-Tab Case," *Arctic Sounder*, April 29, 2004.

63. Letter from B.B. Mozee, Superintendent Central District, to Jonathan H. Wagner, Chief of the Alaska Division, Bureau of Education, Aug. 14, 1924.

64. 1930 Annual Report, Eklutna Industrial School. Alaska Division. Bureau of Education. Department of the Interior. Historical Album 1925, 1929–1931.

65. Executive Order No. 4778 (Dec. 5, 1927).

66. Davis, *A Tanaina Indian Village*, at 49–50.

67. Ch. 52 SLA 1963.

68. "Here's How Voters Cast Their Ballots," *Anchorage Daily Times*, Sept. 18, 1963.

69. 47 *Fed. Reg.* 53130, 53134 (1982).

70. Affidavit of George Ondola, March 26, 2007, submitted to Chairman, National Indian Gaming Commission, in support of the gaming ordinance that the Native Village of Eklutna submitted to the Chairman on April 2, 2007.

71. Sansonetti Opinion, Jan. 11, 1993, at 129.

72. Letter from Robert Anderson, Associate Solicitor for Indian Affairs, to Michael Cox, General Counsel, National Indian Gaming Commission, May 17, 1995.

73. "Natives' Casinos Faltering," *Anchorage Daily News*, May 19, 1995.

74. Constitution of Native Village of Eklutna, Jan. 27, 1996.

75. Section 223, Amended Gaming Ordinance of the Native Village of Eklutna, April 26, 2006.

76. Letter from Senator Rick Halford, President, Alaska Senate, and Representative Brian Porter, Speaker, Alaska House of Representatives, to the Hon. Gale Norton, Dec. 10, 2001.

77. Letter from Senator Lyda Green and Representative John Harris, Speaker, Alaska House of Representatives, to the Hon. Dirk Kempthorne, May 1, 2007.

78. "Stevens Backs Request on Tribal Status," *Anchorage Daily News*, Jan. 30, 2002.

79. "Eklutna Class II Gaming Hopes Bring Backlash for Alaska Natives," *Indian Country Today*, May 18, 2007.

80. Letter from Marissa Flannery and Colin Cloud Hampson, Sonosky, Chambers, Sachese, Enderson & Perry, to Philip Hogen, Chairman, National Indian Gaming Commission, June 25, 2007.

81. Letter from Don Young, Congressman for All Alaska, to Associate Deputy Secretary James Cason, Nov. 21, 2017.

82. Letter from Ethan Berkowitz, Mayor, Municipality of Anchorage, to Associate Deputy Secretary James Cason, Jan. 16, 2018.

83. Letter from John Tahsuda, Principal Deputy Assistant Secretary of the Interior for Indian Affairs, to Aaron Leggett, President, Native Village of Eklutna, June 18, 2018.

84. *Native Village of Eklutna v. U.S. Department of the Interior*, Memorandum Opinion, at 10, 2021 WL 4306110 (D.D.C., Sept. 22, 2021).

Conclusion

1. Anderson, "Sovereignty and Subsistence," at 223, 226.

2. On June 25, 2021 the U.S. Supreme Court issued *Yellen v. Confederated Tribes of the Chehalis Reservation*, 141 S. Ct. 2434, a decision in which, by a vote of 7 to 3, the Court held that the Ninety-third Congress intended to include ANCSA regional and village corporations in the definition of the term "Indian tribe" in the Indian Self-Determination and Education Assistance Act. In her majority opinion, after noting that "at the time [the Self-Determination Act] was enacted, some doubted whether ... Alaska Native villages could be federally recognized," Justice Sonia Sotomayor added a footnote in which she stated that "That doubt was resolved in the villages' favor in 1993." In his dissenting opinion, Justice Neil Gorsuch agreed, stating: "Over time, the vast majority of Alaska Native Villages went on to seek—and win—formal federal recognition." But whether in 1993 or at any other time Native residents of Native villages had been lawfully designated as "federally recognized tribes" was not at issue in the dispute the Court's decision in *Yellen* resolved. Because it was not, the question was not briefed for the Court, nor was it debated during oral argument. As a consequence, Justice Sotomayor's and Justice Gorsuch's statements are obiter dicta. As Black's Law Dictionary (11th ed.) explains, an obiter dictum is "a judicial comment made while delivering a judicial opinion, but one that is unnecessary to the decision in the case and therefore not precedential."

Bibliography

Archival Collections

Anthony J. Dimond Papers, Alaska & Polar Regions Collection & Archives, Elmer E. Rasmuson Library, University of Alaska Fairbanks, Fairbanks, Alaska.

Bureau of Indian Affairs, Record Group 75, National Archives, Washington, D.C.

Edward Lewis "Bob" Bartlett Papers, Alaska & Polar Regions Collection & Archives, Elmer E. Rasmuson Library, University of Alaska Fairbanks, Fairbanks, Alaska.

Felix S. Cohen Papers, Yale Collection of Western Americana, Beinecke Rare Book and Manuscript Library, Yale University, New Haven, Connecticut.

William Lewis Paul Papers, Special Collections, Allen Library, University of Washington, Seattle, Washington.

Printed Works

Alaska Rural Justice and Law Enforcement Commission. 2006. *Initial Report and Recommendations.* Anchorage: Alaska Rural Justice and Law Enforcement Commission.

________. 2012. *Report to the United States Congress and the Alaska State Legislature.* Anchorage: Alaska Rural Justice and Law Enforcement Commission.

American Indian Policy Review Commission. 1977. *Final Report.* Washington, D.C.: Government Printing Office.

Anderson, Robert T. 2016. "Sovereignty and Subsistence: Native Self-Government and Rights to Hunt, Fish, and Gather After ANCSA," 33 *Alaska L. Rev.* 187 (2016).

Angell, John E. 1981. *Public Safety and the Justice System in Alaskan Native Villages.* Anchorage: Justice Center, University of Alaska Anchorage.

Berger, Thomas R. 2002. *One Man's Justice: A Life in the Law.* Seattle: University of Washington Press.

________. 1985. *Village Journey: The Report of the Alaska Native Review Commission.* New York: Hill & Wang.

Case, David. 1978. *The Special Relationship of Alaska Natives to the Federal Government: an Historical and Legal Analysis.* Anchorage: Alaska Native Foundation.

________. 1987. "Listen to the Canary: A Reply to Professor Branson," 4 *Alaska L. Rev.* 209.

Cohen, Felix S. 1942. *Handbook of Federal Indian Law.* Washington, D.C.: Government Printing Office.

Davis, Nancy Yaw. 1965. *A Tanaina Indian Village.* Fairbanks: Rasmuson Library, University of Alaska Fairbanks.

de Laguna, Frederica. 1960. *The Story of a Tlingit Community: A Problem in the Relationship Between Archeological, Enthnological, and Historical Methods.* Washington, D.C.: Smithsonian Institution.

Deloria, Vine, Jr., and Lytle, Clifford. 1984. *The Nations Within: The Past and Future of American Indian Sovereignty.* New York: Pantheon Books.

Field Committee for Development Planning in Alaska. 1968. *Alaska Natives and the Land.* Washington, D.C.: Government Printing Office.

Golovin, Pavel N. 1983. *Encounters: The Worldly Travel Letters of an Imperial Russian Navy Officer, 1860–1861.* Portland: Oregon Historical Society.

Hess, Bill. 1993. *Taking Control: The North Slope Borough, The Story of Self-Determination in the Arctic.* Barrow: North Slope Borough.

Hoxie, Frederick E. 1984. *A Final Promise: The Campaign to Assimilate the Indians, 1880–1920.* Lincoln: University of Nebraska Press.

Hu-DeHardt, Evelyn. 1984. *Yaqui Resistance and Survival: The Struggle for Land and Autonomy,* 1821–1910. Madison: University of Wisconsin Press.

Hunt, William R. 1987. *Distant Justice: Policing the Alaska Frontier.* Norman: University of Oklahoma Press.

Kendall-Miller, Heather. 2011. "State of Alaska v. Native Village of Tanana: Enhancing Tribal Power by Affirming Concurrent Tribal Jurisdiction to Initiate ICWA-Defined Child Custody Proceedings, Both Inside and Outside of Indian Country." 28 *Alaska L. Rev.* 217.

Kizzia, Tom. 1991. *The Wake of the Unseen Object.* New York: Henry Holt and Company.

Kvasnicka, Robert M. and Viola, Herman J. (eds.). 1979. *The Commissioners of Indian Affairs, 1824–1977.* Lincoln: University of Nebraska Press.

Marston. Marvin R. "Muktuk". 1969. *Men of the Tundra: Eskimos at War.* New York: October House.

Miller, G.R. 1956. "Banishment—A Medieval Tactic in Modern Criminal Law," 5 *Utah L. Rev.* 365.

Mitchell, Dalia Tusk. 2007. *Architect of Justice: Felix S. Cohen and the Founding of American Legal Pluralism.* Ithaca: Cornell University Press.

Mitchell, Donald C. 1997. *Sold American: The Story of Alaska Natives and Their Land, 1867–1959.* Hanover: University Press of New England.

________. 1997. "Alaska v. Native Village of Venetie: Statutory Construction or Judicial Usurpation? Why History Counts," 14 *Alaska L. Rev.* 353.

________. 2001. *Take My Land Take My Life: The Story of Congress's Historic Settlement of Alaska Native Land Claims, 1960–1971.* Fairbanks: University of Alaska Press.

________. 2016. *Wampum: How Indian Tribes, the Mafia, and an Inattentive Congress Invented Indian Gaming and Created a $28 Billion Gambling Empire.* New York: Overlook Press.

Miller, Gerald R. 1957. "Banishment — A Medieval Tactic in Modern Criminal Law," 5 *Utah L. Rev.* 365.

Murray, Peter. 1985. *The Devil and Mr. Duncan: A History of the Two Metlataklas.* Victoria: Sono Nis Press.

Naske, Claus-M. 1973. *An Interpretative History of Alaskan Statehood.* Anchorage: Alaska Northwest Publishing Company.

Newton, Nell Jessup (ed.). 2012. *Felix S. Cohen's Handbook of Federal Indian Law.* San Francisco: LexisNexis.

Oswalt, Wendell H. 1980. *Historic Settlements Along the Kuskowim River, Alaska,* Alaska State Library Historical Monograph No. 7. Juneau: Alaska Division of State Libraries and Museums.

________. 1963. *Mission of Change in Alaska.* San Marino, California: Huntington Library.

Petroff, Ivan. 1882. *Report on the Population, Industries, and Resources of Alaska.* Washington, D.C.: Government Printing Office.

Prucha, Francis Paul. 1962. *American Indian Policy in the Formative Years: the Indian Trade and Intercourse Acts, 1790–1834.* Lincoln: University of Nebraska Press.

Rusco, Elmer R. 2000. *A Fateful Time: The Background and Legislative History of the Indian Reorganization Act.* Reno: University of Nevada Press.

Scherer, Kyle E. 2021. "Alaska's Tribal Trust Lands: A Forgotten History," 38 *Alaska L. Rev.* 37.

Shinn, Charles Howard. 1884. *Mining Camps: A Study in American Frontier Government.* New York: Charles Scribner's Sons.

Snider, William Garth. 1998. "Banishment: The History of Its Use and a Proposal for Its Abolition Under the First Amendment," *24 New England Journal on Criminal & Civil Confinement* 455.

Stewart, Robert Laird. 1908. *Sheldon Jackson.* New York: Fleming H. Revell Company.

Viola, Herman J. 1974. *Thomas L. McKenney: Architect of America's Early Indian Policy, 1816–1830.* Chicago: Sage Books.

Wilkins, David E. (ed.). 2006. *On the Drafting of Tribal Constitutions: Felix S. Cohen.* Norman: University of Oklahoma Press.

Williams, Gerald O. 1991. *Alaska State Troopers: 50 Years of History.* Anchorage: Alaska State Troopers Golden Anniversary Committee.

Wood, Darryl. 2000. *Turnover Among Alaska Village Public Safety Officers: An Examination of the Factors Associated With Attrition.* Anchorage: Justice Center, University of Alaska Anchorage.

Zuckerman, Michael. 1970. *Peaceable Kingdoms: New England Towns in the Eighteenth Century.* New York: Alfred A. Knopf.

Other Books by the Author

Sold American: The Story of Alaska Natives and Their Land, 1867–1959 (1997 and 2003)

Take My Land Take My Life: The Story of Congress's Historic Settlement of Alaska Native Land Claims, 1960–1971 (2001)

Wampum: How Indian Tribes, the Mafia, and an Inattentive Congress Invented Indian Gaming and Created a $28 Billion Gambling Empire (2016)

Index